Independence Edition

VOLUME I

THE PAGEANT OF AMERICA

A PICTORIAL HISTORY OF THE UNITED STATES

RALPH HENRY GABRIEL

EDITOR

HENRY JONES FORD   HARRY MORGAN AYRES

ASSOCIATE EDITORS

OLIVER McKEE

ASSISTANT EDITOR

<table>
<tr><td>CHARLES M. ANDREWS</td><td>ALLEN JOHNSON</td></tr>
<tr><td>HERBERT E. BOLTON</td><td>WILLIAM BENNETT MUNRO</td></tr>
<tr><td>IRVING N. COUNTRYMAN</td><td>VICTOR H. PALTSITS</td></tr>
<tr><td>WILLIAM E. DODD</td><td>ARTHUR M. SCHLESINGER</td></tr>
<tr><td>DIXON RYAN FOX</td><td>NATHANIEL WRIGHT STEPHENSON</td></tr>
</table>

ADVISORY EDITORS

DAVID M. MATTESON

INDEXER

Drawn expressly for *The Pageant of America* by Gregor Noetzel, American Geographical Society, New York.   Inset from the sculpture by H. A. MacNeil at Portland, Oregon

THE PAGEANT OF AMERICA

ADVENTURERS IN THE WILDERNESS

BY
CLARK WISSLER
CONSTANCE LINDSAY SKINNER
WILLIAM WOOD

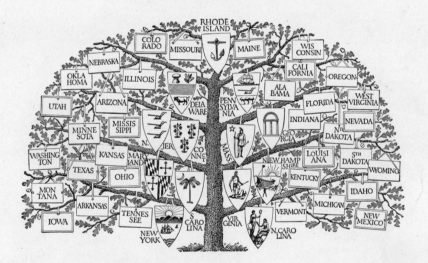

NEW HAVEN · YALE UNIVERSITY PRESS
TORONTO · GLASGOW, BROOK & CO.
LONDON · HUMPHREY MILFORD
OXFORD UNIVERSITY PRESS
1925

TABLE OF CONTENTS

THE AMERICAN INDIAN

A S the sun came up out of the Atlantic on the twelfth of October, 1492, an unwonted bustle stirred aboard three small and somewhat weather-beaten Spanish ships pushing westward. Crews, plainly worried and surly, crowded the rails to discover what the watch had seen. For weeks the masts had bent before the steady trade winds blowing the boats farther and farther into the unknown ocean. For weeks the Spanish sailors had watched the western horizon with a growing dread of what monsters might be hidden behind it. There they saw on the morning of the twelfth a blurred spot in the slanting morning light. "Land!" was shouted from ship to ship. Superstitious fear relaxed into excitement. A little later, Columbus, clad in armor over which he had thrown the crimson robe of an admiral of Castile, with sword and banner in hand, stepped from the ship's boat on to a sandy beach. There was a ceremony; he knelt and kissed the earth and took possession in the name of the Spanish king. A little knot of officers and men looked on, glad to have a chance to stretch their legs on shore and vaguely thrilled at the drama of the landfall. All, including the admiral, were ignorant of the true significance of the thing that had come to pass.

Columbus, cruising amid the islands he had discovered, lost no time in searching out the people that he might learn where lived the mighty monarch for whom he bore a letter from the Spanish king. He did not find the cities that Marco Polo had said were in China and India but only a primitive people living in little villages of huts. It was a strange scene, that first meeting of the red and white races. Neither had any comprehension of the identity of the other. Columbus thought the redmen Orientals and misnamed them Indians; no record has been left of the terrifying thoughts that passed through the minds of the natives as they gazed upon the beings that had come to their country. Scores of centuries stood between the white man and the chief with whom he tried to communicate and neither could cross the gulf.

Columbus, setting out on his pioneering voyage, had left behind him a civilization that expressed itself in a Venice, a Divine Comedy or a Rheims cathedral, and in the New World had stumbled upon a primitive forest people. The Indian hunted his quarry and built his lodges and council fires amid the trees. He seemed to be the very child of the woods, his untutored impetuosity born of its wild life, his strength the fruit of centuries of conflict with the rough forces of nature, his gods articulate in the whistle of the winds in the evergreens. The rhythm of the wilderness beat in his ceremonies and dances. During the years when Europe saw the rise of Greece and Rome and later, the states of modern Europe, the redman in America remained little more than a forest hunter — in a land unsurpassed in climate and wealth of natural resource. The soil which was one day to make America the greatest of agricultural nations, he left uncleared. His squaw scratched it with a sharpened stick. The storehouses of mineral wealth that were to furnish the sinews of a later civilization the Indian never unlocked. For thousands of years destiny seemed to hold before him a priceless opportunity and he let it slip. Because of this failure to utilize the resources of his environment, the redskin has frequently been put down as belonging to an inferior race and as incapable of achieving

1

civilization. In these later days, when scholarship has drawn the veil a little aside and men can look back over the long vista that marks the trail of human progress, the strange story of the Indian begins to appear. We can see now the catastrophe that cast its long shadow over practically the whole history of the red race in America.

The Indian did not originate in America. Far back in the dim twilight, we can make out shapes moving eastward from Asia by way of the Bering Strait. We cannot see clearly what urged them on; we can only see them coming, making their way southward and spreading finally over the whole continent. The Indian plunged into the vast forest and found subsistence there; he ventured out on the broad grasslands, and followed the wandering herds of bison there.

His people differentiated into a multitude of tribes speaking a multitude of languages. He threw away his early weapons of stone for new ones more beautifully and skilfully wrought. In places he dragged copper from its native bed and worked it. The prairie peoples who hunted the bison drew colored pictures, developed to a high state of perfection, on the skin coverings of their tipis. In the forested valleys of the Ohio and the Mississippi, the early Algonquins built mounds of heroic proportions. The traveler of today may see them, one an almost perfect circle a thousand feet in diameter, another a serpent five hundred feet in length with writhing body, an elaborate head and a coiled tail. To the eastward, the tribes of the Iroquois built up a confederation worthy to be compared with many whose origin is better known, a piece of statecraft that withstood the shocks of more than two centuries, and then only collapsed when the white menace could be fought off no longer. Throughout his long racial history in America the Indian made progress. But the acme of his development came south of the Rio Grande.

In Guatemala and the peninsula of Yucatan, partially sheltered from the attacks of invaders, the Mayas through many centuries developed a culture that, with its written language, crossed the boundary of civilization. During the centuries in which Rome was passing from the splendor of world empire to defeat at the hands of barbarian invaders, the Mayas were building great cities on the plains just back of the western shore of the Caribbean Sea. They erected truly noble temples of masonry, embellished with beautiful and effective sculpture. Beside these sanctuaries stood impressive monolithic monuments profusely carved. Maya astronomers calculated the calendar of the sun and the moon with an accuracy greater than that of their Roman contemporaries. Maya chroniclers set down the dates of the passing centuries in picture writing sometimes chiseled in the temple wall, sometimes painted on it in polychrome designs and sometimes recorded on the paper pages of a book. But when the whites first stumbled upon the western continent, the civilized Mayas were gone. Gold-seeking Spaniards found in Yucatan the ruins of splendid cities, but the Indians who dwelt in the region did not live in them, and knew little or nothing of their origin. The Cross was set up; the Spaniard proclaimed a victory for Christendom. He had no time to speculate on ruins.

But the man of a later day cannot escape the thought, as he pores over the remains of that vanished culture and pictures to himself the active, beauty-loving people who once worshiped in those temples: what would have been the history of the New World had that Maya civilization lived; had it spread northward, like the Roman culture in Europe, to the plains Indians, the mound-building Algonquins and the empire-building Iroquois. What if Columbus had found in America the fabled seven cities and discovered the redman harnessing the mighty resources of the continent? But the Mayas passed away. The Aztecs of Mexico and the Incas of Peru fell short of their achievements and, for the most part, the American Indians remained plains nomads or forest hunters. The culture of the Mayas is the high point in the race history of the Indian. It demonstrates beyond the shadow of a doubt the redman's intellectual capacity to achieve civilization. It raises insistently the question, why did he not do so in that rich environment where in three centuries the white race created the modern United States of America. Much of the answer may be found in a catastrophe which occurred at the very beginning of the career of the red race on the continent of North America.

In distant geologic ages before man appeared, North America became the home of a number of mammals, like the horse, the elephant and the camel, that were one day to be important factors in human progress. In those far-off days a land-bridge is believed to have bound Alaska to Siberia and another, stretching eastward from Labrador, spanned the north Atlantic. Over these, animals and plants migrated from continent to continent. At the height of the epoch of mammalian evolution, glaciers as broad as continents and thousands of feet deep moved out of the north, grinding their slow way southward in North America as far as the Ohio valley. The forests and grasslands gave place to a waste of ragged ice. Not once, but four times they came, and the land was green in the intervals. In one of these the first Indians probably came to America. Four times the wild creatures of America were inexorably pushed before the advancing ice sheets. Unable to withstand such colossal changes of climate practically all those animals which, like the elephant, the camel and the horse, were sufficiently tractable and intelligent to be domesticated, had either made their way to other continents or had perished. Just before the advance of the first glacier, the land-bridge across the north Atlantic had foundered. When the warm sun of a changing climate had driven northward the last of the ice sheets, Bering Strait joined the Pacific to the Arctic Ocean. America was isolated.

It was a strange destiny that cut off the western continents from the rest of the world almost at the time when man first appeared upon them. The redman faced the long task of racial evolution with no source of power outside the human body to aid in subduing the natural environment. He did not accept the handicap without a struggle. He sought to domesticate all manner of beasts and birds; he tamed bears, deer, hawks and turkeys. The bison was too fierce and too stupid. With the exception of the dog and the llama and alpaca of the Andean highland, he failed. Even the city-building Mayas had no beasts to do their work or to augment their food supply. Living on the edge of the tropics, the Maya tribes could raise crops with a minimum of labor. But, without draught animals and the plows and carts that make the strength of such animals useful, the civilization of the Mayas was built upon an inadequate foundation. It crumbled apparently because of a slight change in the climate. Even more conspicuously than among these Maya cities, the disaster of the Ice Age tied the hands of the Indian. He had no flocks of sheep or goats to furnish him with materials for weaving cloth, no herds of cattle to give him milk or hides or meat. He had no beasts of burden to haul his property or till his fields. All such beasts had perished as he was coming to North America. Had they been in America, doubtless he would have tamed them, for he found wild, food-bearing plants and domesticated them: gourds, beans, sunflowers, tobacco, corn. The gardens that the white men discovered beside the Indian villages were the fruit of thousands of years of intelligent effort. But half the value of this great achievement was lost because he had no beasts to aid him in the struggle for existence.

He could never shake off his dependence upon wild animals for meeting part of the needs of life. He could not pass from the hunting to the agricultural stage of culture; he was caught between the two. No large population could grow up, no lasting civilization could be built upon so insecure a foundation. The achievement of the lost Mayas was merely the measure of how near to an impossible goal the redman came.

Elements of tragedy may be found in this story of the American Indian. There was bitter irony in the destiny that put him so well equipped physically and mentally, yet with hands tied, in one of the richest environments of the world, and that spurred him on, ignorant of the disaster which blocked his progress, to make the best of a bad situation. At the end, without warning, he was brought face to face with a more fortunate race which had achieved the civilization that he could not. The ancient law of life began to operate; a struggle developed; and the weaker race gave place to the stronger. The familiar hunting grounds, the garden plots, the graves of his ancestors were all obliterated. His fate even compelled him to be the tutor of his conquerors. They borrowed from him the American plants which he had domesticated and learned how they were raised; he taught them where to hunt and how to fish; from him the adventurers from the villages and cities of Europe learned the art of living in the forest. When the English had mastered it well enough to make their little coast settlement permanent, there began that ceaseless westward pushing of the white frontier which was not to end until the Pacific had been reached and the Indian engulfed. For the redman, it meant that a futile racial struggle had been brought to a cruel end; for America, it signified that the culture of Europe was to be the culture likewise of the New World.

RALPH H. GABRIEL

INDIANS OF THE FOREST

IN prehistoric times the forests of North America spread in one continuous sweep from Florida to Alaska. They touched the Pacific coast below the Aleutian Island chain, extended thence inland across the region of the Great Lakes to the Atlantic and stretched onward to the Gulf of Mexico. Yet this vast forest was not one uniform tract of woodland. There were coniferous trees in the north, deciduous areas in the middle, and evergreens in the extreme south. When Europeans first reached the Atlantic coast, they found many separate tribes of Indians living in villages scattered here and there throughout these woodlands. Though these tribes differed much in their modes of life, yet, because they lived in the forest and got their sustenance from it, they all had much in common and were thereby distinguished from the Eskimo and the Barren Ground peoples of the extreme north and from the tribes of the open plains and prairies to the west.

The forest Indians were pre-eminently hunters, and deer was their principal game. In favorable regions they fished, but only as a supplement to the chase. Supplemental also were such attempts as they made at agriculture. The hunt was the most important task, and it was man's work. Searching for berries, fruits, and edible roots fell to the lot of the women, as well as caring for the little garden plots near the lodges.

The forest peoples, except for occasional pets, had no domestic animals but the dog, and it was only in the far north that they used him for draft or burden. They traveled on foot over forest trails or by canoe on forest-bordered streams. From the woods came their food, and the materials from which they made their clothing and habitations. The forest was their home, and its influence was felt in every phase of their life.

1 *The Primitive Marksman*, bronze figure by Fernando Miranda Casellas (1842–1925), in The New York Historical Society

2   From the bronzed plaster study in the United States National Museum, for *The Chippewa Family*, by John J. Boyle (1852–1917) in Lincoln Park, Chicago

A TYPICAL FOREST INDIAN FAMILY

IN a forest that stretched down to the water's edge, the Indian, strange and unexpected inhabitant of an unknown continent, faced the first white man to set foot on shore. Hunter, warrior and man of peace, held by circumstance to a culture far behind that of the new-comer, the redman marshalled all his experience and all his knowledge in an attempt to understand and appraise the new, strange people. And the European, on his part, watching the native glide noiselessly among the trees or seeing him lounge about his squalid huts, dubbed him a savage, a noxious creature of the forest like the wolf or the wild cat, to be guarded against and ultimately exterminated.

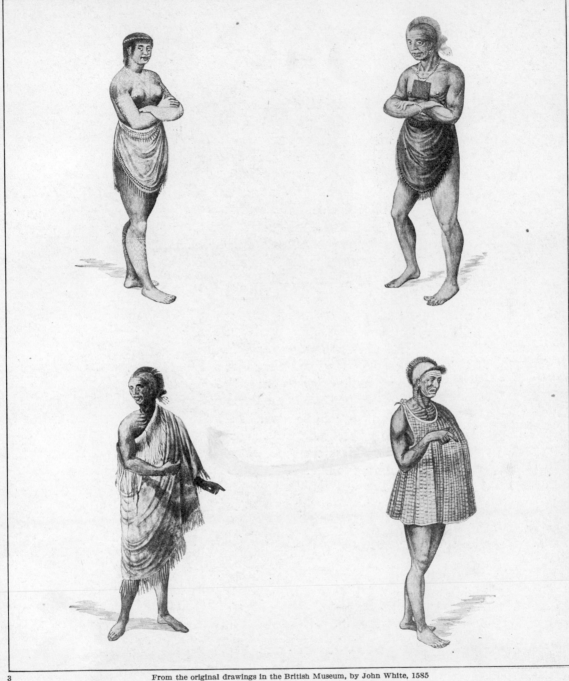

From the original drawings in the British Museum, by John White, 1585

JOHN WHITE'S INDIAN FIGURES

ABOUT 1585 an Englishman, John White (or Wyth) by name, made a series of remarkable portraits representing the Indians of Virginia and vicinity. The four drawings, done with the most careful attention to detail, represent (above) a woman and a chief, (below) an old man and a priest, in their ordinary garb; the first two with aprons of deerskin, the universal garment, the old man in a robe of dressed skin, and the priest with a cloak. Though all are barefoot, moccasins were frequently used by the Indians. Naturally the costume varied with the climate and the season of the year. Moreover, there were special costumes for ceremonial occasions. Nowhere among the forest Indians, however, did the garb attain the barbaric splendor to be found on the Western plains.

4   From the original drawings, 1585, in the British Museum

INDIAN TYPES BY JOHN WHITE

MOST picturesque of the figures in the Indian tribe was the magician, or medicine man, who claimed the magical power of communing with the spirits of another world. White drew him dancing according to the rites of his primitive religion, a bird charm on his head and a bag of charms in his girdle. So equipped, he fought off the evil spirits that lurked in air and earth and water. The equipment of the warrior was different, and his body was finely tättooed. The costume of the figure with the bowl may have been modified by the artist, since the fringe shown belongs to a robe. The group of pictures gives a vivid idea of how the tribes from Virginia to Florida appeared to the first explorers.

A

B

C

D

From Thomas Jefferys, *Collection of the Dresses of Different Nations*, London, 1757–72

INDIAN COSTUME, 18TH CENTURY

THE Indians of the forest had no beasts of burden but carried their packs on their backs, partly supported by a strap passing over the forehead. To the women fell most of this labor, for the men must be left free to hunt and fight. The tribes to the north of Virginia needed more and heavier clothing to protect themselves against the sharp frosts of winter, when for many moons the snow lay white beneath the leafless trees. For the most part the skins of animals were used.

A. MOUNTAIN INDIAN NEAR HUDSON'S BAY   *B.* A WOMAN OF THE CRISTIANOUX [CREE] INDIANS
C. WYANDOT WOMAN WITH PAPOOSE ON BACK   *D.* MOHAWK INDIAN SMOKING PIPE

CHIEF OF THE SIX NATIONS
IN COLONIAL COSTUME

WHEN the whites came, the redmen acquired new costumes of borrowed finery. Sometimes in garments in which little of the aboriginal remained, they met their new and dangerous neighbors in solemn conclave, while at home among their fellows they wore the native garb. Yet everywhere the coming of the Europeans wrought changes in costume, for the redman preferred the highly colored cloth of the trader, and for their own purposes the French and English competed in presenting to the chiefs shoes, fine uniforms, and beads — gifts fraught with danger.

This portrait was done in London and is one of four Iroquois chiefs who were brought to England by Philip Schuyler in 1709. They were presented to the Queen and to the Archbishop of Canterbury who wrote them a Christian message. The costume may have been one provided in England or it may represent merely the artist's fancy.

Te Yee Neen Ho Ga Row Emperour of the Six Nations

6   From a mezzotint by Simon, in the American Antiquarian Society, after an original drawing about 1710 by Simon P. Verelst, London

FORTIFIED VILLAGES

No Indian tribe could ever tell when war with a neighboring people might break out or when its braves might be called upon to defend the village against a hostile raid. Even before the whites came, the palisade had been developed. Jacques Le Moyne came to America about 1564, as a member of a little colony of French Huguenots planted in what was then known as Florida. When the Spanish wiped out the settlement, Le Moyne was among the few who escaped. His picture, drawn from intimate knowledge of the Florida peoples, shows the council house in the center of the village, the sturdy stockade, and the fortified entrance which could be defended with ease. John White, a few years later, found and drew a similar village in Virginia (see p. 29). The houses shown in both pictures were common to the eastern forests, each constructed with a framework of poles covered with mats and bark. Close to the huts were the gardens of the Indians, and the surrounding forest was the tribal hunting ground.

7   From Theodore de Bry, *Grands Voyages*, Part II (Florida), Frankfort, 1591, after a drawing by Jacques Le Moyne, 1564

8   From the model designed by Dr. W. H. Holmes, 1920, in the United States National Museum

AN IROQUOIS VILLAGE

THE Iroquois of the north, ablest of the eastern forest peoples, built habitations very like those in the south. On the Finger Lakes, as in the deepest valleys of the southern New York plateau, their shaggy villages were set in little clearings amid the trees. Within the stockades centered their work and their play. Here the hunter brought home his game, and here his squaw tended the hearth. Here children were born who would add to the strength of the tribe, and from here the dead were borne out to their final resting-place.

9   From *Valentine's Manual*, New York, 1858

A MODERN CONCEPTION
OF A MANHATTAN VILLAGE
(IROQUOIS)

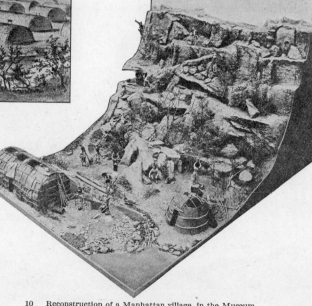

INDIAN VILLAGE
OF MANHATTAN

EVERYWHERE within the eastern forests the bark huts of the Indians were much the same. Thatch was also in common use. Their chimneys were holes in the roof whence issued the smoke of the hearth fire and the odor of the meat, corn bread, and succotash.

10   Reconstruction of a Manhattan village, in the Museum
of the American Indian, New York

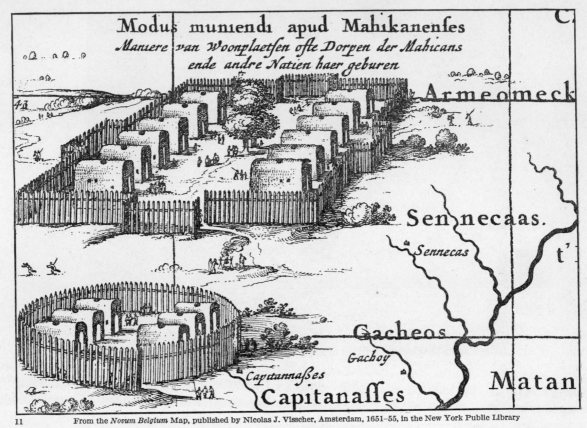

Modus muniendi apud Mahikanenses
Maniere van Woonplaetsen ofte Dorpen der Mahicans
ende andre Natien haer geburen

Armeomeck

Sennecaas.

Sennecas

t'

Gacheos

Gachoy

Capitannaſses

Capitanaſses

Matan

11   From the *Novum Belgium* Map, published by Nicolas J. Visscher, Amsterdam, 1651-55, in the New York Public Library

A MINISINK VILLAGE, 1651

WOOD was the universal building material of the eastern forest Indians. Their culture had not advanced to a point where they were able to erect temples of masonry like the Aztecs in Mexico or the Mayas in Guatemala. Their only enduring monuments are the mounds of earth piled up in the Mississippi valley. The picture, a representation taken from an old map, shows the typical village surroundings of the Iroquois, who developed the greatest confederation among the eastern Indians. Such primitive habitations had no influence on the development of American architecture.

12   From H. R. Schoolcraft, *Indian Tribes of the United States*, 1851-57, after a drawing by J. C. Tidball, U.S.A.

ERECTING A CHIPPEWA BARK LODGE

To make a bark lodge, slender poles were planted in the ground, bent over, and tied. Sheets of bark were then added for the covering. Building the lodge was woman's work. The drudgery of the camp was hers, but the tremendous exertion of the hunt and the dangers of battle fell to the man. The division of tasks was not unequal. Such flimsy habitations easily caught fire. Burning arrows to fire an enemy village were commonly used in war.

13   From the painting, *Out of the Silence,* by George de Forest Brush (1855–). © Curtis & Cameron

THE FOREST HUNTER

THE Indian was above all a hunter. When game failed, starvation stalked through the camp. Equipped with flint-tipped spears and arrows, the redman matched his wits and skill against the instincts and cunning of the birds and beasts. Moose and deer were especially difficult to kill, and a favorite device was to attack them in deep water.

14   From the painting, *The Moose Chase,* by George de Forest Brush (1855–), in the United States National Museum

CATCHING GAME

CHAMPLAIN's record depicts two common devices of the forest hunters. In trails were set snares to be jerked up by a small tree bent over as a spring. A hunting party armed with devices for making a noise would beat through the woods stirring up the game and driving the animals before it. The deer were directed toward a fence and, as they leaped over it, were speared by hunters concealed behind. The spear made of a straight, strong shaft tipped with a sharp flint point was an effective weapon that could be turned to the uses of war as well as peace.

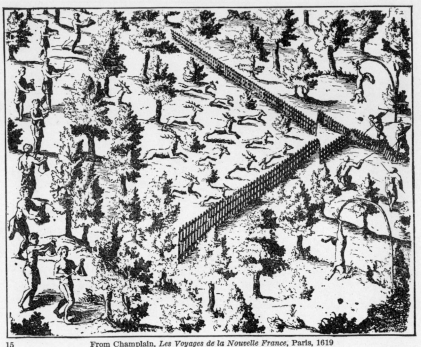

15   From Champlain, *Les Voyages de la Nouvelle France*, Paris, 1619

STALKING DEER

THE bow and arrow were the chief dependence of the redskin in his pursuit of game. The development of this weapon was a triumph of inventive skill and was the product of a development running through many generations. The bow and arrow had advantages over the crude matchlock which the first settlers brought to the American forest. The arrow sped silently on its mission. The weapon could be used many times in rapid succession. It was light and required no awkward rest for aiming. Oftentimes the white hunter adopted the Indian device. Stalking game was practised by all the forest tribes. Dire necessity drove the Indian hunter to the quest of food and forced him to devise divers ways and means to secure his catch, for if he returned home empty-handed, there were many mouths that would go unfed. Sometimes he concealed himself with skins. Patiently he watched by forest paths and drinking places. The central idea of Le Moyne's somewhat fanciful sketch is correct.

16   From Theodore de Bry, *Voyages*, Part II (Florida), 1591, after a drawing by Jacques Le Moyne, 1564

17   From the group in the State Museum, Albany, by Caspar Mayer and Henri Marchand, background painting by David C. Lithgow

RETURN OF THE HUNTER

To a hunting camp of the Senecas, one of the Six Nations, the hunter returns successful. The women are preparing venison and dressing skins. To tan deerskins for clothing was a laborious process, and a woman's standing among her people was gauged by the quality and number of skins she tanned. The smoked venison was dried on poles for the long cold months of winter, when the snow made hunting difficult and game scarce. The division of labor between the sexes made for greater economic efficiency within the tribe.

FISHING

In early days fish were abundant in the lakes and streams and in the inlets of the sea, and at times from convenience or necessity the forest Indians became fishermen. They used neat hooks of bone and spears with sharp bone points. Some tribes devised a three-pronged spear, like Neptune's trident, which would catch and hold the fish securely.

Some tribes made annual pilgrimages to the fishing grounds when the fishing season was on, just as they went on hunting trips in the autumn. Such seasonal migrations led many early observers to think that the forest Indians were nomadic. On the contrary, the activities of a village were normally confined to a restricted area.

18   From the sculpture by Louis Philippe Hébert (1850–1917), for the Parliament building, Ottawa

19   From M. H. Eastman, *American Aboriginal Portfolio*, 1853, after a drawing by Seth Eastman (1808–75)

SHOOTING FISH

Sometimes, where fish were abundant and the water clear, the Indian killed his fish as he did his game, with sharp arrows shot with practised aim.

THE "MANNER OF FISHYNGE IN VIRGINIA"

John White observed the fishing customs of the Virginia and Carolina natives. He noted the Indian weirs for guiding the fish into a trap, the spear, and the dugout in the midst of which a fire was often built on an earthen hearth to warm the fishermen and to cook the catch. All the practices in his faithful representation were customary on the Atlantic coast. But the Indians never ventured beyond the shallow waters immediately adjoining the shore. Unlike the Polynesians of the Pacific islands they developed no ocean-going canoes. The discovery of the cod banks off New England and Newfoundland was left to the whites.

De Bry's reconstruction of White's picture illustrates the liberties which de Bry frequently took with his originals.

20   From the drawing by John White, 1585, in the British Museum

JOHN WHITE'S ORIGINAL

21   From Theodore de Bry, *Voyages*, Part I (Virginia), 1590

DE BRY'S REDRAWING OF JOHN WHITE'S PICTURE

COOKING FISH

"AFTER they haue taken store of fishe, they gett them vnto a place fitt to dress yt. Ther they sticke vpp in the grownde 4. stakes in a square roome, and lay 4 potes [poles] vppon them, and others ouer thwart the same like vnto an hurdle, of sufficient heighthe, and layinge their fishe vppon this hurdle, they make a fyre vnderneathe to broile the same.... And when as the hurdle can not holde all the fishes, they hange the Rest by the fyrres on sticks sett vpp in the grounde a gainst the fyre, and than they finishe the rest of their cookerye. They take good heede that they bee not burntt. When the first are broyled they lay others on, that weare newlye broughte, continuinge

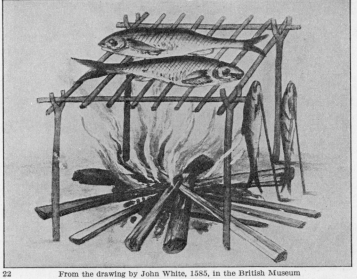

22   From the drawing by John White, 1585, in the British Museum

the dressinge of their meate in this sorte, vntill they thincke they have sufficient." — THEODORE DE BRY, *Grands Voyages*, Part I (English), 1590.

23   From the drawing by John White, 1585, in the British Museum

"THEIRE SITTING AT MEATE"

"THEIR manner of feeding is in this wise. They lay a matt made of bents one the grownde and sett their meate on the mids thereof, and then sit downe Rownde, the men vppon one side, and the woemen on the other. Their meate is Mayz sodden, in suche sorte as I described yt in the former treatise, of verye good taste, deers flesche, or of some other beaste, and fishe. They are verye sober in their eatinge, and drinkinge, and consequentlye verye longe liued because they doe not oppress nature." — THEODORE DE BRY, *Grands Voyages*, Part I (English), 1590.

24   From the group in the State Museum, Albany, by Caspar Mayer and Henri Marchand, background painting by David C. Lithgow

A WORKSHOP OF THE IROQUOIS

THERE is a fascination in looking back across the intervening years at the simple yet busy life of the wild people who dwelt in forests that have long since given place to farms and cities. The scene is in the Iroquois country. In the midst a stoneworker chips out flint blades and arrowheads and grunts a tale to which the rest listen, while carrying on their own work. Another man finishes the hollowing of a wooden bowl. Two of the women are making skin clothing; one braids a pack strap from cords of twisted bark fibre, and another weaves baskets from wooden splints. Raw materials gathered from the forest are being transformed into things useful in the primitive life of the redman. Common enough were such scenes to the wandering traders and Jesuit missionaries.

25   From the group in the State Museum, Albany, by Caspar Mayer and Henri Marchand, background painting by David C. Lithgow

THE CORN HARVEST

THE Indians were also farmers, and every village had its garden wherein corn was the chief crop. Corn meal and smoked and dried meat were the two staples of diet. To the women fell the work of husbandry, the preparing of the crops for storage, the grinding of the meal, and the cooking. For hundreds of years this simple life, unchanged by progress, had characterized the forest Indian.

HOME INDUSTRY — IROQUOIS WEAVING, COOKING, AND GRINDING

In the villages of the Indians, rough and rude though they seem to us, many industries were practised, for Indian life required the making of many things: clothing, tools, weapons, and stores of food preserved for future use.

The sketch from Lafitau represents to a certain extent the work of all the forest Indians of the south: cooking, weaving, pounding and winnowing meal, dressing skins, and grating and pressing roots. The hammock and the grating and pressing are not typical of all the forest tribes, but the method of weaving is. The warp was suspended from the limbs of trees or some other support. So far as is known, the forest Indians did not use a bar loom but wove downward. Cloth could not be made in this way, but only bags and soft baskets. Elsewhere in North America were Indian peoples who had perfected the art of weaving durable cloth ornamented with attractive designs.

26   From J. F. Lafitau, *Mœurs des Sauvages Amériquains*, Paris, 1724

27   From M. H. Eastman, *American Aboriginal Portfolio*, 1853, engraving after the drawing by Seth Eastman

INDIAN MAPLE SUGAR CAMP

Long before the days of Columbus maple sugar was made by the forest Indians. The art was learned by the colonists and is therefore one of the contributions of the Indians to our practical knowledge. The sketch shows an Indian camp after the trade days, when iron kettles and wooden barrels were available.

"THE MANNER OF MAK- INGE THEIR BOATES"

"THE manner of makinge their boates in Virginia is verye wonderfull. For where- as they want Instruments of yron, or other like vnto ours, yet they knowe howe to make them as handsomelye, to saile with whear they liste in their Riuers, and to fishe withall, as ours.

"First they choose some longe and thicke tree, ac- cordinge to the bignes of the boate which they would frame, and make a fyre on the grownd abowt the Roote

28   From Theodore de Bry, *Voyages*, Part I (Virginia), 1590, after the drawing by John White

therof, kindlinge the same by little and little with drie mosse of trees, and chipps of woode that the flame should not mounte opp to highe, and burne to muche of the lengte of the tree. When yt is almost burnt thorough, and readye to fall they made a new fyre, which they suffer to burne vntill the tree fall of yts owne accord. Then burninge of the topp, and bowghs of the tree in suche wyse that the bodie of the same may Retayne his iust lengthe, they raise yt vppon potes [poles] laid ouer crosswise vppon forked posts, at suche a reasonable heighte as they may handsomlye worke vppon yt.

"Then take they of the barke with certayne shells: they reserue the innermost part of the lengte, for the nethermost parte of the boate. On the other side they make a fyre according to the lengthe of the bodye of the tree, sauinge at both the endes. That which they thinke is sufficientlye burned they quenche and scrape away with shells, and makinge a new fyre they burne yt agayne, and soe they continne somtymes burninge and sometymes scrapinge, vntill the boate haue sufficient bothowmes. Thus God indueth thise sauage people with sufficient reason to make thinges necessarie to serue their turnes." — THEODORE DE BRY, *Grands Voyages*, Part I (English), 1590.

A PUBLIC GRANARY IN FLORIDA, 1564

AT harvest time corn and vegetables and nuts were often brought easily from a distance by canoe to the tribal granary, where pro- visions were kept for the long winter. Meat was preserved by smoking and drying, and corn was fre- quently kept in great bas- kets woven especially for the purpose. The artist has Europeanized some of the utensils.

29   From Theodore de Bry, *Voyages*, Part II (Florida), 1591, after the drawing by Jacques Le Moyne, 1564

30   From the model in the United States National Museum

INDIAN ARROWMAKERS

CULTURALLY, the forest Indians lived in a stone age. Flint was the most useful, and boulders of this material were sought in bluffs of rivers and in other likely places. Fortunate indeed was the tribe that controlled a supply; not only were its weapons assured but it had a commodity of the greatest value to trade. Chunks were fractured from the native rock to be chipped later into knives, scrapers, or arrow points. The work of shaping the stone tools and weapons fell appropriately chiefly to the men.

INDIAN FLINT QUARRIES

ONE of the most extensive areas where the Indians excavated flint has been found in Ohio. From this multitude of pits came the raw material for countless beautifully shaped arrowheads and spear points.

"The ancient pittings cover hundreds of acres, and in numerous cases are still open to a depth of from 10 to 20 feet. About the pits are ridges and heaps of débris and many shop sites where the implement forms were roughed out, and masses of fractured flint and flakage, as well as countless hammerstones used in the shaping operations." — W. H. HOLMES, in *Handbook of American Indians*, Washington, 1912.

We have come to think of the Indian almost entirely as a hunter and warrior. To walk among these pits and piles of debris is to realize what an important factor in the tribal life was the artisan.

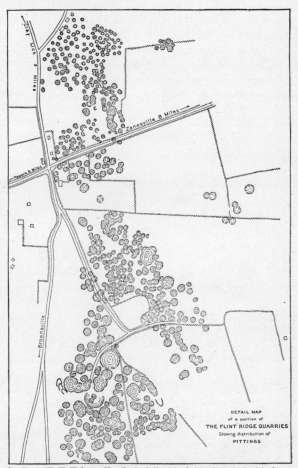

DETAIL MAP
of a portion of
THE FLINT RIDGE QUARRIES
Showing distribution of
PITTINGS

31 From W. H. Holmes, *Handbook of Aboriginal American Antiquities* in *Bulletin* 60, Bureau of American Ethnology, Washington, 1919

CHIPPING FLINTS

THE first step in the process of turning the rough flint or chert as it came from the quarry into an arrow point or a knife was the shaping of the piece. Large flakes were struck off with a hammerstone until the crude outline of the final tool appeared.

From W. H. Holmes, *Handbook of Aboriginal American Antiquities, Bulletin* 60, Bureau of American Ethnology, Washington, 1919

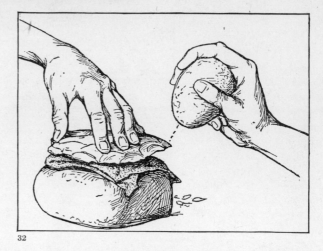

32

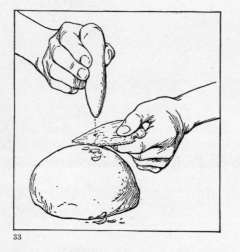

33

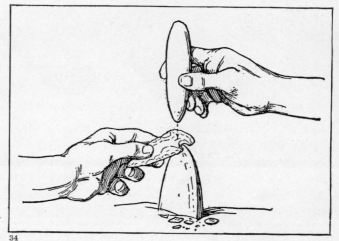

34

HERE fracture is accomplished by resting a blade upon an anvil and tapping it from above with a hammer.

NOTCHING a blade by resting it on a sharp-edged anvil and tapping it with a hammer.

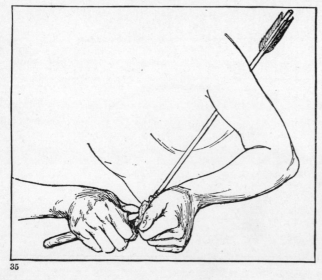

35

ARROW SHARPENING

THE illustration shows how an arrow point is sharpened by chipping with a bone point. This method is capable of trimming the edges of flakes or of blades already well advanced, but is apparently incapable of specialization of any other kind, unless, indeed, a sharp-edged rest is employed as shown above (No. 34). By this method it is possible to chip out notches of considerable depth, by reversing the piece to be chipped, from time to time.

A FLINT QUARRY

THE redman had but the simplest tools with which to make his excavations. Because he had no means of carrying heavy loads, much of the raw flint was worked up near the pit. The remains of these old "shops" give a vivid impression of the tremendous amount of work done by patient labor with crude tools.

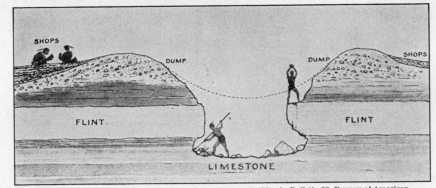

36   From W. H. Holmes, *Handbook of Aboriginal American Antiquities*, in *Bulletin* 60, Bureau of American Ethnology, Washington, 1919

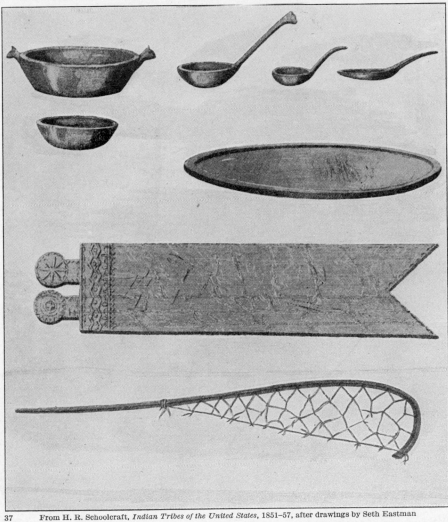

37   From H. R. Schoolcraft, *Indian Tribes of the United States*, 1851–57, after drawings by Seth Eastman

IMPLEMENTS MADE OF WOOD

At the top are bowls and ladles; the two large pieces are for cutting tobacco; the lower object is a lacrosse stick. These were the more important wooden objects of the forest Indians.

38   From H. R. Schoolcraft, *Indian Tribes of the United States*, 1851–57, after the drawing
by Seth Eastman

POTTERY

ALL the Indians of the forest, except in Canada, made some pottery. "The clay used was mixed with various tempering ingredients, such as sand or pulverized stone, potsherds and shells; the shapes were extremely varied and generally worked out by hand, aided by simple modeling tools.... As a rule, the baking was done in open or smothered fires or in extremely crude furnaces, and the paste remained comparatively soft."
—W. H. HOLMES, in *Handbook of American Indians,* Washington, 1912.

39   From Theodore de Bry, *Voyages,* Part II (Florida), 1591; after a drawing by Jacques Le Moyne, 1564

GAMES OF FLORIDA INDIANS

IN archery the test of highest skill was to hit an arrow shot from the bow of another. Sometimes an arrow or a braid of grass was tossed up to be shot at. Foot races were common. The peculiar game shown here, with a basket on a pole, may be fanciful.

SPORT

THE Indians, like most primitive peoples, were fond of games, and old and young joined in the sports of the village. There were tests of skill and endurance which often provided a useful training for hunting and war. Archery and a kind of handball were common. The picture showing the ball and curved sticks is, no doubt, lacrosse, a favorite sport of the woodlands. The children's games differed from those of the adults and consisted of top spinning, mimic fights and other imitative sports that were of use in their preparation for the duties of later life.

40   From J. F. Lafitau, *Mœurs des Sauvages Amériquains*, Paris, 1724

41   From Walter James Hoffman, *The Menomini Indians*, in 14th *Annual Report*, Bureau of Ethnology, Washington, 1896, drawing by M. I. Wright

THE MOCCASIN GAME

GAMES of chance were well known to the Indians, as to practically all primitive peoples, and gambling was often carried to excess. A favorite game was one in which the player concealed a bone or button in one of several moccasins, his opponents guessing its whereabouts. There were many variations of this type of guessing game. The Indians represented are of a later period.

THE CHALLENGE

MANY of the old Indian fights were little more than raids or skirmishes. The redman's code usually required the attacking tribe to notify its enemy. Sometimes the method was planting arrows secretly at night, or sometimes the sending of a sheaf of arrows as the Narragansett chief, Canonicus, did to the Pilgrims. Whatever the form, the symbolism and the hostile intent were clear.

The Indians recognized two kinds of warfare; on the one hand, fighting for the protection of women and children, the home and the village, and, on the other hand, the going forth on expeditions to avenge injuries or to take spoils.

42   From Theodore de Bry, *Voyages*, Part II (Florida), 1591, after a drawing by Jacques Le Moyne, 1564

43   From Theodore de Bry, *Voyages*, Part II (Florida), 1591, after a drawing
by Jacques Le Moyne, 1564

THE ATTACK

THE forest Indians fought from the cover of trees. They had little military organization. The war chief directed the action in a general way, but an Indian battle was little more than a series of individual encounters. When a fortified village was assaulted, the attackers strove to fire the lodges and to drive the defenders into the open.

In this picture the attack is being made with flaming arrows in order to set fire to the houses within the palisade.

THE IROQUOIS WARRIOR

LIFE for the redman was a sharp contest not only with nature but with neighboring tribes, who might covet his possessions or try to drive him from his hunting grounds. War was a part of his life.

Unhappy was the lot of him whom some physical defect kept from the reconnoissance or the fight. He must live among the women only to be despised by all the village warriors. The powerful

Iroquois organized a federation that built up a subject empire. Their power was the most feared among the forest Indians.

44   From the sculpture by Louis Philippe Hébert,
on the Maisonneuve monument, Montreal

THE LAST STAND

VALOR and heroism were the ideals of the forest Indian, and to die in battle was considered the best possible way to end life. When a war party was trapped, they seldom surrendered but fought on to the end. With the scalps of the vanquished as trophies, the victors returned to their village to be applauded by the old men and the women, while the forest echoed with the shrieks and howls of the victory dance.

45   From a wax group by Dwight Franklin (1888-),
in his possession

46   From H. R. Schoolcraft, *Indian Tribes of the United States*, 1851–57, after a drawing by J. C. Tidball, U.S.A.

THE SECRET SOCIETY

AMONG the redmen of the northern forests was a secret society called Midewin. The initiation was an impressive occasion. A war party approaches with scalps, asking to be initiated. A pole adorned with scalps is raised in the middle of an open space. The members of the society are seated about the outer wall awaiting the ceremony. Later a tribesman will show the candidates the sacred medicine bag. As they gaze upon the holy object, he will simulate the shooting of a small shell from the bag into their bodies and they will fall as dead. When revived, they will spit out shells upon the ground as proof that magic power has entered into them.

PRISONERS OF WAR

MANY times when the fight was over or the enemy's village captured, a group of unhappy prisoners followed the victors homeward — women and children to be adopted into the tribe of their successful adversaries, and warriors to be tortured or sometimes adopted. Torture was an accepted custom and was governed by code. Rarely did the Indian appear to better advantage than when he stood silent, immovable, victor over the anguish that his captors inflicted upon him. To die without a cry of pain was to achieve greatness.

47   From J. F. Lafitau, *Mœurs des Sauvages Amériquains*, Paris, 1724

THE CALUMET

IF the tomahawk was the symbol of war, the calumet
stood for peace. The picture represents the peace
ceremony between Bienville and the hostile tribes
of Louisiana.

"The peace calumet has a stem at least a foot
and a half long; it is adorned with the skin of the
neck of a duck, 'branchu' (?) — whose plumage of
many different colors is very beautiful — at the
end is a bowl. At the same end is fastened a sort
of fan made of the feathers of a white eagle, a
quarter of a circle in form, at the end of each feather
is a tuft of 'poit' or bright red. The other end of the
stem is uncovered to allow for smoking." So wrote
Bienville of the pipe he saw. Inevitably when a formal
meeting occurred between members of different tribes
the calumet passed from hand to hand. It was solemnly puffed by each person. This ceremony was one
of the most impressive of the Indian formalities.

AN IROQUOIS COUNCIL HOUSE

MANY symbolic terms borrowed from the Iroquois
have enriched our language, as the "council fire,"
"keeper of the wampum," "the sachem," "burying
the hatchet," etc., and here we have a glimpse of
the council at work. The young man at the right
is a messenger ready to carry the belt of wampum
that may mean peace or war, as the case may be.
Every Indian village throughout the forest land had
some kind of a building in which the older men and
sometimes the women also met to exercise the functions of government. Its usual place was in the
center of the village.

48   From Le Page du Pratz, *Histoire de la Louisiane*, Paris, 1758

49   From the group in the State Museum, Albany, by Caspar Mayer and Henri Marchand, background painting by David C. Lithgow

VILLAGE CEREMONIES

TRULY remarkable in its comprehension is this representation of Indian village life. The redman felt compelled to adjust himself to the requirements of two worlds — that which he saw and touched and heard about him, and the invisible world of the spirits mingling with the other as the mist mingles with the air. The Elizabethan draftsman has caught this dual aspect of the Indian life.

The cornfields with the shelter for the watcher who scared away the birds, the hunters returning through the forests, the lodge with the beds for sleeping, the fire for cooking and warmth, and the cooked meal ready for eating, all portray the redman's adjustment to the material world.

But fittingly in the foreground are the tomb of the dead chieftain, the fire which is the "place of solemne prayer," and a religious dance about posts carved with faces. Here mortal man comes close to the world of the spirits and adjusts himself to their requirements.

THE FALSE FACE CEREMONY

RELIGIOUS practices developed among the Indians as the years passed. No false face ceremony was known among the Iroquois until about 1700, when the custom shown appeared. Without warning, men with wooden masks burst into the lodge. One addresses a boy or girl; the other takes up ashes from the hearth. In a moment they are gone, and are entering the next lodge. They are driving the evil spirits out of the houses of the village. Such wearing of masks was not usual among the forest Indians.

50   From the original drawing by John White, 1585, in the British Museum

51   From the group in the State Museum, Albany, by Caspar Mayer and Henri Marchand, background painting by David C. Lithgow

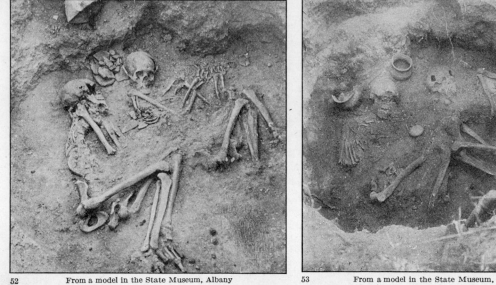

52   From a model in the State Museum, Albany   53   From a model in the State Museum, Albany

IROQUOIS GRAVES

THE most common method of burial among the forest Indians was in a grave.   Sometimes the grave was in a mound raised above the surrounding earth.   Sometimes it was merely a pit or even a cave. Among some peoples the graves were lined with stones, with a stone roof to keep the earth from falling in upon the body.   With the dead were interred the things that he had used and prized in life — his bow and arrow and spear, his pottery utensils, his amulets and perhaps the decorations that he wore. With unquestioning faith the redman believed that the grave was the beginning of a new life to be lived after the ancient manner of the tribe.   So, with solemn ceremony, the departing warrior was given the things necessary to meet the needs of the existence beyond death.

INDIAN RELIGION

THIS world of ghosts was the basis of the Indian's religion, and religion was a powerful factor in his life.   It prescribed long ceremonies which were carried out with meticulous care for detail; it laid down strong taboos.   It was one of the most important disciplinary factors in his life.   Closest to the spirit world was the medicine man, who was usually a juggler and kept close-guarded tricks which his fellow tribesmen could not comprehend.

The picture shows an anxious chief consulting such a priest as to the outcome of a projected war excursion.   With violent contortions the medicine man, who is sometimes a pure fraud but frequently self-deceived, induces visions and so makes a prophecy.   The chief, believing implicitly in this message from the spirit world, undertakes his enterprise with assurance.

54   From Theodore de Bry, *Voyages*, Part II (Florida), 1591, after Jacques Le Moyne, 1564

55   From Theodore de Bry, *Voyages*, Part II (Florida), 1591, after a drawing by Jacques Le Moyne, 1564

DEATH AND MOURNING

DEATH to the redman meant a passing over to the spirit world. In his dreams sometimes an Indian saw one who had died and talked with him; therefore, he reasoned, the dead must live. The land of spirits was not far away but close at hand, about the very village which the departed had known so well. The things of the new life were like the old, save that the spirit of the dead had become more powerful than in life and capable of doing greater mischief to those who remained. Sometimes the house of a dead man was burned for fear that he would molest another who used it. For the same reason relatives cut their hair and disfigured themselves to escape recognition.

A ceremony of lamentation at the grave honorably ushered the dead man into the new life pleased with his former friends and not angry at any want of respect. Moreover, the Indians, in spite of frequent representations to the contrary, were an emotional people. It was part of their code to stand unmoved in the face of torture by an enemy. From childhood they were trained to this form of self-control. But beyond this they gave vent to their feelings without restraint. So they mourned the death of friend or relative.

56   From the original drawing by John White, 1585, in the British Museum

AN INDIAN TOMB

IF a chieftain died, his power as a spirit was regarded as in proportion to his influence in life. John White, the English traveler, found among some southern Indians this sepulchre for their great men. The bodies were prepared according to savage custom. Beside them sat a wooden image to guard them through the passing years.

Under the "scaffolde some one of their priests hath his lodginge, which Mumbleth his prayers night and day, and hath charge of the corpses. For his bedde he hath two deares skinnes spredd on the grownde, yf the wether bee cold hee maketh a fyre to warme by withall." — THEODORE DE BRY, *Grands Voyages*, Part I (English), 1590.

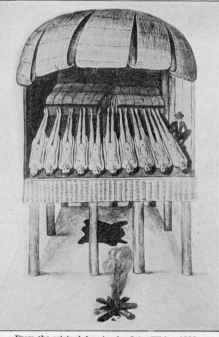

57   From the original drawing by John White, 1585, in the British Museum

AN ALGONQUIN BURYING GROUND

INDIAN burial customs varied considerably among the different tribes. Many times bodies were put in trees or, as in the picture, upon scaffolds. Wolves and other carrion-eating animals could not disturb the remains and hence cause displeasure to the spirits of the departed. Precautions were taken against depredations by the birds. Such a burying ground was a sacred place to the people of the tribe. What would the spirits think if it came into the hands of the white invaders? The Indian must fight desperately to ward off such a fate. Yet, if he were driven off and forced to seek new hunting grounds, the ghosts of the dead went with him, still to be propitiated and appeased.

58   From H. R. Schoolcraft, *Indian Tribes of the United States*, 1851–57, after the drawing by Seth Eastman

"THEIR MANNER OF PRAINGE VVITH RATTELS ABOWT THE FYER"

WHITE in Virginia noted the custom of offering thanksgiving to the spirits after good fortune. "Vvhen they haue escaped any great danger by sea or lande, or be returned from the warr in token of Ioye they make a great fyer abowt which the men, and woeman sitt together, holdinge certaine fruite in their hands like vnto a rownde pompion or a gourde, which after they haue taken out the fruits, and the seedes, then fill with small stons or certayne bigg kernells to make the more noise, and fasten that vppon a sticke, and singinge after their manner, they make merrie: as my selfe obserued and noted downe at my beinge among them."— THEODORE DE BRY, *Grands Voyages*, Part I (English), 1590.

59 From the original drawing by John White, 1585, in the British Museum

PROPHET'S LODGE

AMONG the tribes around the Great Lakes were seers who shut themselves in a tubular lodge and performed incantations. The medicine man had magic formulae and magic implements which gave him control over the spirits. He fell into trances and communed with them. In this sacred seclusion of the tubular lodge the medicine man spoke to the spirits above the lodge and brought to his solemn questioner a knowledge gained from the world beyond the grave. Not all the spirits, however, were ghosts of the dead. There were spirits of animals, particularly the tribal totem animal. There were spirits everywhere about the living, in trees and stones, in streams and the whistling wind. The circle of darkness about the evening fire was full of them.

60 From H. R. Schoolcraft, *Indian Tribes of the United States*, 1851–57, after a drawing by J. C. Tidball, U.S.A.

61   From the mural painting in the State Museum, Albany, by David C. Lithgow

THE SUN WORSHIPPERS

PERHAPS the Indian's religion seems to us today to be crude and packed with superstitions. The same, however, is true of all primitive religions out of which our finer faiths have developed. Yet it was a powerful agency for good among the tribes. It disciplined the savage and taught him the folly of depending solely upon his own strength. It explained for him the strange and terrifying things of life and calmed his fears with the belief that, if he performed certain ceremonies or wore certain amulets, he would be safe. After all, comfort, hope, and the sense of a power, greater than himself, with whom he could communicate — the elements of religion — were there.

INDIANS OF THE PLAINS

THE forest mantle in which the forest Indians lived stretched across what is now central Canada from the Rocky Mountains to Labrador and then extended southward along the Atlantic coast plain and the Appalachian mountains to the Gulf of Mexico. Climate made some differences but, in general, the Indians of this vast wooded area were much alike. Quite different were the tribes dwelling in the grass-covered plains in the center of the continent. Bounded on the west by the towering Rockies, extending northward to the Saskatchewan river and almost to Lake Winnepeg, reaching eastward as far as the Illinois river and southward almost to the Nueces in Texas lay a country in which trees were rarely found. Here grazed vast herds of bison and multitudes of prairie dogs dug their burrows. Packs of wolves ranged the plains seeking their prey and coyotes howled through the nights. In this environment dwelt the plains Indians.

They differed from their forest neighbors because their surroundings were different and because, as a result, their whole mode of living was different. Yet they belonged to the same race and, like the forest Indians, had not progressed beyond the neolithic stage of culture. In general the Indians of the plains were a vigorous, capable people. There were few weakling tribes. These had been driven off the low country in the fierce competition of the bison hunters and many of them had taken refuge in the sheltered recesses of the mountains. Like the forest Indians, the peoples of the plains, while divided into many tribes and speaking a number of languages, belong to a common group because the way of life was essentially the same from Texas to the Saskatchewan.

In 1832–34, a German scientist, Maximilian, Prince of Wied-Neuwied, left behind him the frontier of the young United States, which had barely crossed the Mississippi, and worked his way up the Missouri to its headwaters. Week after week he journeyed through the country of the plains and the bison, home of the plains Indian, who was as yet scarcely touched by the influence of the white. Maximilian took with him Carl Bodmer, an artist who left posterity a priceless heritage of Indian portraits and pictures.

62   Fort Clark on the Missouri, February, 1834, from Maximilian, Prince of Wied-Neuwied, *Travels in the Interior of North America* (Translation), London, 1838–43; lithograph after the drawing by Carl Bodmer

63   From Maximilian, *Travels*, lithograph after the drawing by Carl Bodmer

INDIANS OF THE NORTHERN PLAINS

THE Indians of the plains differed in costume from their brothers of the forest. They dressed their hair differently, and for their clothing they depended almost solely upon the bison. The hide took the place of cloth, while bones and horn furnished ornaments. With rare accuracy Bodmer has depicted the characteristics not only of the Indian's dress but of his countenance. In the upper picture from left to right are represented a Blood, a Piegan and a Kootenay; in the lower, a Missouri, an Oto and a Ponca (Poncha).

64   From Maximilian, *Travels*, lithograph after the drawing by Carl Bodmer

66   From the model in United States National
         Museum, Division of Ethnology

SIOUX WARRIOR IN FULL COSTUME

65   From Maximilian, *Travels*, London, 1838–43, lithograph after the drawing
                              by Carl Bodmer

MANDAN INDIANS

YOUNG warriors dressed brilliantly, fully muffled in buffalo robes, hair-side in and decorated on the outside with broad bands of porcupine quill work. Similar work appeared on their leggings and moccasins and on the long trailers to their heels. They wore elaborate hair ornaments and carried a fan of eagle's wing. The forest Indians did not dress so gaily, perhaps because theirs was a less open country. The decorations were not without their use for, upon meeting a brave, a stranger could gain the measure of the man by reading in his head-dress and the marks on his blanket the important deeds which he had performed.

A SIOUX WOMAN

THE buffalo robes worn by Sioux women were painted on the flesh side in an elaborate pattern. The leggings and moccasins were ornamented with quill work, but in no case were the women so gaudily dressed as the young men. The women were the drudges. Their work was about the lodges, cooking and preparing the game which the men took, striking and making camp and carrying the luggage when the tribe moved. Their status was not so high as among peoples who have passed to the agricultural stage of development.

67   From Maximilian, *Travels*, London, 1838–43,
         lithograph after the drawing by Carl Bodmer

68   From the *North American Indian Portfolio*, London, 1844, lithograph after the drawing by George Catlin (1796–1872)

STALKING THE HERD

THE old trick of stalking in disguise brought down many a beast. Concealed under the skin of a wolf or a coyote, the hunter crept up on the herd. Such a method was fraught with grave risk, for a buffalo could be a dangerous animal at close quarters. The Indian and his family, however, must live. If a man were not skilful enough to bring down his game, he had better lose his life, for he was of little value to the tribe.

THE HUNT

ALMOST the whole economy of life of the plains Indian depended upon the bison. Other large animals, such as antelope and bear, were also caught, but they were of small consequence in comparison with the bison. In the days before the horse, the fleet antelope and the fierce and wary bison presented difficult problems to the hunter afoot. The pictures show familiar methods of the old days.

69   From Le Page du Pratz, *Histoire de la Louisiane,* Paris, 1758

THE EARLY BUFFALO HUNT

70   From Le Page du Pratz, *Histoire de la Louisiane,* Paris, 1758

THE EARLY ANTELOPE CHASE

71   From the painting, *The Buffalo Hunt*, by Charles Wimar (1828–63), in the City Art Museum, St. Louis

THE KILL

AFTER the herd had been sighted by the advance scouting party, a council of the leaders was held to work out a plan of approach that would give each hunter a good chance. When all was ready, the word was given and the onslaught began. Then it was that the skill and prowess of the individual were brought into play, and he succeeded or failed as a result of his own efforts.

72   From the *North American Indian Portfolio*, London, 1844, lithograph after the drawing by George Catlin

BISON HUNTING IN WINTER

WHEN the snow lay deep in the hollows of the northern plains, the bison was at the mercy of his human enemy. Wallowing through the unbroken drifts, he could not escape the hunter whose snow-shoes bore him swiftly and safely over the surface.

DEVICES FOR CATCHING WILD ANIMALS

THE "buffalo pound" was an early device. The pound itself was roughly fifty feet on a side and was built of trees piled up to a height of five feet. At the entrance was thrown up a bank of earth with a gradual incline, up which the animals were to be driven. The inner part of the wings was formed of trees or bushes; the outer part by men lying on the ground under buffalo skins, each holding a stick aloft.

"Every preparation being made, three or four men set off on foot to find a herd of cows, for the bulls they think not worth their trouble. These they drive easily along till they arrive within the vicinity of the pound, when one man is dispatched to give notice to the other Indians, who immediately assemble on horseback on each side of the herd, keeping a proper distance for fear of frightening the animals. By this means the herd is brought within the exterior line of poles.

"It frequently happens that they will go out, to prevent which the men who are placed at the foot of each pole shake their skins, which drives the herd to the opposite side where the others do the same; so that at last they arrive at the pound and fall in headlong one upon the other, some breaking their necks, backs, etc. And now the confusion becomes so great within that tho the height of the building shall not exceed five feet, none will make their escape." — UMFREVILLE, *Present State of Hudson's Bay*, London, 1790.

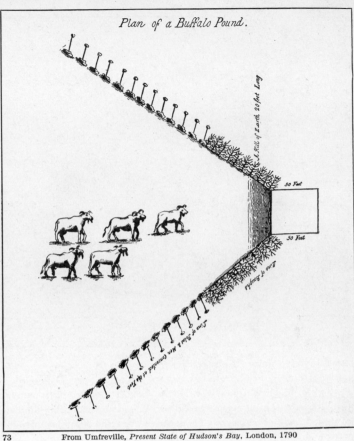

Plan of a Buffalo Pound.

73 From Umfreville, *Present State of Hudson's Bay*, London, 1790

THE BUFFALO POUND

74 Crees Driving Buffalo into a Pound, from Henry Youle Hind, *Narrative of Canadian Red River Exploring Expedition of 1857*, London, 1860, after a sketch by John Fleming

75   From the *North American Indian Portfolio*, London, 1844, lithograph after drawing by George Catlin

THE HAZARD OF THE HUNT

THE life of the man who lived by the chase was full of peril.   The bison was a fierce though stupid animal and fought, when brought to bay, with a deadly ferocity.   His bulk and speed and the sharp horns with which he was equipped demanded of the Indian the best of horsemanship.   More terrible still was the grizzly, hunted where the plains merged into the mountains.   The qualities which made for success in such a life developed that courage and firmness which made the redman of the plains one of the greatest of Indian warriors.

76   From the *North American Indian Portfolio*, London, 1844, lithograph after drawing by George Catlin

ATTACKING THE GRIZZLY BEAR

77   From the painting by Charles M. Russell (1865–), courtesy of the artist

THE ADVANCE GUARD OF A BLACKFOOT HUNTING PARTY

THE hunting of the bison developed in the plains Indian a capacity for effective co-operation not often found in the redman of the forest. He was compelled to organize. In the hunt different persons did different things. Such habits of organization stood the redman in good stead when attacked by his enemies.

CATCHING WILD HORSES

HORSES escaped from the first Spanish expeditions. Thus began the wild herds which were soon to

become an important element in the Indian life of the plains, for the hunters soon became skilful in capturing, in taming, and in riding these horses. Catlin's picture shows a capture of a wild horse in true Indian fashion made by a half-breed in the party with which the artist was crossing the plains. The advent of the horse suddenly and profoundly changed the Indian's mode of life.

78   From the painting, about 1840, by George Catlin, in the United States National Museum

79   From Catlin, *Manners, Customs and Condition of the North American Indians*, London, 1841

HORSEMANSHIP OF THE COMANCHE

THE old name for these Indians was "Horse Indians." They were the most fearless of riders.

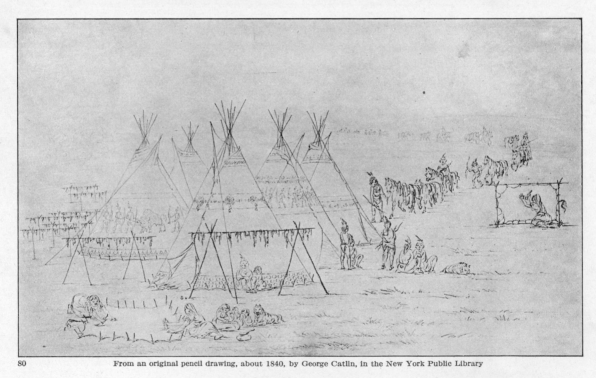

80   From an original pencil drawing, about 1840, by George Catlin, in the New York Public Library

DRESSING SKINS

THE proper dressing of skins was an art in which the Indian excelled. The fresh skin was first stretched out on the ground, hair-side down, fleshed and dried. If to be fully dressed, it was then turned over and the hair was scraped away. If a robe was to be made, the skin was treated to a softening process and was sometimes stretched on a frame.

81   From Maximilian, *Travels*, London, 1838–43, lithograph after the drawing by Carl Bodmer

INDUSTRIES, UTENSILS, AND ARMS

MANY of the things that the Indians of the plains made were exceedingly well wrought. Like the redmen of the forest they used weapons and tools of stone, but they were particularly adept in the use of skins. There was a certain dash of ornamentation that set their work off from that of their forest brothers.

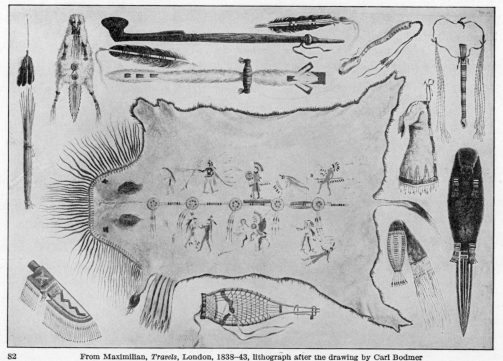

82   From Maximilian, *Travels*, London, 1838–43, lithograph after the drawing by Carl Bodmer

83   From M. H. Eastman, *American Aboriginal Portfolio*, 1853, engraving after the drawing by Seth Eastman

VILLAGE OF THE EASTERN DAKOTA

SOME of the Dakota Indians near the forest line in Minnesota and Wisconsin made occasional use of bark cabins. "The summer houses of the Dacotas are made of the bark peeled from trees. The building of the house is the work of the women. . . . For these houses the bark of the elm tree is principally used. There is a quantity of this sort in the Sioux country. In the spring, the bark peels off easily in large pieces. The women have only to plant poles in the ground, fasten the bark to them, and the summer house is soon made. In the roof there is a hole cut that answers the purposes of a chimney. The fire in a Sioux or Dacota lodge is always kindled in the centre. A place in the lodge is allotted to each member of the family. The wife has hers near the door; being servant as well as wife, she is by custom placed where she can conveniently go in and out. The husband has his place near the fire." — MRS. MARY H. EASTMAN.

84   From Maximilian, *Travels*, London, 1838–43, lithograph after the drawing
           by Carl Bodmer

MANDAN VILLAGE

EXCEPT during the summer hunt of the bison, some of the tribes along the Missouri lived in oval, dome-shaped houses covered with earth. Frames or stages were erected upon which meat and food were dried, out of the reach of dogs and horses. For crossing the river a curious boat was used, made by stretching a fresh buffalo skin over a basket-like framework of poles. These boats were later used somewhat by the trappers and fur traders who ventured into the Indian region. They were soon discarded for they capsized easily and were difficult to steer. The habitations of the Mandans differed from those of the great majority of the Plains Indians.

85   From Maximilian, *Travels*, London, 1838-43, lithograph after the drawing by Carl Bodmer

A TRIBAL CAMP

As herds of bison moved from place to place in search of pasture, the Indians of necessity followed them. In the plains, during the summer months, a whole tribe was often organized as a moving cavalcade, striking its tents at command and pitching them again at night, perhaps in some sheltered valley where the adjoining grassland promised good hunting. In the picture can be seen the form of the camp and the life of the people — the women engaged in their daily routine, the hunters returning with game, and the warriors lounging about, ready for any alarm.

86   From an original pencil drawing about 1840, by George Catlin, in the New York Public Library

THE DOG AND THE HORSE

BEFORE horses came, the Indian of the plains traveled on foot accompanied by dogs bearing the lighter parts of his baggage. Even tent poles were dragged by the dogs and sometimes they carried the babies as well. Such a use of dogs was not possible in the forest. After horses came, following the establishment of the Spanish colonies, they also were trained to draw the *travois* and the tent poles.

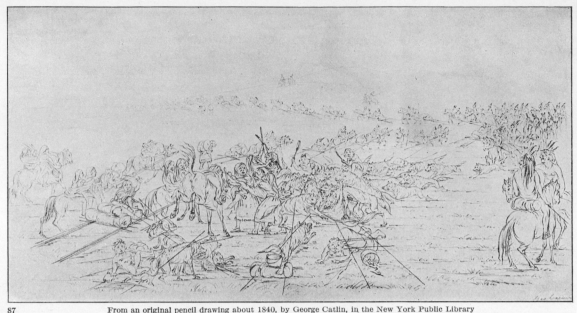

From an original pencil drawing about 1840, by George Catlin, in the New York Public Library

INCIDENTS OF A COMANCHE MARCH

"I should also have given the reader, a sketch of one of these extraordinary scenes, which I have had the good luck to witness. . . . Each horse drags his load, and each dog, *i.e.* each dog that *will* do it (and there are many that will not), also dragging his wallet on a couple of poles; and each squaw with her load, and all together (notwithstanding their burthens) cherishing their pugnacious feelings, which often bring them into general conflict, commencing usually amongst the dogs, and sure to result in fisticuffs of the women; whilst the men, riding leisurely on the right or the left, take infinite pleasure in overlooking these desperate conflicts, at which they are sure to have a laugh, and in which, as sure never to lend a hand.

"These people, living in a country where buffaloes are abundant, make their wigwams more easily of their skins than of anything else; and with them find greater facilities of moving about, as circumstances often require; when they drag them upon the poles attached to their horses, and erect them again with little trouble in their new residence." — GEORGE CATLIN.

88   From Maximilian, *Travels*, London, 1838–43, lithograph after the drawing by Carl Bodmer

PASSING THE PIPE

THE reception of a guest was a matter that called for etiquette. A pipe was passed with dignity and according to a fixed custom. The picture shows a Mandan chief receiving visitors in his earthen lodge. When the pipe had gone round, relations of friendship and amity had been established, if the visitor were a stranger, or renewed, if he were an old acquaintance.

"The Indians are not fond of large fires," wrote Maximilian of his visit to the Mandans. "The inmates sit around it, on low seats, made of peeled osiers, covered with buffalo or bear skin."

89   From the group in the United States National Museum

GAMES

WE see here "a play tent and games of the Kiowa Indians of which these children have a variety. The girl and boy in the foreground are bantering as to a play in the wheel and dart game. Boys in the background are playing with whip toys. The girl and the little boy, the latter dressed in imitation of his warrior father, are in the act of surprising their sister, who is playing doll in the tent. The girl, laying aside her miniature papoose cradle, lifts the flap of the tent while the boy, joining in the sport, emphasizes the surprise by a war whoop." — WALTER HOUGH, in *Smithsonian Report*, 1920.

90   From the painting, *Lacrosse Playing among the Sioux Indians*, 1857, by Seth Eastman, in the Corcoran Gallery, Washington

BALL PLAY

THIS ancient game is known as "ball and racket," the object being to carry the ball by the racket over the goal of the opposing side.

91   From Maximilian, *Travels*, London, 1838–43, lithograph after the drawing by Carl Bodmer

THE HOOP AND POLE GAME

THOUGH the various forms of this game are aboriginal, they are still found in all parts of the plains. The ring, or hoop, is rolled and as it falls the players try to thrust their poles underneath, and according as the markings on the fallen ring coincide with the pole, the count is made. Frequently arrows are used instead of poles. It is a gambling game.

92   From Maximilian, *Travels*, London, 1838–43, lithograph after the drawing by Carl Bodmer

FORT UNION ON THE MISSOURI

THE whites, as they worked their way westward across the forest country, pushed their trading-posts out into the plains. Fort Union was built by the American Fur Company in 1829, near the spot where the Yellowstone enters the Missouri. Bodmer, to whom we owe this picture, saw it five years later. Powerfully built and well armed, it furnished a place where the trader could deal in safety with the plains people. Within the inner quadrangle were the residences of the interpreters and clerks, the stores and supplies of goods for trade, the skins that had been received in barter, and rooms for receiving and entertaining the Indians. In such strongholds the frontier civilization of young America met the barbarian of the plains.

93   From Maximilian, *Travels*, London, 1838–43, lithograph after the drawing by Carl Bodmer

TRIALS OF AN INDIAN TRADER

THE life of a trader was full of trials and critical incidents. The wild Indians were often difficult to keep within bounds. Surprise attacks had to be balked with readiness and cunning matched with cunning. Experience taught the trader to sleep with one eye open and to be ready for anything.

SIGNALS

PICTURE writing was one way of communicating among the Indians. The great distances of the open country required signals of several kinds. Perhaps an enemy was in the offing; perhaps there were wild horses and the distant tribe must be given the information. When the Ponchas or Omahas discovered bison the watcher stood erect on a hill, with his face toward the camp, holding his blanket with an end in each hand, his arms being stretched out (right and left) on a line with his shoulders. The signals of the plains Indians were an adjustment to the vast treeless grasslands whose slightly undulating surface often hid the animals which the redskin sought as prey.

94   From Col. Garrick Mallery, *Sign Language among North American Indians*, in *Annual Report*, 1879–80, Bureau of Ethnology, Washington, 1881

PICTURE WRITING —LONE DOG'S WINTER COUNT

THE writing of the plains Indians was made up of pictures, and in this way they could convey much information. The heroic deeds of a warrior were inscribed upon his buffalo robe or on the walls of his tipi. Everyone would then know what degree of recognition to give him. The pigments were mineral in origin, mixed with water and applied with a stick.

The picture represents a calendar of the Dakotas covering the years from 1799 to 1870. The narrative begins at the right of the center and goes outward in a spiral. The first entry consists of three rows of lines which indicate that in 1799 thirty Dakotas were killed by the Crows. In the following year small-pox broke out, as shown by the dotted human figure. The story of the tribe unfolds in order: the Dakotas stole horses with shoes; they stole horses with curly tufted hair; they had a medicine dance and went to war, as shown by the pipe stem ornamented by feathers; Crow In-

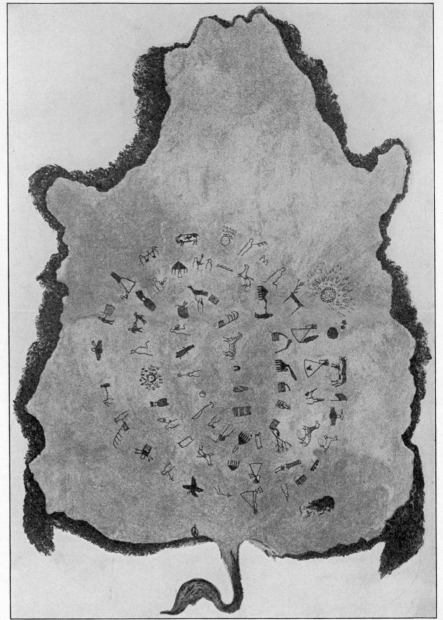

95   From United States Bureau of Ethnology *Annual Report*, 1882-83

dians killed eight Dakotas; a Dakota killed an Arikara, as he was about to shoot an eagle; Chief Red Coat was killed; and so on through the years.

The last three entries, made in the years when the armies of the United States were beginning to move against the people of the plains, represent the bringing of Texas cattle to the Dakota country, the eclipse of the sun in 1869, and an attack by the Dakotas on a Crow fort. Perhaps in no better way than in this simple story of the great events in tribal history can people of a different day and culture catch a glimpse of what life meant to the Indians of the plains.

Living in the region which still bears their name, the Dakotas, the main tribe of the Sioux, were the greatest, physically, mentally and probably morally, of the plains Indians. Their bravery was unquestioned. Their form of government was superbly adapted to the needs of their life. Their chiefs, chosen for fitness rather than by heredity and limited in power by the Band Council of the tribe, led their warriors to victory after victory until every rival except the Chippewas had been driven from their hunting range.

THE SIGN LANGUAGE

As there were many tribes on the plains, so there were many languages and dialects. The frequent contact of tribe with tribe made some sort of common language necessary and the sign language grew up as an adaptation to the peculiar conditions in the open country. The Indian on the rock in the distance asks, "Who are you?" by raising the right hand, palm in front, and slowly moving it right and left. Answer is made with, say, the tribal sign for Pawnee. The sign for peace is made by the Indian laying down his weapons and raising his hands high above his head. In such ways the tribe from the headwaters of the Missouri could communicate with a people from the Rio Grande for the sign language was a universal language of the plains. Its development was an intellectual achievement of great importance.

96   From Col. Garrick Mallery, *Sign Language among North American Indians*, in *Annual Report*, 1879–80, Bureau of Ethnology, Washington, 1881

97   From Col. Garrick Mallery, *Sign Language among North American Indians*, in *Annual Report*, 1879–80, Bureau of Ethnology, Washington, 1881

98   From the bronze statuette, *A Cheyenne*, by Frederic Remington (1861–1909)

WAR

ROVING from place to place as they followed the bison, the tribes of the plains came frequently into contact and conflict with one another. Early in Indian history the weakling tribes were driven from the open places to the shelter of rough mountain valleys, and the fierce and warlike tribes were left to dominate the grasslands. As the tribe was organized for the hunt, so it was organized for war. Skilful horsemen and courageous fighters, the Indians of the plains left a rich heritage of tales of heroism and fortitude. This oral tradition, however, has been mostly lost because the Indians could not write and what records they left are wordless.

99   From Maximilian, *Travels*, London, 1838–43, lithograph after the drawing by Carl Bodmer

INDIANS IN A FIGHT

FROM the walls of Fort Mackenzie, in the background, Bodmer in August, 1833, saw this fight. A band of Blood Indians, come to trade, fought an enemy tribe outside the stockade. The fierce and bloody character of the hand-to-hand struggle is vividly portrayed. Even in the midst of the fray the warrior takes time to strip off a scalp. Both sides hastily remove the wounded. The affair is soon over, but it leaves the rankling enmity of the blood feud.

100   From the painting by Frederic Remington, 1908, in the Museum of Art, Toledo, Ohio

INDIANS DISGUISED AS BUFFALO

IN the open plains country a scout could not conceal himself in a tree or in the underbrush at the crest of a hill, for when he climbed to a high point for observation, his figure would be silhouetted against the sky. So ingenious devices were used to disguise the scout. Sometimes, concealed by skins, he stalked the buffalo or crept close to an enemy.

THE WOUNDED

IN every war the wounded present a problem. "If it is a long distance to go home from the field of battle, a litter is prepared to carry the wounded. The warriors take two poles, having a blanket or buffalo skin fastened to them, so as to form a sort of cot, upon which the wounded man is placed. An Indian at each end raises the poles, and, by means of a strap tied to the ends and thrown over his shoulder, he is enabled to bear it for miles before resting. Two Indians can thus transport a wounded man from thirty to forty miles a day."—M. H. EASTMAN.

101   From M. H. Eastman, *American Aboriginal Portfolio*, 1853, engraving after the drawing
by Seth Eastman

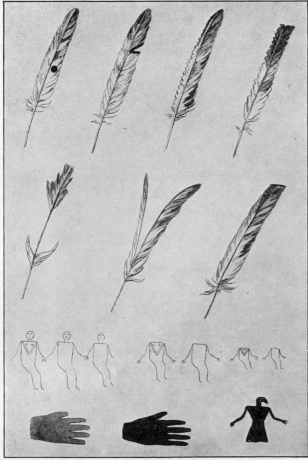

102   From H. R. Schoolcraft, *Indian Tribes of the United States*, 1851–57,
after drawings by Seth Eastman from the originals

BADGES OF HONOR

A FEATHER in the head stood for a deed according to its marking: "an eagle's feather with a red spot denotes that the wearer has killed an enemy, a notch cut in it and edges of the feather painted red, indicates that the throat of an enemy has been cut. Small consecutive notches on the front side of the feather without paint, denote that the wearer is the third person that has touched the dead body. Both edges notched, that he is the fourth person that has touched it; and the feather partly denuded, that he is the fifth person that has touched the slain. The split feather denotes that the wearer has received scars from the hand of an enemy. The feather clipped off, and the edges painted red, are also indicative of the cutting of an enemy's throat."— H. R. SCHOOLCRAFT. When painted on robes or tipis, human figures with heads represent the number of prisoners taken; those without heads, the number of killed, adults and children. Hands and birds vary much in their meanings. So the Indian brave, like the modern soldier in full regalia, displayed the history of his achievements in his costume. His status in the community was largely dependent upon his record.

103   From Maximilian, *Travels*, London, 1838–43, lithograph after the drawing by Carl Bodmer

THE BULL DANCE

WAR led to advancement in the secret societies which were part of the tribal organization. The Indians of the plains developed societies that were very elaborate. The young men joined the lowest society and, passing from rank to rank, might eventually as old men reach the highest, the Bull Society. At stated times each organization brought out its regalia and gave its dance in public. The picture shows a ceremony of the Mandan Bull Society. Very impressive to adolescent youth was this ceremony of the veteran warriors. Eagerly they looked forward to the time when they should earn the right to share in the secrets and mysteries of the great society.

THE SCALP DANCE

WHEN a war-party returned to camp successful over their adversaries, the women celebrated their exploits with the scalp dance. The warrior who had brought back a scalp gave it to his wife or sweetheart to carry in the ceremony. Other trophies, such as captured war-bonnets, were worn. The wild excitement of the battle was transmuted into the savage rhythm of the dancing.

104   From Maximilian, *Travels*, London, 1838–43, lithograph after the drawing by Carl Bodmer

DEATH

Self-controlled as he was in the face of danger and suffering, the Indian was at heart strongly emotional. Emotion permeated his wild dances and filled his religious ceremonies, but it was never more marked than when he stood in the presence of death. Sometimes the relatives, gathering about the lifeless form of one who had gone, would call upon him, reproach him for leaving them, vow vengeance on his enemies, and exaggerate his virtues. Sometimes they would cut off their hair, lacerate their limbs, and tear their clothing already crimson with their own blood.

Rolled in a skin or blanket, the body would be placed with gentle solemnity upon a scaffolding to keep it away from the wolves. By it were placed food and water, to be frequently replenished as the birds hovering around consumed the supply. Then all repaired to the preparation of one of their most solemn feasts. Sometimes the bereaved wife would carry a bundle representing the husband, and night and morning she would wail in solitary places.

105   From H. R. Schoolcraft, *Indian Tribes of the United States*, 1851–57,
after a drawing by Seth Eastman

106   From a wood engraving in Col. Richard I. Dodge, *Our Wild Indians*, 1882, after a drawing by Ernest Griset

107   From M. H. Eastman, *American Aboriginal Portfolio*, 1853.
engraving after the drawing by Seth Eastman

THE MEDICINE MAN

THE medicine man was both priest and doctor to his people. Called to the bedside of the sick, he brought his sacred rattle and his sacred medicine bag. It might be that, according to their simple belief, some animal had entered the body of the victim and was eating away his vitals. If so, the medicine man made a little bark image of the animal and directed the young men to shoot it. Perhaps the water-spirit had frowned on the sick one or the thunder-birds were angry with him; perhaps a medicine man or a woman of another clan hated him and was holding over him the evil eye.

All of these things the medicine man considered and prepared to counteract. Nothing was left undone. He shook his rattle with howls and grunts and groans. He crawled on hands and knees and made frightful faces. Suddenly changing, he would begin a slow and solemn chant. Sometimes he gave the patient a magic potion, which often had real medicinal value. His purpose in all these operations was to drive out the evil spirit that was troubling the sick one.

THE CALL TO THE GREAT MYSTERY

AT least once in his life the Indian of the plains alone made an offering and supplicated the Great Unknown to show Himself, to speak to his poor child, to give him faith and courage to be a man. The more religious did this many times during their lives. Bodmer caught the spirit of these tense moments in picturing an Indian out alone in the gathering gloom, where he had set up an altar and an offering.

Sometimes the suppliant fasted and prayed for four days, or even longer, until he was granted a vision or heard the voice of the Great Mystery, giving him a formula by which his life was to be guided in the future.

108   From Maximilian, *Travels*, London, 1838–43, lithograph after the drawing
by Carl Bodmer

THE OFFERING OF A FINGER

AT the time of the Sun Dance ceremony, held once a year by the Plains tribes, those who in time of great trouble or danger had vowed to give a finger to the sun redeemed their pledge according to a ritual. In such self mutilations we can catch a glimpse of the power which his religion had over the redman. He had entered into a compact with a spirit and, when his prayer had been answered, it was only right and proper that he make good his engagements.

109   From the painting about 1840, by George Catlin, in the United States National Museum, Washington

THE TORTURE

SOME, who had made a vow to be tortured, were held by a thong attached through a cut in the skin until they swooned or received a vision. This latter experience caused them to be regarded as holy men and gave them great influence among their people.

110   From the painting about 1840, by George Catlin, in the United States National Museum, Washington

THE SACRED BUNDLE

"WHEN an old-time Blackfoot makes camp, the first thing to go up is the tripod from which is hung his sacred medicine bundle (usually a raw-hide case decorated with paint and fringe and containing the sacred objects) — then the tepee. Here behind his tepee this Blackfoot man stands in the first chill of an October evening, eagle-tail in hand, regarding his medicine. The meditative, vaguely reverential poise of the figure suggests the pathos of the Indian who still clings to the sacred mystery of his ancient dream." — MAYNARD DIXON.

111   From the painting by Maynard Dixon (1875–), in his possession

A HUPA INDIAN FAMILY, CALIFORNIA

WEST of the plains lay the Rockies and beyond them a wilderness of jagged mountains and arid plateaus. Almost on the edge of the Pacific was the rich valley of California. Through all this country Indians lived, the wretched Utes of the Central Basin and the primitive tribes of the coast. In the desert of Arizona and New Mexico the Pueblos built their great communal houses. Further south, in Mexico, were the Aztecs and, beyond their country, the ruins of the vanished culture of the Mayas.

Nature has given California a great diversity of climate and topography — mountains and lowlands, forests, plains and deserts. Indian life varied with these; some tribes wandered over the plains country and others were isolated in little mountain valleys. There were more different languages here than in any other part of the country. The Hupa live in the north in the rough and forested country.

112   From a group in the United States National Museum, Washington

113

114

CALIFORNIA BASKETS

THE old prints illustrate the uses of baskets among the Indians of California. As they made no pottery, there were no other vessels. It is hard to realize that many of these finely woven baskets were cooking pots. Stones were heated and then dropped in to make the contents boil. The pictures illustrate basket-making (No. 113), gathering grass seed (No. 114), carrying water and seed (No. 115), and cleaning seed (No. 116).

115   116

Four drawings by Seth Eastman after sketches by E. M. Kern in H. R. Schoolcraft, *Indian Tribes of the United States*, 1851–57

117   From the group in the United States National Museum

THE DIGGER INDIANS

In eastern California the Indians made extensive use of edible roots, and as they were everywhere seeking for these and grubbing, they were called "Digger." Like other California tribes, they gather and store acorns from which they make meal for baking into bread. A storage platform stands on the right of the lodge. No doubt these dwellings have been modified by contact with whites but are still primitive in form.

118   From the group in the United States National Museum

NAVAJO HOGANS

The house of the Navajo is called a hogan, made by setting up logs and covering them with earth. The Navajos are an agricultural people whose life differs profoundly from that of the former nomadic hunters of the plains. Their culture stands between that of the tribes to the north of them and that of the old Aztecs and Mayas on the south. The Spaniards brought sheep to the Navajo and taught them to be shepherds. Then they learned to weave the unique blankets now so familiar.

119 From M. H. Eastman, *Chicora and other Regions of the Conquerors and the Conquered*, 1854, drawing by Seth Eastman, after sketch by R. H. Kern

LAGUNA

IN New Mexico and Arizona one may still see the villages of the Pueblos. They were first described by Coronado in 1540 "as excellent good houses of three or four lofts high, wherein are good lodgings and fair chambers," and were no doubt about what they are now, great apartment houses.

120 From Lewis H. Morgan, *Houses and House Life of the American Aborigines*, 1881, after restoration by W. H. Jackson

BONITO

MANY similar buildings were in ruins when the Spaniards came, indicating that this type of architecture is ancient. We see here the restoration of Bonito, the most famous ruin in the southwest. Note that the successive stories are stepped back, facing the court, and that one ascends to the roofs by ladders.

121   From Lewis H. Morgan, *Houses and House Life of the American Aborigines*, 1881

ROOM IN A ZUÑI HOUSE

EACH room in a pueblo house was the home of a family. Agriculture was highly developed, so that these Indians depended upon their fields rather than upon hunting. The country was dry, but they understood irrigation. They also domesticated the turkey. The Zuñi, still living in their ancestral home, are a quiet, industrious people who still cling tenaciously to their ancient religion.

122   From a model in the United States National Museum

ZUÑI POTTERS

POTTERY was the art in which the Pueblos excelled. No wheel was used anywhere in America, but the vessels were built up free-hand by coiling rolls of clay. The design was painted on and the pot then fired.

123   From the painting, 1913, by Lon Megargee (1886–) in the Arizona State Capitol

THE CEREMONIAL SNAKE DANCE OF THE MOQUIS

THE religions of the Indians of the southwest were filled with the same nature worship and spirit fear that characterized the beliefs of their neighbors on the plains. The Moqui snake dance is one of the more striking of the dramatic ceremonies of the Indian worship. "The striking features of the complicated secret rite are the gathering of snakes from the world-quarters, the making of the sand altar, the snake washing, the snake drama, and the races which occur on the mornings of the days of the public 'dance' of the Snake fraternity." — WALTER HOUGH, in *Handbook of American Indians*, Washington, 1912.

END OF THE MOQUI SNAKE DANCE

THIS is the last act in the Moqui snake dance, but really a prayer for rain. The whole ceremony continues for nine days, and this running figure typifies the last moment of the dance when the snakes are being returned to the snake clan that handles the snakes. This Moqui has grabbed a bunch of them and is off down the *mesa* at top speed, speeding out to the four points of the compass to deposit the snakes in their desert home.

124   From the sculpture by Hermon A. MacNeil (1866–)

125   From a plaster study by Cyrus E. Dallin
       (1861–), in his possession

126   Navajo Orator, from the sculpture
      by Hermon A. MacNeil

THE PASSING OF THE REDMAN

THE Indian possessed great dignity
and a peculiar reverence for the mysteries of nature. It is because of
these appealing characteristics that
he is so frequently represented in both
sculpture and painting. He is, in
fact, the greatest distinctly American
element in the art of the nation by
whom he was dispossessed of his
princely heritage.

127 The Sun Vow, from the sculpture by
    Hermon A. MacNeil in the Metropolitan
    Museum of Art, New York

ADVENTURERS IN THE WILDERNESS

IN the year 1298, the jails of the little seaport town of Genoa were bulging with some seven thousand prisoners. The belligerent Genoese had bagged most of the fighting fleet of Venice, burned the bulk of it, and sailed the rest triumphantly home overloaded with captives. Among them was a Venetian gentleman who had of late achieved some notoriety because he had recently returned from a long sojourn in China and because he told tales of that far-off country which were beyond the wildest imaginings of mediæval Europeans. Waiting in prison for the feud between the rival commercial cities to be settled, Marco Polo turned his tales into one of the most famous books of travel of all time. In its pages his fellows caught a glimpse of a civilization older and, in some respects, more advanced than their own. There were canals and rivers in Cathay full of boats, and great cities teeming with population. There was a powerful emperor, Kublai Khan, presiding over a rich and luxurious court. Men looked up from Polo's pages at the bare walls of feudal castles; at fortified trading towns; at kings struggling to found small nations, England, France. There were more silks and spices, more gold and silver and precious stones in China and India than in all of Europe. Polo set men to coveting the luxuries of the Orient, and the trade that had already sprung up increased.

Between the East and the West lay that vast, sub-arid plateau of central Asia which Polo had crossed and whence fierce, fighting tribes had more than once come into China, India and Europe. West and East were developing, each in its own way and in accordance with the needs of its own life. Europe's culture was the youngest but within it lurked a discontent and vigor that the others lacked. Its life, though somewhat crude, was running full and strong, while that of China and India was passing into quiet, perhaps stagnant, pools. China, rich in herself and close to India, had bred a race of landsmen, but Europeans, from the time of early Phœnicia, had been familiar with the sea. So it came about that Europe took the initiative in building closer trade relations between the East and West. She utilized the overland routes along which the slow caravans moved back and forth; her sailors felt out the long passage about the south of Africa; they sailed westward across the Atlantic and found America. How different might have been the story of the world had the great civilization of China developed a seafaring race, and had an adventurous Mongol, making his way eastward from island to island, been the first to sight the New World. But China had no Mediterranean in which to train sailors, and already the Chinese were content with living unto themselves and looking back to their ancestors for guidance. The return of Columbus from his first voyage marked for the Orient the passing of a supreme opportunity.

Yet Columbus was not the first European to bring home news of America. About the year 1000 Leif Ericsson of the Vikings made his way westward from Iceland to

Greenland and from Greenland to Vinland, where he camped a space. There is a certain fitness in the fact that his little boats sailed the whole way above that old, sunken land-bridge which, long ages ago, had made the wild life of the two continents one. But America's time had not yet come. Leif left only the memory of a glorious adventure; the famous Genoese was no braver, only more fortunate. So it happened that a few Spaniards, captained by an Italian dreamer making his way outward in search of new sea routes, stumbled upon a strange continent in the midst of the Atlantic and, by so doing, sealed the doom of the red race and snatched from the yellow peoples an opportunity that would never return.

Yet many years passed before the Europeans grasped the full significance of their treasure-trove. Much wealth and many lives were squandered in the search for routes around or through America to the spices and the silks of Asia. But the search was not in vain, for it brought to light the outline of the continents and called into being one of the greatest feats of all time, Magellan's pioneering voyage around the world. Then precious metals were found in the American mountains. There was excitement in Spain and all manner of men set sail for Cuba, for Mexico, and for the Isthmus of Panama, and Peru. No man could tell what the vast hinterland beyond the shore might bring forth. The size, the uncertainties, the possibilities for wealth and empire in the new country excited the imaginations of the sovereigns of Europe directing the new nations arising out of the feudalism of the Middle Ages. It became a day of fantastic visions; adventure and romance were in the air. The Atlantic, which had so long been a terrifying barrier limiting the expansion of Europe, became in one short century a broad highway. Across it stretched a shining silver trail from the American Cordilleras to the kingdom of Castile.

Over this trail from west to east strained Spanish galleons, sails bulging, masts bending and holds packed with the precious metal that was making the Spanish king master in Europe. Englishmen watched this fleet grow in size and the Spaniard in arrogance. Then the Anglo-Saxon turned buccaneer. English sea-dogs began to prowl in the Atlantic and to lighten the galleons of their silver ballast. There was a fight in 1588, less than a hundred years after Columbus had taken possession of an unknown coast in the name of the Spanish king, and the Armada limped home amid the jeers of the British. The New World was to be English as well as Spanish.

Trade stirred the imagination of the English, as gold and silver did that of the Spaniards. The markets of the world were being opened up and the Briton was everywhere seeking his profits. Even the American wilderness offered opportunities to drive good bargains. Following the behests of trade, England came, somewhat unwittingly, into possession of an empire. From Maine to Georgia a chain of frontier settlements appeared which gave allegiance to the British king. But hardly were the first enterprises under way when the island kingdom found herself facing in the wilderness her ancient enemy France.

The French had set up the fleur-de-lys on the banks of the St. Lawrence and, with a true genius for empire, had plunged into the exploration of the interior. They were, in the main, fur-traders, missionaries, and soldiers. The foundations of New France rested on the forest, not on the soil. While the British were digging in almost within earshot of the Atlantic, the French swept down the Mississippi valley to the Gulf and planted stations on the way. Their plan was nobly conceived and nobly accomplished, but it was futile. Old international feuds rose from their graves and were aggravated by new rivalries. There were almost a hundred years of intermittent war. Then New France fell to England. Meanwhile the Spaniards had advanced steadily northward from Mexico into the Arizona desert and on to California; and small nations, like the Netherlands and Sweden, had been brusquely pushed aside in their colonial ambitions.

There is a fascination in looking back from the vantage point of a later century to those rude beginnings of civilized life in America. The peoples of Europe had just passed through that great intellectual awakening known as the Renaissance, which marked the close of the Middle Ages and the beginning of the modern world. New thoughts and new ambitions stirred in men's minds, and the world presented a different aspect after the days of Columbus and Magellan. Luther had defied the Pope, and the Protestant revolt against the great Roman church was setting Europe by the ears. Feudalism was slowly but inevitably giving way to nationalism. Out of such a Europe came the first peoples who built their cabins in the American forest. They were French, English, Dutch and Spanish, bringing with them the ideas and points of view of their homelands. In the main they were humble folk from the vills of the feudal manors and the trading centers. They came, following no great Columbian vision, but from very simple human motives; to win wealth from gold or the fur-trade; to own a bit of land, to find a remote place where they might worship without fear of molestation. There were almost no great figures among them. Perhaps a few, like La Salle or Penn, could be ranked among the leading minds of their day, but for the most part European leaders remained at home fixing their minds on such problems as Europe had not seen for a thousand years. The management of the settlements in America was left to lesser men.

Yet in reality these early settlers were a picked group. The ocean, still full of terrors in the seventeenth and eighteenth centuries, acted as a great selective force. The timid and the physically unfit were kept at home. Only the strongest in mind and body could meet the rigorous demands of the wilderness. Death took a heavy toll of those people who came to build their homes in the edge of the forest. The little burying grounds, so often laid out as soon as the fort, were mute evidence of the risks of the venture.

Simple folk from quiet village communities where life had run its course with little change from generation to generation were plunged into an environment where all was strange. They knew neither the forest nor its wild life and, in the main, they were unfamiliar with the sea. Yet this first American frontier was set between the two, a line of tiny settlements, like beads on a string, following the water's edge. Dirty, painted Indians grunted in the streets of the hamlets. There was always the possibility of war — war in which quarter was neither asked nor given. The menace of the savage, the danger of disease in the isolated cabin, rough labor, loneliness, — these were the price of life in the New World. The pounding of the sea on the desolate coasts served to remind the new-comers of the distance that lay between them and home. The fact that they persisted in the new life until they succeeded was the measure of the quality of the folk who first brought the civilization of Europe to America. Their pioneering spirit laid the foundations on which was to be built out of that culture a new civilization in a new world. And the personal experience of cutting loose from all that was familiar and dear and putting everything to the hazard in a little-known wilderness far across the ocean was the first step in the making of the American.

RALPH H. GABRIEL

CHAPTER I

THE VIKING ADVENTURERS

STRANGE is the story of how the destiny of Europe was first linked with that of America. In northern Scandinavia in the ninth century lived a rugged people, individualistic, warlike, ruled over by petty chieftains like the thanes of early England. Over them was a king whose power varied with his personal ability. A wild hinterland drove these Vikings seaward from their homes at the head of deep-set, high-walled fjords. They built better ships than their neighbors. Without a compass they abandoned cautious land-hugging and struck out into the open water. The rough free life at home and familiarity with the sea in all its moods schooled the Viking in courage and initiative; he became a freebooter, a pirate, and also a colonizer.

A ferment stirred in Norway in the ninth century. The North Sea was dotted with the sails of their little open ships. From the chronicles of Christian lands which suffered from the scourge of the Northmen has been gleaned most of what is known of these aggressive seafarers. They sailed to England and to northern France; they established themselves in Baltic Russia. Landsmen were no match for the sailor warriors from the north, and for a time the Vikings upset the balance of northern Europe. In vain church bells tolled; in vain the litany ascended, "From the fury of the Northmen good Lord deliver us." In their day of greatness they settled Iceland where they founded a commonwealth; from Iceland they crossed to Greenland where they established two frontier settlements; and from Greenland they sailed to Vinland.

The location of Vinland must forever remain a mystery. Whatever news Leif brought home is recorded in sagas set down long after the event. But the early sagas were deliberate attempts at historical narrative and in them is to be found most of what is known of the earliest history of Iceland. With some detail they record Leif's exploit, but their geographical descriptions cannot with assurance be attributed to any known coast. That part of the continent of North America — the coast of Labrador — was explored by the Vikings was demonstrated by the MacMillan Arctic expedition in the summer of 1925, when ruins were found on the mainland on the fifty-sixth parallel of north latitude. Had the Vikings been merely pirates, they must have sunk into oblivion. There was in them, however, a greatness which left its indelible impress upon Europe. But their discovery of America was premature; neither they nor their neighbors were prepared to develop the continent which lay beyond the ocean.

128   Model of a Viking Ship, in the United States
National Museum, Washington

THE VIKING SHIP

"Foes are they fierce beyond other foes, and cunning as they are fierce; the sea is their school of war, and the storm their friends; they are sea-wolves that live on the pillage of the world." So a Roman poet sang of the Anglo-Saxons, the first great wave of Northmen to engulf a Latin civilization. His verse is equally descriptive of their kinsmen, the Vikings of a later period.

129   From the painting, owned by Herr Wittig, Prague, by H. R. M. Hendrich (1856–)

THE OSEBERG SHIP, VIKING RELIC, 8TH CENTURY

The Norse queen or chieftainess was a Viking too, as well as her husband and her male kin. Here is pictured the remains of a queen's pleasure-boat unearthed at Oseberg, now in the Museum of the University of Oslo, Norway. The potter's clay in which the vessel was buried, preserved it. In it were found the queen's body and that of her maid who had been sent on the final journey with her; and the queen's household possessions, spinning wheels, a loom, balls of thread, and wax, a millstone, sledges, chests, cooking utensils, beds and feathers and down from pillows. Around the ship were the skeletons of her horses, dogs, and oxen, which had been killed and sent into the unknown with their mistress.

130   © E. M. Newman

BOW OF THE OSEBERG SHIP

The body of the ship is seventy-one feet long and sixteen and a half feet at its middle breadth. It has fifteen oars to a side. The original gangplank lies on deck. The mast is set amidship into the keel and is given extra support by a large arched beam. The rudder is fastened by an osier band and the rudderhead is held in the gunwale by plaited rawhide. This boat is flatter bottomed than the warships, indicating its use as a pleasure craft on the fjords. Its date is probably about 1100 A.D.

131 © E. M. Newman

THE GOKSTAD VIKING SHIP — 800 TO 1000 A.D.

Not even death could part the Viking from the sea. Sometimes his vessel with his body aboard was driven off shore in flames as a floating pyre. Sometimes it was buried on the beach, with its skipper in full armor, his weapons and drinking cups at hand. Thus through the nether darkness the Viking steered out upon invisible waters, master of the sea forever, with Valhalla, the realm of his fierce gods, his destination.

132 Photograph by Vaering, Oslo

CONJECTURAL ROUTES
OF THE
NORSEMEN
(800 — 1000 A.D.)

NORSEMEN:
——————— NORWEGIAN
—·—·—·— SWEDISH
— — — — DANISH
·············· FRENCH

133   Drawn expressly for *The Pageant of America* by Gregor Noetzel, American Geographical Society, New York

PATHS OF THE NORSE SEA ROVERS, 800–1000 A.D.

FOR several hundred years the Scandinavian peoples exhibited a remarkable power of racial expansion. The movement was at its height from about the year 800 till nearly the middle of the eleventh century, the so-called Viking period.   They crossed the Baltic, penetrated the vast wilderness of Russia by way of the Dnieper, and threatened Constantinople.   They took northern France, which under their rule became Normandy.   They settled in England, Scotland, and Ireland.   The Northman, Canute, ruled from London the British Isles, Norway, and Denmark, the first great northern empire and the first British empire in history.   From Norway and the Hebrides the Vikings colonized Iceland, from Iceland they discovered and colonized Greenland, and from Greenland they sailed to America.   The conjectural Vinland is somewhere on the northeastern coast of the North American continent.

The following were drawn upon in the construction of the above chart:
Meyers' *Historical Atlas*, Leipzig and Vienna, 1911.
C. F. Keary, *The Vikings in Western Christendom*, London, 1891;
  and the works of North Ludlow Beamish, London, 1841; William Hovgaard, New York, 1914; H. P. Steensby, Copenhagen, 1918; Eben Norton Horsford, Boston, 1891; Joseph Fischer (translated by Soulsby) London, 1903, and E. J. Payne, in *Cambridge Modern History*, 1902.

THE FIRST MENTION OF VINLAND

ADAM of Bremen was a great historian and geographer of the eleventh century. His *Historia* is a source of information not only for Baltic and German lands but for the activities of the Vikings as far west as America. Here is the first recorded reference (seventh line) to Vinland (Winland). Before the setting down of the Norse sagas, the stories of the Vikings had reached even Germany.

134   From Adam of Bremen's Ms., 11th Century, in the Staats Bibliothek, Vienna

135   From William Hovgaard, *Voyages of the Northmen to America*, New York, 1914

A PAGE OF THE SAGAS

THE adventure stories of the early Vikings are preserved, for the most part, in the sagas, the earliest literature of Scandinavia. When the art of writing became known, the sagas or legends which story-tellers had passed on by word of mouth from generation to generation were gathered into books. Story-telling was introduced into Iceland from Norway with the early settlers. In the older country it served for entertainment in kitchen or nursery but in Iceland it became a chief source of information as well as entertainment. The story-teller assumed a quasi-professional character. The *Flatey Book*, in which the page appears, is a collection of sagas with poems and shorter tales, composed and compiled between 1387 and 1395 partly by the priest Jón Pordárson. This gives the fullest version of the Vinland episode which occurred nearly four hundred years before.

Another, and older, version of the Vinland story appears in the *Saga of Eric the Red*, dating from the thirteenth century. Although several authorities have questioned the reliability of both versions, there is little doubt that there is a considerable core of fact in both stories.

NORSE RUINS, GREENLAND

ERIC THE RED was an outlaw from Norway who took refuge in Iceland. Hearing of a land to the westward, said to have been seen by some storm-driven mariners, he went in search of it and afterwards returned with tidings of a new country which, to attract settlers, he named Greenland. In 986 he sailed for this new region with twenty-five

136

ships, only fourteen of which made land, and there he planted a colony. Later a second settlement appeared, and the two endured for over 400 years. The Greenlanders raised many cattle. One settlement alone numbered 190 farms. They shipped butter, cheese, and hides to Norway and brought back timber, with which they built permanent habitations. Above are the ruins of the cathedral and bishop's house of one of the chief villages.

137

VIEW FROM BRATTAHLID OVER ERICSFIORD

ON the shores of this narrow arm of the sea dividing the snow-capped Greenland mountains, Eric the Red and Leif Ericsson built their habitations.

A GREENLAND CHURCH

THIS is the best preserved ruin of the churches of the Greenland Vikings. Like most of the others, it is built of granite in the old Irish style of architecture. The ruins at the fifty-sixth parallel discovered in 1925 have not been thoroughly investigated. Donald MacMillan believes they prove Norse exploration of the Labrador coast in that latitude.

138   The above three photographs by Mogens Clemmensen, Copenhagen

THE FLEET OF LEIF ERICSSON

ACCORDING to the Sagas, in the year 999, Leif Ericsson, son of Eric the Red, visited the court of Olaf Tryggvesson, King of Norway. The young Viking found that the Dusk of the Gods had fallen on Scandinavia. Odin had given place to Jehovah, Baldur to Christ. Olaf, who had been converted by an Anglo-Saxon monk in the Scilly Islands, had vowed to spread Christianity. Leif adopted the new faith and resolved to introduce it into Greenland. The next year he turned homeward on his sacred mission. But destiny had first another plan for this Christian Viking. Storms took the sails of his fleet and sped them far from every hitherto known coast.

LEIF ERICSSON DISCOVERING VINLAND

THROUGH the dark days and starless nights the hardy Sea-wolves battled with the sea. After weeks had

139   From the mural painting by Ezra Winter (1886–). © 1921 Twenty-five Broadway Corporation

passed thus they at last saw a shadowy outline lifting through the thinning mist and heard the boom of breakers on a shore. Land stretched north and south as far as eye could reach. Not Greenland, but a new land — Vinland.

140   From the painting by Christian Krohg (1852–), in the National Gallery, Oslo

141   From the mural painting by Harry W. Rubins (1865–), in the Blake High School, Minneapolis

LEIF ERICSSON — THE LANDING IN VINLAND

"THERE was dew upon the grass; and having accidentally got some of the dew upon their hands and put it to their mouths, they thought that they had never tasted anything so sweet. . . . As soon as their ship was afloat they took the boats, rowed to the ship, towed her up the river, and from thence into the lake, where they cast anchor, carried their beds out of the ship and set up their tents." So, in part, runs the story of Leif's discovery as told in the Icelandic sagas.

The sagas tell of other voyages to Vinland. There was even an attempt to colonize the new land. But the only result of these desperate adventurers was to spread abroad among the Viking folk the tradition of a fruitful land to the westward, Vinland the good, which Leif the Lucky had found. So the curtain thus raised for a moment upon the prologue to the drama of American history was lowered again. The significant discovery of America was to fall to the lot of another people.

142   Leif Ericsson, from the statue
at Boston, by Anne Whitney
(1821–1915)

CHAPTER II

CONTACTS WITH THE EAST

THE story of Vinland passed into legend and, outside of Scandinavia, was forgotten. Mediæval Europeans lived out the cycle of their lives ignorant of even its existence.

The Dark Ages were a time of confusion, of quarrels, forays, and wars. The nobility was an aristocracy of arms on land, and armored knights clashed in battle and in sport. The system of feudalism maintained what law and order existed. The stone castle of the feudal baron was a center of offense and defense for the people who lived about it and who did homage to the lord for his protection of them. Walled towns where dwelt artisans and men of commerce closed their gates at night against enemies from without. Nations, vague shadows of what they were later to become, were forming and dissolving. Steadfast above confusion stood the church, a super-state, the greatest stabilizing force of the time. Symbols of its power and aspirations were the cathedrals lifting throughout Europe their towers toward the heavens.

Barbarism had been left far behind by mediæval Europe. Modern languages were taking shape, and a new literature and art were appearing. Education was not yet general. A few could read books laboriously copied by hand in the monasteries, but the masses of the people looked to the officers of the church for their instruction. The mental horizon of the average man was pitifully limited. Yet in this crude and undeveloped Europe there was the promise of a future greatness.

Need is the starting-point of progress. Mediæval Europe in its daily life needed products which its own environment, rich though it was, could not supply: spices to season a diet of bread and salted meats; drugs for medicine; silks, precious stones, silver, and gold to gratify the demands of luxury as the standard of living rose. Peoples living in sub-tropical lands to the eastward produced these goods. Europe slowly became aware of it. Trade sprang up. Then began an expansion which carried Europeans not only to the civilizations of the East but westward to America, as explorers brought back tidings of rich lands across the Atlantic.

143 Temple of St. Sophia, Constantinople, from
G. J. Grelot, *Relation Nouvelle d'un Voyage de
Constantinople*, Paris, 1680

144   From the painting by Sir John Gilbert (1817–97), in the Victoria and Albert Museum, London

CRUSADERS ON THE MARCH, 1096–1270

MUCH of the first knowledge of the East came to the West through the Crusades. The earliest contacts of feudal Europe with the oriental peoples who began in the twelfth century to attend the annual fairs in Europe resulted from that supreme romance — the Crusades. Religious fervor, love of adventure, passion for war, characteristic of the Middle Ages, found vent in the great effort of the Christian world to wrest the Holy Land from the infidel. Between 1096 and 1270, seven Crusades were undertaken in vain against the Saracens. Much of the chivalry and youth of Christendom perished by sword and disease while the beloved quest, the tomb of Christ, remained in the possession of the Moslem Arabs. But those brave knights who lived to return brought back reports of Eastern splendors and samples of Eastern arts and crafts. Whither the knights had gone to fulfill a dream, followed the merchants to fill their coffers.

SAINT FRANCIS OF ASSISI, 1181–1226

THE second contact with the East came through the religion of love. About the year 1206 Francis Bernadone, son of a wealthy Italian merchant, forsook the world for a life of poverty. To possess nothing, to serve the poor, the outcast, and the leper, were the ideals on which Francis of Assisi founded his order of Friars Minor, the Franciscans. He went with the Crusaders for the purpose of preaching Christ to the Mohammedans. On his death-bed Francis rejoiced to learn of the martyrdom of two of his followers in the pagan East. Thus before 1226 had begun that glorious tradition of service to the heathen, of heroism, and of charity, which has made the Franciscans famous and beloved among the missionaries of the Catholic Church. As the missionaries went out bearing the gospel to foreign lands, they learned much of strange peoples and civilizations.

145   From the painting on wood by Lippo Memmi, ca. 1357, in the Lindenau Museum, Altenburg, Germany

JOANNES DE PIANO CARPINI,
ca. 1182–1252

THE thirteenth century saw descend upon Europe a pagan terror as disquieting as the Saracens themselves. In 1218 Genghis Khan, leader of the Mongol hordes which roamed the plateau between China and Siberia, had conquered China and Hindustan. Under his successors the Tartar wave swept westward, over Russia, Poland, and Hungary, where at last its advance was stopped by the combined forces of western Europe. In 1245 the Pope sent his countryman Carpini, who had been one of the companions of St. Francis, on a mission to the Great Khan. One of the earliest of European

146   From Pieter Vander Aa, *Naaukeurige versameling der Gedenk Waardigste Zee en Land-Reysen na oost en West-Indien,* Leyden, 1707

explorers of the Mongol empire, he made an overland journey north of the Caspian into the heart of Asia. For forty days, he says, his food was "nought but millet with salt and water" and his drink "snow melted in a kettle." The mission was unsuccessful, but his book gave Europe the first authentic description of the land ruled by the Mongols.

147   From Pieter Vander Aa, *Zee en Land-Reysen,* etc., Leyden, 1707

A FRANCISCAN FRIAR IN CHINA

IN 1253, Louis IX of France sent the Francisan friar, William de Rubruquis (1215–70), to offer to the Great Khan the Christian religion and the advantages of diplomatic relations. The friar and his party set out from Budak on the Crimean coast and crossed the steppes to Mongolia with horses and carts, a journey of five thousand miles. The Khan, however, did not accept the moral benefits offered by Louis. But good Friar William, like Carpini, wrote a book which contributed to European knowledge of the East and stirred anew the dream of an Orient to be explored, won, and redeemed by the Occident.

BAS–RELIEF EFFIGY OF FRIAR ODORIC, *ca.* 1286–1331

IN May, 1330, in a Franciscan convent in Padua, there might be seen a group of eager friars listening to the marvelous tales told by Brother Odoric, the greatest traveler of his time, while his companion, Friar James of Ireland, watched to see that no valuable fact or miracle was omitted by Friar William of Salagna who was taking down Odoric's words, and perhaps translating them into homely Latin as he went along. Odoric's travels had taken him from Trebizond to the Persian Gulf; and from Ormuz (Milton's "Ormus") to Bombay, where four Franciscans had just been killed by the Mohammedan governor. Odoric, taking their bones with him, had then passed through Malabar, Madras, Ceylon, and had sailed by junk to Sumatra, Borneo, Java, and Canton. By land from Canton he had visited Fuchow, Hangchow, and Peking. He had turned homeward through Asia, had seen Thibet and probably Lhassa itself, and finally had wound down to Venice by way of Persia and the Levant.

148   From Henry Yule, *Cathay and the Way Thither,* in Hakluyt Society Publications, 1866

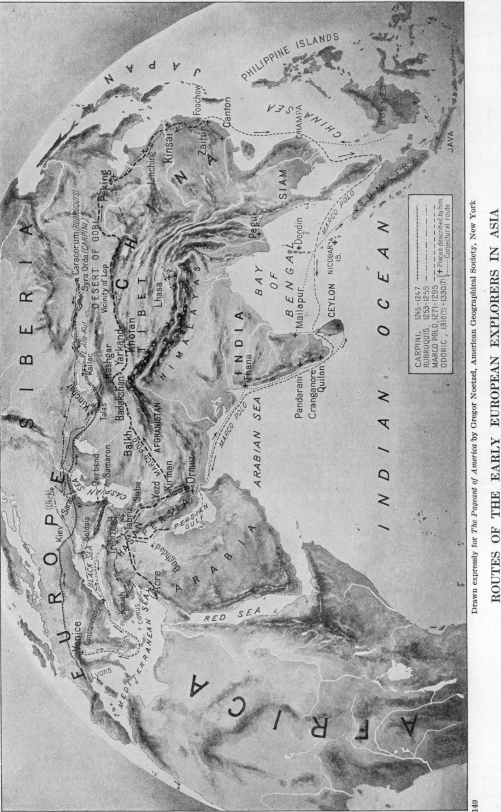

Drawn expressly for *The Pageant of America* by Gregor Noetzel, American Geographical Society, New York

ROUTES OF THE EARLY EUROPEAN EXPLORERS IN ASIA

THE travels of these ancient explorers who passed from Europe into Asia are beyond the possibility of reconstruction by the modern imagination. We cannot see life from the restricted viewpoint which was theirs. We can only vaguely imagine the dangers and hardships which they confronted in their astonishing overland journeys across central Asia. We cannot share their complete amazement at the wonders of the civilizations which they encountered. This map shows in a general way the routes that four men took and the places they visited.

149

Licommence li liures du grannt Caam qui parole de la grannt Seimeur de perse
et decertauns et dynte. Et des graunt mierueille qui p le monde sont ...
Dur sauoir la pure verite des ⚬ bites tauz vide meucouge. Et chescais qui ce liure ona

150   From a miniature on a late 14th century Ms. in the Bodleian Library, Oxford

THE POLOS LEAVING VENICE

In the winter of 1271, Marco Polo, aged seventeen — "the young bachelor," as he calls himself in his book — set out from Acre with his father, Nicolo, and his uncle, Maffeo, on their return visit to Cathay. The first plan of the Polos was to make China by sea, but they changed their minds and started overland through Persia, which was now a Tartar realm ruled by the brother of Kublai Khan of Cathay. In the spring of 1275, young Marco first saw the Khan at his summer seat, Shang-tu, north of the Great Wall. "The young bachelor" so endeared himself to Kublai that the Khan kept him in his service for twenty years, entrusted him with diplomatic and military commissions, and made him governor of a city.

KUBLAI KHAN *

In Xanadu did Kubla Khan
A stately pleasure dome decree,
Where Alph, the sacred river, ran
Through caverns measureless to man,
Down to a sunless sea.
              — S. T. Coleridge: *Kubla Khan* (1797)

Kublai Khan was the first of his race to rise above barbarism. He was keenly interested in all that the Polos could tell him about the outside world. In 1286, he sent a message to the Pope asking him to send missionaries. In response, the Franciscan, John of Montecorvino, set out in 1289, accompanied by a Dominican who died on the way. Father John went by way of Persia and India, as he was also charged with missions to rulers in those countries. It was not until 1294 that he reached Peking, only to find that Kublai Khan had just died, but he was hospitably received and by 1299 had established a church. He remained in Peking until his death about 1328, prior to which other Franciscans had joined him and he had been raised to the rank of archbishop.

151 From Henry Yule, *Book of Ser Marco Polo, the Venetian*, London, 1871, after an engraving in a Chinese encyclopedia, Bibliothèque Nationale, Paris

* This is the spelling adopted by Asiatic scholars.

QUAINT ILLUSTRATIONS OF EARLY TRAVELS IN ASIA

A FRENCH artist's fancy has pictured here the Polos in far Cathay. Chinese castles rise with Norman towers; the streets climb and wind as in Fiesole; the river craft of mediæval Europe float on an Indian river; the trusty little Italian donkeys add an intimate and homely touch. The mind of the mediæval European could not conceive civilization so different as that of China. Polo helped to break down this provincialism.

152   Illustration from *Livre des Merveilles*, Paris, 1916, after late 14th century miniatures in the Bibliothèque Nationale, Paris

MAFFEO AND NICOLO POLO IN CHINA

"THE GREAT KHAN received them with great honor and hospitality, and showed much pleasure at their visit, asking them a great number of questions. First, he asked them about the Emperors, how they maintained their dignity, and administered justice in their dominions; and how they went to battle, and so forth. And then he asked like questions about the Kings and princes and other potentates."

THE ANCIENT CITY OF PEKING

MARCO POLO writes that it has two fine towers. "One of them has been covered with gold a good finger in thickness so that the tower looks as if it were all solid gold; and the other is covered with silver in like manner. The upper part is girt all about with bells, the top of the gold tower with gilded bells and the silver tower with silvered bells."

153   Illustration from *Livre des Merveilles*, Paris, 1916, after late 14th century miniatures in the Bibliothèque Nationale, Paris

154   Illustration from *Livre des Merveilles*, Paris, 1916, after late 14th century miniatures in the Bibliothèque Nationale, Paris

MARCO POLO IN INDIA

POLO writes of an Indian prince: "He wears also a fine silk thread strung with 104 large pearls and rubies of great price. The King wears on his arms three golden bracelets thickly set with pearls of great value, and anklets also of like kind he wears on his legs, and rings on his toes likewise. So let me tell you what this King wears between gold and gems and pearls, is worth more than a city's ransom."

— Quotations from Henry Yule,
Book of Ser Marco Polo, London, 1903.

MARCO POLO,
ca. 1254–1324

155 From Henry Yule, *Book of Ser Marco Polo,* London, 1903, from the painting in the gallery of Monsignor Badia, Rome, by Giuseppe Gnoli, probably in the 16th century

156 From an engraving in the Nuremburg (1477) Edition of *Marco Polo,* Grenville Collection, British Museum

IN Venice still stands a passage and a decorated archway of the old Ca' Polo, the mansion of the Polos. At the door under that arch, one day in 1295, three strangers in fantastic and travel-worn garb knocked for admittance. The Asiatic travelers had returned and, sewed in the seams of their garments, was a fortune in precious stones. Soon the whole city was agog to hear the tales they told, tales which perhaps might never have been written down had Marco not shipped in a fleet that put off to fight the rival Genoese. The day was lost to Venice, and Polo was one of a host of prisoners carried off to Genoa. He whiled away the weary months in prison by dictating the book which has kept his memory alive through the centuries. One Rusticiano (or Rustichello) of Pisa, also a captive of the Genoese and otherwise a respectable literary hack, wrote the manuscript. Within less than a year the captivity was over and Polo was restored to his home. At this point in his life Marco, save for one or two glimpses of him, drops out of the historical record. Even his tomb, erected, in accordance with his will, in the Church of St. Lorenzo, has disappeared.

MARCO POLO'S BOOK — PRINTED IN LATIN

"THE pen is mightier than the sword," and "there is a power in books." For the truth of these two old platitudes look to Marco Polo, the Venetian. The book about the wealth and splendor of the East which Polo dictated had an influence, hardly to be overestimated, upon the discovery of the western world. Here at last was a book, but not by a friar who might be suspected of gilding facts for the purpose of moving Christian sovereigns to the conquest of a heathen realm for the Church. Nay, here was a book by a trader, the son and nephew of traders, a practical man who would not lure any to ruin for the sake of an ideal. Kings and princes read it and forthwith coveted the treasures of the Khan; merchants read it, figured the value of the jewels and stuffs of this distant realm and sighed, seeing as yet they had but touched the hem of profits; mariners read it, tried to visualize that great sea washing the beaches of Cathay and in imagination sailed upon it — to what shores beyond?

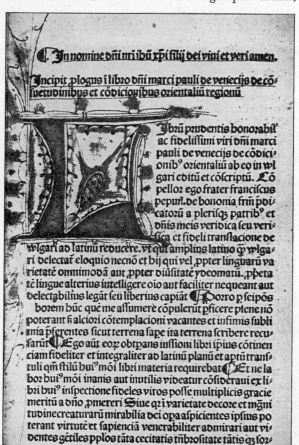

157 First page of *Marco Polo* (The Travels of) printed by Gerard Leeu, probably at Gouda, in 1484. In the New York Public Library

158   Detail from a facsimile of the Catalan map, 14th century, in the New York Public Library

THE CARAVAN

THOUSANDS of caravans of camels and horses brought the goods of Asia over the long land routes to the sea ports where they could be picked up by Europeans. The picture shows the caravan of a Tartar chieftain with his retainers.

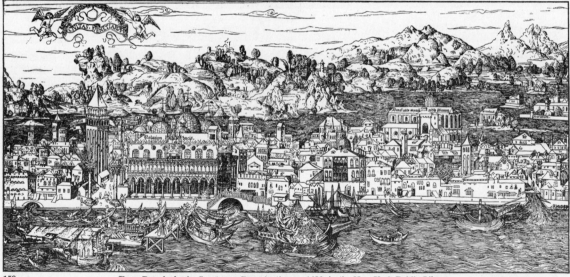

159   From Breydenbach, *Sanctarum Peregrinationum*, 1486, in the New York Public Library

VENICE, 1486

As the contacts with the East grew in numbers, trade increased in volume, Europeans sought more and more the spices, the silks and fabrics, the porcelain and the precious stones of Asia. The Mediterranean was dotted with a constantly growing fleet of merchantmen. Venice and Genoa became the great distributing centers of southern Europe, gathering the riches of Asia from the Black Sea and the eastern Mediterranean, and sending them at a handsome profit to the towns and manors of feudal Europe. Suddenly, in 1453, when the invading Ottoman Turks took Constantinople, Asiatics had entered upon conquest in Europe.

MOHAMMED II

MOHAMMED II, famed for his cruelty, led the
Turks in their final assault upon Constantinople, the city founded in 330 by Constantine
the Great, the first Christian emperor, as the
capital of the Christian Roman Empire.
When Constantine XII, Emperor on that
fateful day, May 29, 1453, saw the Moslem
banners carried over the walls, he threw
away his weapons and cast himself upon the
swords of the foe. But the Turk, in shattering
an old empire, helped to stir Europe to the
discovery of a new world.

CONSTANTINOPLE

"ALL these products, 'cloths of silk and gold,'
and many more besides, so attractive to the
unjaded mind of Europe, celebrated in
chronicle and romance from the thirteenth to
the fifteenth century, were to be found in
those cities of the Levant — in Constantinople, in Antioch or Jaffa or Alexandria —
which were the western termini of the long
established trade routes to the Far East.
Wares of China and Japan and the spices of
southern Moluccas were carried in Chinese
or Malay junks to Malacca, and thence by
Arab or Indian merchants to Paulicut or
Calicut in southern India. To these ports

160   From the portrait by Gentile Bellini (1429–1507), in the National
Portrait Gallery, London

came also ginger, brazil-wood, sandal-wood, and aloe, above all the precious stones of India and
Persia, diamonds from Golconda." — CARL BECKER, *Beginnings of the American People*, 1915.

161   From Grelot, *Relation nouvelle d'un Voyage de Constantinople*, Paris, 1680

TRADE ROUTES
OF
MEDIAEVAL COMMERCE
IN
EUROPE

HANSEATIC LEAGUE   VENETIANS   GENOESE

MOST OF THE BLACK SEA COMMERCE
WAS IN THE POSSESSION OF THE
VENETIANS AND GENOESE.

162   Drawn expressly for *The Pageant of America* by Gregor Noetzel, American Geographical Society, New York

TRADE ROUTES

THE long trade routes from Asia, by land and sea, led eventually to the Black Sea and the Mediterranean. Chinese and Japanese junks and Malay boats brought goods to the Moluccas, and Indian and Malay traders carried them to Calicut, whence they were taken up the Persian Gulf to Basra and overland, by caravan through Bagdad and Damascus, to the Mediterranean. Other goods went by way of the Red Sea to Suez. Such were the southern routes. A central route crossed central India, Afghanistan, and Persia to Asia Minor. A third came from China and, going north or south of the Caspian, reached the Black Sea. This widespread network of commercial routes fell into collapse when the adventurous Portuguese discovered the ocean route from Europe around Africa to the Orient.

163   Mohammedans at prayer, from G. J. Grelot,
*Relation nouvelle d'un Voyage de Constanti-
nople*, Paris, 1680

CHAPTER III

THE PORTUGUESE NAVIGATORS

PORTUGAL is a narrow region with navigable rivers flowing westward and a long coast indented by fine harbors. Such a country seems fashioned to breed men for the sea. It was from her ports that the Arabs, after the Northmen the boldest of mediæval mariners, had made their explorations when the Moors held sway. The tradition of their voyages and of the new lands which they had discovered — the Madeira and Cape Verde Islands — lingered to redound to the glory of her harbors in later days.

The dawn of the fifteenth century found Portugal once more Christian and independent. By the valor of her arms she had expelled the Moor and had stopped the ambitious aggressions of Spain. She was quick with the old spirit of the Crusades. The Faith had blessed her sword and had given her power among the nations. The aggrandizement of that power was therefore to the Portuguese a mission hardly less sacred than that of spreading the Faith.

Hostile Spain, lying east and north of her, blocked her from land communication with Europe. Already Portuguese commerce with England, Flanders, and Germany had made a virtue of necessity and had been successfully carried on by sea. The accomplishment of both her sacred missions, then, must be by way of the sea.

164 The Cross-staff, from John Seller,
Practical Navigation, London, 1680

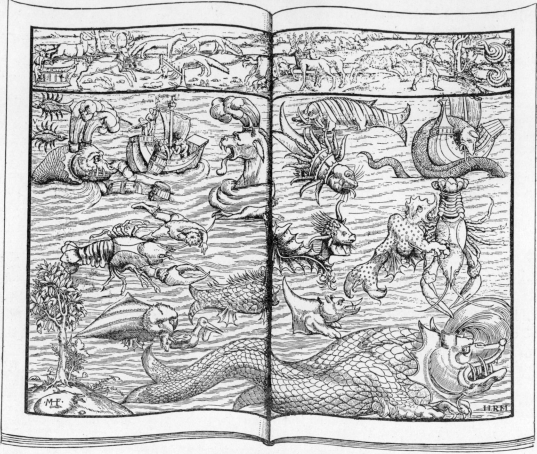

165   From Sebastian Münster, *Cosmographiae Universalis*, Basil, 1544

THE SEA OF DARKNESS

An unknown sea stretched away southward and to the westward from the coasts of Europe touching somewhere, perhaps, upon the Golden Cathay of Marco Polo's travels or upon richer lands unseen as yet by Christians. Somewhere this ocean received the waters of the "Western Nile" flowing through the realm of the mythical Christian King, Prester John, who — so ran the legend — ruled in the heart of Africa, beset on all sides by Islam and awaiting his rescue by Catholic Europe.

But medieval superstition, a deadlier power than Spanish steel, barred the Portuguese empire from that sea, which the ancients had justly named "The Sea of Darkness." Out beyond its horizon line, luring though that might be, this Sea of Darkness was held to be the home of weird monsters that dragged down ships, a place of thick and noisome vapors that strangled men and forever blew their thin ghosts about, lost wanderers in a chill and supernatural fog.

166   From Olaus Magnus, *Historia de Gentibus Septentrionalibus*, Rome, 1555

HENRY THE NAVIGATOR
1394–1460

A SAINT GEORGE to slay this sea-dragon of superstition was the need of the hour. He came in the person of Henry, later surnamed the Navigator, fourth son of John I of Portugal. Henry was one of the first scholars in Europe, a warrior of renown, and a man of devout Christian life. He had, moreover, enough Norse blood in him from his grandfather, "Old John of Gaunt, time-honor'd Lancaster," not to fear the sea. Moreover, he had Marco Polo's book and a rare collection of maps, the one to inspire and the other to assist him in piercing the mystery of the Sea of Darkness that men so feared. Prince Henry did not dissipate his energies in many enterprises. With iron determination, each year he advanced farther and farther toward his one great objective.

THE "SACRED PROMONTORY," WHERE PRINCE HENRY STUDIED

IN 1419 Henry went to Sagres, a rocky promontory at the southernmost tip of Portugal. Here he erected an observatory and drew about him scientists and seasoned mariners. There were many questions to be answered. Was this world really flat, with its doming sky and far crescent of sea? Where did the

167   From a miniature in Gomes de Azurara, *Une Chronique de la Découverte et de la Conquête de Guinea*, 1448–53, in the Bibliothèque Nationale, Paris

off-shore waves end? What of ebb and flow? By study of the heavens, man would master the tides, said the Arabs whose chief science was astronomy. To Henry, the Christian, seeking nightly for that answer in the sky, seeking through the patient years while the names of fool and blasphemer were hurled at him, this saying had a twofold meaning. For was it not decreed in the beginning by the God who charted the heavens and gave the Gospel for a light to the mind that man should have dominion over the sea and its terrors? To Henry the Navigator the answer seemed within his grasp. During his lifetime the Navigator saw the results of his work change profoundly the mental outlook of Europe.

168   From Oliveira Martins, *The Golden Age of Prince Henry the Navigator*, E. P. Dutton & Co., 1914, after a drawing by Commander R. N. Shore

HENRY AT THE SAGRES OBSERVATORY

YEAR after year Henry sent out ships that worked their way farther and farther down the hot and inhospitable African coast. They passed the land of the tawny Moors and came upon the white sands of the Sahara. Further they sailed and left behind even the bounds of Islam. Then in 1445 Diniz Diaz pushed beyond the desert to the green country of the Soudan. He found and named Cape Verde. Beyond this promontory where the coast begins to fall away, Henry's navigators turned their prows eastward, and excitement ran high, for surely now, they thought, they were rounding Africa. Black natives on the shores peered in wonder at the strange ships. And to Africa, as to America, woe and injustice came by sea, for some of these dark men were brought back to Portugal, and ere long a profitable slave trade sprang up. Henry had nerved his captains to conquer the superstition of the Sea of Darkness; but mariners who feared not the monsters of the deep must be persuaded to forego the profits of the new trade.

169   From Antonio Ennes and others, *Historia de Portugal*, Lisbon, 1876-83

170 From the original in the Sociedade
de Geografia de Lisboa, Lisbon

FRAGMENTS OF A *PADRÃO* SET UP BY BARTHOLOMEW DIAZ

HENRY's seamen followed the African coast for two thousand miles, here and there planting stone columns as milestones to mark their progress on the sea lane to India. From the long voyage they brought back ivory, gold, and slaves, three fateful gifts of Africa to the white explorer. Explorations that proved so profitable did not cease with Henry's death. In 1482 Diego Cam discovered the Congo. Six years later Bartholomew Diaz rounded the Cape. Because of the cruel winds he had encountered he called it "The Cape of Storms." But when King John II heard the joyful news that the long wall of continent had at last been passed and eastern waters entered, he renamed it "The Cape of Good Hope." The illustration shows fragments of a stone set up by Bartholomew Diaz in 1487 on the coast of Africa.

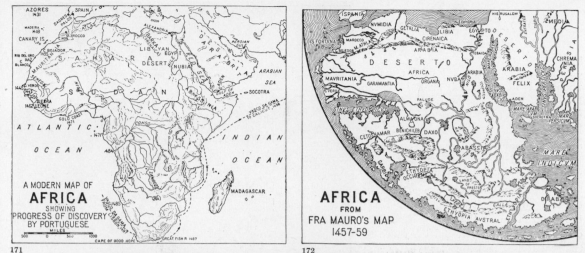

171

172

Drawn expressly for *The Pageant of America* by Gregor Noetzel, American Geographical Society, New York

PORTUGUESE VOYAGES DOWN THE AFRICAN COAST

PRINCE HENRY firmly believed that, if the African coast were followed south, a cape would be discovered which the mariner could round and then start for India. So great was his influence that his belief was imparted to his followers. It was accepted by Fra Mauro, working at Venice, in the years 1457–1459, on a map of the world. An examination of the northern part of the map makes clear its surprising accuracy. The north shore of "Sinus Ethyopicus" is that along which the Portuguese captains turned eastward after passing Cape Verde. Across the map Egypt and the Red Sea, "Mare Rubrum," are shown in their proper relations. The southern part of Africa is pure conjecture, in the midst of which is put the land of the mythical Prester John, the isolated Christian engulfed in a Mohammedan flood. Because it was carefully done and based on the best information obtainable, this map had wide influence on the navigators of the day. It beckoned them to further voyages down the African coast and around the southern point to India and Persia.

KING JOHN IN THE SHIPYARD

HENRY went to his tomb no longer the scorned but the honored of his nation. Because Henry's faith held stanch through twelve years of mockery and failure, when even his captains betrayed him and sometimes, fear-driven, fled back to Sagres, King John II stood in a later day in the shipyard directing the building of the Indian fleet. Neither demons nor darkness should assail those galleons. And, at the end of the voyage, waited the opulent markets of the East.

173
Drawn expressly for *The Pageant of America* by H. A. Ogden (1856–)

VASCO DA GAMA, *ca.* 1460–1524

JOHN died before the fleet for India sailed. His successor sent out Vasco da Gama, who after many days upon an uncharted sea dropped anchor in the harbor of Calicut, west coast of India, on May 20, 1498. When Vasco turned homeward the prows of his ships he left a marble column on the shore to announce that Portugal had added a second continent to her empire. In 1499, seven years after Columbus' famous voyage, the Portuguese government smilingly informed the Spanish court that a "nobleman of our household" had found the route to the real Indies, and the "large cities, and great populations" which Columbus had failed to discover; in proof of which he had brought home "cinnamon, cloves, ginger, nutmeg, pepper, also many fine stones of all sorts; so that henceforth all Christendom in this part of Europe shall be able, in large measure, to provide itself with these spices and precious stones."

Da Gama's discovery of an all-water route to the Orient revolutionized commerce. It was far cheaper to ship the freight of the East around the Cape of Good Hope than to carry it with several rehandlings overland by caravan. The new route was more important than the coming of the Turks in diverting trade from the Mediterranean to Portuguese ports on the Atlantic.

174   From the portrait by Christovao de Utrecht (born 1498), in the
Museu Nacional de Arte Antiga, Lisbon

175   From Montanus, *De Nieuwe en Onbekende Weereld*, 1671

CABRAL'S SHIPS OFF THE COAST OF BRAZIL

IN 1500 Pedro Alvarez Cabral, another intrepid adventurer of the day, set out from Portugal for India. Cabral, however, stood far out from the coast on this voyage and was blown westward to the shore of Brazil, where he planted the standard of Portugal. Brazil, it is true, had already been discovered in 1499 by Vicente Yañes Pinzón, who commanded the little *Niña* on Columbus' first voyage. But, by the Pope's arbitrary line of division and the subsequent treaty between Spain and Portugal, Brazil lay in Portugal's half of the world.

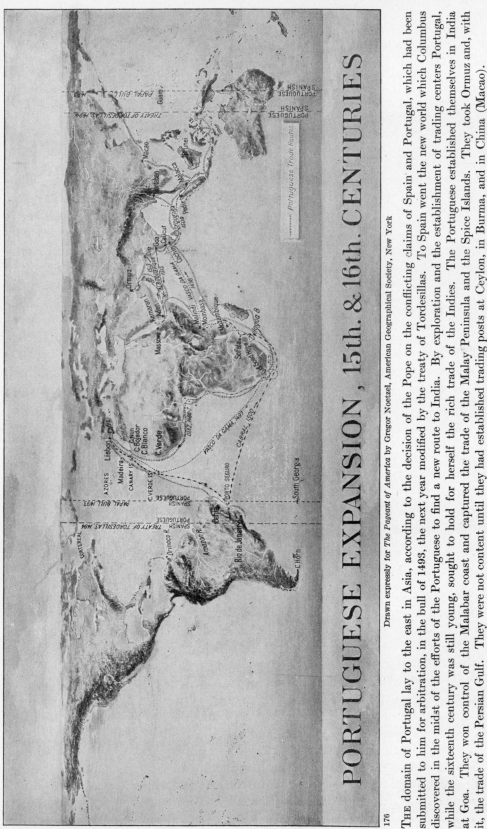

PORTUGUESE EXPANSION, 15th. & 16th. CENTURIES

Drawn expressly for *The Pageant of America* by Gregor Noetzel, American Geographical Society, New York

176

THE domain of Portugal lay to the east in Asia, according to the decision of the Pope on the conflicting claims of Spain and Portugal, which had been submitted to him for arbitration, in the bull of 1493, the next year modified by the treaty of Tordesillas. To Spain went the new world which Columbus discovered in the midst of the efforts of the Portuguese to find a new route to India. By exploration and the establishment of trading centers Portugal, while the sixteenth century was still young, sought to hold for herself the rich trade of the Indies. The Portuguese established themselves in India at Goa. They won control of the Malabar coast and captured the trade of the Malay Peninsula and the Spice Islands. They took Ormuz and, with it, the trade of the Persian Gulf. They were not content until they had established trading posts at Ceylon, in Burma, and in China (Macao).

The expansion of Portugal marked the passing of the commercial importance of the Italian cities, Genoa and Venice. The Mediterranean was no longer the chief water route between the West and the East. Trade routes now ran across the open ocean.

The Portuguese captains not only added much to the geographical knowledge of the time but made exploration popular. They had actually reached the fabled East. They had trained up a school of daring navigators willing to risk the dangers of an unknown sea. But they neither proved nor disproved the theory of a round earth. Columbus, who embarked on his first voyage in the midst of the Portuguese activities on the west coast of Africa, could get no data from them as to the probability of reaching India by sailing west.

CHAPTER IV

CHRISTOPHER COLUMBUS

WHILE Portuguese captains were venturing down the African coast in search of a water route to the East two monarchs, Ferdinand and Isabella, were welding Spain into a nation. The union of the separate kingdoms of Aragon and Castile was but one of the problems that confronted the Spanish rulers. Seven centuries before, hordes of African Mohammedans had crossed the Straits of Gibraltar and conquered their way into Europe. The Moors, as they were called, had been thrown back in long and bloody wars. In 1481, the armies of Ferdinand and Isabella moved against Granada, the last stronghold of the infidels. The task was difficult. Not until eleven years had passed were the Spanish arms successful. At last, on January 2, 1492, Granada surrendered and the Moor passed finally out of Europe.

One of those who watched the surrender ceremony was an Italian navigator, Christopher Columbus. Nearly five years before he had first presented to the Spanish court a plan for sailing westward across the unknown ocean to Asia. But the Moorish wars had absorbed the attention and depleted the treasury of the sovereigns and little heed had been given to Columbus. Yet he had persisted in his quest. He was familiar with the best thought of the time that the earth was round, and shared in that belief. He was profoundly convinced that great discoveries would follow a voyage westward.

Columbus had been born in Genoa, the son of a weaver. Doubtless, as a boy, along the wharves of the busy Italian port, he had heard from returned sailors strange tales of distant lands. The sea attracted him and when he was but fourteen he was sailing before the mast. Most of the details of the early life of the great navigator are lost in the mists of the past. The origin of the idea that was to dominate his career will probably never be known. When he was twenty-five he made a voyage to England. In February of the following year, according to his own account, he ventured "a hundred leagues beyond the island of Thule [Iceland]." Perhaps he came into contact with the old Norse tradition of Vinland. In the ports of Portugal and Spain tales of mysterious islands beyond the Canaries were bandied about. The maps of the day gave them form. Perhaps this gossip of the seaboard awakened in the mind of the imaginative Genoese the vision of lands that lay to the west. He had read the travels of Marco Polo; perchance he also might reach Cathay.

The world into which Columbus had been born was full of new thoughts. In the cities of his own Italy had come the Renaissance that was bringing new life to Europe. Men were turning from the cramped philosophy of the Middle Ages to the rich thought of ancient Greece. Freedom and individualism were in the air. Men were exploring the realms of the spirit as well as of the earth. The dreams of Columbus were in harmony with the growth of the age. Others believed in a round world and in lands to the westward, but in the great admiral persistence and fortitude were united with imagination. When he returned from the first voyage, he had broadened immeasurably the horizon of Europe. The Middle Ages had come to an end.

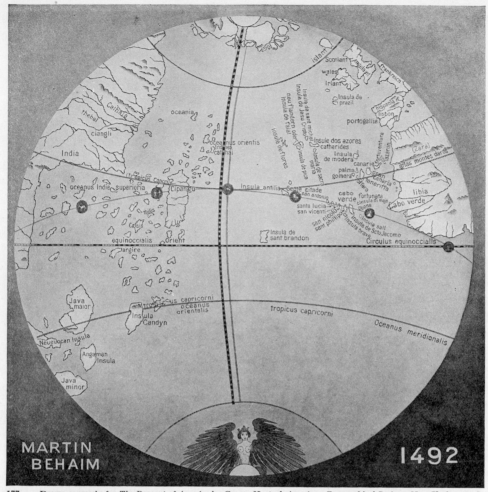

MARTIN BEHAIM

1492

177   Drawn expressly for *The Pageant of America* by Gregor Noetzel, American Geographical Society, New York,
based on a facsimile in the Society

178 From E. G. Ravenstein, *Martin Behaim, His
Life and His Globe*, London, 1908

MARTIN BEHAIM'S GLOBE

COLUMBUS had an intellectual double, Martin Behaim of Nuremberg, a cosmographer. Both believed in a round world. Behaim, to prove his theories, had made a secret voyage westward in partnership with his patron, Estreito of Madeira, but the expedition failed. Returning to Nuremberg, he set forth his ideas in the famous globe which he completed in 1492 before the return of Columbus. It shows the influence of Ptolemy and of the discoveries of Marco Polo. The Atlantic is filled with the islands familiar to the myths of the Middle Ages. There is no evidence that Columbus was influenced by Behaim in his great undertaking. The two men were in Portugal at the same time but no connection between them has been established.

The significance of the Behaim globe lies in its vivid presentation of the ideas that were current at the time when the Genoese opened a new chapter in geographical knowledge.

THE PORTRAITS OF COLUMBUS

So far as is known there is no portrait of Columbus in existence that was painted during his lifetime. Yet many artists have portrayed what they conceived to be the features of the great admiral. The purpose of the following collection of portraits is to show some of the more significant of these attempts.

The Jovius portrait is an engraving which is believed to have been first published in 1575. It is a copy of a portrait that hung in the famous gallery of Paulus Jovius, Archbishop of Nocera (1483–1552). Jovius, a man of vast wealth who spent a fortune in collecting portraits of the great men of his time, was an ardent admirer of Columbus, though but a young man when Columbus died. On Jovius' walls hung a portrait of Columbus which has since been lost. It is inconceivable that Jovius would have been content with less than the most faithful possible portrait of his favorite hero. Perhaps the Archbishop's picture was one which had been painted in Columbus' lifetime. If so, this vigorous engraving of a man in middle life must approximate the features of the discoverer of America. No portrait with

179   From Paulus Jovius, *Elogia Virorum Illustrium*, Basil, 1595

better claims has yet appeared, and it is interesting to be able to trace the influence of the first attempt to portray the Discoverer, as is seen in the Jovius portrait, on all of the subsequent paintings of Columbus.

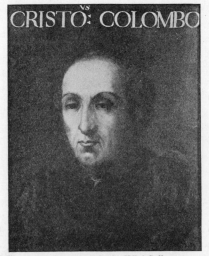

180   From the portrait in the Uffizi Gallery, Florence

THE FLORENCE PORTRAIT (180)

CERTAINLY since 1567 and probably since 1552, this portrait has hung in the Uffizi Gallery at Florence. It is believed to be a poor copy of the Jovius portrait and has been called the oldest perfectly authenticated picture of Columbus.

THE PIOMBO PORTRAIT (181)

THE inscription at the top reads: "This is the admirable effigy of the Genoese Columbus, the first who entered in a ship into the world of the Antipodes."

181   From the portrait by Sebastino del Piombo (1485?–1547) in the Metropolitan Museum of Art, New York

182 From the portrait in the Biblioteca Nacional, Madrid

THE YAÑEZ PORTRAIT (182)

A STRANGE story clings to the Yañez portrait. In 1763 the Spanish government bought from Señor Yañez of Granada four portraits, including one of Columbus, all painted by the same hand. Many years later the Columbus portrait was found to have been altered before its purchase. With great skill the daubs that concealed the original were cleared away and the portrait as here reproduced was brought to light. It bears unmistakable marks of the Italian school of the sixteenth century. Strong claims have been made that this is the Jovius portrait, the engraving of which it strongly resembles. This Yañez portrait is perhaps the only one in which are presented complete the characteristics of Columbus which those who knew him personally have described. Yet too little is known of it to establish its authenticity.

183 From the portrait, 1838, by Charles Legrand, in El Museo Naval, Madrid

184 From the portrait in the possession of Dr. Alessandro de Orchi, Villa Muggio, Albate, Italy

THE MADRID PORTRAIT (183)

THE Madrid portrait was painted in 1838 at the order of the Spanish government. The artist seems to have used the old Capriolo engraving for his model.

THE DE ORCHI PORTRAIT (184)

THE painter of the de Orchi portrait is unknown. Its likeness to the Florence portrait has led to the belief that the two had a common original. Claims have been made that this is the lost Jovius portrait.

THE CAPRIOLO PORTRAIT (185)

THE Capriolo portrait is evidently derived from the Jovius. The Madrid portrait shows striking resemblances to it.

THE DE BRY PORTRAIT (186)

DE BRY claimed that this was made from an artist's copy of a portrait painted by order of the Catholic kings before Columbus set sail on his first voyage. According to de Bry, the original was stolen and taken to the Netherlands. The story is considered a bit of advertisement for de Bry's work.

185 From Aliprando Capriolo, *Ritratti di cento capitani . . . illustri*, Roma, 1600

186 From de Bry, *Grands Voyages*, Part V. Frankfort, 1595

TOSCANELLI'S CHART

THE great Florentine astronomer, Paolo Toscanelli, also believed in a small round earth. The story ran that Toscanelli set forth his ideas in a chart (since lost) of the Atlantic and sent it with a letter to Columbus. But this report is no longer unquestioned. His chart, of which a restoration appeared in *Das Ausland*, 1867, has here been adapted to show by shaded lines the actual location of the western continent. The sketch is based on *Das Ausland*, Ruge, Justin Winsor, and John Fiske.

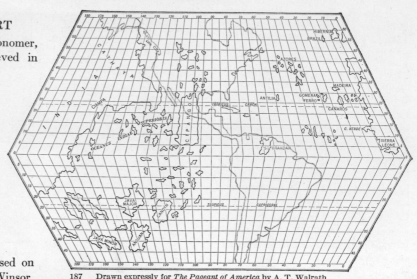

187   Drawn expressly for *The Pageant of America* by A. T. Walrath

188   From Henry Harrisse, *Notes on Columbus*, 1866

PIERRE D'AILLY'S *IMAGO MUNDI*

THE geographer d'Ailly set forth, in his *Imago Mundi*, ideas of a round earth. Because the book was printed in 1480, many have thought that Columbus derived his ideas from it. A copy annotated in the handwriting of Christopher, or in that of his brother Bartholomew, is among the Columbian relics at Seville, but there seems to be no evidence that Columbus read or used it before his epoch-making voyage of 1492.

FERDINAND, 1452–1516, KING OF ARAGON

EARLY in 1486 Columbus interviewed the Spanish sovereigns at Cordova. The time was not propitious. It is true that Ferdinand, by his marriage with Isabella, had united the crowns of Aragon and Castile and had thus strengthened his kingdom against the heathen, but the Moors still held the southwest. All Ferdinand's resources were at this time consecrated to the task of European conquest and could not be diverted to outfitting Columbus for the purpose of attempting transatlantic discovery.

189   From the portrait on wood, painter unknown, in El Museo Naval, Madrid

THE PRESENTATION AT COURT

IN his later years Columbus complained that in his struggle for recognition in Spain "everybody had derided him, save two Monks, Marchena and Pérez." Laughed at he was, but probably not so much because of his theories of the earth, which many others held, but because of the stupendous rewards which his great ambition led him to demand in case he should be successful. To be governor of the lands he discovered, to have one tenth of all the trade exchanges within those lands, to be admiral of the "Ocean Sea" that washed the shores of distant Cathay, and to be made a nobleman — such aspirations for the son of a Genoese weaver seemed ridiculous. They had already hurt his cause

190   From the painting signed "M. Crespo, Madrid, 1889," artist and location not known. Photograph by Roig

with King John of Portugal, to whom Columbus had first made his proposition for a voyage westward into the Atlantic ocean.   When Columbus had failed in Portugal, he turned to Spain.

THE COUNCIL OF SALAMANCA, 1486–87

THE court referred the project of Columbus to Hernando de Talavera, who thereupon called a council of ecclesiastics, scientists, and mariners to consider it.   After nearly five years the council reported adversely. Meanwhile, Christopher's brother, Bartholomew, had appealed in vain to Henry VII of England and was now importuning Charles VIII of France.   To France Christopher resolved to go; but first he determined to visit the convent of la Rabida near Palos in Andalusia.   Here he had a friend, Antonio de Marchena, the former guardian, and in his care Columbus planned to leave his little son, Diego.

191   From the painting, 1887, by Nicolo Barbarino (1832–91), in the Orsini Gallery, Genoa

THE CONVENT OF LA RABIDA

AT Santa Maria de la Rabida, Columbus arrived in poverty and in dejection of spirits. But St. Mary of the Frontier was to be for him that boundary of failure from which the last successful march upon achievement is made. Marchena and the officiating guardian, Juan Pérez, heard his story with enthusiasm. Who could be more eager to discover new lands than Franciscans? Already their Order had a glorious roll of explorers, crusaders, missionaries,

192   From a photograph by Diego Calle, Huelva, Spain

in the East, among the Saracens and with the Portuguese in Africa.

COLUMBUS AND THE FRIARS OF LA RABIDA

COLUMBUS, Marchena, and Pérez devised a plan whereby the Italian navigator, using Palos as a center, should gather together in the maritime section of Spain all possible information regarding voyages into the Sea of Darkness. At Santa Maria a pilot told him that he had recently sailed due west from Ireland and had sighted land, probably Labrador. Another pilot in Palos itself, at the very doors of La Rabida, recounted a voyage west with "a Prince of Portugal" to discover new lands and his encounter with the leagues of weed floating in the Sargasso Sea, which compelled a return. Columbus also learned something of the exploration plans of the most important man in maritime affairs at Palos, Martin Alonso Pinzón, then absent in Rome marketing a cargo of sardines and incidentally scanning documents in the Papal library.

193   From the painting, 1873, by Félipe Maso (1851–), owned by the Provincial Committee of Huelva, Spain

ISABELLA, QUEEN
OF CASTILE, 1451–1504

WHATEVER news Pinzón brought home presently was enough to send Pérez off at dead of night, riding on a mule, to see Isabella. Pérez had been the Queen's confessor. He knew her to be an ardent Catholic, an ambitious queen, a power with Ferdinand, and rich enough to finance the venture for which Pinzón and Columbus had now joined forces. Her imagination fired by Pérez's tale, Isabella summoned Columbus and called a council to arrange ways and means.

With success almost in his grasp the navigator came to the court, not as a poor suitor, but still persistent in his demands for high offices and great emoluments as the price for his services.

ON THE BRIDGE OF PINES:
THE RECALL OF COLUMBUS

BUT Ferdinand, no less haughty than John of Portugal, although the Spanish flags now waved at Granada to proclaim the final overthrow of the Moors, refused the honors which Columbus demanded. Again the disappointed navigator turned away, defeated. But on

194   From a life-portrait of Isabella, attributed to Juan Flamenco, in the Royal Palace, Madrid

the Bridge of Pines, two leagues from Granada, he was overtaken by a messenger from Isabella. For the queen had relented and had decided to give her aid despite the aloofness of her husband.

195   From the painting by Augustus G. Heaton (1844–), in the Capitol, Washington

196   From the painting, 1877, by Antonio Muñoz Degrain (1849–), in the Senate Chamber, Madrid

ISABELLA OFFERING HER JEWELS

THE story that Isabella, to win the consent of the Court for the great undertaking, offered to sell her jewels, seems to be one of those bits of pure romance that so often creep into the historical narrative and lend fictitious color to it.

197   From the painting, 1884, by Vacslav von Brozik (1851–1901), in the Metropolitan Museum of Art, New York

COLUMBUS SIGNING THE CONTRACT

HAD Pérez whispered a fact not before revealed? The hard-headed treasurer of Aragon, Louis de Santangel, and the King's chamberlain, Cabrera, had reasons other than sentiment for attempting to break down Ferdinand's opposition. It was a small risk and a possible inestimable gain. Resentful at the price, the Spanish monarch on April 17, 1492, reluctantly saw the Genoese mariner affix his name to the document which would make him, if he succeeded, almost second to the crown in power.

198   From Bernhardus de Breydenbach, *Sanctarum Peregrinationum*, Mainz, 1486

SHIPBUILDING IN THE 15TH CENTURY

THE contract of Columbus called for armed vessels. The German picture of a Venetian shipyard shows the type of ship built in the Admiral's time.

199   From the painting, 1873, by Ricardo Balaca (1844–80), in the Provincial Museum, Cadiz, Spain

THE DEPARTURE OF COLUMBUS FROM PALOS

IT is sunrise on August 3, 1492. With what joy in the hearts of friar and mariner the last mass is celebrated! The boats put off under the benediction of that good angel, Pérez, who doubts not that Santa Maria de la Rabida attends the fleet to draw the frontier line of Church and State across the glittering East.

200   From a reconstruction of the original *Santa Maria*, made for the Columbian Exposition at Chicago, 1893

THE *SANTA MARIA*, FLAGSHIP OF COLUMBUS

COLUMBUS, in supreme command, is on the *Santa Maria*, which is sailed by her owner, Juan de la Cosa, a cosmographer of Palos. She carries two pilots, a grand constable, a physician, an archivist and — as a wise forethought! — an interpreter. Martin Alonso Pinzón captains his own *Pinta*, and his brother, Francisco, pilots her. His youngest brother, Vicente Yañes, commands the little *Niña*, and her owner, Pero Alonso Niño, goes as pilot. Some ninety seamen man the fleet, caught by Pinzón's cry along the wharves of Palos: "Friends, come with us! . . . You will find the houses with roofs of gold, and you will return rich and prosperous!" To the Canaries first they sailed, then west, west, on the trail of the sinking sun.

THE ASTROLABE AIDS COLUMBUS

OUT into the Sea of Darkness sailed three small ships, sturdy and seaworthy, but with only crude equipment for crossing the great, mysterious Atlantic. For their direction the pilots had the compass. The astrolabe, an ancient device for taking the altitude of sun, moon, and stars, and recently perfected for use at sea, aided in determining the ship's position. The prevailing winds and currents were unknown, since the distance to land ahead was a baffling mystery. Yet these pioneers were willing to risk the venture with such instruments and the knowledge they had.

The astrolabe was the forerunner of the modern sextant. It consisted of a circular disk marked with the degrees of arc on the circumference and was suspended from a ring, so as to hang vertically. The observation was made through two uprights at the ends of a bar, pivoted at the center. The axis of these uprights was pierced with small holes for sighting through, and the elevation of the object was read on the divided circle on the edge. From this reading the latitude was easily calculated.

201 Reproduction of Champlain's astrolabe. Courtesy of
          Samuel V. Hoffman, New York

202   From the painting, about 1840, by Christian Ruben (1805–75), in the possession of Erwein Nostitz, Prague, Czechoslovakia

THE LANDFALL OF COLUMBUS

"THE weather was like April in Andalusia," the smooth sea "like the river at Seville," and "nothing was wanting but to hear the nightingales." Thus the admiral later wrote. But day after day passed with the same monotonous winds driving the ships westward. His crews became frightened. Weeks passed without the promised land. Mutiny was secretly plotted among the men. But Columbus remained master of the situation. On October 7, Pinzón persuaded Columbus to alter the course from west to west-southwest. In the dawn of the twelfth, land was sighted — the faint shadow of a new world. The story goes that Columbus, on deck and watching intently for any sign of land, thought he saw a light moving in the distance. He pointed it out to a companion. The moon was up, and, about two o'clock, a sailor, watching from the *Pinta*, in the white light clearly discerned the dark line of a sandy shore. The cry of land was shouted from ship to ship. The greatest landfall in history had taken place. The fears of the crew which had almost led to open revolt were now banished, and with joyous anticipation they awaited the dawn. Columbus later claimed the reward offered to the first man who sighted land. The gray line on the horizon was the vindication of Columbus' dream and the reward of his persevering courage. It meant glory, wealth and power; he would now be "admiral of the Ocean-Sea." This voyage of Columbus has rightfully taken its place as one of the great adventures of history. Its conception and execution displayed a scientific spirit that was quite at variance with the habits of the mediæval mind. Columbus amassed all the data obtainable with regard to the shape of the earth and the existence of land to the westward. From these facts he inferred that a voyage into the unknown ocean would eventually bring him to a shore at its western edge. His moral qualities are shown in his willingness to risk his life to prove that his conclusions were correct. Few geographical discoveries have brought about so widespread and so sudden a mental readjustment as did that of Columbus. The attention of Europe and, to a certain extent, of posterity has been centered upon his discovery of land. It should be remembered, however, that he began with outlining and determining the characteristics of an ocean. In a very real sense Columbus was the discoverer of the Atlantic as well as America.

203   From the painting, 1842, by John Vanderlyn (1776–1852) in rotunda of the Capitol, Washington

THE LANDING OF COLUMBUS

WRAPPED in the scarlet cloak of a Castilian Admiral, Columbus stepped ashore, dropped to his knees, and kissed the sand. Then rising, he drew his sword, unfurled the royal standard, and named this new Spanish possession San Salvador. The scene was strange and impressive. An Italian navigator with the ceremony and pomp of Spain claimed a wild beach washed by an unknown ocean for the King and Queen who had made his voyage possible. But hidden from those who shared the emotions of that happy landing was the fact that they were beginning a new page in the history of men. They did not know and could not

dream even a little of the significance of what they had accomplished. No more could the frightened natives, who after a time fearfully approached them, understand that on that day destiny sealed the red man's doom. The Indian name of the island was Guanahani, now generally identified with Watling.

A MODERN SKETCH
OF THE BEACH
OF WATLING ISLAND

From original sketch by Rudolf Cronau (1855–) in his *Amerika, Die Geschichte Seiner Entdeckung von der ältersten bis auf die neuste Zeit,* Leipzig, 1892

204

205   From the painting, 1892, by José Garnelo y Alda (1866–), in possession of the artist, Madrid

THE LANDING OF COLUMBUS: A Spanish Conception

"The whole company kneeled on the shore and kissed the ground for joy, returning God thanks for the great mercy they had experienced during their long voyage through seas hitherto unpassed, and their now happy discovery of an unknown land. The admiral then stood up, and took formal possession in the usual words for their Catholic majesties of this island, to which he gave the name of St. Salvador.

"Numbers of the Indians or natives of the island were present at these ceremonies; and perceiving them to be peaceable, quiet, and simple people, the admiral distributed several presents among them. To some he gave red caps, and to others strings of glass beads, which they hung about their necks, and various other things of small value, which they valued as if they had been jewels of high price.

"After the ceremonies, the admiral went off in his boat,

206   From facsimile of the *Narrative of Columbus;* an Italian poem by Guiliano Dati; Florence; 1493, in the New York Public Library, original in the British Museum

EARLIEST PICTORIAL REPRESENTATION OF THE LANDING

and the Indians followed him even to the ships, some by swimming and others in their canoes, carrying parrots, clews of spun cotton yarn, javelins, and other such trifling articles, to barter for glass beads, bells, and other things of small value." — Ferdinand Columbus.

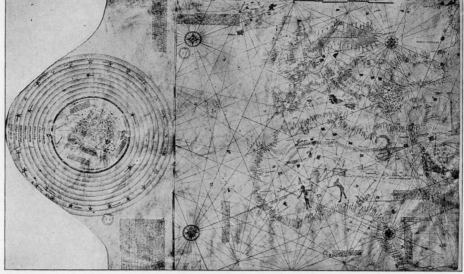

207   From the original in the Bibliothèque Nationale, Paris

COLUMBUS' CHART

In 1924 there was brought to light in the Bibliothèque Nationale in Paris an old map drawn on calfskin and still showing the vivid red, blue and green of the colors when first applied. M. Charles de la Roncière, the distinguished Director of Documents in the Library, has dated the map between 1488 and 1493. He believes that the evidence in the map proves it to be the chart that Columbus showed the Spanish sovereigns and that the real aim of the expedition was not India, but the legendary island of the Seven Cities.

208   From the painting, 1876, by Ricardo Balaca (1844–80), in la Biblioteca de Sevilla, Seville

COLUMBUS RECEIVED BY FERDINAND AND ISABELLA AT BARCELONA

It is a fair day in March, 1493, in Barcelona. The streets swarm with people and are gay with streaming flags. The great admiral has returned. He has discovered Cathay — India, too, perhaps; enormous riches, certainly. The sovereigns will receive him as a prince.

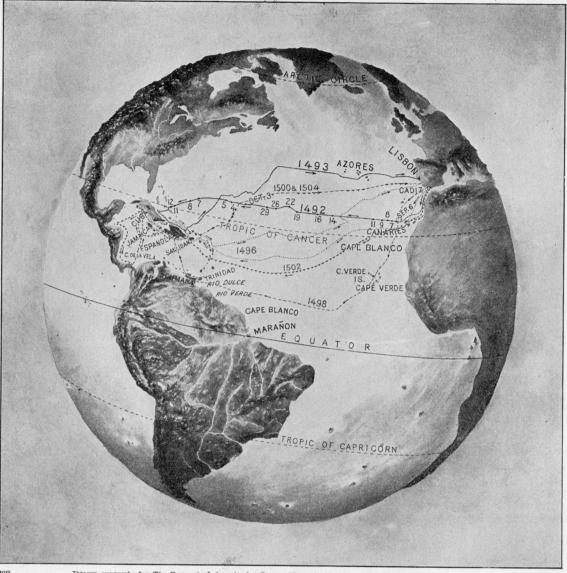

Drawn expressly for *The Pageant of America* by Gregor Noetzel, American Geographical Society, New York

MAP OF COLUMBUS' VOYAGES

THE numerals on the line of the voyage which Columbus made in 1492 are the dates of important incidents. On the 11th of September, the explorer saw a large piece of a mast; on the 14th, a tern and boatswain bird; on the 16th, much weed; on the 22nd, sandpipers; on the 29th, man-of-war birds; on the 3rd of October, more weed; on the 5th, flying-fish; on the 7th, men on the *Niña* thought they sighted land; on the 8th and 9th, ducks were seen; on the 11th, a green rush and a pole and at night a light ahead. Other dates relate to rains, to climatic conditions, or to variations of the compass.

The story of the remaining voyages is one of mingled triumph and humiliation. In the second voyage, which lasted from 1493 to 1496 he discovered Porto Rico and Jamaica and visited Cuba, compelling his entire ship's company to swear that they believed it to be the mainland. The third voyage, 1498 to 1500, brought Columbus to the mainland of South America, his greatest achievement next to his original discovery.

The purpose of the fourth voyage was to find a strait through the lands he had discovered to the Portuguese sea. He accomplished nothing more than to skirt the coast of Central America. When he returned, in 1504, his patroness, Isabella, was dying.

COLUMBUS' LETTER TO SANTANGEL

"SIR, as I know that you will have pleasure from the great victory by which our Lord hath given me my voyage, I write you this, by which you shall know that in thirty-three days I passed over to the Indies with the fleet which the most illustrious King and Queen, our Lords gave me; where I found many Islands peopled with inhabitants beyond number. And of them all I have taken possession for their Highnesses. . . . To the first which I found I gave the name Sant Salvador, in commemoration of his High Majesty, who marvellously hath given all this."—From *Original Narratives of Early American History*, New York, 1906.

So begins the letter, written by Columbus to Luis de Santangel on his return voyage in 1493. It is believed to be a copy of the first edition of the letter printed in Barcelona in April, 1493. It was discovered in Spain in 1889. It consists of two leaves of very coarse paper printed in Spanish blackfaced type.

210   From the original printed at Barcelona, 1493.   In the New York Public Library

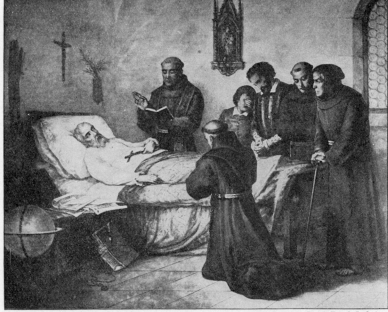

211 From the painting by Luigi Gregori (1819–96), in Notre Dame University, South Bend, Ind.

THE DEATH OF COLUMBUS

COLUMBUS discovered an ocean as well as a new world. Yet his day of favor was brief. He did not bring back from his voyages the riches of the East. Da Gama did this for the rival Portuguese in 1498. On May 20, 1506, in a humble dwelling in Valladolid, deserted and practically forgotten by all but his sons and a few friars, the great discoverer breathed his last, not realizing the true significance of his great achievement.

CHAPTER V

SEARCH FOR THE WESTERN ROUTE

IN one and the same year, 1498, Vasco da Gama circumnavigated Africa and reached India, and Columbus discovered the South American continent blocking his path to that part of Asia where riches lay. Asia had been reached by the African route and its wealth had been sampled; but the African route was ten thousand miles long, and it was dangerous. Columbus believed that south of the limit of his explorations there was a passage beyond the American mainland. But the great dream of reaching the East by way of the West now stirred the hearts of venturesome seamen in other lands than Spain. It had, indeed, been the talk of seamen ever since Diaz had come home to tell of the eastern ocean beyond the "Cape of Storms." There were those who thought that a river flowed from China through this new continent of America; others believed that there was no continent but rather a group of very large islands, and that among these islands lay the passage which presently came to be spoken of as the Strait of Anian. Where lay this strait — whether to the north or the south or, perhaps again, just to the west of the land found by Columbus — no one knew. Its importance, however, none failed to grasp. The nation which should discover that strait and fortify it would be master of the world. Therein lay the motive of the struggle which followed, a struggle in which all gained — England, Portugal, Spain, Holland, and France. Around this contest centers much of the early history of America. From it emerged two mighty continents, no longer mere barriers to the riches of the East, but a vast and far-flung arena where the colonial schemes of rival European powers were to clash for the next two hundred years.

212   The Student of Navigation, from Martin Cortés, *Breve Compendio de la Sphera*, Sevilla, 1556

JOHN CABOT AND HIS SON
SEBASTIAN

JOHN CABOT (1450–98) was an Italian who had given his allegiance first to Venice, then to England. He was a captain in the employ of the Merchant-Venturers of Bristol in 1496, the year when Henry VII gave him "full and free authoritie, leave, and power, to sayle to all partes, Countreys, and Seas, of the East, of the West, and of the North," and also "licence to set up Our banners and ensignes in every village, towne, castel, yle, or maine lande, of them newly founde." Whether Cabot was prompted by the discoveries of Columbus or had, even so early as 1490, dreamed of finding his way to the, perhaps, not distant Cathay, is uncertain.

In the springtime of 1497, Cabot sailed from Bristol and in the little *Matthew*, with a crew of eighteen, he braved the storms of the North Atlantic. On the 24th of June, he reached the shores of North America somewhere between the modern Halifax and Hudson Strait, and planted St. George's Cross for England on what he believed to be the territory of the Great Khan. Thus the British flag first came to continental America.

213   From the original model for the bronze group by John Cassidy (1860–), exhibited in London, 1897

214   From the painting by Ernest Board (1877–), in the Bristol Museum and Art Gallery (England)

DEPARTURE OF JOHN CABOT FROM BRISTOL

IN the port of Bristol hangs a painting to commemorate the significance of the first transfer of British power across the Atlantic. Cabot sailed as a master mariner on the roster of the Merchant-Venturers of Bristol. Most important in his instructions was the charge to find the route to Asia; but he found a continent instead.

SEBASTIAN CABOT
1476?–1557?

JOHN CABOT sailed a second time for America and never returned. One of the most important results of his first voyage was the opening up of a route from northern Europe to the rich fisheries of Newfoundland. Not many years after Cabot's famous trip the summer months saw the Grand Banks dotted with Portuguese, French, Spanish, and English fishing boats. Some historians doubt the old statement that Sebastian accompanied his father. In after years the son became a figure of consequence, so more may have been attributed to him than was his due.

JUAN DE LA COSA'S
MAP, 1500

PAINTED in brilliant colors and hanging now in the Museo Naval at Madrid is the La Cosa map made in 1500, the oldest map known to have been drawn subsequent to the discovery of America. The Spanish, English, and Portuguese flags record the discoveries of those nations. In this map, as in so many that follow it, the coast line of northern North America is carried

215 From the copy by Cephas G. Thompson, 1841, of a portrait by Hans Holbein (1497–1543), in the New York Historical Society

much too far to the east. Perhaps the reason was that the men of this time did not know that the magnetic pole lies south of the true pole and therefore deflects the compass westward.

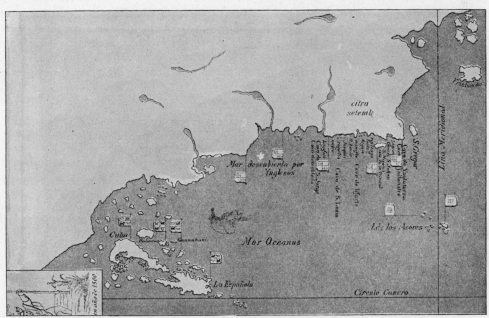

216 From J. G. Kohl, *History of the Discovery of Maine*, 1869, based on La Cosa's map of the world, 1500. In *Collections* of the Maine Historical Society

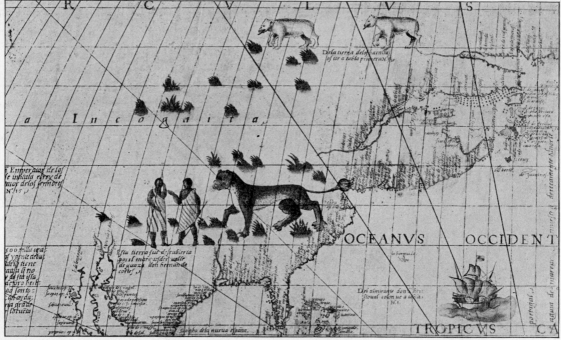

217   From the original (1544), in the Bibliothèque Nationale, Paris

THE CABOT MAP — SECTIONAL VIEW

THE Cabot map, found in 1855 in Germany, is a large engraved map of the world, in several sheets.   Who made it is not known, but that it was done by the hand of Sebastian Cabot is not believed by all scholars. It is full of errors, and its chief interest lies in the fact that it bears out the theory of the discovery of the North American continent by John Cabot.   Printed in Latin at the side appears the statement, referring to Newfoundland, that "This land was discovered by John Cabot, a Venetian, and Sebastian Cabot his son, in the year of the birth of our Saviour Jesus Christ, M. CCCC. XCIIII (1494), the twenty-fourth day of June (at 5 o'clock) in the morning; to which land has been given the name of The Land First Seen (*terram primum visam*); and to a great island, which is very near the said land, the name of St. John has been given, on account of its having been discovered the same day."

218   From the portrait, date and artist unknown, in the Uffizi
                    Gallery, Florence

AMERIGO VESPUCCI, 1451–1512

A CLOUD of mystery envelops the figure of Vespucci, whose Christian name in its Latin form was given to the New World.   A few facts stand forth; he was a Florentine who drifted to Spain; he visited Española and the mainland in a search for pearls with the Spaniard, Ojeda, in 1499; and he wrote a letter in which he called the western lands "Mundus Novus" rather than Asia.   Perhaps he was not always truthful. Whatever his shortcomings, however, it was not he who suggested the honor which his name received.   The latest critical study of Vespucci develops the thesis that he, before Columbus, discovered the mainland and that he was the first to realize that Mundus Novus (South America) was wholly distinct from Asia and was, in fact, a new world.

THE ORIGIN OF THE NAME "AMERICA"

It chanced that at St. Dié in the Vosges Mountains there was a little collegiate institution which was both a center of geographical learning and the possessor of a new printing press. Two of its fac-

> Nũc v̄o & hę partes funt latius luftratæ/& alia quarta pars per Americũ Vefputiũ(vt in fequentibus audietur)inuenta eft/quã non video cur quis iure vetet ab Americo inuentore fagacis ingenɲ viro Amerigen quafi Americi terrã / fiue Americam dicendã:cũ & Europa & Afia a mulièribus fua fortita fint nomina. Eius fitũ & gentis mores ex bis binis Americi nauigationibus quæ fequuṽ liquide intelligidatur.
>
> **Ameri-ca**

219 From Waldseemüller, *Cosmographiae Introductio*, St. Dié, May, 1507. In the New York Public Library

ulty, Mathias Ringman, a Latinist, and Martin Waldseemüller, a geographer, were preparing a new edition of Ptolemy's *Geographia*. Before its publication, however, they printed a little essay called *Cosmographiae Introductio*, to which they added the letter of Vespucci. It was in this essay that Waldseemüller offered the suggestion which was destined to make the name of Amerigo Vespucci famous forever.

THE PORTUGUESE IN THE NORTH ATLANTIC

As early as 1500, Caspar Cortereal, a Portuguese nobleman of the Azores, embarked on the great search for a route to Asia. Believing that the coveted passage lay to the north, he sighted the American coast at Newfoundland and explored as far north as Hudson Strait. Next year he was back again with three ships. Probably they made land at Cabot's Cape Breton; and there Cortereal saw Venetian rings in an Indian's ears, which led him to believe that he had arrived in Asia in the wake of some European trading vessel. Leaving two of his ships, he went exploring northward and was heard of no more. The next year his brother Miguel came in search of him; but Miguel and his ship, too, were never seen again.

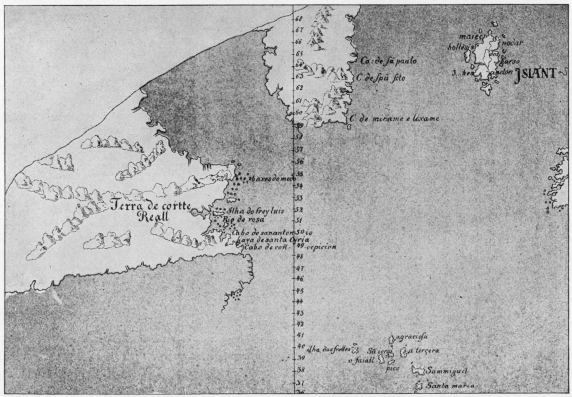

220   From J. G. Kohl, *History of the Discovery of Maine*, 1869. In *Collections* of the Maine Historical Society

221   From Rudolf Cronau, *Amerika, Die Geschichte seiner Entdeckung von der ältersten bis auf die neuste Zeit* . . . 1892, drawing by Rudolf Cronau

THE ISTHMUS OF PANAMA (JUNGLE OF DARIEN)

Vasco Nuñez Balboa was a bankrupt and from Española he smuggled himself out to sea in a cask or the bunt of a sail. He was put off on the mainland at a little Spanish colony. In a short time Balboa made himself the leader of the wretched colony, beset by hunger and Indians. He adopted a shrewd policy of friendship with the Indians, who were peculiarly dangerous enemies on account of their poisoned arrows. From the Indians he heard of a great sea to the west, and set out on the adventure of discovering it, partly to retrieve himself for usurping command in the colony and partly in the hope of finding riches.

222   From an original painting by C. W. Jefferys
      in possession of the publishers

BALBOA DISCOVERS THE PACIFIC, 1513

> . . . When with eagle eyes
> He stared at the Pacific — and all his men
> Looked at each other with a wild surmise —
> Silent, upon a peak in Darien.

From the peak in Darien, where on his knees he had rendered thanks for the new ocean seen afar, Balboa sent Pizarro to find the shore. On September 29, 1513, with drawn sword and lifted banner, Balboa marched alone into the mighty waters of the Pacific and claimed them for his King. Thus Balboa discovered that the New World, in one place at least, was but a slender isthmus and that an ocean washed its western side. Through such a narrow country as this there must be a strait, he thought, linking the two seas and offering the route to Asia.

FERDINAND MAGELLAN
ca. 1480–1521

WHEN Balboa discovered another ocean but forty-five miles west of the Atlantic, he gave a tremendous impetus to westward exploration. The general impression now was that America was a huge peninsula, like a larger India, and doubtless was joined by Asia on the north. At its southern extremity the two oceans must meet. In this belief a Portuguese, Ferdinand Magellan, a nobleman and fighting mariner who had already voyaged to India and Malay, set out in 1519, with a Spanish fleet of five old and rotten boats manned by motley crews, to reach India by the western route. November found him at Brazil. January he spent exploring Rio de la Plata, hoping that it was the strait he was in search of. Disappointed, he continued southward. One of his ships was lost.

From April to August 24, he was in Patagonia, so named by him because of the big feet of the natives. Here with great difficulty he crushed a dangerous mutiny. On October 21, he discovered Cape

223   From the portrait, date and artist unknown, in the Real Academia de Bellas Artes de San Fernando, Madrid, Spain

Virgenes, at the eastern entrance of the strait which separates Patagonia from the Island of Tierra del Fuego. Here Gomez, one of his captains, deserted with his ship, leaving Magellan with three ships.

224   One of Magellan's ships, the *Victoria*, from Hulsius, *Sammlung von Schiffahrten*, Nurnberg, 1603

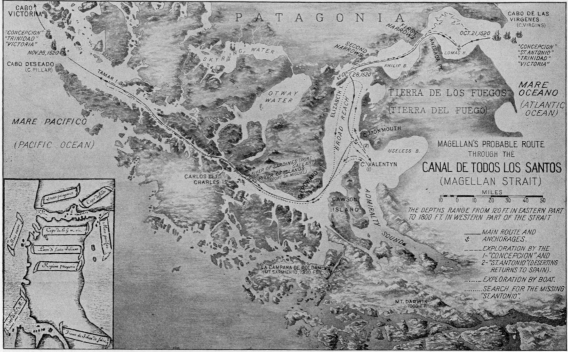

225   Drawn expressly for *The Pageant of America* by Gregor Noetzel, American Geographical Society, New York

HOW MAGELLAN FOUND THE WAY TO THE PACIFIC

THE new strait found by Magellan, 360 miles long and as crooked as a serpent, is one of the most dangerous stretches of navigable water on the globe. For many days Magellan, with his three shiploads of fear-stricken men smouldering with rebellion, sailed onward through a labyrinth of precipitous rocks. On the thirtieth day the men held a council. Should they go on with this madman or compel him to turn back? But the iron will of their commander prevailed. The ships went on. Presently a swifter boat was sent ahead to spy out the course of the waterway. At last, thirty-eight days after entering the strait, Magellan emerged upon the Mar del Sud, the Sea of the South, to which, because of the peace of its vast waters, he gave the name "Pacific."

(The inset on the map is after a sketch of the Straits by Pigafetta, who was with Magellan. It appears in A. E. Nordenskiöld, *Periplus*, 1897, after the sketch in the Amoretti edition of Pigafetta, Milano, 1800.)

226   View of the Straits of Magellan, from the United States Hydrographic Office

FIRST VOYAGE AROUND THE WORLD, 1519-22

Drawn expressly for *The Pageant of America* by Gregor Noetzel, American Geographical Society, New York

AFTER Magellan had passed through the Straits he steered northwestward on an unknown sea. Hunger and disease were added to the crew's terrors. For ninety-eight days across the Pacific the men were put to such hardship that they ate the rats in the ship's hold and even the leather casings of the spars. On March 6, 1521, Magellan reached the Ladrones, probably at Guam. Ten days later he discovered the Philippines, touching at Samar Island. He explored the archipelago and named it St. Lazarus. After innumerable perils endured on his heroic quest, he was killed on April 27 by natives of Maktan Island. The *Victoria*, commanded by del Cano, was the sole survivor of the three ships to reach home. She rounded the Cape of Good Hope in the summer of 1522 and anchored in Spanish waters. At last a passage to the East had been found, and men lived to tell the tale.

The voyage of the *Victoria* is one of the great exploits of history. A tiny vessel, when viewed by the standards of the twentieth century, had not only threaded the uncharted Straits of Magellan but had crossed the unknown Pacific. The return of del Cano to the home port in Spain was the first conclusive demonstration that the earth is round. The knowledge which such voyages as that of the *Victoria* kept bringing to sixteenth-century Europe caused profound readjustments in the intellectual centers of the Continent. The broadening of the mental horizon of European leaders was the fore-runner of the migration of European people.

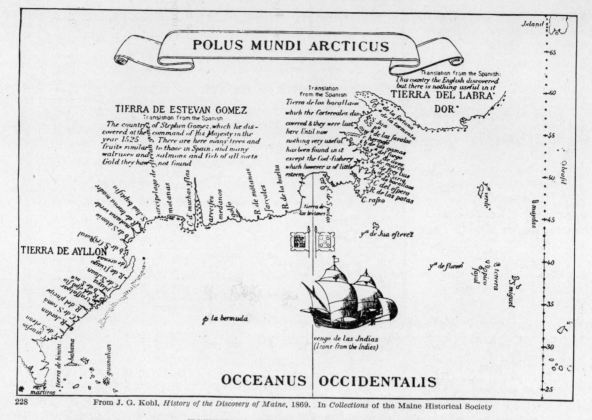

POLUS MUNDI ARCTICUS

TIERRA DE ESTEVAN GOMEZ
Translation from the Spanish
The country of Stephen Gomez, which he discovered at the command of His Majesty in the year 1525. There are here many trees and fruits similar to those in Spain, and many walruses and salmons and fish of all sorts. Gold they have not found

Translation from the Spanish:
Tierra de los bacallaos which the Cortereales discovered & they were lost here until now nothing very useful has been found in it except the Cod-fishery which however is of little esteem

Translation from the Spanish:
This country the English discovered but there is nothing useful in it

TIERRA DEL LABRA·DOR·

TIERRA DE AYLLON

p la bermuda

vengo de las Indias (I come from the Indies)

OCCEANUS OCCIDENTALIS

228   From J. G. Kohl, *History of the Discovery of Maine*, 1869. In *Collections* of the Maine Historical Society

ESTEVAN GOMEZ SAILS NORTH

Two years after del Cano's return, the Portuguese, Estevan Gomez, who had deserted his commander at the eastern gate of Magellan Straits and had put back for home and safety, sailed to the northern coast of America. Gomez explored the Atlantic coast from the Penobscot River to Newfoundland. But he found no pearls, no gold, no spices, and no strait — only natives poorly dressed in furs and living precariously amid forbidding forests of pine.

229   From the portrait, about 1536, by Titian (*ca.* 1477–1576), in the Louvre, Paris

FRANCIS I, KING OF FRANCE,
1494–1547

THE lure of the new lands and the route to Asia kindled the imagination of France. Francis came to the throne in 1515, full of ambition. The known world had been doubled in size during his lifetime, doubled and then divided between Spain and Portugal, with not a morsel left for France, east or west. He wrote sarcastically to Charles of Spain: "Show me, I pray you, the will of our Father, Adam, that I may see if he has really made you and the King of Portugal his universal heirs." As reports reached him from America of gold, pearls, spices, he remarked to his courtiers: "God has not created those lands solely for Castilians."

VERRAZANO'S REPORT TO THE KING OF FRANCE, 1524

(A page from the *Cèllere Codex*)

IN 1524 Francis I, eager for his share of the New World, sent out Verrazano to find the strait and as many rich islands as possible.   Verrazano coasted from Florida or Georgia to Nova Scotia, discovered the mouth of the Hudson River (to which he referred as "a very large river," — *una grandissima riviera*), peeped into the Gulf of St. Lawrence, and then returned home, richer in geographical knowledge than in pearls and precious stones.

230   From facsimile in I. N. P. Stokes, *The Iconography of Manhattan Island*, Vol. II, 1916, from original Codex in the J. P. Morgan Library, New York

231   From an original painting by C. W. Jefferys in possession of the publishers

CARTIER LOOKS FOR THE STRAIT

AFTER a humiliating defeat and imprisonment at the hands of Spain, Francis once more bethought him of Spanish territory in the New World and of the strait leading to Asia, not by the hazardous way Magellan went, but by that short northwestern passage supposed to run between America and Asia.   From among his Norman and Breton fishermen, who were going yearly to the cod banks discovered by Cabot, Francis chose Jacques Cartier, "The Mariner of St. Malo," corsair and sea-rover, who had already made voyages to Brazil and to the Newfoundland Banks, pirating Spanish and Portuguese ships by the way.

Cartier set forth and, in 1534, passed Newfoundland and traversed the Gulf of St. Lawrence.   On a second voyage he went farther up the river, hoping that it was the long-sought strait.

Cartier was the forerunner of French power in the New World.   But his discoveries did not result in the immediate setting up of a French empire in the American wilderness.   Not until three quarters of a century had passed did the continuous history of New France begin with Champlain's founding of Quebec in 1608.

FROBISHER AMONG THE ESKIMO

YEARS of exploration served to show more clearly the outlines of the continent that blocked the way to Asia. As bay after bay on the Atlantic coast proved to be but an arm of the ocean, the chance of finding the strait was limited to the north. There, in quest of the northwest passage sailed a succession of daring seamen — Frobisher, Davis, Hudson, Baffin, and the rest. But the cold and the ice floes blocked the northward way to the wealth of the Indies, and Magellan's great exploit could not be duplicated under the fringe of the polar cap.

THE NEW WORLD

THIS map, one of the first to set forth the outlines of the new continents, appeared in Hakluyt's edition, 1587, of Peter Martyr's *De Orbe Novo*. The search for the western route and other exploring expeditions had brought together a great body of information regarding the coast lines of the New World. The Americas stood revealed, and men could now set down their outlines upon paper. This is the first general map on which the name Virginia appeared.

232   From a contemporary sketch of northern exploration, in the British Museum

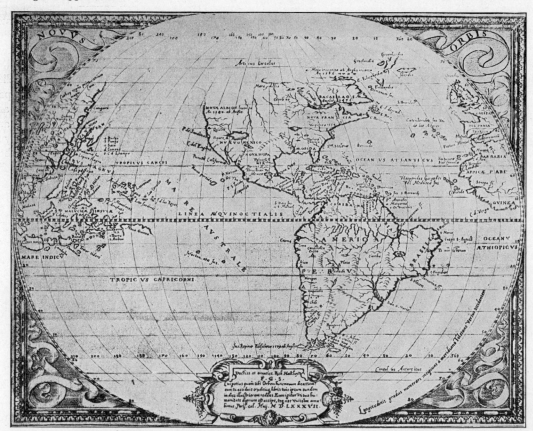

233   From Richard Hakluyt's revised Latin edition, Paris, 1587, of Peter Martyr's *De Orbe Novo*, 1534

CHAPTER VI

THE FOUNDING OF NEW SPAIN

IT fell to the lot of the Spaniard to be the first to push Europe's frontier westward across the ocean. It is not strange that such should have been the case. Eight centuries of struggle against the Moors had bred in Spain a hardy and energetic military class. Over these warriors the ideals of mediæval chivalry still held sway. In their pride and fierce courage, their prodigality and their cruelty, their readiness to set out upon adventures, they represent the same blend of virtues and of faults that everywhere characterized the mediæval knight.

But in Spain the Moorish power was broken. A national monarchy had been established. Frontiersman for eight centuries, the Spanish knight saw the frontier recede from him. The sword sheathed, chivalry's occupation was gone. At the new court chances were limited and preferment went to the man of subtle intrigue and not to the best sword arm and the frame trained to endure the hardships of the field. On the one hand poverty and comparative inaction; on the other, a chance at a new frontier, a career worthy of the talents which the cavalier of Spain knew as his only birthright.

The new frontier Columbus had opened. The urge toward it was as irresistible as the later rush for Californian gold.

In 1493 Columbus had planted on Española (Hayti) a settlement which he named Isabella. Twenty years later there were seventeen chartered towns on the island. Española was thus the first frontier colony in the New World and the mother of the first American frontiersmen. It was chiefly a mining frontier. Under vigorous governors who knew the one road to kingly favor, gold mines were worked by enslaved natives; and plantations of cotton and sugar were also put under cultivation. The new Land of Promise was rich enough to yield a fortune to every Spanish knight who had the hardihood to plunge with horse and sword and pack of slave-hunting dogs into the hills behind the settlements.

234 Silver Mining in Peru, from Theodore de Bry,
Voyages, Part IV, 1596

235   From Carolus Allard, *Orbis Habitabilis*, Amsterdam, *ca.* 1690

SANTO DOMINGO

SANTO DOMINGO dates from 1496. It was the capital of "Little Spain," and for thirty years, until the gold failed and the natives were nearly exterminated, the center of Spanish culture in America. From its harbor sailed Nicuesa and Ojeda, pioneers on the Isthmus of Panama, and Juan de la Cosa, whose search for the Golden Fleece was ended by a poisoned arrow in Venezuela; and hence, too, sailed Velasquez and Garay to govern and colonize, respectively, Cuba and Jamaica. These narrow streets knew them all: Coronado, Ayllon, the iron De Soto, swarthy and proud, handsome Balboa, drawing all eyes, grizzled Ponce with his fierce Bezerillo, the most talked of dog in the city, Pánfilo Narváez, and Pizarro. Here before the house of the official "Marker of the Gold" loitered Hernando Cortés, fingering an empty purse, while Indian and negro slaves trooped by, bearing the shining bars down to the treasure-ships, and men gambled away the portions they were waiting to receive.

236   From Beaumont (*Pablo de la Purisima Concepcion*), *Cronica de Mechoacan.* Transcript of Ms. about 1750. In the New York Public Library

SPANISH PUNISH–MENTS FOR IN–DIAN OFFENDERS

FRIAR BEAUMONT was a surgeon who later came to New Spain and taught anatomy and surgery in the royal hospital in Mexico City. The drawings which appear in his manuscript show the punishments which the conquerors meted out to the Indians in a less humanitarian age than ours, to correct such evils as licentiousness, murder, disobedience, and sorcery.

EMPEROR CHARLES V, 1500–1558

THE Spanish frontiersmen across the western ocean were to serve a greater empire than Ferdinand's. In 1516, at the age of nineteen, Charles ascended the throne, to be the most powerful monarch in Europe. Charles' European possessions included Spain, the Netherlands, and Hapsburg dominions in Germany and Austria, Navarre, Artois, and Burgundy in France, and Naples, Sardinia, and Sicily in Italy. And all the New World was his except Brazil. With the treasure wrested from the New World, he paid for the wars which strengthened his power in the Old.

BEGINNING OF EUROPEAN SETTLEMENT ON THE AMERICAN MAINLAND

WITH the island of Española as a center New Spain expanded year after year. New settlements appeared in Cuba, Porto Rico and Jamaica. The irregular coast of the mainland was explored and towns were established, Cartagena, San Sebastian, Nombre de Dios, Trujillo, Vera Cruz, Panuco. Expeditions plunged into the hinterland and, in the case of Cortés and Pizarro led to dazzling conquests. The "Mar del Norte" became dotted with the sails of galleons hurrying westward and eastward on courses that daily grew more familiar.

237   From the portrait, 1547, by Titian in the Pinakothek, Munich

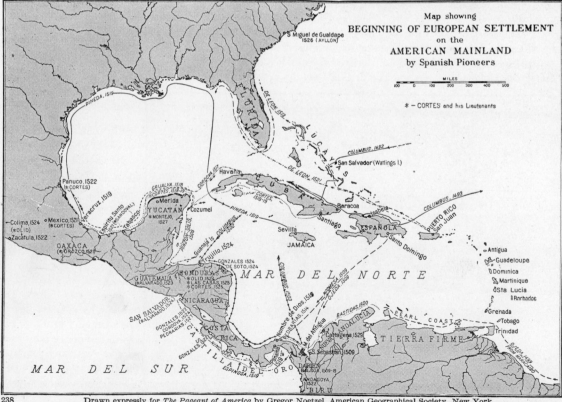

Map showing
BEGINNING OF EUROPEAN SETTLEMENT
on the
AMERICAN MAINLAND
by Spanish Pioneers

MILES

* — CORTES and his Lieutenants

239   Drawn expressly for *The Pageant of America* by Gregor Noetzel, American Geographical Society, New York

1	PONCE DE LEÓN	1513		10	CORONADO	1540-42
2	CORTES	1519-21		10a	DIAZ	1540
3	PINEDA	1519		10b	CARDENAS	1540
4	GÓMEZ	1525		10c	ARELLANO	1541
5	AYLLON	1526		11	ALARCÓN	1540
6	NARVAEZ	1528		12	CABRILLO	1542-43
6a	DE VACA	1533-36		12a	FERELLO	1543
7	PIZARRO	1531-33		13	RODRIGUEZ	1581
8	ULLOA	1539		14	ESPEJO	1582
9	DE SOTO	1539-42		15	ONATE	1596-1605
9a	MOSCOSO	1540-43		16	VIZCAINO	1602-03

THE SPANISH ADVANCE, SIXTEENTH CENTURY

THE Spaniards pushed northward across Mexico and into regions which later became the United States.
The great finds of Cortés and Pizarro lured other men to search the mountains and the deserts for gold
and silver. Every fantastic Indian tale was eagerly listened to. Many a life and reputation were sacrificed
in the wilderness on trails that had no end.

PONCE DE LEON, 1460–1521, DISCOVERER OF FLORIDA

JUAN PONCE DE LEON, of whom no authentic portrait is known, had come with Columbus on the voyage of 1493. Ponce heard of an isle where a magic spring washed old men young. Obtaining from Charles the necessary grant, he set out to find the magic land. In April, 1513, Ponce de Leon landed on a balmy floral shore, which he named Florida. He explored his new "island," not without Indian interference, to Pensacola Bay. On the way home he discovered the sheltered Bahama Channel, which thereafter became the route for treasure ships.

In 1521 Ponce de Leon returned to colonize Florida. He landed near Charlotte Harbor, but the Indians made such a fierce attack upon his forces that they had to retreat, and ere night his caravel was sailing homeward carrying Ponce mortally wounded.

240   From Herrera, *Historia General de las Indias Occidentales*, 1728

JUAN DE GRIJALVA, WHO EXPLORED THE GULF COAST

THREE objectives stirred the Spaniards of Santo Domingo to action: treasure, slaves, and the strait leading to Asia. Two colonies, San Sebastian and Nombre de Dios, were founded in the isthmus of Panama but did not endure. Grijalva was sent out by Velasquez, the governor of Cuba, and coasted from Yucatan to Panuco River. He came back with a store of gold. Grijalva was impressed with the scenery of the Coast he passed and with the fact that on the islands off the shore of the mainland were mounds, piled up in the form of pyramids, ascended by stone steps and each surmounted by a temple. Obviously the natives were of no mean cultural development! The Grijalva expedition along the shore led directly to that of Cortés from Vera Cruz into the interior. In 1526, Ayllon of Española sailed to the Carolinas with five hundred colonists, but starvation and disease brought death to the leader and ruin to the colony. By 1525 Spanish activity had made known a large part of the North American coast. There is no known authentic portrait of Grijalva.

241 From Herrera, *Historia General de las Indias Occidentales*, 1728

HERNANDO CORTÉS, 1485–1547, CONQUEROR OF MEXICO

THE expedition of Grijalva filled Don Diego Velasquez with the desire for a rich conquest on the mainland. But he was governor of Cuba, a valuable territory, where he had already established Habana (though not on its present site), Baracoa, Trinidad, Puerto Principe and Santiago. His place, therefore, was at home. Looking around for someone to take the risks of expedition and to yield the glory to the governor, his choice fell upon Hernando Cortés, an adventurous young soldier, belonging to a noble family that had destined him for the law. Born in Medellin, a small town of Estremadura, in 1485, he was sent at fourteen years of age to the University of Salamanca, but he broke away and sought military service, in which he soon displayed marked skill and address. He was one of Velasquez' lieutenants when Velasquez became governor of Cuba, and he displayed great ability on several trying occasions.

242   From the portrait (probably contemporary) in the Hospital de Jesús, Mexico City

THE CUBAN CAPITAL — FOUNDED 1514

ON the eve of Cortés' departure from Santiago, Velasquez, accompanied by the court dwarf, Francisquillo, stood on the shore surveying his ships. Francisquillo, looking about, said slyly, "Have a care, Diego, Diego, lest this Estremaduran captain of yours make off with the fleet!" Into the ambitious soul of Velasquez entered, too late, a doubt. He sent messengers to recall Cortés, and even issued an order for his arrest, but the latter was in such high favor with his troops that it could not be executed, and he went on with his expedition in spite of the governor. He reached land on March 4, 1519, and advanced along the Mexican coast, overawing the natives who sent ambassadors with presents. Cortés thus learned that there was in the interior a native sovereign called Montezuma, who ruled an extensive empire. The news so excited Cortés' ambition that he decided to attempt the conquest of that empire. He founded Vera Cruz, caused himself to be elected captain-general of the new colony, burned his vessels to show his soldiers that they must conquer or perish, and began his march toward the city of Mexico, where Montezuma lived.

243   From Arnoldus Montanus, *Die Nieuwe en Onbekende Weereld*, Amsterdam, 1671

THE AZTEC OVERLORD, MONTEZUMA II, 1466–1520

"Montezuma is lord of many kings; his equal is not known in all the world: in his house many lords serve barefooted with eyes cast down to the ground. . . . Montezuma dwells in the most beautiful, the largest, and the strongest city in the world — a city built in the water. . . . Hither flock princes from all the earth, bringing incalculable riches. No lord however great is there who does not pay tribute, and no one so poor is there who does not give at least the blood of his arm." Thus spoke the Totonac chief, Olintetl, enemy of Montezuma, who received Cortés in friendly fashion at Cempoalla, north of Vera Cruz.

AZTEC ARTISTS PICTURE THE ARRIVAL OF THE SPANISH

The news was carried apace to Montezuma that gods in guise of men, who bestrode fierce swift animals, and carried thunder in their hands, had come to land from "floating towers in the waters of heaven." Aztec artists pictured for their amazed lord the ships, the horses, the cannon, and the bearded Spaniards.

244 From a fictitious portrait, date and painter unknown, in the National Library, Mexico City

245 From the painting by Isidro Martinez in the Municipal Palace, Toluca, Mexico

246   Drawn expressly for *The Pageant of America* by Gregor Noetzel, American Geographical Society

CORTÉS' MARCH TO MONTEZUMA'S CAPITAL

VERA CRUZ lies in the hot lowlands, the Tierra Calienta. Cortés plunged into the tropical forest and crossed the narrow coastal plain. He then climbed a steep escarpment down which the rivers tumble in great falls. Each day of ascent brought a cooler and more invigorating climate. Finally he reached the high plateau, surrounded by a ring of mountains where then, as now, lived the greater part of the Mexican people.

247   From the painting, 17th century (artist unknown), in the National Museum, Mexico City

CORTÉS MEETS THE EMBASSY OF MONTEZUMA

THE strange gods, Montezuma learned, were hungry for gold. Therefore, thought he, let them be given gold enough to content them, so that they will go away. But the two great cartwheels of gold and silver, the embroidered cottons, the jeweled feathers, the helmet filled with gold dust from Montezuma's storehouse only strengthened Hernando's purpose to conquer the land and to possess its treasures. Cortés learned that the Aztecs held sway over conquered tribes and pueblos whose people were intensely hostile toward their overlords. The subject Indians not only paid tribute but, at the time of their conquest, had seen their young men and maidens taken away to the capital city, Tenochtitlan, where most of the men and some of the women became sacrifices to satisfy the blood lust of the Aztec war god. Cortés sensed the fear and hatred of the subject peoples. He posed as their deliverer. Passing one after another of the subject cities on the plateau, Cortés marched straight for the center of Aztec power. His allies increased in number and enthusiasm. When he reached Tenochtitlan, Montezuma dared not call out the Aztec warriors to oppose him openly.

248   From the painting, 1885, by Juan Ortega, in San Carlos Academy of Fine Arts, City of Mexico

CORTÉS RECEIVED BY MONTEZUMA

CORTÉS would not be bribed by these gifts to depart, nor would he be put off from an audience with Montezuma. He learned that the Aztec empire was shot through with dissension and filled with allies of the enemies of Montezuma. He pushed on as rapidly as possible over the path by which the gold and silver cart wheels had come and, on November 8, 1519, he entered the city. In the street now named El Rastro, Montezuma met him, clad in a robe of sky blue, shod with golden sandals, and holding crimson roses in his hand. It was as high priest of the War God that the Indian met the Spaniard.

249 From Braun and Hogenberg, *Civitates Orbis Terrarum*, Vol. I, 1576

TENOCHTITLAN, THE CITY OF MEXICO

TENOCHTITLAN, which Cortés entered as guest, god, and conqueror-to-be was a city of perhaps 70,000 souls, spreading over two marshy islands at the western end of Lake Tezcuco. Three long causeways supplied with sluice-gates connected it, west, north, and south, with the mainland. Bridged canals intersected the four quarters of the town. In the center was the great square, entered by four gates in a high stone wall ornamented with serpents. The square was the place of trade, of festivals, and merrymaking, and of human sacrifice. There were four principal types of buildings — huge commercial dwellings of one or two stories, *tecpans* or government offices surmounted by observation towers, "houses of darts" or armories, and pyramidal temple structures. All were built of reddish stone covered with white stucco so brilliant that the Spaniards at first believed the city to be made of silver.

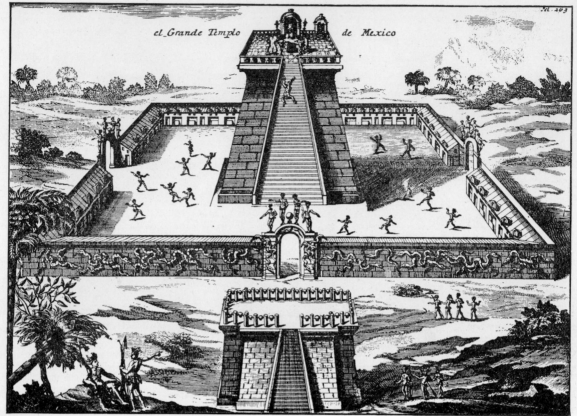

el Grande Templo de Mexico

250   From Herrera, *Historia General de las Indias Occidentales*, 1728

THE GRAND TEMPLE OF MEXICO

FEARFUL gods were worshipped in Tenochtitlan. Chief among them was the war-god, Huitzilopochtli, to whom thousands of victims were sacrificed annually. Captives in war, the choicest youths and maids of vassal provinces, were driven up the stairs of the rude stone pyramid of the war-god's temple, which towered above the great square. The priests seized the victims, tore out their hearts with stone knives, and flung the bodies down for the cannibal rites. Herrera's sketch is fanciful. The Spaniards completely destroyed the temple.

EARLIEST SKETCH OF MEXICO CITY, 1520

THIS drawing seems to have been the source of the late sixteenth-century sketches of the city like the one shown on page 131.

251 From Cortés, *Praeclara . . . de Nova maris Oceani Hyspani Narratio . . .* Nuremberg, 1524

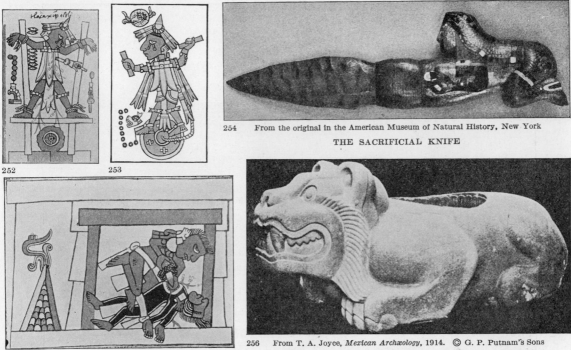

252   253

254   From the original in the American Museum of Natural History, New York
THE SACRIFICIAL KNIFE

255   From the Codex Nuttall, courtesy of the American
Museum of Natural History

256   From T. A. Joyce, *Mexican Archæology*, 1914. © G. P. Putnam's Sons
STONE VASE FOR HOLDING VICTIMS' HEARTS

MEXICAN METHODS OF SACRIFICE

An Aztec painter pictures here, primitively, but realistically, three methods of sacrifice. First (No. 252) is the arrow sacrifice, where the victim, bound to posts within the wooden oratory atop the pyramid, is shot through the heart by an arrow. The second (No. 253) is the gladiatorial sacrifice, in which the victim is allowed a wooden sword. The third (No. 255) is the sacrifice by tearing out the heart, which has already (p. 132) been described. The hearts of the slaughtered were placed in carved stone vases. The knife for the sacrifice had a blade of obsidian and a handle of wood encrusted with mosaics.

257   From H. J. Spinden, *Ancient Mexican Archæology*, American
Museum of Natural History, New York, 1917

AZTEC MUSICIANS

The Aztecs had developed many of the arts to a high degree. Among musical instruments they had long drums and shell rattles (No. 257), also flutes of reed and flageolets of clay, wood, and bone. In embroidery and feather work Aztec artists were masters.

258   From T. A. Joyce, *Mexican
Archæology*, 1914, courtesy of
G. P. Putnam's Sons

AZTEC ARTISANS

Here the native artist (No. 258) shows the leather worker, the goldsmith, and the stone-bead maker at their tasks. The goldsmith is using a reed blow-pipe. Animals, birds and fishes were modeled in gold with the utmost delicacy. The bead-maker fashioned beads of stone, agate, jade, and wood overlaid with gold. The priests (No. 259) are making fire for the sacrifices. Next to the warriors they were the most important figures in the Aztec community.

259   From T. A. Joyce, *Mexican
Archæology*, 1914, courtesy of G. P.
Putnam's Sons

260   From the painting by Rodrigo Gutierrez (1848–1903), in the San Carlos Academy of Fine Arts, Mexico City

THE AZTEC SENATE

MONTEZUMA's palace consisted of hundreds of rooms built around three open squares — a structure so vast, says one of the Spaniards, that he wandered about it four times till he was tired, and yet had not seen all of it. Practically the whole machinery of government was housed under the king's roof. Here met the Aztec senate, consisting of the nobles of the land. Here the judge held court, the supreme court of the country, for other cities had their lower courts. The criminal code was barbarously severe, death by some horrible torture being the penalty for a small offense.

261 From Baron von Humboldt, *Vues des Cordillères et Monuments des peuples indigènes de L'Amérique*, Paris, 1810

AZTEC WARRIOR WITH CAPTIVES

AN Aztec warrior in all his glory was a formidable spectacle. He is here pictured, from a relief carved on stone, with ornamented head-dress and standard, with captives crouching at his feet, with dead foes' heads at his belt — a flower dangling below one of them — and a loin cloth or skirt of jaguar's skin. His foot covering recalls that of Greek and Roman soldiers. The tassels on his cape indicate that he has already distinguished himself before this campaign by the capture of enemy hearts for Huitzilopochtli. Practically all the able-bodied men among the Aztecs, save the priests, were warriors. There were rough grades among them based on prowess in battle. The Aztec conquerors of the tribes on the Mexican plateau were the Romans among the American Indians.

ARMS OF THE AZTECS

THE Aztec warrior's weapons — bow, bone-tipped arrows, sling, obsidian or bronze spearheads and javelins, stone tomahawk, and heavy clubs, plain or studded with stone spikes — were, however, no match for Cortés' cannon. The Aztec science of war was better at fortifications than in tactics.

SCULPTURED FACE OF QUETZALCOATL, THE FAIR GOD

BELIEVING that Cortés might possibly be the Fair God who, according to the ancient tradition, was to return over the water from the East, Montezuma hesitated to offend him. Cortés, however, lost no time in imprisoning his host, who was later slain on the parapet of his palace by his own people. Cortés captured some of the war chiefs of the outlying districts as well as some of the chief men of the Aztec confederacy.

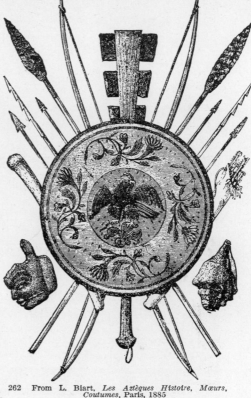

262 From L. Biart, *Les Aztèques Histotre, Mœurs, Coutumes*, Paris, 1885

263 From T. A. Joyce, *Mexican Archæology*, 1914, courtesy of G. P. Putnam's Sons

He then forbade human sacrifice. The Aztec war chiefs who remained at large took command and roused their people to resist the invader.

264 © Underwood and Underwood

THE "TREE OF THE DOLEFUL NIGHT"

AT this point in his enterprise Cortés received a blow from behind. Don Diego Velasquez, deeply offended by the arrogant proceedings of Cortés, sent a force under Pánfilo Narváez to take him prisoner. Narváez, through his emissaries, offered to support the Aztecs. Cortés therefore divided his army, leaving part in Tenochtitlan under Alvarado, and with the rest marched against Narváez. Cortés brought him back a prisoner and along with him most of Don Diego's second expedition, which he had won over to himself as he had already won the first. Alvarado, meanwhile, roused by tales of conspiracy, without warning set upon the Mexicans celebrating a religious festival and massacred them ruthlessly. Cortés, returning, found the Aztec fully roused to their danger. For a space he remained in the capital, then, by night, sought to steal out over the causeway with the fewest sluiceways. The move was discovered. A desperate fight occurred where a bridge over the sluiceway had been removed. With a loss of four hundred and fifty killed and captured, Cortés escaped. It was the *noche triste*, the "doleful night."

265   From the painting, 1887, by Manuel Ramirez Ibañez (1857–), in the Provincial de las Palmas, Canary Islands

THE VICTORY OF CORTÉS AT OTUMBA

THE Aztecs pursued the Spaniards to the mainland but were beaten off in a fierce scrimmage called the battle of Otumba, July 7, 1520. Cortés thereupon prepared to retake the city. He made friends with the vassal peoples, who hated their Aztec lords; he set guards at the road to Vera Cruz as a protection against Don Diego; and he constructed a fleet of shallow boats. In May, 1521, with nine hundred Spaniards, thousands of native allies, eighty-six horses, and eighteen guns, Cortés began the siege of Tenochtitlan by land and water, and on the 13th of August entered the city.

266   From Oexmelin, *Histoire des Avanturiers*, Paris, 1686

THE SPANISH AT PANAMA, 1519

ANOTHER conquest, and one which would presently provoke rivalry against Cortés, was under way in Central America. Pedrarias de Avila had arrived in Darien as governor in 1514, and five years later, after quarrels and reconciliations with Balboa, had beheaded him on the charge of treason. In 1519, the year in which Cortés founded Vera Cruz, Pedrarias established Panama and made it his capital.

267   From Carolus Allard, *Orbis Habitabilis*, Amsterdam, *ca.* 1690

NOMBRE DE DIOS, PORT OF THE SPANISH TREASURE FLEET

PEDRARIAS refounded Nombre de Dios — first planted by Nicuesa and subsequently abandoned — and opened a road to the Pacific, a road to become historic because of the wealth of gold, silver, and jewels which would be transported over it. Pedrarias then cast an avaricious eye upon the territory north of Darien. Cortés, however, was also looking at it southward from Mexico. Under Pedrarias' banner, Gil Gonzalez Dávila and Andrés Niño explored Nicaragua and returned to report thirty-two thousand baptisms and to exhibit thousands of dollars worth of pearls and gold. Pedrarias now set about conquering Nicaragua for

himself, with the assistance of Hernando de Soto and Pizarro, and, in 1527, he was made governor of that province. Meanwhile, in Guatemala and Honduras agents of Pedrarias encountered those of Cortés. But Cortés got the better of his rival and spread his conquests over the disputed territory and Yucatan.

FRANCISCO PIZARRO BEFORE CHARLES V

PIZARRO was born in Estremadura, the illegitimate son of an army officer. As a youth, he made his way across the Atlantic to New Spain. In the rough and tumble of life in America he pushed himself forward until he gained an opportunity to explore the unknown western coast of South America. Reports of a great empire situated in the mountains he succeeded in verifying. Unable to influence the colonial governor, however, he went to Spain to plead his cause with the emperor. His request was granted and he returned to America armed with the powers of a viceroy over the lands to be conquered.

268   From the painting, exhibited at the Exposition, Madrid, 1881, by Angel Lizcano (1846–)

269   Drawn expressly for *The Pageant of America* by C. W. Jefferys

270   From Herrera, *Historia General de las Indias Occidentales*, 1728

EL INGA ATAHUALPA ULTIMO REY.
del Peru.

PIZARRO'S FIRST SIGHT OF THE INCA EMPIRE

IN the autumn of 1532 Pizarro led his little army up the rocky heights of the Andes until he could look down into the protected valley where the Peruvian Incas ruled. His force seemed small indeed for the conquest of the populous cities that lay below him.

THE INCA, ATAHUALPA, LAST KING OF PERU

WHEN the Spaniard dragged his army over the gigantic Andean wall, he knew very little of the extent of the Peruvian empire or of the numbers of its warriors. He knew only that gold was there in amounts, it was to be hoped, far exceeding the Aztec treasure. In November, at Caxamarca, Pizarro met Atahualpa, the Inca, child of the sun. Scornful of the dusty little band of travel-worn Spaniards and secure in his own divinity, Atahualpa, attended by nobles in blue garments with metal broideries — and but a handful of warriors — gave Pizarro a haughty greeting. Pizarro and the Inca chieftain supped together, then the Spaniard suddenly made the Indian prisoner. The native courtiers were too dazed to offer resistance. Atahualpa's lot was hard. Though in captivity, by one means and another he sought to oppose the Spaniards. Finally he was brought to a trial which in itself was a farce, as the decision to kill him had already been made. His end came in August, 1533, when, in the plaza of Caxamarca, he was strangled with a bowstring.

271   The Inca's Soldiers on a vase, from Reiss and Stübel, *The Necropolis of Ancon in Peru*, 1880–87

PERUVIAN ARTS AND CRAFTS

THE Peruvian civilization was of a higher type than the Aztec. It bore a certain analogy to the Persian; its religion was sun-worship; its government was despotic, with all authority centralized in Cuzco and in the person of the Inca, and enforced by means of governors, garrisons, military highways, and the Quichua language of the rulers, which was imposed on all conquered peoples. The caste system prevailed.

In the arts the Peruvians excelled, especially in weaving, in pottery, and in metal work. They composed dramas, poems and hymns, and their musical instruments were numerous. The cyclopean architecture of the Incas was superior to all other examples of the same type, and their fitted and polished stonework was unsurpassed. They were better husbandmen and better engineers than even their conquerors. They raised corn and vegetables and cotton. They had domesticated the llama, which provided wool for garments which they made in many beautiful patterns and various colors. They smelted gold and silver ore from which they made decorated armor and intricate jewelry. They displayed an infinite variety of design in their work with metals and as potters. As cultivators of the soil and as engineers they were superior to the Spaniards who conquered them. They built roads with post houses which ran for hundreds of miles over deserts and the roughest mountain ranges.

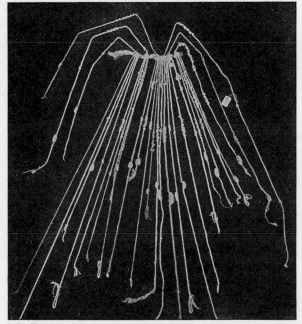

272   From an original in the American Museum of Natural History, New York

THE QUIPUS,
A PERUVIAN KNOT RECORD

THE Peruvians had no writing as the Mayas and the Aztecs had. The Spaniards found them keeping their records with knotted cords known as the *quipus*. The base of the *quipus* was a heavy cord some two feet in length from which a series of knotted strings hung like the fringe of a garment. There were white strings signifying silver or sometimes peace, yellow strings for gold, and red ones for war. The number and size of the knots and their distance from one another all had meanings. In this way the Inca kept a rough record of births and deaths and even of the events in the history of the tribe. Couriers ran from the central capital to the chiefs of outlying provinces carrying orders knotted in *quipus*. Perhaps it was used when strange white men mounted on strange animals suddenly invaded the mountain empire.

273   From Reiss and Stübel, *The Necropolis of Ancon*

WEAVING TOOLS

FEATHERED
HEADDRESS

GOLD BREAST-
PLATE FROM
CUZCO

274   From Reiss and Stübel, *The Necropolis
of Ancon*

275   From C. R. Markham, *The
Incas of Peru*, London, 1910

276   From Reiss and Stübel, *The Necropolis of Ancon*

277   From originals in the American Museum of Natural History,
New York

WOOLEN GARMENT

PERUVIAN MUSICAL INSTRUMENTS

PIZARRO, THE CONQUEROR OF PERU, *ca.* 1471 OR 1475–1541

ATAHUALPA, to gain his freedom, offered to fill a room of the palace with gold and a smaller room twice with silver. In three months Pizarro had collected gold objects worth a fortune. In August, 1533, Atahualpa was murdered and Pizarro, his little army of 183 men and 27 horses somewhat reinforced, marched to Cuzco, which he entered in November. In 1536 the Inca made a determined attempt to drive out the foreign invader. For two months they besieged the Spaniards in Cuzco before relief came to the defenders. Then the Europeans fell to fighting one another for the booty of Peru. Pizarro and his disgruntled lieutenants made peace, broke peace, and then embraced again. On June 26, 1541, the gray conqueror, 63 years old now, was alone in the government house and unarmed. A score of the malcontents suddenly rushed upon him and hacked him down. With his blood Pizarro traced a cross on the floor, kissed it, and died.

278 From *Retratos de los Españoles Ilustres con un epitome de sus Vidas*, Madrid, 1791, engraving by Rafael Estevez y Vilella (1772–1841), after portrait by J. Maca

279 From the portrait study sculptured by Herbert Adams (1856–), for the Louisiana Purchase Exposition, 1903

PÁNFILO NARVÁEZ, *ca.* 1480–1528, ILL-FATED GOVERNOR OF FLORIDA

MEANWHILE, Pánfilo Narváez — tall, red-bearded, one-eyed — obtained from Charles V in 1527 a grant to Florida. He was to colonize, to convert, to seek the Strait, to bear the title of "Adelantado," all at his own expense. On April 14, 1528, Narváez landed at St. Clement's Point, north of Tampa Bay. In a deserted Indian hut he found a little golden ornament. No more was needed to lure him onward in the search for treasure.

For three months Narváez and his three hundred men plunged through the Florida forests, beset by mire and morass, by hunger and Indians. In September they camped at Appalachee Bay, and here they built five boats as best they could. They killed their horses for food, preserved the leg skins entire for water-bottles, and used the tails and manes for ropes. Setting sail from the "Bay of Horses," two boats went ashore on the Texas coast, and the men in the other boats were captured and killed by Indians. Narváez' boat was lost in a storm.

CABEZA DE VACA IN THE DESERT

CABEZA DE VACA and eighty men of Narváez' colony, hungry, sick, and shivering in the November cold, were cared for by friendly Indians on an island now thought to be Galveston. By spring all but fifteen had died, and the living were soon scattered. Only Vaca and one other were left on the island; the others were taken away by Indians from the mainland. Vaca gained the confidence of his masters and was presently trusted to carry articles of trade to the mainland tribes. On his journeys he always sought news of the West and of the nature and extent of the territory between him and Mexico, for to Mexico he had resolved eventually to go.

He waited six years for his timid companion, Oviedo, to dare the venture with him, and, when at last they had gone a hundred miles, Oviedo ran back. Vaca, however, kept steadfastly on. Happily he encountered two Spaniards, Dorantes and Castillo, and a Christianized Moor, Estevanico, the remnant of those taken away by the mainland Indians several years before, and the reunited four pressed on together.

280   From the painting for *Collier's Weekly*, March 18, 1906, by Frederic Remington. © P. F. Collier & Son Co.

281   Title-page from Alvar Nuñez Cabeza de Vaca, *Relación*, the Zamora Edition (1542)

VACA'S BOOK ON HIS TRAVELS

VACA'S medical skill, his cures by prayer and his unselfish character, impressed the savages so deeply that they passed him and his friends in safety from tribe to tribe, fed, clothed and guarded them.

Vaca thus traversed the sand belt between the Nueces and the Rio Grande, and crossing the river pressed on to Chihuahua. He crossed the sub-arid grasslands of northern Mexico. He made his way through the great mountain barrier now known as Sierra Madre Occidental. He traversed nearly half the length of the Sonora desert, skirting the foothills at the western base of the mountains.

At last he reached a Spanish outpost of Sinoloa after one of the most remarkable land journeys of the century. Vaca thereafter went home to Spain and wrote an account of his wanderings. This was the first book about America by a traveler. Of his cures by prayer he wrote: "Our method was to bless the sick, breathing upon them, and recite a Pater-noster and an Ave Maria, praying with all earnestness to God our Lord that he would give health and influence them to make us some good return."

HERNANDO DE SOTO, 1496?–1542
THE DISCOVERER OF THE MISSISSIPPI

HERNANDO DE SOTO, unlike many of his companions, had returned from Peru with honor unsullied and with so much wealth that he was able to ingratiate himself with Charles by lending money to that monarch, who conferred on him the governorship of Florida. In that wild region, where Narváez had failed to find another Mexico, de Soto now set out to seek another Peru. Vaca's return, with a handful of turquoise and with Indian tales of silver cities and jeweled doors, sent de Soto's countrymen flocking to his standard. Nobles sold their castles and estates to join him, and his nine ships could not hold them all.

282 From a copy in the Wisconsin State Historical Society of the portrait in Madrid, date and artist unknown

DE SOTO AT THE MISSISSIPPI, 1542

DE SOTO and his companions forced their way through what is now Florida, Georgia, Carolina, Tennessee, Alabama, and Mississippi. In May, 1541, near Chickasaw Bluffs, de Soto reined in on the east bank of the Mississippi. (The line of this historic march through the wilderness is indicated in the map on page 126.) Hunger, disease, and Indian hostility had thinned his band to half its original number. The survivors were in tatters under their armor. De Soto's iron pride and his iron will held them to the search for gold.

283   From the painting by W. H. Powell (1823–79), in the Capitol rotunda, Washington

284   Drawn expressly for *The Pageant of America* by H. A. Ogden (1856–)

THE BURIAL OF HERNANDO DE SOTO

DE SOTO's men built barges, crossed the Mississippi, and marched on into Arkansas and Oklahoma. Then, discouraged, they turned back. Again in May, a year later, they were on the bank of the great river. And here, Hernando, convinced at last of defeat, fell into a fever and soon died. His little band of followers were fearful of attack from the Indians, if it became known their leader was dead. In the blackness of night de Soto's body was taken from concealment, sewed in fur "shawls," weighted with stones, and sunk in the depths of the river. Luis de Moscoso, designated their commander by de Soto, now led his men into Texas in futile search of a way out, and then back to the Mississippi, where he set them to building brigantines. In their rudely constructed fleet, they floated down the river, crossed the Gulf, and made Mexico in safety.

THE FIGHT AT THE ZUÑI PUEBLO, 1539

IN search of a western entrance to the Strait of Anian, Fray Marcos de Niza, a Franciscan, set out in 1539 with an Indian band and the Moor, Estevanico, bound for New Mexico — where rose the fabled Seven Cities of Cíbola. The frontier passed, Estivanico was sent ahead to find the route, and as he

went he came to the Zuñi pueblo of Hawaikúh. The new-comers were well received by the wondering Indians. Gifts and tribute were brought to the Moor. But the mood of the barbarian redskins changed. "The sun was about a lance high" when the people of Hawaikúh let fly with arrows and stones upon the invaders. The Moor's army, fleeing, looked back and thought they saw him fall.

285   From R. E. Twitchell, *Leading Facts of New Mexican History*, 1911, after a drawing by
Kenneth M. Chapman (1875–)

286   From the painting by Frederic Remington for Henry Inman, *Old Santa Fé Trail*, 1898, published by Crane & Company, Topeka, Kansas

CORONADO'S MARCH THROUGH THE SOUTHWEST

THE reports of Fray Marcos incited Coronado, Governor of the Mexican frontier, to assemble an army at Compostela in February, 1540, with three hundred nobles and a thousand Indians. Coronado, in the second week in July, reached Hawaikúh, which he captured after a sharp fight. Great was the general rage and disappointment when this silver city of Fray Marcos' description was entered and explored. But captives told Coronado of richer cities further on. He crossed the Texas plains on his futile search and then went north to Great Bend, Kansas, where he set up a cross and turned back. After two years he reached Mexico again, poorer in spirit and wiser in experience. "He lost his reputation, and shortly thereafter his government of New Galicia" tersely states Castañeda, the historian with the expedition.

287   From the portrait in the National Museum, City of Mexico

DON ANTONIO DE MENDOZA,
FIRST VICEROY OF NEW SPAIN, 1480-1552

ANTONIO DE MENDOZA, who had been sent out in 1535 as Viceroy of Mexico or New Spain, as it was called, was an ambitious, energetic man. He had received Vaca and had been inspired by his story to send out Fray Marcos, Alarçon, and Coronado. The failure of Coronado did not daunt him.

In June, 1542, he sent a Portuguese mariner, Cabrillo, and two ships up the west coast and, in November, despatched an expedition "West towards China or the Spice Islands," under Villalobos. Villalobos took possession of the Philippines but died on his journey. Cabrillo discovered the bay of San Diego and the northern harbor later called Drake's Bay. He, too, died on the voyage. But Ferrelo, his pilot, continued north as far as Rogue River, Oregon, and then turned home, without having found the Strait of Anian.

ALARCÓN'S SHIPS IN THE GREAT BORE OF THE COLORADO, 1540

To co-operate with Coronado and to explore, when found, the western end of the Strait of Anian, Viceroy Mendoza had sent out two vessels under Hernando de Alarcón. Alarcón went up the coast to the head of the Gulf of California and then battled with the fierce tide which rushed up and down the Colorado. He presently sent his ships back to the sea and proceeded by boats as far as Fort Yuma, where he buried letters for Coronado.

288   From F. S. Dellenbaugh, *The Romance of the Colorado River*, 1902, after a drawing by the author

289   From the model in the American Museum of Natural History, New York, constructed under the direction of C. A. Reeds and E. O. Hovey

GRAND CANYON OF THE COLORADO

DURING his journey news was brought to Coronado of a great river and a race of giants that lived along its banks. He sent Don Garcia López de Cárdenas with twelve men to discover it. At last, after a difficult desert journey, the party stood on the brink of the Grand Canyon and, looking down, saw the Colorado a thin line thousands of feet below. After several days of exploration they returned with the report that the canyon presented an impassible barrier.

CHAPTER VII

FRENCH DEFIANCE IN FLORIDA

SPAIN had established the centers of her American empire in the West Indies, on the Isthmus of Darien and in Mexico. From Mexico the Spaniard had steadily pushed northward toward the regions that came to be known as Texas and California. But Spanish claims did not end with the southern areas of the continent. They extended indefinitely to the north. So, when the news came to the West Indies that a party of Huguenots from France were planning a settlement on the western shore of the Atlantic not far north of Cuba, the Spaniards were bound to bestir themselves. In spite of more than one exploring expedition the Spaniard had failed to establish himself on the mainland of North America either in Florida or northward. The reason was not hard to find. The gold and silver which was the life of New Spain did not exist on the Atlantic coast plain which Ponce de Leon and others had explored. New Spain was, therefore, not well prepared to meet an invasion of this region by the French.

The Huguenots were Frenchmen who had come under the influence of the Protestant movement that had originated in Germany in the sixteenth century. René de Laudonnière was a Huguenot who, in June, 1564, led a fleet to what is now the coast of Carolina. Most of the people with him were folk of the new Protestant faith and they came to found a colony in the New World.

But Laudonnière was merely carrying out the work which Jean Ribaut of Dieppe, a seaman of renown, had begun. Two years before, he had crossed the sea to explore the American coast and had sighted land near the present St. Augustine. He had nosed his way northward along the shore until he came to what seemed to him a great river which he called the "River of May" because it chanced to be May Day when he entered the estuary. It is now known as the St. John's. Landing here, the Frenchmen found the region "the fairest, fruitfulest, and pleasantest of all the world." They believed that the famed Cíbola with its seven cities was but twenty days' journey away. Leaving the River of May without attempting to reach the Seven Cities, Ribaut skirted the coast to the northward and finally turned east to France. He left at Port Royal Sound a force of thirty volunteers to hold the land. But hunger and mutiny broke up the colony. Killing their leaders, the mutineers put to sea in a rough boat they had shaped, and undertook the desperate adventure of a voyage across the Atlantic.

Laudonnière, coming out with a fleet in 1564, was attempting to advance the French claim which Ribaut had established. But the colonists were taking grave risks. They were trespassing on soil claimed by a rival nation, and most of them belonged to the Protestant faith, between which and the Church which Spain defended was a growing enmity. They must expect to fight to maintain their foothold.

290 From the portrait by Jan van Ravesteyn (*ca.* 1572–
1657), in the Louvre, Paris

THE HUGUENOT LEADER, GASPARD DE COLIGNY, ADMIRAL OF FRANCE, 1519–72

COLIGNY, a distinguished soldier, and a man of noble Burgundian family, was made Admiral of France in 1552 at the age of thirty-three. We do not know at what date he joined the Huguenots; John Calvin's first letter to him was written in 1558. Four years later the religious wars broke out. The party of the Guises and the Queen-Mother, Catherine de Medici, strove to eradicate Protestantism as representing primarily a new political power. In 1572 occurred the Massacre of St. Bartholomew, in which Coligny fell.

THE HUGUENOTS, LED BY JEAN RIBAUT, LAND IN FLORIDA, 1562

To revive the fallen glory of France, to protect his co-religionists, and to strike a blow at Spain were Coligny's three chief aims. In the first he had all Frenchmen with him. On French maps of the New World there was a tract marked, since Verrazano's time, "Terre des Bretons." This was, approximately, Nova Scotia; but so vague were current notions of geography that the French may have thought it included Florida, territory which had been recently declared by Spaniards unfit for white habitation. To Florida Coligny dispatched a colony composed chiefly of Huguenots, under Jean Ribaut of Dieppe.

291
From Theodore de Bry, *Voyages*, Part II (Florida), 1591, after a sketch by Jacques Le Moyne

SATURIBA AND LAUDONNIÈRE AT RIBAUT'S COLUMN

RIBAUT reached St. John's River on the coast of Florida on May 1, 1562, and named it for the day, "The River of May." Here he erected a column which he had with forethought brought from France. He then sailed north, landed his colony on the Broad River, under the charge of René de Laudonnière, and sailed home to get supplies. Civil war, however, was again

292   From the original drawing by Jacques Le Moyne de Morgues (*ca.* 1564) in the possession of La Marquise de Ganay, Paris

convulsing France, and Ribaut found himself unable to return to America. His colonists, starving, started homewards in a ship which they could not manage, and were at last picked up by an English vessel.

In 1564 Coligny sent a second colony under Laudonnière which landed at St. John's River and built Fort Caroline. Here Saturiba, an Indian chief, led Laudonnière in state to Ribaut's column to show him the garlands and offerings of maize with which his tribe had honored it. For lack of adaptability this French colony also starved in fruitful Florida and was about to depart in a ship purchased from the English seaman, John Hawkins, when, in August, 1565, Ribaut opportunely arrived with supplies and more colonists and soldiers.

THE BUILDING OF FORT CAROLINE

LAUDONNIÈRE, enchanted with the land in which he had established his colony, wrote a description, touched

293   From Theodore de Bry, *Voyages*, Part II (Florida), Frankfort, 1591

with imagination and philosophy, of "cedars red as blood" and "bay trees of so sovereign an odor that balm smells nothing like in comparison," in short, of a place "so pleasant that those which are melancholic would be enforced to change their humor." In the midst of this pleasant prospect, the French built Fort Caroline. The fortification was needed, for the Spaniards sent their treasure ships home through the Bahama channel and were bound to attempt to wipe out a French settlement, so placed that it could be used as a refuge and base for privateers preying on the silver galleons.

294   From the portrait by Titian in the
          Museo Nazionale, Naples

PHILIP II OF SPAIN, 1527–98, ORDERS MENÉNDEZ TO FLORIDA

PHILIP was as fanatical about his own power and glory as he was about his religion. As Spanish king no less than as royal Catholic, he felt that Protestantism was a wicked rebellion that must at all costs be put down. To Spain the presence of armed Frenchmen and "Lutheran heretics" in Florida was an insult unendurable and a political threat to be promptly answered. King Philip ordered Pedro Menéndez de Avilés, an able naval commander fanatically loyal to Crown and Church, to extirpate the French from Florida and found in their stead a Spanish colony. On August 28, 1565, the day of Ribaut's arrival at Fort Caroline, Menéndez anchored to the south in a harbor which he named St. Augustine, and set out northward in search of the French.

295   From *Retratos de los Españoles Ilustres,*
          etc., Madrid, 1791

PEDRO MENÉNDEZ DE AVILÉS,
1519–74

MENÉNDEZ CHALLENGES RIBAUT'S SHIPS

EARLY in September, Menéndez with five vessels came upon four of Ribaut's ships at the mouth of St. John's River. Ribaut himself was ashore. Menéndez sailed into the midst of the French, determined on battle before reinforcements should arrive. His trumpets sounded a salute; the French trumpets responded. Menéndez's *San Pelayo* now lay alongside Ribaut's *Trinity*. "Gentlemen, from where does this fleet come?" "From France," answered a voice from the *Trinity*. "What are you doing here?" The voice answered that the French were building a fort for the King of France. "Are you Catholics or Lutherans?" "Lutherans, and our general is Jean Ribaut." Menéndez thereupon ordered his men to draw swords and board. But the Normans, more agile seamen than their foes, cut their cables and made out to sea unscathed.

296   Drawn expressly for *The Pageant of America* by C. W. Jefferys

297   Drawn expressly for *The Pageant of America* by C. W. Jefferys

THE FOUNDING OF ST. AUGUSTINE BY MENÉNDEZ, 1565

MENÉNDEZ put back to the bay of St. Augustine. On the 6th of September he disembarked his colonists and supplies and himself went ashore in state. Flags, trumpets, and drums did him honor; the chaplain, carrying a cross and chanting the *Te Deum*, advanced to meet him. Menéndez now took formal possession in the Spanish king's name. Mass was celebrated. During these ceremonies two of Ribaut's ships, which had fled through the Spanish fleet at St. John's River and had then turned and followed it, appeared at the mouth of the harbor and challenged the *San Pelayo* and the *San Salvator*, anchored outside the bar because they were too large to cross it safely. Menéndez's vessels, however, refused the combat, and the French sailed away.

ST. AUGUSTINE — PLAN OF THE FIRST SPANISH FORT

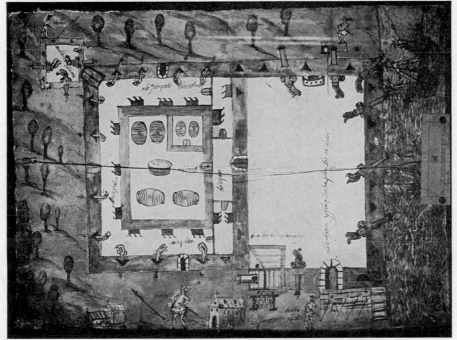

MENÉNDEZ was instructed to establish fortified towns one of whose functions would be to protect the Bahama channel. The fort at St. Augustine was begun with the founding of the colony. The position was well chosen and strongly maintained. So it happened that St. Augustine became the first permanent town within the boundaries of what is now the United States.

298   From the original (*ca.* 1593) in the Archives of the Indies, Seville

299   Drawn expressly for *The Pageant of America* by C. W. Jefferys

THE MASSACRE OF THE FRENCH

RIBAUT, conscious of the Spanish peril, set sail for St. Augustine but was blown out to sea by a storm. Menéndez, equally active, marched overland, surprised Fort Caroline, and killed all but a handful of the small garrison that Ribaut had left. Then came the news of the wreck of two of the French ships at Matanzas. Losing no time, the Spanish commander marched to the spot and by fair promises disarmed and bound the one hundred and forty survivors. Going ahead of them, he drew a line in the sand behind a dune. Dusk was falling when the shipwrecked party reached the mark. The rising sun next day saw their headless bodies already attracting carrion birds. Later Ribaut and the rest of the French, who also met with shipwreck at the same place, were hacked to death beside the same bloody mark in the sand.

300   From Theodore de Bry, *Voyages*, Part II, 1591, after sketch by Le Moyne

HUGUENOTS PLEADING WITH MENÉNDEZ

301   From the painting, in the Royal Palace, Madrid, *Philip Receiving an Embassy from the Low Countries*, by Santiago Arcos y Megalde

PHILIP RECEIVING AN EMBASSY

To Philip wrote Menéndez: "They came and surrendered their arms to me, and I had their hands tied behind them, and put them all excepting ten (Catholics) to the sword." And on the back of Menéndez' report Philip scrawled: "As to those he has killed, he has done well, and as to those he has saved, they shall be sent to the galleys." To Menéndez he wrote: "We hold that we have been well served."

GOURGUES' ATTACK ON SAN MATEO

THE victorious Spaniards changed the name of Fort Caroline to San Mateo. In 1568, Gourgues, an ex-soldier of France, landed quietly in Florida, made an alliance with the chief Saturiba, and fell upon San Mateo with the aid of his Indian allies. Against this attack the cannon in the fort were of no avail. As many as possible of the garrison were taken alive.

When Gourgues left, their bodies swung from the branches of the southern forest. Gourgues said they were executed "not as Spaniards" but "as traitors, robbers and murderers." The expedition was an act of private revenge which led neither to war nor to the establishment of permanent French settlements in the neighborhood of the Bahama channel.

302   From an engraving in Van der Aa, *Zee en Land-Reysen*, Leyden, 1706-27

303   From the original Mestas map in the Archives of the Indies, Seville

THE EARLIEST VIEW OF
ST. AUGUSTINE

THE Mestas map may now be found among papers which were carried to Spain in 1594–95 by Hernando de Mestas. Mestas had been sent by the Florida colony to the Spanish court to plead for many things the colony wanted, particularly new fortifications. Because of the fact that it was taken to Spain under such circumstances, the map has usually been dated 1595.

Recent research has unearthed evidence which strongly points to a date perhaps as much as thirty years earlier. The enlarged section of the map here reproduced may represent the St. Augustine that Menéndez knew. Before the rough church is a curious device for holding the chimes. Beside the wharf is a small protecting fort just beyond the end of which a bell is hung from an upright — perhaps for sounding the alarm in time of war or fire. Behind the wharf and to the right is a house for the governor. The squares in the background are the cultivated fields. The map remains the earliest authentic representation of St. Augustine, Florida.

304 From the original Mestas map in the Archives of the Indies, Seville

CHAPTER VIII

ENGLAND'S CHALLENGE TO SPAIN

SPAIN grew in power as a result of the riches her galleons brought across the Atlantic from Nombre de Dios and Vera Cruz. Other factors contributed to make her at times in the sixteenth century the most powerful nation in Europe. Unswervingly Spain upheld the ancient faith. She sent her missionaries to convert the conquered peoples in America and set her face steadily against the Protestants of Europe. England under the Protestant Elizabeth became the chief of her enemies.

It happened that Spain's day of greatness coincided with England's. The nation north of the Channel was no longer a wholly agricultural and fishing people. Long before Elizabeth's time they had begun to send traders into far distant regions. Englishmen were pooling their capital in joint-stock companies that were trading in Europe and even in central Russia and the Levant. In the Elizabethan era this commercial development came into full flower, and a new wealth poured into London and the lesser cities. The laden Spanish galleons ploughing eastward across the Atlantic from Mexico and Darien were at once a threat and an opportunity.

Elizabethan England was fully alive to the Spanish menace. Never before had the English people produced such a brilliant array of leaders. The mariners who became famous for trading and for their depredations in the Spanish Main found their counterpart in the statesmen and the men of letters. Richard Hakluyt began his collections of narratives of exploration in unknown lands and Walter Raleigh began to dream of an English empire in America.

Of such quality was the England that Philip II of Spain faced. He saw English buccaneers, increasing in numbers with the years, prowl along the sea routes that the galleons traveled, every now and then cutting out a rich ship. Though the two nations were at peace the English carried their attack to the Spanish ports in North America. War was the inevitable result. England had challenged Spain's monopoly of the western hemisphere and the two must fight it out for a place in the New World.

305   An English Galleon; from Vischer's engravings, representing
      the defeat of the Armada, published in Holland about 1588

QUEEN ELIZABETH,
1533–1603

ELIZABETH had the fortune to rule in a day of England's greatness. Never before had the island kingdom produced such a wealth of men of ability and daring. Merchants were trading to the far corners of the earth; adventurers were seeking plunder in the Spanish Main and new routes to the Orient; men of letters were writing dramas, poems and essays that have enriched the literature of the world.

Elizabeth was a great figure in a great age. "Nothing, nothing, no worldly thing under the sun, is so dear to me as the love and good will of my subjects," she said to her first Parliament. All her gifts were devoted to rallying the nation to the support of the throne as the best means of promoting prosperity and security.

When the test came, in 1588, the Spanish Armada found the English invincible. From that date Elizabeth more and more withdrew from her people, but the prosperity and brilliance of her reign continued to its end in 1603. So well had England's world position been established that only four years after the passing of the great queen, the first permanent English colony was founded on the continent of North America.

306 From the portrait attributed to Federigo Zucchero (Zuccaro) (1543–1609), in the National Portrait Gallery, London

SIR JOHN HAWKINS, 1532–95

IN 1562 John Hawkins, the son of an English merchant, formed a joint-stock company for trade with the Spaniards. His first trip out was made in three small vessels. An old account gives the following story. "At Teneriffe he received friendly treatment. From thence he passed to Sierra Leona, where he stayed a good time, and got into his possession, partly by the sword and partly by other means, to the number of 300 Negroes at the least, besides other merchandises. . . . With this prey he sailed over the ocean sea unto the island of Hispaniola [Hayti] . . . and here had reasonable utterance [sale] of his English commodities, as also of some part of his Negroes, trusting the Spaniards no further than by his own strength he was able to still master them." He sold all his negroes and with a load of hides, ginger, sugar and some pearls started for home. Queen Elizabeth made him a knight, and gave him a coat of arms with the crest: "A demi-Moor, bound and captive." Sir John Hawkins was one of the most daring mariners of his time. He led the way in the English attack upon the Spanish monopoly of the trade with the West Indies and the mainland of America.

307   From C. B. Markham, *The Voyages of Hawkins*, issued by the Hakluyt Society

MARTIN FROBISHER, *ca.* 1535–94

MARTIN FROBISHER as early as 1560 had formed a resolution to look for a northwest passage to Cathay. One of his companions on his first voyage, writing in 1578, says Captaine Frobisher is "thoroughly furnished of the knowledge of the sphere, . . . and being persuaded of a new and neerer passage to Cataya, than by Capo d'buona Speranza, which the Portugalles yeerly use. He began first with himselfe to devise, and then with his friendes to conferre, and layde a playne platte unto them, that that voyage was not onely possible by the north-weast, but also, as he coulde prove, easie to bee performed."

Elizabeth gave him farewell at Greenwich June 7, 1576, whence he sailed with the *Gabriel* and the *Michael*, of twenty to twenty-five tons each. Frobisher passed along the Labrador coast, crossed the entrance of Hudson Strait, and coasted along Baffin Land, entering the inlet now known as Frobisher's Bay. He brought back a large stone, "black earth," which it was claimed contained gold, and the queen and others subscribed liberally to the founding of the Company of Cathay, which was to have a monopoly in all lands to the westward where Englishmen had not traded before. Expeditions went under Frobisher in 1577 and 1578, but the minerals brought back proved to be worthless.

308 From a portrait by Cornelis Ketel (1548–1616), in the Bodleian Library, Oxford

SIR HUMPHREY GILBERT, *ca.* 1539–83

SIR HUMPHREY GILBERT, step-brother of Sir Walter Raleigh, who had been writing, talking, and petitioning on the subject of "discovering of a passage by the north to go to Cataia, [Cathay]" finally received a charter granting for six years a monopoly of discovery and colonization in America. In 1578 his fleet was twice scattered by storms and the attempt abandoned. But in 1583 Gilbert sailed to the coast of Newfoundland and took possession in the name of the queen. On the return voyage his ship, the *Squirrel*, foundered in a storm north of the Azores. Gilbert and all hands perished.

309   From Henry Holland, *Herwologia Anglica*, London, 1620

BARTHOLOMEW GOSNOLD AT CUTTYHUNK

IN 1602, Gosnold, a venturesome exploring mariner, sailing for Sir Walter Raleigh, coasted the shore of the present states of New Hampshire and Massachusetts and made landings at Cape Cod, which he named, and on the island of Cuttyhunk (Buzzards Bay). Returning home with a cargo of furs and sassafras, he warmly urged colonization. In 1606, King James granted charters to the London and Plymouth companies. The next year Gosnold commanded one of three vessels which carried the first permanent English col-

310   From Vander Aa, *Beschryvinge van der Englische na oost Indien*, Leyden, 1706–27

ony to America.   Vander Aa's sketch represents the ideas held a century later of the exploring expedition.

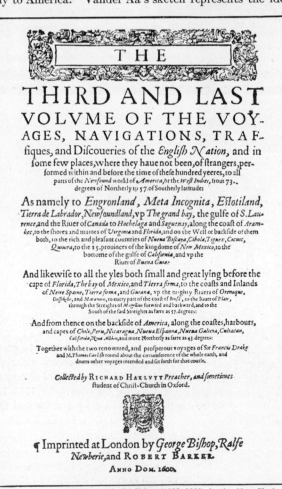

311   From a copy of the original edition (1598–1600) in the New York Public Library

HAKLUYT'S *VOYAGES*

RECORDS of the voyages of the explorers in American waters, and whatever other accounts of American adventurers were obtainable, were collected and published by Richard Hakluyt, the English geographer, who even as a youth had resolved "to prosecute that knowledge and kind of literature." By his books and his discourses he worked incessantly to popularize and extend English colonization in America. He published the first map showing the name "Virginia"; and, in 1606, as Archdeacon of Westminster, he was one of the leading spirits in the London, or Virginia, Company, which planted Jamestown.

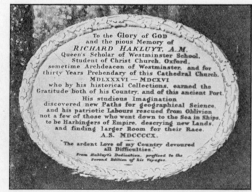

312   From the marble tablet in the Bristol (England) Cathedral

MEMORIAL TO RICHARD HAKLUYT

313 From the portrait attributed to Federigo Zucchero (Zuccaro), in the National Portrait Gallery, London

SIR WALTER RALEIGH,
ca. 1552–1618

POET, master of prose, soldier, statesman, and patriot, Sir Walter Raleigh stands out as a great figure in a great age. He was a crusader for an ideal, whether leading his troop of English volunteers in the cause of the French Huguenots, or expending his resources and his strength in American ventures. He was the first Englishman to catch the vision of America as a place not for plunder or primarily for trade, but as a new region where English homes and English speech and English law might flourish. "I shall yet live to see it an Inglishe nation," he prophesied.

A phrase in Raleigh's charter, repeated from that to Sir Humphrey Gilbert, granted his colonists "all the privileges of free denizens and persons native of England in such ample manner as if they were born and personally resident in our said realm of England." This guarantee, renewed in the Virginia charter of 1606, became one of the bases of the struggle for colonial freedom which eventually led to independence.

THE COUNTRY SEAT OF WALTER RALEIGH

OF the several properties presented to Raleigh in his day of favor, the estate at Sherborne in Dorsetshire was apparently first in his affections. There he built a fine example of the domestic architecture of the day.

314   From the mural painting by C. Y. Turner (1850–1918), in the Hotel Raleigh, Washington

315   From the mural painting by C. Y. Turner in the Hotel Raleigh,
Washington

THE DEPARTURE OF RALEIGH'S COLONISTS

In 1584, Raleigh received a patent and sent two ships to
America. Following the southern route they finally landed
at Roanoke Island. In 1585 Raleigh sent out his first
colony, under Ralph Lane as governor, to the domain
which he had named "Virginia." The colonists established
themselves on Roanoke Island, but there they fared so ill
that they were glad to sail home next year with Francis
Drake, who had been raiding the Spanish Main. Just
after Drake had left, a ship of Raleigh's "freighted with
all maner of things in most plentiful maner" dropped
anchor before Roanoke. The relief expedition "after some
time spent in seeking our Colony up in the Countrey, and
not finding them, returned with all the aforesayd provision
into England." Nothing daunted, Raleigh sent out another
colony in 1587.

CHART OF THE COAST OF VIRGINIA,
1585–86

John White, the artist who accompanied Lane's colony,
has outlined in this remarkably faithful map the country
which was the scene of Raleigh's ill-fated endeavors.
Amidas and Barlowe in 1584 had landed at "Wococon"
(Collington Island), taking possession for the queen under
Raleigh's patent. Here Lane's colony the next year made
their first landing. Explorations before proceeding to
"Roanoac" involved the destruction of the Indian village
of "Aquescgoc" for an alleged theft, an act that made
enemies of the Indians of the region. From Roanoke
exploring expeditions had been sent up the river, one of
which proceeded as far as "Morataic" in the hope of finding
a route to China, but was forced to return because of the
hostility of the natives.

316   From the original drawing by John White in the
British Museum, London

From Theodore de Bry, *Voyages*, Part I, Frankfort, 1590

ENGLISHMEN LANDING AT ROANOKE

THUS writes Thomas Hariot of the English arrival at Roanoke: "Wee came unto a Good bigg yland the Inhabitants thereof as soone as they saw us began to make a great and horrible crye. . . . But beenge gentlye called backe wee offered them of our wares, as glasses, knives, babies [dolls] and other trifles, which wee thought they delighted in . . . then they brought us to their village in the iland called, Roanoac . . . such was our arrivall into the parte of the world which we call Virginia."

THE TREE INSCRIBED "CROATOAN"

THE second colony to Virginia was led by Governor John White. After building a fort and seeing his colonists safely housed, White went home for supplies. At this moment, however, the menace of Philip's Armada

and the necessary preparations for the great struggle on the sea balked White's efforts to return to the relief of his colony. Two years passed before he was able to sail again for Roanoke. Silence greeted his arrival. The only sign that Englishmen had been there before was the word "Croatoan," the name of a neighboring island, carved upon a tree. All trace of the colonists had disappeared, and White and his crew were left in the uncertainty of surmise as to the fate of their fellow-colonists.

Drawn expressly for *The Pageant of America* by H. A. Ogden

SIR FRANCIS DRAKE, *ca.* 1545–95

ONE of the ablest contemporaries of Raleigh was Francis Drake, the most famous of Elizabeth's seadogs. At ten the red-haired, blue-eyed lad was already a sailor. Ten years later he commanded one of Hawkins' ships in a disastrous encounter on the Spanish Main. Yet he was destined to harass the Spaniards as no other man yet had done. Not the least of his adventures was his attack upon Nombre de Dios in 1572, and his capture of a mule-train of gold and jewels. From that day onward Spanish fear and hatred of the English scourge ran high.

DRAKE'S GREATEST ASSAULT UPON THE SPANIARDS

ONE of the most stirring and significant episodes in the story of the clash between England and Spain was Drake's voyage around the world. His incursions in the Caribbean region had caused the Spanish in that region to look well to their ports and ships. Drake now proposed to attack in an unexpected quarter. This old map of the world showing the scene of his new operations in the Pacific is said to have been corrected by Drake himself. The whole region of the Caribbean Sea was prepared for defense against Drake and the other English free-booters. As a result the profits of privateering began to fall.

319 From the portrait, probably by Abraham Janssen, 1594, in Buckland Abbey, Yelverton, Devonshire, England

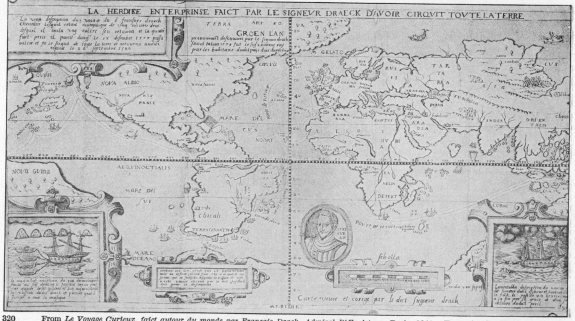

320   From *Le Voyage Curieux, faict autour du monde par Francais Drack, Admiral D'Engleterre*, Paris, 1641. Engraving by Nicola van Sype in the Hispanic Society, New York

THE *GOLDEN HIND*

On December 13, 1577, Drake slipped quietly out of English waters with his little fleet of five vessels. The *Golden Hind*, his flagship, was of only 100 tons. The ships were abundantly stocked with ammunition and carried 350 men, among whom were some gentlemen adventurers out for a lark. The fleet turned south along the African coast picking up some Portuguese and Spanish vessels. Then Drake turned his prows across the southern Atlantic. He was following, in a general way, the route of the great Magellan. Englishmen who had helped to finance the enterprise awaited expectantly the return of the fleet laden with rich booty. Weeks passed as the little flotilla sailed through the steady trades, crossed the equatorial belt of calms, and ran down the south Atlantic with the continent of South America on the starboard side. On board the ships, musicians, whom Drake, with much foresight, had brought along, broke up the monotony of the long ocean voyage.

321   From the mural painting by Ezra Winter. © Twenty-five Broadway Corporation

DRAKE CAPTURES THE TREASURE SHIP

Reaching the Straits of Magellan, Drake essayed the hazardous channel. Only one of his ships, the *Golden Hind*, got through. In this sea-worn flagship he sailed into the Pacific and northward along the Spanish coast of South America. Drake made several rich hauls. He pursued the pride of the Spanish treasure fleet, *Nuestra Señora de la Concepción*, "the chiefest glory of the whole South Sea," carrying a rich cargo of gold, jewels, and silver. Don Anton, her captain, seeing the unexpected sail on the horizon and never dreaming that any other than a Spanish ship had entered the Pacific, slackened speed and ordered up wine for his visitor. Drake, however, came not as guest but as master. "Accept with patience the usage of war," said the new-comer as he took possession. The western coast was thrown into consternation.

322   Drawn expressly for *The Pageant of America* by C. W. Jefferys

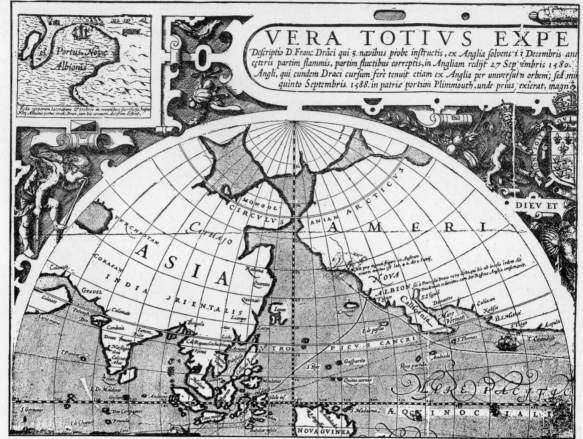

323   From the original of Jodocus Hondius, *Vera totius expeditionis nauticae Descriptio D. Franci Draci*, 1595, in the British Museum, London

HONDIUS MAP SHOWING DRAKE'S BAY

As a result of Drake's disquieting captures, the whole Spanish coast was now on the alert for the red-bearded marauder. Now, if ever, thought Drake, should the long-sought Strait of Anian prove a short and safe route home. Accordingly he sailed northward looking for it, as far as British Columbia. Then turning back, he anchored in Drake's Bay north of San Francisco and took possession of this new land for his sovereign, naming it New Albion. Thence he steered westward for the East Indies, rounded the Cape of Good Hope and by more familiar waters came at length home, having made the "encompassment of all the worlde."

ELIZABETH KNIGHTS DRAKE

ON the *Golden Hind*, lying off London, Drake gave a banquet to the queen "finer than has ever been seen in England since Henry VIII." Elizabeth came wearing her crown, the most gorgeous of her gowns, and in her merriest mood, for she knew that Philip was gnashing his teeth over his losses. She lifted a gilded sword and bade Drake kneel. "He [Philip] hath demanded Drake's head of me," she said gaily, "and here I have a gilded sword to strike it off." Then, after the customary tap of the sword on the kneeling man's shoulder, she pronounced the formula, "I bid thee rise, Sir Francis Drake." And an English poet wrote:

The Stars of Heaven would thee proclaim
If men here silent were,
The Sun himself could not forget
His fellow-traveller.

324   From the painting, 1922, by Howard Davie,
courtesy of Raphael Tuck and Sons, Ltd., London

THOMAS CAVENDISH, ca. 1555–92, SAILS AROUND THE WORLD

To live at court as he would — that is, to shine there — Thomas Cavendish, gentleman, needed more money than he possessed. In search of fortune, he set out for the Spanish Main in 1585, and thence started to circumnavigate the globe, the third man to attempt the feat. In the Pacific he made a rich haul and captured the *Santa Ana*, the pride of the new Spanish treasure fleet.

He made Plymouth in 1588, and, according to an old story, with his sailors dressed in silks, his sails of damask, and his topmast covered with cloth of gold. The sight of Spanish treasure was hailed with rejoicing and drew fresh adventurous spirits into the queen's navy.

Three years later Cavendish was again in straits. He organized a second expedition into the Atlantic and Pacific. But this time fortune was unkind. The enterprise was an utter failure, due, in part, to Cavendish himself. On his way home, in 1592, declaring falsely with his last breath that his partner, John Davis, had deserted him, Cavendish died, and was buried at sea. His only important contribution to knowledge as a result of his two great expeditions was the discovery of "Port Desire" on the coast of Patagonia.

THOMAS CANDISH ARMIGER

Animum fortuna sequatur

325   From Henry Holland, *Herwologia Anglica*, 1620

326 From W. L. Clowes, *The Royal Navy*, London, 1897, engraving after the portrait by Federigo Zucchero (Zuccaro)

CHARLES HOWARD, 1536–1624, LORD EFFINGHAM: LORD HIGH ADMIRAL

CHARLES HOWARD, Lord Effingham, was the titular head of the fleet, of which Drake was the brains. English raids upon the Spanish colonies and treasure-ships had become unendurable. It was clear that in his good time Philip would attempt to clean out the nest of pirates and heretics, and Howard is said to have remarked to the queen:

"For the love of Jesus Christ, Madame, awake thoroughly and see the villainous treasons round about you, against your Majesty and your realm, and draw your forces round about you like a mighty prince to defend you. Truly, Madame, if you do so, there is no cause for fear. Put down whatever of treason lies at home and prepare for foreign war."

If this quotation is correct, the advice was good. Spain was steadily and rapidly growing in power and ambition. The same was true of England. The rival interests of the two powers made for an inevitable clash on the Atlantic. England sought to trade with all the world; Spain excluded all foreigners from her oversea possessions and for the trade between Old and New Spain made the severest restrictions.

DRAKE AT SANTO DOMINGO, 1585

IN 1585 the trouble brewing between England and Spain broke into open hostilities. In that year Drake set off for the Spanish Main, not for plunder but for war. Late in the autumn his ships dropped anchor in the harbor of Santo Domingo. The fortifications of the town were formidable and strongly defended, but the British smashed their way in. When they left, this ancient center of Spanish authority in the New World was a smoking ruin.

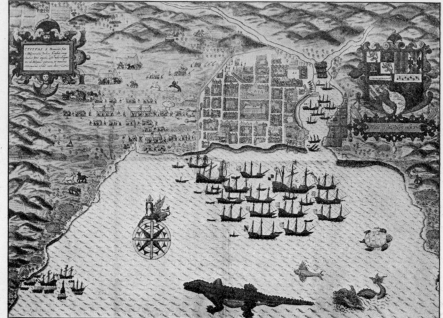

327   From *Expeditio Francisci Draki*, etc., Leyden, 1588. In New York Public Library

After burning Santo Domingo, Drake went over to Cartagena, took the town from the Spaniards, and held it for a heavy ransom. Then he made for St. Augustine. There was no rich loot to be taken here, but Spanish Florida was a menace to Virginia; so Drake set St. Augustine afire and destroyed it. Then sailing north to Roanoke, he took Raleigh's first colony aboard and turned homewards.

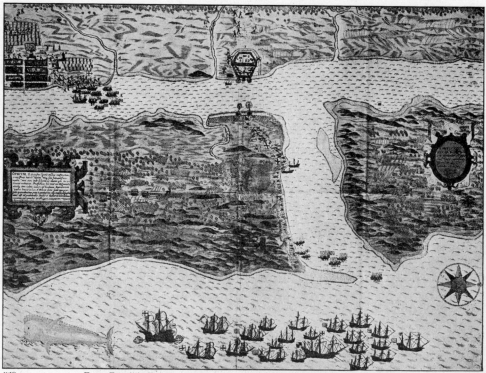

328   From *Expeditio Francisci Draki*, etc., Leyden, 1588. In New York Public Library

DESTRUCTION OF ST. AUGUSTINE, FLORIDA, BY DRAKE — 1586

329   From the painting by Sir John Seymour Lucas (1849–) in the National Gallery of New South Wales, Sydney, Australia

THE ARMADA IN SIGHT

IN 1580 Philip had conquered Portugal and had joined her fine fleet to his own.   Eight years later he was ready to send his Armada against England.   But Elizabeth's navy was prepared.   On Friday, July 19, 1588, runs an old story, Drake and Howard were playing a game of bowls on Plymouth Hoe, when up rushed the Captain of the *Golden Hind* with news that the Spanish Armada was in sight.   Noticing the terror of the crowd of townsfolk and realizing that his first duty was to quiet it, Drake, after whispering an order, called out "There's time to end our game and beat the Spanish, too."

TAPESTRY PICTURES OF THE GREAT BATTLE

THE next morning Drake, with a fleet of fifty-four vessels, sighted, through a thickening mist and drizzling rain, the Armada near the Eddystone.   But instead of risking an engagement, he allowed the Armada, consisting of one hundred and twenty-eight ships, to advance up the Channel in the famous eagle formation, and then attacked it from the rear, with the advantage of a favorable wind.   John Pine of London, who in 1739 engraved the Armada pictures, says in his "Account" that the engagements between the two fleets were "represented in ten curious Pieces of Tapestry, with the Portraits of the several English Captains, taken from the Life, worked in the Borders, which are now placed, some in the Royal Wardrobe, some in the House of Lords."

330   From *The Tapestry Hangings of the House of Lords* (Second Day), by John Pine, London, 1739

THE FOURTH DAY

"A GREAT galleon," having fallen "foul of another vessel in the hurry and confusion" and dropped behind, was thereupon captured by Drake, who had her sent to Dartmouth. In actual size and numbers the Spanish fleet was superior at first. But, as the running fight progressed during the week, reinforcements brought up the strength of the English equal to that of the foe.

331   From John Pine, *The Tapestry Hangings of the House of Lords*, London, 1739

332   From John Pine, *The Tapestry Hangings of the House of Lords*, London, 1739

THE SEVENTH DAY

"THE next morning, July 25, both Fleets being come over against the Isle of Wight (which the Spaniards had resolved to make themselves Masters of) and not above a hundred yards asunder, a terrible Fight began." — JOHN PINE.

THE BATTLE OF GRAVELINES, JULY 29, 1588

BY a surprise attack of fire ships in the dead of night, the great Armada, driven out of a temporary resting place at Calais, rushed in confusion up the Channel toward the North Sea. Drake led the pursuit and inflicted heavy losses. When the day was done, the Spaniards were in full flight and the command of the sea was in the hands of England.

333   From John Pine, *The Tapestry Hangings of the House of Lords*, London, 1739

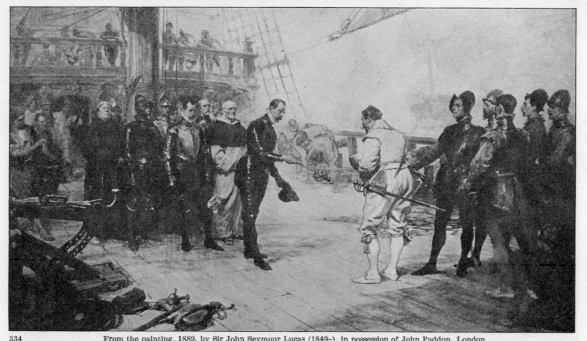

334   From the painting, 1889, by Sir John Seymour Lucas (1849–), in possession of John Paddon, London

THE SPANISH ADMIRAL SURRENDERS TO DRAKE

ONE of the dramatic incidents in this great final battle between England and Spain for mastery of the seas was the personal encounter of Drake with the Spanish Admiral, Don Pedro de Valdes. When the command to surrender came from the *Revenge*, Don Pedro's galleon was about to sink, but the brave Spaniard refused. Then, learning that it was Drake in person who challenged him, he surrendered. Don Pedro tendered him his sword, saying that it was an honor to yield it to the greatest seaman in the world.

THE BURIAL OF SIR FRANCIS DRAKE

IN August, 1595, Drake led another fleet out to harry Spain's American possessions. In the Mosquito Gulf, fever attacked the men, and Drake himself was stricken. On his orders to "take the wind as God had sent it," the ships moved to the harbor of Puerto Bello, twenty miles from Nombre de Dios. Here in January, 1596, Drake came to his end. "Amid the thunder of the guns whose voice he knew so well, and surrounded by consuming pyres afloat and on the shore, his body was committed to the deep, while muffled drums rolled out their last salute and trumpets wailed his requiem." His men then burned Puerto Bello, the Spanish ships they had taken, and two of their own vessels, for the ravages of fever had not left them sailors enough to man the ships.

335   From the painting by W. R. Davison in the Plymouth Art Gallery (England)

ROUTES OF THE
ELIZABETHAN SEA ROVERS
16TH & 17TH CENTURIES

The Golden Hind

C -----	CAVENDISH, 1586-88, 1591
Da -----	DAVIS, 1585, 1586, 1587
Dr -----	DRAKE, 1572-73, 1577-80, 1585-86
F -----	FROBISHER, 1576, 1577, 1578
Gi	GILBERT, 1583
Go -----	GOSNOLD, 1602
H -----	HAWKINS, 1562-63, 1564-65, 1567-69
R	RALEIGH, 1595

336   Drawn expressly for *The Pageant of America* by Gregor Noetzel, American Geographical Society, New York

ROUTES OF THE ELIZABETHAN SEA ROVERS

THE trails of the English seamen of the sixteenth and seventeenth centuries lay thick upon the Atlantic with two across the vast Pacific. They tell the tale of the activity and the daring of the sea rovers of England in a way that nothing else can do. The English were both privateers and explorers. They challenged Spain's claim to the exclusive possession of the new lands which Columbus had first brought to the knowledge of the world. They opposed the commercial provisions which Spain established to govern the trade between the home country and the over-sea colonies. One commercial fleet a year should go from Seville to Vera Cruz and one to Nombre de Dios. No Spaniard might trade with the continent save through these fleets. No foreigner should trade at all with Spanish America. But the British of Elizabethan England would not sit quietly by and watch Spain wax in wealth and power by means of the treasure from the New World. Nor were they content to accept the continent of North America as a barrier between England and India and China. Diligently they sought a passage through or around it on the north. These were the men who helped to bring down the sea-power of Spain and who gained for England a foothold on the North American continent. Their achievement is one of the greatest in the English annals of the sea.

CHAPTER IX

"AND OURS TO HOLD VIRGINIA"

IN 1603 Elizabeth died and the powerful Tudors gave place to the House of Stuart. England had prospered under her "good Queen Bess." The interests and thoughts of her people had reached out to distant parts of the world. Raleigh's scheme of settlement had come to naught, but the fall of Spanish sea-power had removed the chief menace to the English on the sea lanes that led to the New World. New companies of merchants and investors had carried English trade into Russia, the Levant and India.

Three years after James came to the throne two more companies, the London and the Plymouth Companies, were formed for colonization and trade in North America. Both almost at once turned their energies to procuring colonists for their great undertakings. In three months the Plymouth Company had things in readiness, and in August, 1606, sent out a trial ship followed two months later by another. But the first was captured by the Spaniards, and the second, after skirting the American coast, sailed home without making a settlement. The tidings brought back, however, stimulated the Company to a greater effort, and in August, 1607, two ships dropped anchor at the mouth of the Sagadahoc, or Kennebec river on the Maine coast. After a sermon by the preacher, the reading of the instructions from the Company in England revealed George Popham president of the colony. A fort was built and fortified with twelve pieces of ordnance. Inside, a church, a storehouse and fifteen cabins were erected. A shipbuilder constructed a pinnace which was afterward used in Virginia.

But many of the colonists became discouraged, and half went back to England when the ships returned in December. The winter was a time of suffering and terror for the little handful of men on the frozen Kennebec. Their storehouse burned and with it most of their provisions. Their leader, Popham, died. In the spring, when a ship came again from England, with one accord the colonists resolved to return. "And this," in the words of the chronicler, Strachey, "was the end of that northerne colony upon the river Sagadahoc." Meanwhile, to the southward on the James had been established the first permanent English settlement in America.

337 Bronze tablet at Cape Henry,
Va., marking the first landing by
the Jamestown colonists

THE POPHAM COLONY, MAINE, 1607

THE Popham colony was an attempt to extend the English trading area to a part of the American coast hitherto unoccupied. The promoters of the enterprise were quite ignorant of the conditions which a colony would have to face in America. They were aware of the necessity for defense against the Indians and other enemies of the forest but to plan such a fortifica-

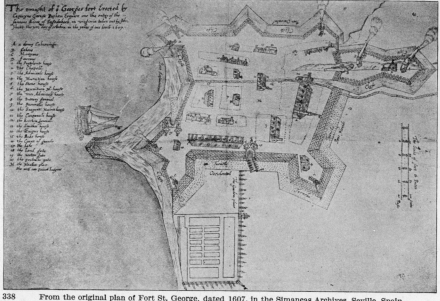

338   From the original plan of Fort St. George, dated 1607, in the Simancas Archives, Seville, Spain

tion as Fort St. George was to attempt to put a citadel adapted to European conditions in the American wilderness. Such a fort should be contrasted with the simple palisade defenses about the frontier town of Boonesborough in the latter part of the next century. Whether the actual fort approximated this ideal plan may well be doubted.

339   From a contemporary engraving, 1663, in the collection of J. H. Innes, Nyack, N. Y.

THE LONDON CUSTOMS HOUSE

DURING the great days of Elizabeth and especially after the fall of Spanish sea-power, commerce, that new handmaid of British agriculture, spread apace. East, south, and west, farther and farther from the Thames went the adventurous traders of England. The old customs house in London received the cargoes of a swiftly growing merchant fleet. England was taking a new place in the world.

340   MERCHANTS ADVENTURERS   341   MUSCOVY COMPANY

THE FIRST TRADING COMPANIES

BRITISH capital was meagre, and the hazards of trading in distant, often half-civilized, regions was great. Merchants therefore pooled their resources and distributed the risks. They organized companies incorporated by the Crown. Each company had a monopoly of the trade of the particular part of the world assigned to it. There was the company known as the Merchants of the Staple, incorporated by Edward III, and trading in wool across the Channel. The Merchants Adventurers were incorporated by Elizabeth to trade also across the Channel. The Muscovy Company traded with the dark interior of Russia. The Levant Company held the monopoly of the Near East. Greatest of all was the East India Company which, by its charter, received sole rights to trade with all nations east of the Cape of Good Hope to the Straits of Magellan. These are but a few of the many merchant enterprises, among which the Virginia Company of London of 1606 was organized to colonize and trade in Virginia, and which was destined to play so prominent a part in the establishment of English power on the North American continent.

LEVANT COMPANY   THE EAST INDIA COMPANY

342   343

From John Stowe, *Survey of London*, 1633

COAT–OF–ARMS OF THE VIRGINIA COMPANY OF LONDON

THE escutcheon is quartered with the arms of England and France, Scotland and Ireland, crested by a maiden queen with flowing hair and crown. The motto means "Behold Virginia gives a fifth" [Kingdom]. After the union of England and Scotland, "fifth" was changed to "fourth." With a slight alteration, the coat was used by Virginia until the Revolution, the arms of the Georges being presently substituted for those of the Stuarts. The London Company (1606) was enlarged in 1609 under the name of the Virginia Company, and its great colonizing venture was backed by all England. Its stockholders included bishops, lords, mayors, knights, merchants, and the workers' guilds.

In 1606, when the company was first founded, another company, the Plymouth Company, also received a charter. Each company was to have land for fifty miles north and south of its first settlement, a hundred miles out to sea and a hundred miles inland. Neither was to settle within a hundred miles of the other. The companies were to have the right to mine gold, silver and copper; the king was to receive a fifth of the precious metals, but only a fifteenth of copper. So the Spanish fortune in the south influenced the ideas of the English. The charters followed another Spanish precedent in providing that Christianity should be taught to the natives.

344   From John Smith, *Generall Historie*, London, 1624

SIR THOMAS SMYTHE

AMONG the most influential commercial backers of England's great enterprises was Sir Thomas Smythe. He was the first governor of the East India Company and long directed its affairs. He was also a governor of the Muscovy Company, and was interested in the Levant Company and other similar enterprises. Such was the commercial training of the man who became the first treasurer of the London Company and the director of the Virginia enterprise during its most critical years. In August, 1606, an advance agent was sent to Virginia to choose a site for the settlement, but he was captured by the Spaniards. In the last days of 1606, the company sent out three ships, the *Sarah Constant*, the *Goodspeed* and the *Discovery*, to establish a colony in the New World. Late in April, 1607, the little flotilla sailed for the first time into Virginia waters. Sixteen of the one hundred and twenty settlers who embarked had been buried at sea.

345 From an engraving by Simon van de Passe, 1616, in Hakluyt Society Publications

JAMES I, 1566–1625

WAR with Spain did not come to an end until 1604, after James I had begun his reign. Perhaps the uncertainties which were an inevitable part of the conflict had retarded the establishment of English settlements. Perhaps Raleigh's conspicuous failure had kept English companies from further venturing in the Virginia wilderness. Whatever the causes, almost three years passed after the conclusion of peace before the little flotilla of the Virginia Company set sail. The undertaking was a private enterprise. James' government looked on with interest and favor but did not participate. Gentlemen and laborers, on the whole representative Englishmen, were sent out to America.

346 From the portrait by Paul van Somer (1570–1621), in the National Portrait Gallery, London

347 Letters Patent of James I for the Colonization of Virginia. From a copy in British Museum, Add. Mss. 30567, f.207.

THE BUILDING OF JAMESTOWN — 1607

"THE six and twentieth day of April, about foure a clocke in the morning, wee descried the Land of Virginia," says Percy. They sailed through Chesapeake Bay and Hampton Roads (where they landed and set up a cross, and some "were assaulted by five Salvages"), naming Capes Henry, and Charles and (Old) Point Comfort on the way; and so on up James River, named for their king, to a peninsula about thirty miles from its mouth.

Here they went ashore on May 24 and began at once the building of Jamestown in a country where forests, streams, and meadows were of such beauty that, says Percy, they were "almost ravished at the first sight thereof."

The choice of the site of Jamestown was most unfortunate. The water was bad and the forest was infested with malarial mosquitoes. With practically no previous knowledge of the conditions that they would have to meet, these servants of the Virginia Company undertook the dangerous task of adjusting themselves suddenly to a wild environment and an unfamiliar climate, with their base of supplies distant two months' fast sailing.

348   Drawn expressly for *The Pageant of America* by H. A. Ogden

349   From the mural painting by C. Y. Turner in the County Court House, Cleveland

THE TRIAL OF JOHN SMITH

THE Virginia Company had no more comprehension of the realities of American life than did the settlers. An ineffective system of government was established with the result that, on the voyage over, before it had been set up, quarrels on ship-board had resulted in making John Smith a prisoner. After the landing a trial straightened the matter out but did not alter the ineffectiveness of the arrangement. The control of affairs

in Virginia was put in the hands of a Council of which Edwin Maria Wingfield was president and Smith a member.

SMITH'S *A TRUE RELATION*

LACKING a strong controlling hand the colonists soon fell into confusion, which was increased by the tasks laid upon them by the Company, whose main motive was profit. The colonists were to search for gold and for a possible route to the Pacific. Valuable time and energy were expended in largely fruitless wanderings among the Virginian woods and rivers. The one gain from these was the establishing of contact with the Indians and the beginning of trade.

But at Jamestown little real progress was made in putting the settlement on a solid foundation. The colonists were servants of the Company. Whatever profit they made went to the Company. That powerful incentive, opportunity for private gain, was conspicuously absent. Inevitably, the colonists were disinclined to work. When disease and death weakened the Council, the confusion became complete. The food began to run low. The coming of new supplies was uncertain. The fact was brought home to every man that the colony faced destruction. Under such circumstances a natural leader, John Smith, arose for a few months. His *True Relation* contains his vivid account of the founding of Virginia. It is a story of privation, of desperate suffering, and of courage.

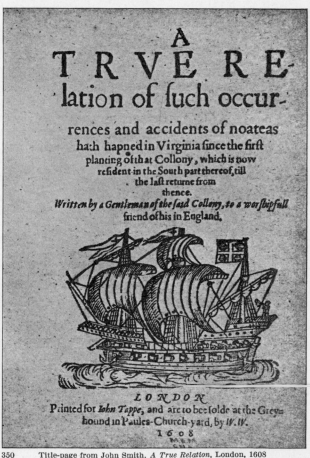

350   Title-page from John Smith, *A True Relation*, London, 1608

CAPTAYNE JOHN SMITH

SMITH finally became President of the Council and proved an energetic and able leader. He explored, traded busily, and set the colonists to raising crops. In a few adventurous months he won for himself lasting renown and also the reputation for telling somewhat exaggerated tales. But neither Smith nor any one else in Virginia was capable of saving the colony. Its fate rested with the Company, which was responsible for its government and support. And the Company strove to rise to the situation. Supplies and colonists were sent out at great expense. But good tidings did not come from Virginia to the London office — only news that the colonists became sick, used up the supplies, and were still unable to support themselves, let alone make a profit for the Company. Virginia was an experiment in colonization made peculiarly difficult because the natural environment was so different from any with which Englishmen were familiar. The Company slowly learned by costly experience and, in the face of the most discouraging conditions, refused to abandon its enterprise.

351 From John Smith, *A Description of New England*, London, 1616, after the engraving by Simon van de Passe (1595–*ca.* 1644?)

THE FIRST WOMEN ARRIVE IN JAMESTOWN

IN the second year of the colony there arrived in Christopher Newport's ship seventy colonists including Master Thomas Forest, a gentleman who brought his wife with him and a maid, Anne Burras, to wait upon her. By winter Madam Forest had lost her maid to John Laydon, laborer, at the first wedding in Virginia. These two brave women came to the banks of the James not long before the colony almost crumbled to ruin. Two years later Sir Thomas Gates described the plight of the settlement. "Cast up this reckoning together: want of government, store of idlenesse, their expectations frustrated by traitors, their market spoyled by the Mariners, our nets broken, the deere chased, our boats lost, our hogs killed, our trade with the *Indians* forbidden, some of our men fled, some murthered, and most by drinking of the brackish water of James fort weakened, and endaungered, famine and sicknesse by all these means increased. . . . Above all, having neither Ruler, nor Preacher, they neither feared God nor man, which provoked the wrath of the Lord of Hosts, and pulled downe his judgements upon them."

352 From the painting by Stanley M. Arthurs (1877–), in his possession

THE LONDON COMPANY SEEKS SUPPORT

In 1609 the London Company was reorganized, and it sent out to America a fleet of nine ships with more than four hundred persons on board, men, women, and children. Already starvation had nearly destroyed the struggling colony. In a great effort to win support for their enterprise, which they conceived to be a patriotic as well as a commercial venture, the management of the Company issued the pamphlet *Nova Britannia*.

AN APPEAL TO INVEST

In *Nova Britannia* the Virginia Company set forth in no uncertain terms the call of America and the character of the men who were engaged in the Virginia enterprise:

"And yet another, and no lesse Argument of Gods fauourable assistance in this, that sundry Noble minded men in their owne persons, doe so willingly vndertake (by Gods permission) the present Conduct and perpetuall Plantation of this People there, as namely the Right honourable and Religious, Sir Thomas West, Lord De la Ware, Lord Gouernour and Captaine Generall, with Sir Thomas Gates Lieutenant Generall; and Sir George Sommers Admiral of Virginia, and Captaine Christopher Newport Viz-Admirall: All beeing well knowne to be Knights and Gentlemen of great worth, for speciall Seruices to God and their Countrie, who besides the furnishing their owne Traine and priuate Prouisions, haue layd downe and brought into the common Stocke, many hundred Pounds in ready money, and for that

NOVA BRITANNIA.

OFFERING MOST

Excellent fruites by Planting in
VIRGINIA.

Exciting all such as be well affected
to further the same.

LONDON
Printed for SAMVEL MACHAM, and are to be sold at
his Shop in Pauls Church-yard, at the
Signe of the Bul-head.
1609.

353 From a copy of the original issue, 1609, in the
New York Public Library

the said Knights, Sir Thomas Gates, Sir George Sommers, and Captaine Newport, with their Shippes, Men and Prouisions aforesaid, are now on their way, and departed the Coast of England: We doe further let you know, that our purpose is (God willing) by the Conduct of the Right Honourable Lord De-La-Ware, with all conuenient expedition, to make a new Supplie of men and Shippes, with all necessary prouisions to second them, in as large and ample manner, and by all the helpe and means we can procure, either of our selues which are already interested, or by any new Associates that will therein conioyne with vs, vpon such hopefull grounds of future good, as by such an effectuall Plantation, may the sooner succeed vnto vs."

And for that wee cannot herein without beeing too tedious describe our proiect more fully, nor shew in particular, how acceptable to Almighty God, how comfortable to so many blinde soules, that liue and die in ignorance for want of light, how profitable to this whole land, and beneficiall to euery one of vs, this enterprise (by Gods blessing) may in short time shew and manifest it selfe; we haue also sent you annexed hereunto, some few of our Printed Bookes, which by reading and diuulging the same among your friends, will further enforme you of each particular.

And whereas you shall therein reade, that we purpose to maintaine and carry all in a Ioynt stocke for seuen yeares, and then to deuide the lands, &c. Yet we thought it meete to let you know, that the Stocke and Marchandize which shall arise from thence, we purpose sooner and so often as the greatenesse of it shall surmount the charge, to make a Diuident and distribution thereof to euery man according to his Bill of Aduenture.

And further wee doe assure you, that it is no way our purpose or meaning, to enforce or cause any man, hauing once aduentured to aduenture or supply any more, except of his owne motion and willingnesse he shall bee so disposed, neyther shall hee loose his former aduenture, for we doubt not (by Gods helpe) but after the second returne from thence, to haue sufficient matter returned to defray all charges of new supplies, and to giue satisfaction to men that haue aduentured

And so leauing it to your wise and best aduised consideration, when we shall receiue your aunswere, which wee pray with your conuenient expedition may be returned to Sir *Thomas Smith* in Phil-pot Lane in London, Treasurer for the Colonie, you shall then finde vs ready to performe in what we may, to your best content.

354   From *Nova Britannia Offering Most Excellent Fruites by Planting in Virginia*, London, 1609

THE FIRST FOOTING IN BERMUDA

SIR THOMAS GATES, commissioned as Governor of Virginia, Sir George Somers, and Christopher Newport were all on board the *Sea Adventure* in the fleet that went out to Virginia in 1609. A storm in mid-ocean separated the *Sea Adventure* from the other ships, and drove her on the Bermuda Islands, the leaking ship a useless wreck. Ten months the Virginia colonists lived among the Bermudas. They built huts. A dog had come ashore with them.

> A thousand hogges that dogge did kill
> Their hunger to sustaine.

From the wrecked ship, fast on a reef but half a mile from land, they brought stores of many kinds. As the weeks passed and no kindly sail appeared to take them off, they built pinnaces, the "brave *Deliverance*" and the *Patience*. So they came to Virginia.

The chance landing on the Bermudas called into being a new English colony. In 1612 the London Company was given jurisdiction over the islands, but two years later they were allotted to a specially incorporated Somers Island Company. In the latter year some six hundred persons were living in the islands, a number which grew to between two and three thousand in the next ten years. The prosperity of Bermuda, like that of Virginia, rested on tobacco.

355   From *The Illustrated London News*, June 13, 1903, after a drawing by R. C. Woodville (1856–)

356   From the portrait in the Virginia Historical Society. Copied by H. L. Smith from the original in Lyon House, Northumberland County, England

GEORGE PERCY, 1586–1632

SEVEN vessels of the fleet of nine from which the *Sea Adventure* had been separated arrived at Jamestown without the governor or the admiral, with well-nigh three hundred persons to add to the hundred there. Smith was still president but, as the winter of 1609–10 drew on, trouble was heaped on trouble. The terrible starving time began in which four hundred Virginians were reduced to sixty. Before this disaster occurred, Smith, wounded in an accident, had been deposed and sent to England. Percy, who succeeded him, now lay ill and unable to keep order. In the spring, Gates and Somers arrived from Bermuda in pinnaces which they had built. They found the colony on the brink of disaster. There was dissension among the officers who remained alive. The Indians, sensing the weakness of the whites, were beginning to attack the settlement. Disease and starvation had laid the colony prostrate. Gates and Somers took charge of the hopeless situation. They decided to wind up the affairs of Jamestown. They loaded the survivors aboard their little pinnaces and dropped down the river, prepared to hazard the voyage across the Atlantic.

THOMAS WEST, THIRD LORD DELAWARE

AT the mouth of the James the departing Virginians met Lord De La Warr with new colonists and fresh supplies. With this new energy Jamestown was rebuilt, and exploration was pushed forward under Captain Argall. The new governor fell ill and soon went home, and in March, 1611, Sir Thomas Dale was sent out as Marshal of Virginia. The coming of Dale and the firm establishment of Virginia destroyed a fondly cherished Spanish hope. Far-seeing Spaniards prophesied that, if Virginia lived, it would become the base for hostile operations against Spanish commerce — a prophecy which time was to fulfill.

ARGALL AMONG THE CHICKAHOMINIES

CAPTAIN SAMUEL ARGALL became a prominent figure in Virginia in Dale's time. In 1609 he had discovered the short transatlantic route via the Canaries, and a little later he brought over more colonists. He dashed north and burned the French settlements at Mount Desert and Acadia. He went up the rivers of Virginia and either cajoled or threatened the Indians into good behavior. Here he is shown powwowing with the Chickahominies.

357 From the portrait, 1877, by W. L. Sheppard (1833–1912), in the State Library, Richmond, Va., from an original portrait (artist unknown) in possession of Earl de la Warr, at Bourne, Cambridgeshire, England

358 From Theodore de Bry, *Voyages*, Part V, 1619

359   Drawn expressly for *The Pageant of America* by H. A. Ogden

SPANISH SCOUTS AT ALGERNOUNE FORT, 1611

THE Spanish ambassador at London, Zuñiga, kept his government informed of the planting of Virginia, but the Spanish authorities underestimated its significance and thought that England was wasting money on a worthless territory.

Two expeditions were despatched, one in 1609 and the second in 1611, to spy out the land and obtain information. The first went to Virginia, but finding a ship anchored in the bay and fearing a trap, withdrew without attempting to reconnoiter. The other, entering the bay, sent a boat ashore with three men, Molina, Pérez, and Francis Lymbry, who were seized and held in captivity by the English there.

THE "IRON GOVERNOR'S" LETTER, 1611

THE "Iron Governor" is a favorite sobriquet for Sir Thomas Dale, who took the reins of power in Virginia when De La Warr went home. The colony was disorganized by disease and lawlessness. Dale introduced order and discipline.

This letter, his first, to the President and Council of Virginia in England, is dated May 25, 1611. In it he notes certain things to be done at Jamestown: the repairing of the falling church and storehouse, the building of a stable and a powder house, "a new well for the amending of the most unholsome water," and "a block house on the north side of our back river to prevent Indians from killing our cattle," a winter shelter for cattle, a forge, a bridge to be constructed, a private garden for each man, and common gardens for hemp, flax, and other necessities.

360   First page of the copy in the Ashmolean collection, Bodleian Library, Oxford

THE NEW COLONY UNDER DALE

DALE instituted a code of "lawes and orders dyvyne, politique, and martiall," for the regeneration of young Virginia. Barbarous punishments were the rule in the seventeenth century; but Dale's colonial laws outdid in severity English laws of the period. His statutes were "cheifely extracted out of the laws for governing the armye in the Low Countreys."

William Strachey compiled the first part of the code; presumably the latter part is the work of Dale, Sir Thomas Gates and Sir Edward Cecil, all of whom had served in the Low Countries. Iron discipline was needed, if this isolated outpost of England were ever to survive, let alone produce a profit for the investors who had risked their money in the London Company. Self-interest was added to discipline as a driving force when Dale allowed the colonists, most of whom were really employees of the Company, to own and cultivate small parcels of land each for himself. The condition of Virginia under these laws is described in *The New Life of Virginea*, a work issued in 1612.

DALE'S NEW SETTLEMENT, HENRICUS

DALE turned energetically to the building of a new settlement named Henricus (Henryville) after the Prince of Wales, on the plateau within Dutch Gap nearly surrounded by the James River. Here he built an inner palisade to surround the town and an outer palisade from bank to bank of the river.

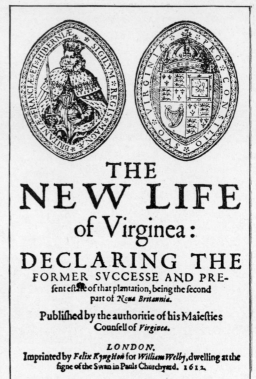

361 Title-page from *The New Life of Virginea*, London, 1612

The town itself had three streets, a church, storehouses, and watch-houses. The curious old chart shows the town of Henricus with its double fortification. This is the earliest map of the settlements that has come to light.

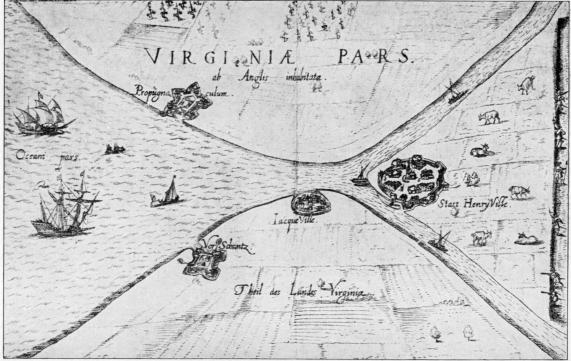

362   From a German "news annual," published in Frankfort in 1613 by Jakob Franck, original in the New York Public Library

THE CAPTURE OF POCAHONTAS, 1613

DALE felt that the colony's desperate situation called for drastic action. Some of the men, chafing under the new régime, ran away from the colony. They were apprehended and, when brought back, some were burned at the stake. Dale also set out to force the Indians about the James to respect the whites. Powhatan's appetite for war speedily diminished. Captain Argall who for a time co-operated with Governor Dale, conceived it a brilliant stroke of policy to capture Powhatan's daughter, Pocahontas, and hold her as a hostage. For the bribe of a copper kettle, one of her kinsmen took her aboard Argall's ship, and Argall, thereupon, carried her off to Jamestown.

363   From Theodore de Bry, *Voyages*, Part X, 1619

DALE AND RALPH HAMOR VISIT POWHATAN AFTER THE CAPTURE OF POCAHONTAS

DURING Dale's régime John Rolfe, gentleman, won fame for himself. His experiments with the raising of tobacco led to the establishment of that crop as the economic foundation of Virginia. With the advent of tobacco the future of the colony was assured. Rolfe also fell in love with Pocahontas. After her capture, he, with Dale and Ralph Hamor, secretary of the colony, went to demand friendship and peace of Powhatan. After the conference Hamor wrote: "And ever since we have had friendly commerce and trade, not onely with *Powhatan* himselfe, but also with his subjects round about us; so as now I see no reason why the Collonie should not thrive a pace."

364   From Theodore de Bry, *Voyages*, Part X, 1619

Ætatis suæ 21. Aᵒ. 1616.

Matoaks als Rebecka daughter to the mighty Prince
Powhatan Emperour of Attanoughkomouck als Virginia
converted and baptized in the Christian faith, and
Wife to the worꟙ Mʳ Tho: Rolff.

365   From the original portrait, 1616, owned by Fountain Elwin, the Manor House, Booton, Norwich, England

POCAHONTAS — A POPULAR AMERICAN HEROINE

THE Spaniards in New Spain freely intermarried with the Indians and such unions were not uncommon
among the French fur traders along the St. Lawrence river. The English, of all the nationalities that came
in large numbers to North America, were the most conscious of race. Intermarriage with the redskins was
very uncommon. Yet, from the beginning, romance has surrounded the figure of the Indian princess who
married one of the chief men of Virginia. She was the center of interest when Rolfe took her to England
and her portrait was painted. Nineteenth-century Americans sentimentalized and idealized this forest
heroine in literature, the drama and various imaginative portraits and pictures of her baptism and marriage.

366 From the portrait, 1830, by Thomas Sully (1783–1872), in the Virginia Historical Society

367 From the portrait by R. M. Sully (1803–55), in the State Historical Society of Wisconsin

368 From an etching after a drawing by Perine about 1840

369 Statue by W. O. Partridge (1861–), at Jamestown Island, Va.

370   From an engraving about 1870 by John McRae, after a painting by Henry Brünckner, location unknown. © Gramstorff Bros.

THE MARRIAGE OF POCAHONTAS

THE bar of her heathen religion removed by her baptism, John Rolfe and Pocahontas were made one.   Their joy was brief.   After two years Rolfe took his wife and infant son to England, where the Indian "princess" caused a great stir.   At Gravesend just before they were to sail for America Pocahontas died of smallpox.

In the parish register at Gravesend stands the entry: "1616 May 2j Rebecca Wrothe, wyff of Thomas Wroth gent, a Virginia lady borne, here was buried in ye chauncell."

SIR EDWIN SANDYS

THE year 1618 was a momentous one in the history of the Virginia Company.   Sir Edwin Sandys became its treasurer and new life was put into the management of the Virginia enterprise.   The next year a liberal-minded governor was sent out to Jamestown to carry on the administration where Dale had left off.   But even under the management of Sandys, one of the great financial figures of his day, the affairs of the Virginia Company did not prosper.

By 1624, reports of mismanagement in the Virginia Company had become so persistent that James I, further aroused by the liberalism of some of the members, revoked the charter and Virginia automatically became a royal colony.

371   From Nash, *Historical Collections for the History of Worcestershire*, 1781–82, engraving by G. Powle after a portrait at Hanley, Eng.

REPORT OF FIRST MEETING OF VIRGINIA BURGESSES, 1619

ON July 30, 1619, the first assembly of representatives in Virginia met in the Jamestown church. Governor George Yeardley and the Council chosen by the Virginia Company sat in the chancel. In the body of the church sat the representatives or burgesses. The session opened with prayer, followed by earnest deliberation upon the all-important questions of defense, Indian relations, agriculture, and religion. The twenty-two burgesses, sitting hat on head, represented James City, Charles City, the City of Henricus, Kecoughtan, Smythe's Hundred, Flowerdieu Hundred, Martin's Hundred, Martin's Brandon, Ward's Plantation, Lawne's Plantation, and Argall's Gift. The English population of Virginia at this date numbered about one thousand souls.

MAP OF EARLY VIRGINIA

VIRGINIA had grown since the terrible days of the starving time. Little settlements had sprung up along both banks of the James. Near neighbors to the English were the Virginia Indians who in 1622 swept down upon the whites in a terrible massacre. It was a heavy blow but so firmly was the colony established that new habitations quickly rose on the ashes of the old and a host of new-comers made good the loss of those who had been killed.

372   From the original record in the Public Record Office, London

EARLIEST ENGLISH SETTLEMENTS
REGION OF POWHATAN OR JAMES RIVER
1607-20
MILES

373   Drawn expressly for *The Pageant of America* by Gregor Noetzel, American Geographical Society, New York

374   From the Farrer map in Edward Williams, *Virginia*, London, 1651, in the New York Public Library

VIRGINIA AND HER NEIGHBORS

THE early London Company had insistently enjoined upon its early colonists the double task of finding gold and searching out a route to the South Sea, as the Pacific was then called. Popular ignorance of America was still such in 1651 as to permit of the publication of this quaint map showing the China Sea "ten dayes march" beyond the Blue Ridge. The long-sought-for passage through the continent appears, save for a small obstruction, in the guise of the Hudson River.

Years of adventure and hardship were to pass before the true outlines of America would be sketched in. Yet this old map with all its curious geography shows the development that had come about on the American continent since the first ships dropped anchor at Jamestown. The land of Carolina lies to the south of Virginia to whose rich lands Virginians are turning their attention.

North of the Potomac (Maryland River) were Baltimore's Catholic settlements. Beyond were the Swedes of the Delaware River, the Dutch in the Hudson valley and, further north, New England and New France.

WESTWARD HO! — SHIPS TO VIRGINIA

THE common ignorance of Virginia in England was great, but there was enough knowledge of the land to entice emigrants thither. While, in 1622, there were roughly twelve hundred settlers, by 1650 the number had increased to more than fifteen thousand souls. From then on the growth was steady and rapid. The initial hazards of settlement were over, and each year the path across the sea became more familiar.

375   From the painting by Carlton T. Chapman (1860–1925),
                        courtesy of the artist

THE ORIGINAL OF THE PICTURE, "JAMESTOWN IN 1622"

INTO the text books on American history has crept an illustration of "Jamestown in 1622, from a contemporary Dutch print." In 1622 occurred the massacre. De Bry published a rather fanciful picture of the massacre in the background of which may be seen a fortified village which is presumably Jamestown. Where de Bry derived his ideas either for the massacre or the village is not known, and his eccentricities were such that, without this knowledge, the authenticity of this sketch must be questioned.

376   From Theodore de Bry, *Voyages*, Part XIII, 1634

THE MASSACRE AT JAMESTOWN, 1622

A STUDY of the picture published by Pieter Vander Aa leads to the conclusion that his sketch was copied practically without variation from that of de Bry. The background shows the same village, even to the same three cannon shooting at the attacking flotilla of impossible Indian canoes.

377   From Pieter Vander Aa, *Naaukeurige versameling der Gedenk-Waardigste Zee en Land-Reysen na oost en West-Indien*, Leyden, 1706–27

"JAMESTOWN IN 1622, FROM A CONTEMPORARY DUTCH PRINT"

A MODERN artist seems to have enlarged the village in either de Bry's or Vander Aa's picture and filled in details to make it appear realistic. On the whole, however, the recent drawing is a remarkably faithful copy of the early print. This drawing becomes "Jamestown in 1622, from a contemporary Dutch print."

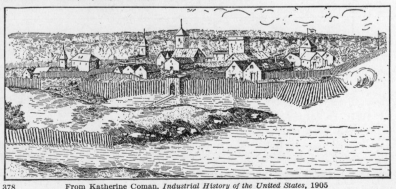

378   From Katherine Coman, *Industrial History of the United States*, 1905

379   From an original drawing by John White in the British Museum

ORIGIN OF THE PICTURES IN *THE GENERALL HISTORIE*

JOHN SMITH published *The Generall Historie of Virginia, New England and the Summer Isles* in 1624, years after his connection with the Jamestown colony had ceased. An unknown artist illustrated his book. The origin of the pictures appears in the group here shown.

John White, while among the Virginia Indians, made a sketch (No. 379) of an Indian dance with all the care regarding costume and detail that characterized his work. De Bry copied White's drawing (No. 380) and, as usual, altered and embellished it. Smith's illustrator seems to have used the de Bry engraving. He has taken out the ceremonial posts and, for one of the three figures in the middle, he has substituted the doughty captain (No. 381). So a religious dance becomes "Their triumph about" Smith.

380   From Theodore de Bry, *Voyages*, Part I (Virginia), 1590

381   From John Smith, *Generall Historie*, 1624

382   From John Smith, *Generall Historie*, 1624

PICTURES IN *THE GENERALL HISTORIE*

SMITH's artist added a fanciful sketch (No. 382) to depict an episode which Smith narrated. The captain told of an exploring trip up the James in the infant days of the colony when he had fallen into the power of the Indians, and had finally been brought before the great chief, Powhatan. Condemned to death, his head was resting on a stone when Pocahontas, the little daughter of the chieftain, begged that his life be spared. The artist seems to have used his imagination freely as, in all probability, Smith did.

Among the three pictures below, White's drawing (No. 383) was apparently made for the purpose of showing costume and tattooing. In de Bry (No. 385) the artist has copied White's figure reversed and then has added a fanciful sketch of a deer hunt. Smith's artist (No. 384) has evidently copied de Bry rather than White. The background has changed from a deer hunt to a battle between whites and Indians, the latter fighting in close order formation after the manner of European soldiers.

383   From John White, 1585

384   From Smith's *Generall Historie*, London, 1624

385   From De Bry, 1590

386   © Rau Studios, Inc.

RUIN OF THE JAMESTOWN CHURCH, BUILT BETWEEN 1676 AND 1684

AMERICA as well as Europe has its historic ruins. This was the third church built in Jamestown, now the only relic of the original settlement. The first church was hardly a building; logs did for seats, a stump with a board topping it served as a reading desk, and sail-cloth roofed it. The second, built of logs with tower and look-out, was the highest building in the colony. There the first shipment of maids married Virginia planters, and there met the first House of Burgesses. The building was destroyed when Nathaniel Bacon flung a torch into Jamestown in 1676.

387   Memorial to the first explorers,
June 10, 1607, on Gamble's Hill,
Richmond, Va.

CHAPTER X

PILGRIMS AND PURITANS IN NEW ENGLAND

IN the same year of 1606 in which the London Company had been founded, the Plymouth Company was chartered with rights to the north of its contemporary holdings. It at once made the unsuccessful attempt to found a colony at the mouth of the Kennebec river in New England. The company did not abandon its interest in the New World. In 1614 Captain John Smith explored and mapped the New England coast and two years later the Plymouth Company made him Admiral of New England. But Smith's attempt to found a settlement also failed. Meanwhile, Sir Ferdinando Gorges, a prominent member of the Plymouth Company, sent fishing and trading voyages into the company's domain. Gorges retained an interest in America when many of his fellow members in the Plymouth enterprise lost heart at the failure of their company to establish a colony. On November 13, 1620, a new organization, the Council of New England, fathered by Gorges, was incorporated to take the place of the older company. In the autumn of the following year the Council sent out to America by the ship *Fortune* a patent for a little body of Separatists that had the year before settled without legal right at Plymouth in New England.

But the Council of New England proved to be not without rivals. It was but eight years old when an association of men in Lincolnshire and London procured, through the assistance of the Earl of Warwick, a patent to lands in the very heart of the domain already granted to the Council of New England. In the same year, 1628, John Endicott led about fifty settlers to Massachusetts. The Gorges interest fought the new enterprise but failed. In 1629 a royal charter confirmed the grant to Endicott and his followers and established a new corporation known as the "Governor and Company of Massachusetts Bay in New England." The Massachusetts Bay Company was a trading company of the same general type as the old London Company, but it met with quite a different fate. Within a year of its founding English Puritans, anxious to escape the growing opposition of Charles I to their movement, bought up the Massachusetts Bay Company, took the charter across the sea and established the headquarters of the company in the New World. Thus the charter of a commercial company became the frame of government for a colony organized as a refuge for a persecuted sect. The Puritans were a group within the Church of England who wished to modify the church service and who stood for a more strict moral code. They were also a political party fighting for the rights of Parliament as opposed to those of the sovereign. They became numerous enough to win the great Civil War.

There was also in England in the early years of the seventeenth century a very small and inconspicuous group of religious radicals who, unlike the Puritans, believed that the reformers should come out of the Church of England and also that Church and State should be separated. These people were known as Brownists or Separatists. One small band of this sect won fame because of its part in the founding of America.

SCROOBY MANOR HOUSE AS IT IS TODAY

SCROOBY MANOR was the property of the Sandys family. Here lived William Brewster, master of the post station where the postman changed horses. Brewster had been in the employ of Elizabeth's secretary, Davison, and had accompanied him on diplomatic missions abroad. At Scrooby met that group of Separatists from which came the Plymouth Pilgrims.

388   © A. S. Burbank

389   From an original watercolor in the United States National Museum

WILLIAM BRADFORD'S BIRTHPLACE AT AUSTERFIELD

WILLIAM BRADFORD, one day to be the historian and governor of Plymouth Colony, was born in 1590 at Austerfield in Yorkshire. Over the meadows and the grassy boundary line between York and Nottingham the boy used to tramp three miles on a Sunday to worship with the congregation at Scrooby, which like the other Separatists had broken from the established church.

OLD CHURCH AT AUSTERFIELD

THIS was the Established Church of which William Bradford's parents were members. He was not yet twelve when his serious, religious nature turned him to the simpler worship of the Separatists. Most of the members of this new sect were from the humbler folk — farmers, artisans, and petty tradesmen.

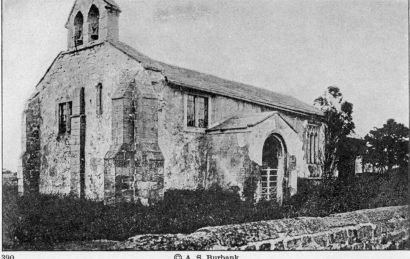

390   © A. S. Burbank

391   Photograph of Leyden Church. © A. S. Burbank   392   Photograph of Tablet to John Robinson, Leyden.
© A. S. Burbank

THE PILGRIMS IN HOLLAND

In 1608 a number of these Separatists, dissatisfied with conditions in England, removed to Holland. They were led by their beloved pastor, John Robinson, who had conducted their meetings at Scrooby. "The most learned, polished, and modest spirit that ever that sect enjoyed," was the comment on him by one of his vigorous opponents. Robinson went with the group to Leyden. He had hoped to follow the Pilgrims who sailed to America in 1620. Death overtook him in 1625.

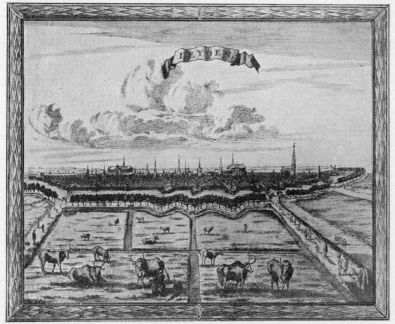

393   From Carolus Allard, *Orbis Habitabilis, ca.* 1690

VIEW OF LEYDEN, 17TH CENTURY

The Pilgrims had been, chiefly, countrymen. But Leyden was a city, and the new life forced them to learn "trades and traffics." Many became weavers, some day-laborers. William Bradford was a silk weaver. William Brewster, whose lovable character as Plymouth's religious leader is so well depicted by Bradford, was a printer. But in danger of being engulfed by the Dutch life about them and fearing to lose their mother tongue and educate their children in Holland, the congregation elected to leave Europe for America, where they could enjoy religious freedom and use their own speech.

THE DOCK AT DELFTHAVEN

FROM Delfthaven the little band of adventurers sailed in the *Speedwell* for Southampton where the *Mayflower* awaited them. They had entered into a financial agreement with some seventy London merchants organized as a voluntary (unincorporated) joint-stock company. The merchants furnished capital; the Pilgrims contributed service. For seven years, while the arrangement was to last, no lands or goods should be divided, in order that the investors might receive a profit. The arrangement proved unsatisfactory; the colonists bought

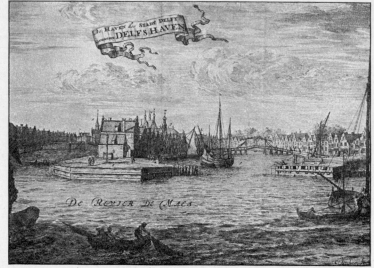

394   From an engraving by C. Decker, about 1680, in the Municipal Archives, Rotterdam

out the interest of the merchants and saddled their settlement with a heavy mortgage.

EMBARKATION FROM DELFTHAVEN

THE Pilgrim venture, unlike most of the enterprises for settling in America, was dominantly religious and the Pilgrims were a sincere and devout people. Most of them lacked education and social position, and were poor in purse, but all were inspired with a great vision. There was rare courage in the little group that knelt on the dock in prayer as they prepared to strike out upon a great adventure. There was but one English settlement in the New World and that but thirteen years old. To Virginia they intended to go, but weariness of the long voyage and the lateness of the year led them to turn in at Cape Cod.

395   From the painting, 1845, by Robert W. Weir (1803–89), in the Capitol, Washington

MODEL OF THE *MAYFLOWER*

396 From the United States National Museum, Washington

THE Pilgrims set out from Southampton in August, 1620, in the *Mayflower* and the *Speedwell*. The *Mayflower* was of about 180 tons burden. The *Speedwell* proved unseaworthy and the two ships put in at Dartmouth for repairs. They started again, but again the *Speedwell* had to put back. At Plymouth, the passengers, except twenty left on shore, crowded into the *Mayflower*, 102 souls all told. For sixty-five days the little ship was buffeted by the Atlantic. But, said the steadfast Pilgrims, "it is not with us as with other men whom small things can discourage, or small discontentments cause to wish themselves home again."

JOHN SMITH'S MAP OF NEW ENGLAND

This congregation of Separatists did not settle on an unknown coast. As ready with pen and compass as with sword and trumpet, John Smith had explored it in 1614 and had named it New England. He had made a map of this new land and had written a book about it. He noted the abundant furs, the good timber, and the rich pastures. He had sowed seeds and later had eaten the "sallets" therefrom. "Of all the four parts of the world that I have yet seen not inhabited, could I have but means to transport a colony, I would rather live here than anywhere; and if it did not maintain itself, were we but once indifferently well fitted, let us starve."

A

DESCRIPTION

of *New England:*

OR

THE OBSERVATIONS, AND Discoueries, of Captain *Iohn Smith* (Admirall of that Country) in the North of *America*, in the year of our Lord 1614: with the successe of sixe ships, that went the next yeare 1615; and the euents befell him among the French men of warres:

With the proofe of the present benefit this Countrey affoords: whither this present yeare, 1616, eight voluntary Ships are gone to make further tryall.

At LONDON

Printed by *Humfrey Lownes*, for *Robert Clerke*; and are to be sould at his house called the Lodge, in Chancery lane, ouer against Lincolnes Inne. 1616.

397 From the original edition of John Smith's work in the New York Public Library

TITLE-PAGE OF SMITH'S

ACCOUNT OF NEW ENGLAND

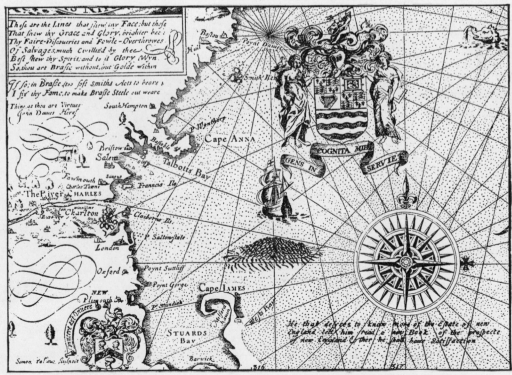

398   A section of the John Smith map, from the Arber edition of John Smith's works, Birmingham, England, 1912

THE FIRST BOAT ASHORE, PROVINCETOWN HARBOR

"After longe beating at sea" says Bradford, "they fell in with that land which is called Cape Cod; the which being made & certainly knowne to be it, they were not a little joyfull." But "they fell among dangerous shoulds and roring breakers." So they decided to bear north for the Cape "and the next day they gott into the Cape-harbor where they ridd in safetie." Captain Standish with fifteen men landed on the shore. "When they had marched about the space of a mile by the sea side, they espied 5. or 6. persons with a dogg coming towards them, who were salvages." The Indians "rane up into the woods." That night the Standish party camped on the shore "& set out their sentinels."

SIGNING THE MAYFLOWER COMPACT

The day before the ship came into Provincetown harbor, the Pilgrims drew up their historic Compact. Says Bradford, "it was thought good that there should be an association and agreement, that we should combine together in one body, and to submit to such government and governors as we should by common consent agree to make and choose; and set our hands to this that follows, word for word."

399   From the painting by H. A. Odgen

The Pilgrims were interlopers in the north without right to land and without a charter allowing them to set up a government. The formal compact was a plantation covenant. It not only established their relations with one another but gave a semblance of legality to their governmental arrangements which might prove useful. In this plantation covenant a respect for law and order that is typically English makes itself manifest.

400   From an unfinished painting by Edwin White (1817–77), in the Yale Divinity School

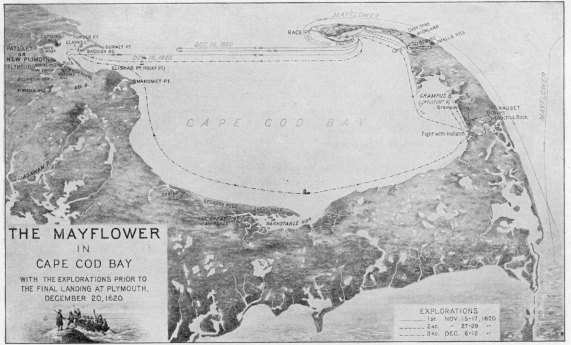

401   Drawn expressly for *The Pageant of America* by Gregor Noetzel, American Geographical Society, New York

THE WANDERINGS OF THE PILGRIMS

THE Pilgrims, sheltered in Provincetown harbor, sent the shallop with a party of men to explore the coast. The boat returned with news of good anchorage and of a place suitable for settlement at Plymouth and, on December 16, 1620, the *Mayflower* crossed the bay and dropped anchor.

402   From the painting by William F. Halsall (1841–1919), in Pilgrim Hall, Plymouth

THE *MAYFLOWER* IN PLYMOUTH HARBOR

FOR many weeks during the winter they lived on shipboard, going back and forth to shore to build their cabins and to spy out the country. When spring and summer came, the Pilgrims found the environment a friendly one so that they had no reason to change their choice of settlement.

403   From J. W. Barber, *Interesting Events in The History of The United States*, New Haven, 1829

404   From Noah Webster's *History of The United States*, 1833

"THE LANDING OF THE PILGRIMS"

In a literal sense no formal "landing" of the Pilgrims ever occurred. Scouts were sent out to explore the country. By gradual stages, life on board ship was changed for life on land. But the "landing of the Pilgrims" has passed into the traditions of the American people as a symbol of the high ideals and the religious faith which were first planted in the New World by this small band of dissenters. There is drama in the story of the wandering Pilgrims. The name Pilgrim itself was a happy choice. The history of their adventure has

405   From the painting, 1815, by Henry Sargent, in Pilgrim Hall, Plymouth, Mass.

entered into the warp and woof of American thought and has been used again and again to recall Americans to high ideals and to religious sacrifice. The "landing" is celebrated at Plymouth annually on Dec. 21.

406   From an engraving, 1854, after the painting, 1847, by Charles Lucy (1814–73)

Plymouth Rock is preserved within a classic marble monument. No American would have it otherwise. The story of the "landing" has taken its place in literature and art. Many generations have symbolized their own ideals in their representations of this beginning in America of the Pilgrim enterprise. Of late years, when America has grown in world significance, foreign artists have contributed to the growing gallery of Pilgrim pictures.

The whole great movement from the Old World to the New was full of drama. Perhaps there is a certain unfairness in selecting one small group for immortality, when so many pioneers in early America endured equal hardships and crossed the ocean from motives equally noble.

407   From the painting by Antonio Gisbert, exhibited at Madrid, 1867, and at the Centennial Exposition, 1876, Philadelphia

A SPANISH CONCEPTION OF THE "LANDING"

408   From the *Illustrated London News*, August 17, 1907, after the painting by C. M. Padday, exhibited at the Royal Academy

AN ENGLISH ARTIST'S CONCEPTION OF THE "LANDING"

THE DEPARTURE OF THE *MAYFLOWER*

HARD was that first winter at Plymouth. Ignorant of the ways of living in the forest and unused to so rigorous a climate, the Pilgrim adventurers saw many of their number fall sick and die. In the spring, when the *Mayflower* hoisted anchor, came the true test of their mettle. The little band so far from home and so thinned by death watched the white sails of the departing ship sink below the horizon, and then bravely returned to the tasks of the new life in the New World. Their

409   From the painting by J. L. G. Ferris (1863–), in Independence Hall, Philadelphia

qualities of heart and their religious idealism have given to the Pilgrims their unshakable place in history.

410   From an engraving after the painting by George H. Boughton (1863–1905)

PILGRIM EXILES

"THER was the mighty ocean which they had passed, and was now as a maine barr & goulfe to seperate them from all the civill parts of the world." — BRADFORD's *History of Plimoth Plantation*.

411 From the portrait in Pilgrim Hall, Plymouth, Mass., after a miniature (1651) attributed to Robert Walker. © A. S. Burbank

412 From C. K. Bolton, *The Founders*, Vol. II, Boston, 1919, from the doubtful portrait on wood owned by Alexander M. Harrison

EDWARD WINSLOW, 1595-1655

EDWARD WINSLOW, one of the founders of Plymouth, was also its first bridegroom, for in 1621 he married Mrs. Susanna White, mother of Peregrine White, the first child born in the colony. He made treaties with the Indians, served as governor, and on several occasions was sent to England to defend the colony against traducers. In 1646 he went to England and held a post under Cromwell for nine years. He died in Jamaica whither Cromwell had sent him to advise with Admiral Penn and General Venables. He wrote much about New England, sometimes perhaps too enthusiastically for strict accuracy.

MYLES STANDISH, *ca.* 1584-1656

"CAPTAIN STANDISH was bred a soldier in the Low Countries," says an early writer. "A little chimney is soon fired; so was the Plymouth captain a man of small stature, yet of a very hot and angry temper." In the first winter at Plymouth, when disease wiped out half the colony, it was to the ministrations of this splendid little fighting man and the gentle Elder Brewster that many of the survivors owed their lives. The portrait comes from an old panel bearing the name "M. Standish," found in a picture shop in Philadelphia. The genuineness has never been proved.

EARLY PLYMOUTH

THE church covenant and organization had from the beginning been the central bond in this group of Pilgrim settlers. They were independent of any established religious organization, and they managed their religious affairs through the congregation. This congregational system was later adopted by the Puritans of Massachusetts who, when they left England, believed they were yet in the Anglican church. This reconstruction of early Plymouth is based on probabilities; few facts are available.

413   Reconstruction from The Chronicles of America motion picture *The Pilgrims*

LEYDEN STREET, PLYMOUTH

THIS reconstruction was based on the following description by Isaac de Rasiere, who visited Plymouth from New Amsterdam in 1627:

"New Plymouth lies on the slope of a hill stretching east towards the sea-coast, with a broad street about a cannon shot of 800 [yards] long, leading down the hill; with a [street] crossing in the middle, northwards to the rivulet and southwards to the land. The houses are constructed of hewn planks,

414   From a drawing, 1891, by W. L. Williams. © A. S. Burbank

with gardens also enclosed behind and at the sides with hewn planks, so that their houses and court yards are arranged in very good order, with a stockade against a sudden attack; and at the ends of the streets there are three wooden gates. In the centre, on the cross street, stands the Governor's house, before which is a square enclosure upon which four patereros [swivel guns] are mounted, so as to flank along the streets. Upon the hill they have a large square house, with a flat roof, made of thick sawn plank, stayed with oak beams, upon the top of which they have six cannons, which shoot iron balls of four and five pounds, and command the surrounding country. The lower part they use for their church, where they preach on Sundays and the usual holidays. They assemble by beat of drum, each with his musket or firelock, in front of the captain's door; they have their cloaks on, and place themselves in order, three abreast, and are led by a sergeant without beat of drum. Behind comes the Governor, in a long robe; beside him, on the right hand, comes the preacher with his cloak on, and on the left hand the captain with his side arms, and cloak on, and with a small cane in his hand, — and so they march in good order, and each sets his arms down near him. Thus they are constantly on their guard night and day. . . . Their farms are not so good as ours, because they are more stony, and consequently not so suitable for the plough. They apportion their land according as each has means to contribute to the Eighteen Thousand Guilders which they have promised to those who had sent them out; whereby they have their freedom without rendering an account to anyone." — From New York Historical Society *Collections*, 2nd Series II, 351.

415   From the bust of Squanto in Pilgrim Hall, Plymouth

THE COMING OF SAMOSET AND SQUANTO

THE Indians, who until now had remained in the background, had been secretly observing the white men at their building; and the colonists feared that an attack was imminent. One day in March a tall savage walked into the settlement and greeted the Pilgrims with "Welcome, Englishmen." This was Samoset, chief of Monhegan Isle, a friend of English traders and fishers. Samoset said that he had sent for two friends of his, Massasoit, the greatest chief of Massachusetts, and Squanto, who had visited England on a trading ship and who could speak English well. Thereupon the Pilgrims made a feast for Samoset and gave him a knife and a ring.

A few days after Samoset's visit, Massasoit came with his warriors and his friend Squanto, and there was concluded a treaty which the Indians did not break for fifty years. Squanto became so enamored of his new friends that he moved into Plymouth, living with one or another of the Pilgrims and sometimes as Bradford's guest. In return for this hospitality he taught them how to fertilize the soil with fish, how to trap beaver, how to stalk game and how to raise corn.

416   From the painting, 1887, by W. L. Williams.   © A. S. Burbank

OLD FORT, BURIAL HILL

In spite of such evidences of harmony, well did these Englishmen know that they lived close neighbors to a barbarous race that might at any time attack their tiny settlement. It was a wise foresight that turned their attention to the building of a fort as one of their first tasks. Whether the illustration represents the type of fort they built is open to doubt. Bradford says that the fort had battlements and ordnance.

INTERIOR OF THE FORT

Within the fort were arms and accoutrements ready for that time — which happily never came to Plymouth — when this should be the citadel for defense against a rising of the Indians. The long, awkward matchlocks with their forked supports were but clumsy weapons against the agile redskins; yet they sufficed. The armor, relic of the fights of mediæval Europe, proved useful against Indian arrows though impeding ease of action. But as fire-arms improved and came into the possession of the redmen, the white settlers gradually laid aside breastplate and helmet and adopted the Indian mode of forest fighting.

417   Reconstruction from The Chronicles of America motion picture *The Pilgrims*

418   From the sculpture at Plymouth by
Cyrus Dallin

MASSASOIT, INDIAN CHIEF

IN Mourt's *Relation* or *Journal* (London, 1622), written probably by Winslow and Bradford, is summed up the early Indian relations: "we have found the Indians very faithful in their covenant of peace with us, very loving and ready to pleasure us . . . not only the greatest king amongst them, called Massasoyt, but also all the princes and peoples round about us, have either made suit unto us, or been glad of any occasion to make peace with us. . . . So that there is now great peace amongst the Indians themselves, which was not formerly, neither would have been but for us; and we, for our part, walk as peaceably and safely in the wood as in the highways in England."

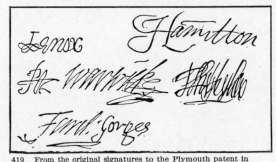

419   From the original signatures to the Plymouth patent in
Pilgrim Hall, Plymouth. © A. S. Burbank

THE PLYMOUTH PATENT

THE patent of Plymouth Colony, the oldest state document in New England, gave the Pilgrims an actual title to the land on which they hitherto had been squatters, but it conferred no powers of government (since from the king only could come such powers), leaving the extra-legal *Mayflower* compact the sole basis for government organization. The patent was issued by the President and Council for New England on June 1, 1621, to John Peirce and his associates (the Pilgrims), and it was brought out to America in the *Fortune* in the same year. The document was signed and sealed by the Duke of Lenox, the Marquis of Hamilton, the Earl of Warwick, Lord Sheffield, and Sir Ferdinando Gorges.

420   From the original in Pilgrim Hall, Plymouth. © A. S. Burbank

BRADFORD'S "*HISTORY OF PLIMOTH PLANTATION*"

BRADFORD, who for so many years was governor of Plymouth, has preserved by his pen for later generations the living story of the Pilgrim adventure. One has but to turn his pages to catch glimpses of the life of those far-off days: Bradford grumbling because the supply of beer is almost exhausted; the difficulty of getting out of the common house the day it caught fire; the man and his dog who held two wolves at bay; the Christmas dinner of wild duck; the difficulties that the colony encountered in dealing with some of the less desirable folk who had come to Plymouth. The Pilgrims were fortunate in their historian as they were in their governor. Bradford's *History* is one of the great documents of the English colonies in America.

421 Photograph of the original Ms. book of Bradford in the State House, Boston

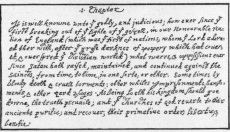

422 From Bradford's original Ms., part of the first page

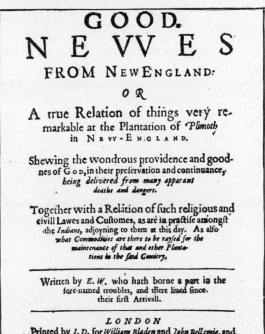

423 From the London, 1624, issue in the New York Public Library

424 From the original edition in the New York Public Library

TWO IMPORTANT CONTEMPORARY ACCOUNTS

MOURT'S *Relation* (No. 424) contains a daily journal kept by Governor Bradford from the discovery of land by the *Mayflower* to April 2, 1621, and also four narratives by Winslow giving an account of the colony down to December 21, 1621. It contains the first published copy of the Mayflower Compact. The publication has received its title from the name "G. Mourt," which is signed to the preface. *Good Newes from New England* (No. 423), written by Winslow, carries on the narrative to September, 1623. These two accounts brought news to Englishmen of the difficulties faced by the little band of Separatists who went out to New England.

425   From the painting by J. L. G. Ferris in Independence Hall, Philadelphia

THE FIRST THANKSGIVING

NOT one day but a week was given to the first Thanksgiving feast in New England, 1621. Bradford sent out men to hunt deer and turkeys and to call Massasoit and his tribe to the Pilgrims' table. The Indians, accustomed to offer a feast of gratitude for their own harvest, entered gladly into the spirit of the affair. They brought deer and corn and birds; they attended the services; then they sang their own songs and played games and ran races with their Plymouth friends. Almost Utopian was this early harmony between the red man and the white. Out of this harvest festival has come the unique American institution of Thanksgiving Day.

THE PILGRIMS' DISORDERLY NEIGHBORS

BUT the Pilgrims soon had neighbors in New England. An ever-merry gentleman named Thomas Morton came to Mount Wolloston in 1622 and by his conduct with his friends and the Indians grievously scandalized the Plymouth folk. While the May-pole he set up, his revels around it, and the slurring bulletins about his good neighbors which he hung upon it were a trial to a Christian's spirit, his rash and illegal trading of fire-arms and liquor to the Indians was a serious menace to the little colonies. Morton was without legal title to the land he occupied. Once he was banished to England by the Pilgrims after Captain Standish had captured him. Returning, he was again sent back; but this time it was the new colony of Massachusetts Bay which exercised authority.

426   From W. A. Crafts, *Pioneers in the Settlement of America*,
Boston, 1876

CHARLES I, 1600–1649

ON the death of James in 1625, Charles became king. As he was a charming and engaging prince, all England hailed him joyously. But ere the year was out, Parliament and King had entered upon the struggle which was to end with his execution. Ultimately Charles dissolved the House, whose members had passed resolutions censuring him. For eleven years he governed without a Parliament by means of his army, sheriffs, judges, and bishops, and he drew his income from autocratic levies on the people. The dismissed Parliament leaders rode up and down England preaching the liberties and rights of Englishmen in every town, port, and country hamlet.

427   From the portrait of Charles I by Sir Anthony van Dyck (1599–1641), in the National Portrait Gallery, London

WILLIAM LAUD, ARCHBISHOP OF CANTERBURY, 1573–1645

LAUD was a High Churchman, who disliked Calvinism in all its forms. He stood well with both Stuarts and, when Charles came to the throne, Laud rose rapidly. In 1633 he became Archbishop of Canterbury. The policy of suppressing all expression of dissent from the established church was now pursued energetically; and Laud, as agent of the royal will, was given full powers. The great exodus of Puritans to New England was largely the result of his zealous activities.

428   From the portrait of Archbishop Laud by Sir Anthony van Dyck, in Lambeth Palace, London

OLIVER CROMWELL, 1599–1658

OLIVER CROMWELL became the military and political leader of the revolt which overthrew the house of Stuart and established the Commonwealth in England. "Ironsides" was the name given to Cromwell by the Royalists after their first encounter with him on the battlefield. He led the troops of Parliament to victory. By diplomacy and the sword he compelled Europe to recognize the Commonwealth. He fought Spain, the traditional enemy, and opposed the rising power of Holland. But during his sway the founding of new English colonies in America, save for the capture of Jamaica, came to an end. Englishmen were too busy with problems at home to seek new enterprises in America.

429   From a contemporary miniature by Samuel Cooper, courtesy of Herbert Dupuy, Pittsburgh

EXECUTION OF CHARLES I

THE Puritans conquered in the civil war that rent England
from 1642 to 1646. Their movement was largely political in
its effects, though centering in an ecclesiastical issue. During
the thirties, in the days of the king's supremacy, thousands
of the Puritan party had left England for Massachusetts and
other New England colonies. When civil war broke out the
exodus stopped. Now that the Puritans were victorious, they
held the king prisoner. Exasperated by the Royalist doctrine
that the king could not be bound by engagements entered
into by him while under duress, and fearing treachery, they
beheaded him. There was joy unstinted in distant Massachusetts when the news was brought across the seas.

430   After the painting, 1894, by Ernest Crofts, R. A.

ROBERT RICH, EARL OF WARWICK, 1587–1658

SOME of the sig-
nificant points in
the origin of the
Massachusetts Bay
Company are lost in
the uncertain past.
New England outside of Plymouth had been granted to the Council for
New England. Sir Ferdinando Gorges, who was a prominent member
of this Council, had schemes for developing the region. But a charter
for a new company granted the very heart of New England to a
trading company of the type of the Virginia Company, and its membership was both Anglican and Nonconformist. That land should be
taken in such manner from one organization and given to another was
probably largely due to the Puritan nobleman, the Earl of Warwick,
one of the most powerful men in England, and one deeply interested
in colonial projects.

431   From the portrait by Anthony van Dyck
in the collection of J. Pierpont Morgan

THE CHARTER OF
MASSACHUSETTS, 1629

THE charter was issued on March 4,
1629, to "the Governor and Company
of the Massachusetts Bay in New England." To them it gave the seafront
from three miles north of the Merrimac River to three miles south of the
Charles, and westward to the "South
Sea," or Pacific. The company remained in England for a year and did
not go to Massachusetts until 1630.

432   From the original in the State House, Boston

433 From the portrait of John Endicott, painted 1665, artist unknown, in the possession of William C. Endicott, Boston

JOHN ENDICOTT, *ca.* 1588–1665

IN the organization of the new company John Endicott was a prime mover. His first step had been to get a land patent from the New England Council to the district between the Charles and the Merrimac. Then he sailed for America with a band of colonists and founded Salem in 1628. The incorporation of the Massachusetts Bay Company followed almost immediately. He was an able but self-righteous and fanatical man, a scourge of "heretics," and an instigator of the persecution of witches — a mirror, indeed, of the strangely blended virtues and dark qualities of that period in the life of the American colonies.

JOHN WINTHROP, 1588–1649

WINTHROP, a Puritan country squire deprived of his office as attorney in the Court of Wards by Charles I's policy toward the Puritans, saw in the new Massachusetts Bay Company an opportunity for himself and his party associates. He decided to give up the old life in England and strike out anew in America.

434 From the portrait of John Winthrop, by Van Dyck, in the State House, Boston

Such was his activity and ability in the new company that, when it was decided to leave England, he was promptly elected governor. The control of this enterprise which the Puritans had bought up now passed to a group which purposed removal to America. On March 29, 1630, at Cowes, England, four ships set sail, followed a week or two later by seven others bearing the rest of the adventurers. With them went the charter. In this way the charter of a trading company became the instrument of government for a colony.

ARRIVAL OF WINTHROP'S SHIPS IN BOSTON HARBOR

ON board the ships were many men of ability and position who were leaving England because of political conditions. A very large number came to get land and to found a new home in the wilderness. A number were not Puritans and a few were in sympathy with the Anglican church. The new colonists did not reach Salem until June and July, 1630. In August they moved to Charlestown, and the first meeting of the company on American soil was held. But, as the water supply proved poor, the settlers moved on to Boston.

In the illustration, the *Arabella*, Governor Winthrop's ship, is being towed to her anchorage in Boston harbor. She carries 26 guns and 52 men. To the left is the *Talbot* and, in the background, the *Jewel*.

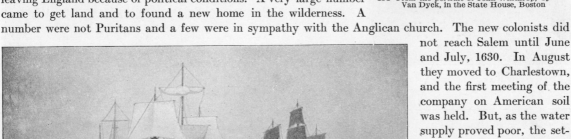

435 From the painting by William F. Halsall, in the possession of Mrs. Walter Bailey Ellis, North Scituate, Mass.

THE SOUTHERN PART OF NEW ENGLAND, 1634

THIS is an exact copy of the first map that was made after Massachusetts was settled. Says Wood in his description of the region, "these be all the towns that were begun when I left for England, which was the 15 of August, 1633." They were, to give their modern names, Boston, Roxbury, Dorchester, Weymouth, Charlestown, Medford, Cambridge, Watertown, Chelsea, Salem, Marblehead, Lynn, Ipswich, Newbury, Nahant. Immigrants were now arriving by hundreds and thousands because of the intolerant policy of Charles I. By 1642, twenty thousand had come. Then, as the power of the king waned, the exodus from England stopped abruptly.

GOING TO CHURCH

THE Puritan leaders were Calvinists who believed firmly in Calvin's ecclesiastical government in Geneva. The little Massachusetts towns that sprang up about Boston were each centered in the church. No one could be a freeman and participate in the political life of the colony who was not a church member, and the membership was carefully restricted and supervised. Rigid laws compelled all to support and attend the institutions of worship.

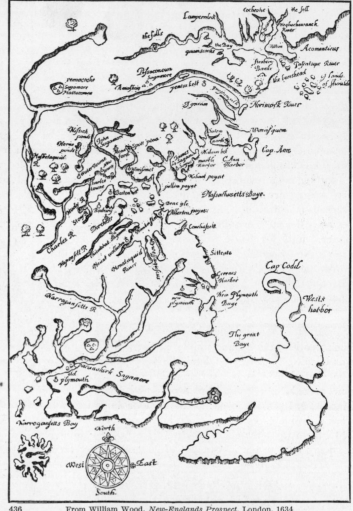

436   From William Wood, *New-Englands Prospect*, London, 1634

437   From the painting *Pilgrims Going to Church*, by George H. Boughton, in the New York Public Library

RICHARD MATHER, 1596–1669

IN England Gorges, of the New England Council, insisted bitterly that the charter of Massachusetts was a direct violation of his proprietary rights. He fought the charter with such success that, in 1635, an investigating commission issued a writ of *quo warranto* against the colony. But disturbed conditions in England prevented the serving of the writ and thus saved Massachusetts.

Persecution of the Puritan party in England drove to Massachusetts a number of men of real ability. Among them were John Cotton and Richard Mather. Mather left behind him in England a reputation for inspirational preaching, and there was rivalry among the churches in Massachusetts to secure his ministration. He went to little Dorchester, which had been depleted by migrations westward, and there he remained until his death. He was one of those who gave shape to New England Congregationalism. Men like Cotton and Mather shared with the civil leaders like Winthrop the control of the colony. The picture is believed to be the first woodcut made in America.

438   From S. A. Green, *Ten Facsimile Reproductions*, after original engraving by John Foster, 1648–81

439   From the portrait by Smibert, about 1735, owned by John E. Thayer, Lancaster, Mass.

THE OATH OF A FREEMAN

THE great immigration to America from England during the thirties of the seventeenth century brought all sorts of people. The "freemen" became a minority, and Massachusetts government assumed an oligarchic form. The great mass of folk who were not Puritans or were only lightly attached to that cause made fertile ground for the sowing of seeds of new religious ideas.

JOHN COTTON: "PATRIARCH OF NEW ENGLAND," 1585–1652

THE real rulers in Massachusetts were a small group of Puritan laymen and ministers. John Cotton, one of the leading Puritans in England, and rector of St. Botolph's Church in Boston, Lincolnshire, fled in disguise from the king's soldiers, took ship for America, and in 1633 was elected teacher to the First Church in Boston, Mass. His influence was like that of a prophet in Israel. He believed firmly in the theocratic state.

THE OATH OF A FREE-MAN.

I (A.B.) being by Gods providence, an Inhabitant, and Freeman, within the Jurisdiction of this Commonwealth; do freely acknowledge my self to be subject to the Government thereof: And therefore do here swear by the great and dreadful Name of the Ever-living God, that I will be true and faithfull to the same, and will accordingly yield assistance & support thereunto, with my person and estate, as in equity I am bound; and will also truly endeavour to maintain and preserve all the liberties and priviledges thereof, submitting my self to the wholesome Lawes & Orders made and established by the same. And further, that I will not plot or practice any evill against it, or consent to any that shall so do; but will timely discover and reveal the same to lawfull Authority now here established, for the speedy preventing thereof.

Moreover, I doe solemnly bind my self in the sight of God, that when I shal be called to give my voyce touching any such matter of this State, in which Freemen are to deal, I will give my vote and suffrage as I shall judge in mine own conscience may best conduce and tend to the publike weal of the body, without respect of persons, or favour of any man. So help me God in the Lord Jesus Christ.

440   From Major John Childe, *New-Englands Jonas cast up at London*, London, 1647

ROGER WILLIAMS, *ca.* 1604–84

THE hand of the clergy lay heavy on early Massachusetts. A small ecclesiastical hierarchy, coupled with a group of magistrates held in office by the freemen who comprised but one-fifth of the adult population, directed the religious and civil life of this frontier community. These men who left England because they would not conform to certain prescribed Anglican practices in turn allowed not the slightest deviation from the worship which they themselves ordained. The first prominent man to revolt against this domination was Roger Williams. Always independent and outspoken, Williams asserted in Salem that the state had no authority over the consciences of men, and that the only valid title to the land of the Colony must be obtained from the Indians. But this was in 1635, and so radical a spirit was banished.

441   From fictitious portrait engraved for Benedict, *History of the Baptists*, 1874

SIR RICHARD SALTONSTALL, 1586–1658

SALTONSTALL, a member of the British gentry, was from the beginning prominent in the Massachusetts Bay enterprise. His liberalism and tolerance caused him many times to differ with the methods and the point of view of the magistrates and clergy. He returned to England within the first year. He later became one of the patentees of the Saybrook settlement (at the mouth of the Connecticut River) and so aided in the founding of Connecticut.

442   From the portrait by Rembrandt (1606–69) owned by Mrs. Saltonstall, Brookline, Mass.

HENRY VANE, THE YOUNGER, 1613–62

443   From the portrait by William Dobson (1610–46), in the National Portrait Gallery, London

VANE, but twenty-three years old, high-born, brilliant and chivalrous, came to Massachusetts in 1635 in connection with a new colonial project of Lords Saye, Brooke, and others. He was elected governor, but lost his popularity in the outlying towns by taking the side of Mrs. Hutchinson rather than that of the clergy. When his year of office was over, the Hutchinson controversy was at fever heat and Vane was defeated for re-election by Winthrop. Disgusted with colonial narrowness, he returned to England. The Massachusetts of that day was obviously no place for a man of his temperament.

ANNE HUTCHINSON PREACHING

IF the banishment of Williams caused no tumult, that of Mrs. Anne Hutchinson did. This remarkable woman, kindly and devout, set the colony by the ears with the teaching which she provided in her Thursday meetings for women who could not go to church. John Cotton, the Boston Church, and even the Governor, young Henry Vane, were on her side, but even they could not prevail against the aroused phalanx of the Massachusetts clergy. Cotton soon lost courage and surrendered. Mrs. Hutchinson was tried by the General Court and was "banished out of our jurisdiction as being a woman not fit for our society." When she said, "I desire to know wherefore I am banished," Governor Winthrop replied, "Say no more; the Court knows wherefore and is satisfied." In 1643, she and her family were murdered by Indians in the neighborhood of what is now New Rochelle, N. Y.

444   From the painting by Howard Pyle (1853–1911), for Woodrow Wilson, *History of the American People*, 1901. © Harper & Bros.

SOME LAWS OF THE COMMONWEALTH

SEVENTEENTH-CENTURY laws in Europe were harsh, as were the punishments meted out for their infraction. They reflect the social development of the time. Those promulgated in Massachusetts reflected strongly the ideas of the Puritans who were in control of the colony. The laws have an Old Testament flavor and rigor that marked the conceptions of a clergy who believed that God was sending more than half of mankind at death to the unutterable terrors of an eternal Hell. If divine justice decreed that the unbaptized infant could not be saved, man must not show softness in the face of carnal offense. In the making of such laws as these the majority of the people had no voice. Large numbers who were neither Puritans nor church members chafed at the severity and the ridigity of the code thus imposed upon them. Almost from the beginning Massachusetts was the scene of a struggle of the people for a greater share in the government. In 1634, the freemen demanded a sight of the charter and then found that for four years they had been deprived of some of their important rights. But as time went on the freemen themselves became a minority. Inevitably dissatisfaction grew.

BY THE COURT:

In the Yeares, 1641. 1642.

Capital Lawes, established within the Jurisdiction of
MASSACHUSETS.

F any man, after legall conviction, shall have or worship any other god, but the Lord God, he shall be put to death. *Deut.* 13. 6, &c. and 17. 2, &c, *Exod.* 22. 20.

2. IF any man or woman be a Witch, (that is) hath, or consulteth with a Familiar spirit, they shall be put to death. *Exod.* 22. 18. *Lev.* 20. 27. *Deut.* 18. 10, 11.

3. IF any person shall blaspheme the Name of God the Father, Son, or Holy Ghost, with direct, expresse, presumptuous, or high-handed blasphemy, or shall curse God in the like manner, he shall be put to death. *Lev.* 24. 15, 16.

4. IF any person shall commit any wilfull murther, which is Man-slaughter, committed upon prnmeditate malice, hatred or cruelty, not in a mans necessary and just defence, nor by meer casualty against his will, he shall be put to death. *Exod.* 21. 12, 13, 14. *Num.* 35. 30, 31

5. IF any person slayeth another suddenly in his anger, or cruelty of passion, he shall be put to death. *Num.* 35. 20, 21. *Lev* 24. 17.

6. IF any person shall slay another through guile, either by poysonings, or other such devilish practice, he shall be put to death. *Exod.* 21 14

15. IF any man shall conspire or attempt any invasion, insurrection, or publike rebellion against our Common-wealth, or shall endeavour to surprise any Town or Towns, Fort or Forts therein; or shall treacherously or perfidiously attempt the alteration and subversion of our frame of Polity or Government fundamentally, he shall be put to death. *Num.* 16. 2 *Sam.* 3. & 18. & 20.   *Per exemplar.* Incre. Nowel, *Secret.*

445   From Major John Childe, *New-Englands Jonas Cast up at London*, London, 1647

QUAFCACANQUEN, 1633(?)
(NEWBURY)

AGAWAM, 1634
(IPSWICH)

CAPE ANN, 1623
(GLOUCESTER)

DANVERS   BEVERLY,
1632(?)   1630

NAUMKEAG
1625 (SALEM)

SAUGUS, 1629
(LYNN)

MUSKETAQUID
1635 (CONCORD)

MYSTIC, 1630
(MEDFORD)

WATERTOWN, 1630

NEWTOWN, 1631 (CAMBRIDGE)

SHAWMUT
TRIMOUNTAIN,
1630, (BOSTON)

MISHAWUM, 1629 (CHARLESTOWN)

ROXBURY, 1630
DORCHESTER, 1630

DEDHAM, 1636

MT. WOLLASTON or
MERRY MOUNT
1625 (QUINCY)

HINGHAM
1635 (INCORPORATED)

WESSAGUSSET, 1623
(WEYMOUTH)

SCITUATE,
1632

DUXBURY, 1632

MASSACHUSETTS ALGONQUIAN TRIBES

EARLY SETTLEMENTS IN MASSACHUSETTS TO 1636

PLYMOUTH, 1620

446   Drawn expressly for *The Pageant of America* by Gregor Noetzel, American Geographical Society, New York

MAP OF EARLY MASSACHUSETTS TOWNS

IN spite of a theocratic government, Massachusetts grew. Thousands of people came in the decade between 1630 and 1640. Some were members of the Puritan party in England, having left the home country because Charles I had the upper hand for the time being and was making life unpleasant for his opponents. Others

447   Drawn expressly for *The Pageant of America* by
C. W. Jefferys

came because the land of America offered opportunities to start life afresh, and pointed the way to the economic and social advance of the individual. Town after town was established. Each followed the precedent established by Plymouth and built the village around the church. The village and the congregation were practically one and the same. Together they formed the social, political and religious unity of the New England settlements. As the frontier advanced northward and westward, the hunting grounds of the Indians diminished year by year.

AN EARLY TOWN MEETING IN NEW ENGLAND

EACH new town that sprang up had its own peculiar problems. The common land must be divided and fields must be allotted; the forest must be cleared; roads and paths must be laid out; a host of things that entered into the everyday life of the people required adjustments that must be worked out. In the town meeting, the men of the community discussed their difficulties and determined their course of action. This institution of the town meeting was coincident with the village organization of New England.

FLIGHT OF ROGER WILLIAMS FROM MASSACHUSETTS

ANXIOUS as were the common people to develop a peaceful and comfortable community life, the bigotry and intolerance of their leaders in Massachusetts was impairing the best interests of the colony. They banished Roger Williams, but ere they could send him to England, he escaped into the wilderness. He spent the winter with his Indian friends planning a new colonial venture over which the Massachusetts clergy should have no control. The following spring saw him at his new settlement, which he called Providence. Thither, during the next two years, came a small group of colonists who found Massachusetts intolerable. Thus began, on the very flank of the Bay Colony, the settlement that was later known as Rhode Island.

448   Drawn expressly for *The Pageant of America* by C. W. Jefferys

ROGER WILLIAMS' BOOK ON THE INDIANS

WILLIAMS was a real friend of the redskins and acquired much influence with them. He prepared this study of them on his first voyage to England to secure a charter for his tiny settlement. He was careful to purchase his lands from their Indian owners. When the Pequot War broke out, he induced his Narragansett allies to join with Massachusetts.

WILLIAM CODDINGTON AND THE RHODE ISLAND SETTLEMENTS

WILLIAM CODDINGTON, who had been among the supporters of Mrs. Hutchinson, was forced as a result of the controversy to leave Massachusetts. He came also to Rhode Island, bought land from the Indians, and established at Portsmouth a settlement which soon moved to Newport. But Coddington, though too liberal for Boston, proved too conservative to live in harmony with Williams. The tiny settlements at Narragansett Bay were rent with dissension until Coddington, over-ambitious in his grasp for power, was forced by his own followers to flee the colony. Later he gave in and returned to the settlement. In 1644 Williams obtained a patent which united under one control the scattered settlements of Rhode Island. So finally was organized the government of the first New England colony to grow up as an off-shoot from Massachusetts.

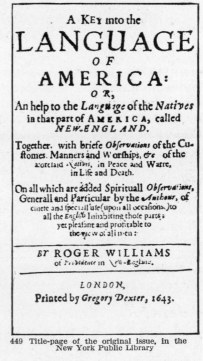

A KEY into the
LANGUAGE
OF
AMERICA:
OR,
An help to the *Language* of the *Natives* in that part of AMERICA, called NEW-ENGLAND.

Together. with briefe *Observations* of the Customes. Manners and Worships, &c of the aforesaid *Natives*, in Peace and Warre, in Life and Death.

On all which are added Spirituall *Observations*, Generall and Particular by the *Authour*, of chiefe and speciall use (upon all occasions.) to all the *English* Inhabiting those parts; yet pleasant and profitable to the view of all men:

BY ROGER WILLIAMS of Providence in New-England.

LONDON,
Printed by *Gregory Dexter*, 1643.

449   Title-page of the original issue, in the New York Public Library

450   From a doubtful portrait in the City Hall, Newport, R. I.   Artist unknown

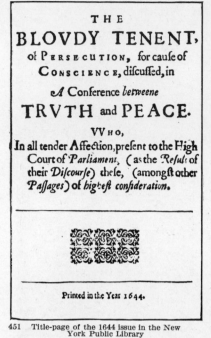

451 Title-page of the 1644 issue in the New
York Public Library

ROGER WILLIAMS, *THE BLOUDY TENENT*, ETC.

WILLIAMS was an active disputant in an age which paid much attention to theology. Not content with helping in the establishment of a colony in America he shared in the arguments of the day when in England. Few men have been more rigid in their theological views and at the same time tolerant of the opinions of others. It may be that his Puritan friends, Milton and Cromwell, were influenced by *The Bloudy Tenent*, London, 1644, in which he argued for liberty of conscience.

STATUE OF ROGER WILLIAMS AT PROVIDENCE, R. I.

A FEW sentences from a letter written by Roger Williams in 1670 bespeak the man. "The matter with us is not about these childern's toys of land, meadows, cattel, government, etc. But here all over this colonie, a great number of weake and distressed soules, scattered, are flying hither from Old and New England; The Most High and Only Wise hath in His infinite wisdom provided this country and this corner as a shelter for the poor and persecuted, according to their several perswasions . . . no person in this Colony shall be molested or questioned for the matters of his conscience to God, so he be loyall and keep the civil peace. Sir, we must part with lands and lives before we part with such a jewell."

452 The Williams statue by Franklin Simmons (1839–1913), in Roger Williams Park, Providence, R. I.

THE HOOKER PARTY MIGRATES TO HARTFORD, 1636

BUT there were others dissatisfied with Massachusetts. In 1634 Thomas Hooker asked leave for himself and others to go to Connecticut, urging "the want of accommodation for their cattle . . . the fruitfulness and commodiousness of Connecticut and the danger of having it possessed by others, Dutch or English: the strong bent of their spirits to remove thither." Boston refused, chiefly on the ground that the exodus of this congregation would weaken Massachusetts "and also divert other friends that would come to us." But under date of May 31, 1636, Winthrop writes: "Mr. Hooker, pastor of the church of Newton, and the most of his congregation, went to Connecticut. His wife was carried in a horse litter; and they drove one hundred and sixty cattle, and fed of their milk by the way." The fertility of the Connecticut valley was doubtless an influence increasing the desire to escape the Massachusetts régime.

453 From the painting, 1846, by Frederic E. Church (1826–1900), in the Wadsworth Atheneum, Hartford, Conn.

THE FUNDAMENTAL ORDERS OF CONNECTICUT

THE Connecticut River towns — Hartford, Wethersfield, and Windsor — were the outgrowth of Hooker's migration. Committees from these met in "a Gen'all cort at Harteford" in 1638–39 and framed the "Fundamental Orders" of Connecticut. Many of the principles of this remarkable document had been set forth by Hooker in a sermon in May, 1638. According to the "Orders," the governor was required to be a church member; the governor was to be elected by the voters; more power was given to the freemen and less to the magistrates. It was a somewhat Utopian attempt to apply the ideal of individual rights as suggested in Hooker's plea, "As God has given us liberty, to take it." But so ideal a purpose could not be maintained, and limitations upon the right to vote were imposed twenty years later.

454   From the mural painting by Albert Herter (1871–), in the State capitol, Hartford, Conn.

SAYBROOK FORT, 1636

As Charles I continued in his efforts to govern England without the aid of Parliament, a group of prominent Puritans, including Lord Saye and Sele, Lord Brooke, Sir Richard Saltonstall, John Hampden, and John Pym, desired to prepare a refuge in America, should the worst menace come true. They supposed they had a grant of land from Warwick in what is now southern New England. Of this territory they appointed John Winthrop, junior, governor. In 1635 Winthrop erected a fort and called the place Saybrook, after two of the chief promoters of the venture. Like other Puritans seeking to found a refuge in America should conditions become so bad as to make one necessary, these leaders avoided the Massachusetts Bay colony on account of its narrow, theocratic character.

455   From an engraving, after a drawing, origin not known, in the Emmet Collection, New York Public Library

LORD SAYE AND SELE, 1582–1662

LORD SAYE AND SELE was a privy councillor, a member of the House of Lords and of the plantations council. He was, according to an unfriendly critic "The oracle of those who were called Puritans in the worst sense, and steered all their counsels and designs." He was one of the chief founders of Saybrook.

456 From the portrait by Paul Van Somer, in the Victoria and Albert Museum, London

457 From the portrait, artist unknown, in the possession of the Winthrop family, New York

GOVERNOR WINTHROP OF CONNECTICUT, 1606–76

JOHN WINTHROP, the younger, governed the territory granted to Lord Saye and Sele and his associates for one year, 1635, under the Warwick patent. Then he returned to Massachusetts and later spent two years in England, chiefly in scientific study. In 1651 he was chosen one of the magistrates of Connecticut, which in the meantime had (as was supposed) acquired title to the territory by purchase of the Warwick patent. He was governor from 1657 to 1658 and from 1659 to his death in 1676. Winthrop had qualities that served him well as governor and magistrate. He was a university man, had toured the Continent and was familiar with the traditions and the ways of court.

THE PEQUOT WAR

HARDLY had Saybrook and the Connecticut River towns been founded when Indian war menaced the new frontier. Massachusetts had sent Endicott into the Indian country to avenge a murder, and had enraged without intimidating the redmen. The River towns, in deadly danger, saw in the Pequots their chief enemy. They struck first in May, 1637. Captain John Mason with ninety men went to Saybrook, where he was joined by Captain Underhill with a handful more. With admirable strategy, they surprised the chief town of the Pequots in a night attack and entered both gates of the village. Mason fired the village and withdrew to the surrounding woods, where his men shot every wretched savage who attempted to climb over the palisade. As the night waned, "five hundred men, women, and children were slowly burned alive." Mason noted that, by the providence of God, there were one hundred and fifty more Indians than usual in the village that night.

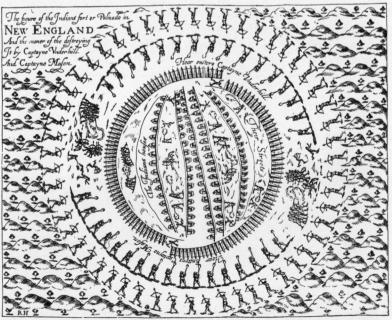

458   Plan of the Pequot Fort, from John Underhill, *Newes from America*, London, 1638, in the New York Public Library

459 From the portrait, artist unknown, in The Yale University School of the Fine Arts, New Haven, Conn.

JOHN DAVENPORT AND THE SETTLEMENT OF NEW HAVEN

THE overthrow of the Pequots opened the way for the settlement of New Haven and the towns near it along the Connecticut shore.   John Davenport, a Nonconformist minister, and Theophilus Eaton, a wealthy London merchant, were the central figures of a distinguished company. Both had been members of the Massachusetts Bay Company, but they now decided to test their fortune by establishing an independent colony beyond reach of the Boston magistrates.   In 1637 Eaton looked over the region of the Quinnipiac and left some men to guard the chosen site during the winter. In the following spring the building of New Haven began.

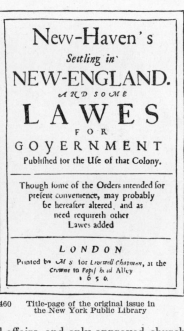

Nevv-Haven's
Settling in
NEW-ENGLAND.
AND SOME
LAWES
FOR
GOVERNMENT
Published for the Use of that Colony.

Though some of the Orders intended for present convenience, may probably be hereafter altered, and as need requireth other Lawes added

LONDON
Printed by *M s* for *Livewell Chapman*, at the Crowne to Popes head Alley
1 6 5 6.

460   Title-page of the original issue in the New York Public Library

NEW HAVEN'S SETTLING IN NEW ENGLAND

THE "Lawes for Government," drawn up by Governor Eaton, outlined a theocratic constitution even more drastic than that of Massachusetts. English statute and common law and trial by jury were excluded from New Haven; the "worde of God was adopted as the onely rule" in civil affairs, and only approved church members were allowed to participate in politics.

THE CONNECTICUT CHARTER

IN 1662 the younger Winthrop, after the distribution of liberal largess among the courtiers of Charles II,

procured a charter for Connecticut.   It legalized the government already existing at Hartford, and gave to the colony a territory extending from the Narragansett River to the Pacific Ocean. The charter produced a quarrel with Rhode Island and resulted in the absorption of New Haven into Connecticut. The charter was so satisfactory that it remained the fundamental law of Connecticut for forty-two years after the Declaration of Independence until the adoption of the present State Constitution in 1818.

461   From the original in the State Library, Hartford, Conn.

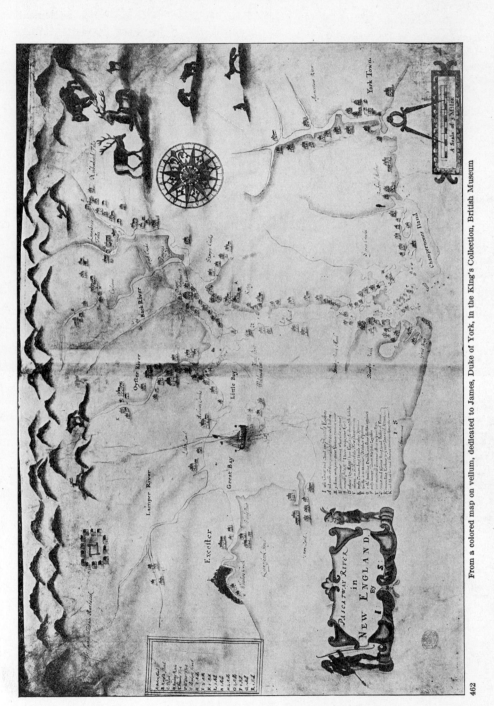

462

From a colored map on vellum, dedicated to James, Duke of York, in the King's Collection, British Museum

NEW HAMPSHIRE—MAP OF PASCATWAY RIVER, IN NEW ENGLAND

NORTHWARD, as well as westward, the frontier was pushed, and towns sprang up along the northern coast. Thus Portsmouth, Dover, Exeter and Hampton came into being. Some of them started independent of the Boston settlement and by direct migration from England. They were peopled in the main by a rough and lawless folk intent on individual profit. Massachusetts discovered in 1652–1654 that one interpretation of the bounds of her charter would include these northern settlements and thereupon added them to her domain. It was clearly an act of usurpation. This old map, bearing an acrostic dedication to James, Duke of York, shows the Exeter region.

ARTICLES OF CONFEDERATION, 1643

To meet the dangers of the new country, the New England Settlements federated. The United Colonies of New England, usually called the New England Confederation, included Massachusetts, Connecticut, New Haven and Plymouth. Rhode Island, that center of religious nonconformity, was excluded from participation. It was not yet considered a respectable member of the New England community. The Confederation endured forty-one years. The articles were agreed upon at Boston on May 19, 1643, John Winthrop, senior, presiding. Provisions were made for joint defense of the colonies and for one standard measure of "eight gallons to the bushell." Letters of remonstrance were written to the Dutch and the Swedes, whose roving cattle had destroyed corn belonging to the colonists.

It was urged that every man give "the fourth part of a bushel of Corne" to maintain the "publike schooles" and that a general fund be created "for the mayntenance of poore Schollers at the Colledge at Cambridge." A sentence passed by one colonial court was to have equal weight in every other. Here was an early form of organization not dissimilar to the Articles of Confederation of 1781. "All the forces which were destined to create the United States were present and at work in connection with the Confederation. Expansion, the sense of need of common action, compromise, and a written agreement to work together were all typical of the later stages of American development."

ARTICLES
OF
Confederation betwixt the Plantations under the Government of the *Massachusets*, the Plantations under the Government of *Plimouth*, the Plantations under the Government of *Connecticut*, and the Government of *New Haven*, with the Plantations in Combination therewith.

WHereas we all came into these parts of *America*, with one and the same end and ayme, namely, to advance the Kingdome of our Lord Jesus Christ, and to enjoy the liberties of the Gospel, in purity with peace, and whereas in our settling (by a wise providence of God) we are further dispersed upon the Sea-Coasts, and Rivers, then was at first intended, so that we cannot (according to our desire) with convenience communicate in one Government, and Jurisdiction; and whereas we live encompassed with people of severall Nations, and strange languages, which hereafter may prove injurious to us, and our posterity: And forasmuch as the Natives have formerly committed sundry insolencies and outrages upon severall Plantations of the English, and have of late combined themselves against us. And seeing by reason of the sad distractions in *England*, which they have heard of, and by which they know we are hindred both from that humble way of seeking advice, and reaping those comfortable fruits of protection which, at other times, we might well expect; we therefore doe conceive it our bounden duty, without delay, to enter into a present Consotiation amongst our selves, for mutuall help and strength in all our future concernments, that, as in Nation, and Religion, so, in other respects, we be, and continue, One, according to the tenour and true meaning of the ensuing Articles.

Wherefore it is fully Agreed and Concluded by and between the parties; or Jurisdictions above named, and they doe joyntly and severally by these presents agree and conclude, That they all be, and henceforth be called by the name of, *The United Colonies of New-England*.

463 From *New-Haven's Settling in New-England, and some Lawes for Government; Published for the Use of that Colony . . .*, London, 1656

JOHN ELIOT, 1604–90

THE advance of the frontier presaged disaster for the Indians. Using legal forms which the Indians could not understand, the whites, ruthless and determined, took parcel after parcel of the Indian hunting grounds and pushed the dispossessed hunters northward and westward into strange forests and among strange tribes. Yet, among the invaders occasionally a man appeared in whom the contact of the races roused a spirit of brotherhood. Intellectual capacity, religious devotion, courage, and selflessness were conspicuous in this "Apostle to the Indians" who arrived in Boston in 1631 and shortly afterward began at Roxbury his life work, the Christianization and education of the redmen. Eliot's translation of the Scriptures into the native tongue was the first Bible printed in the New World. He established towns for his Indian converts who, ere his death, numbered about four thousand.

JOHN ELIOT.
APOSTLE OF THE INDIANS
NASCIT: 1604: OBIT.1690.

464 From a fictitious portrait, artist unknown, in the Museum of Fine Arts, Boston

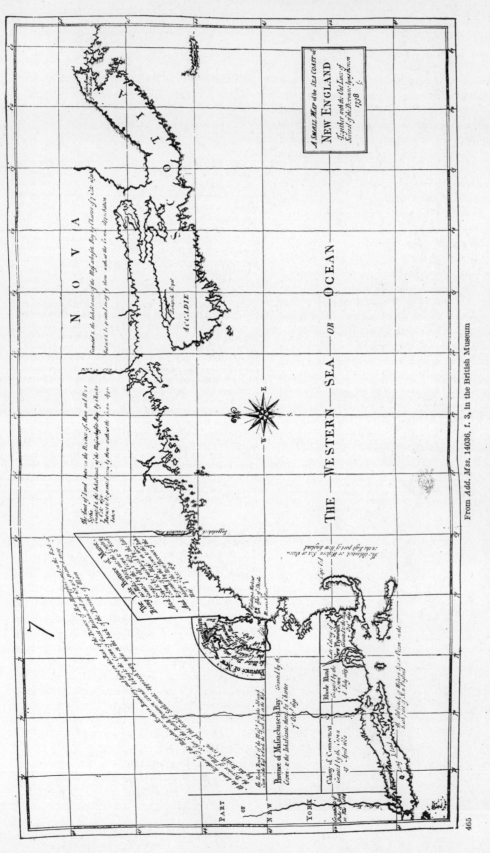

From *Add. Mss.* 14036, I. 3, in the British Museum

THE NEW ENGLAND COLONIES IN 1738

An old map of New England shows New Hampshire as a separate province and the "late colony of New Plymouth" absorbed by Massachusetts October 7, 1691. Maine also has been absorbed by Massachusetts. The colony of New Haven has been made a part of Connecticut and the Connecticut settlements at the eastern end of Long Island have definitely come under the jurisdiction of New York. New England was beginning to establish the political boundaries that were to last, some of them, to the present. The northern frontier remained to be filled with settlements. In this region the boundaries were to depend upon adjustments between neighboring colonies or, at a later period, states, and, in part, upon international agreements.

Drawn expressly for *The Pageant of America* by Gregor Noetzel, American Geographical Society, New York

NEW ENGLAND AND HER NEIGHBORS

To the north and east of New England lay New France. A line of forts and towns occupied the St. Lawrence valley. New England ships sailing for London passed by the ports of Acadia. In the broad expanse of forest between the French and English lived the Indians much as they had for centuries before the advent of the Europeans. But Catholic missionaries were appearing among them and French fur traders were their friends. With increasing apprehension they watched the growth of the English settlements on the south. The map shows the stage set for the bitter struggle between two empires.

CHAPTER XI

NEW NETHERLAND AND NEW YORK

THOSE provinces of the Netherlands lying north of the mouth of the Rhine, and now called Holland, had been swept by the Reformation. The southern provinces, Flanders and Belgium, had remained chiefly Catholic. But both Protestant and Catholic Netherlanders had a common bond in the great commercial prosperity of their land and in the vigor and independence of their own spirit. When Philip II of Spain, however, became King of the Netherlands, he made attempts to stamp out Protestantism and thereby wrecked the commerce and fraternity of that once thriving country. No longer could two hundred and fifty sails be counted on one day at Antwerp, nor could the strange habit of Russian or Levantine merchant be seen in the marts of Bruges or Leyden. Trade came to a standstill; shops were closed; and Spanish helmet and halberd took the place of the merchant's beaver hat and silver-mounted staff.

The independent spirit of the Netherlands, however, could not brook such tyranny. The resistance to the Spaniards' abuse of power was not confined to the Protestant provinces, but it was stronger there. Its moving spirit was William, Prince of Orange, surnamed The Silent. William acquired it by keeping silent when the French King spoke incautiously in his presence of an agreement between Spain and France for destroying Protestantism in the Low Countries. "From that hour," William said later, "I resolved with my whole soul to do my best to drive this Spanish vermin out of the land." The union and independence of the provinces of the north was his work, though he was murdered before that work was consummated. In 1609 a twelve-year truce was signed with Spain. The Spanish would not recognize the independence of the Netherland States for many years to come (1648). But the hardy, stubborn Dutchmen knew that the alien yoke was broken.

During the war the Dutch had built up a navy again, chiefly for the hounding of Spanish treasure ships. These pirate ships, or "Beggars of the Sea," as they were called, were now well fitted for the task of raising Holland once more to its old position of commercial affluence. Even before the true Dutch East India Company had been formed, in 1602, Dutch armed vessels had fought their way to India, Africa, the Spice Islands, and home again with rich cargoes. Nineteen years later the Dutch West India Company came into being to operate in the western hemisphere, and more particularly about the river which Henry Hudson, sailing for the older company, had discovered in 1609. The years of Dutch trading and colonization on the Hudson were the years of Holland's greatness on the sea and in the realm of art and letters. The East India Company established a chain of forts and factories from the Cape of Good Hope to Japan. The West India Company invaded the West Indies and conquered a large part of Brazil. At home, Rubens and Rembrandt painted, Grotius wrote his history, and the great Vondel laid the foundations of a national school of literature.

AMSTELDAM

AMSTERDAM
ABOUT 1690

AMSTERDAM, "the dyke or dam of the Amstel," takes its name from the dam built in 1240 by a Lord of Amstel to keep the sea out of a little fishing village. The canals of the modern city mark the lines of fortified walls built by other lords as the centuries passed. Amsterdam was the headquarters of those sovereign commercial organizations, the Dutch East and West India Companies. It was the center of learning, and was proud of its reputation as a "harborer of all sorts of heresies," where

467   From Carolus Allard, *Orbis Habitabilis*, Amsterdam, *ca.* 1690

the oppressed found a refuge for themselves and their opinions. Financially Amsterdam was the successor of mediæval Bruges and regulated exchange for Europe. It was also a center of literature and art. There Vondel wrote and read his poems. There, in the quarters of the Jewish diamond-cutters, lived Rembrandt and Spinoza. Into its harbor came the sails of the Beggars of the Sea.

THE *HALF-MOON* PASSING THE PALISADES

HENRY HUDSON, English navigator and explorer, sailing for the British Muscovy Company in 1607–08, sought in two voyages a northeast route to the trading centers of Asia and to the coasts of Spitzbergen and Novaya Zemlya. On his return he was commissioned by the Dutch East India Company to seek a route to China. With eighteen or twenty men he sailed on this new quest in the *Half-Moon* on April 6, 1609. A month later he was among the ice near Novaya Zemlya on his old route. Then, disregarding his instructions, he abandoned his attempt for a northeast passage and sought a northwest route past the continent of North America. In June, Hudson was on the Kennebec River, providing a new mast for the *Half-Moon* and having a brush with Indians. He dropped south, and standing in to shore, coasted north. On September 3, he entered the lower bay of New York, and on the 12th saw Manhattan Island.

A majestic river opened before him and he sailed northward to above the site of Albany. Then he turned back, satisfied that this river would not lead him to China. Hudson had found a great river, and exploded the popular myth that in "North Virginia," about the 40th parallel, there was another isthmus like Panama.

468   From the painting by H. A. Ogden. Courtesy of *The Christian Herald*, New York

HENRY HUDSON MEETING WITH THE INDIANS, 1609

On September 5, some days before upper New York bay was discovered, the Indians in "two Canoes, the one having twelve, and the other fourteen men," attacked John Coleman, an Englishman, and four others who had been in the Kill von Kull, sighting Newark Bay, and were on their way back to the *Half-Moon*. Coleman was shot "with an Arrow into his throat, and two more hurt." Coleman was

469   From the painting by J. L. G. Ferris, in Independence Hall, Philadelphia

buried at a point named (Colman's) in his honor, which has been identified with both Sandy Hook and Norton Point.

Hudson, sailing northward, landed somewhere below Albany and was feasted by the Indians. September 22, Robert Juet, mate of the *Half-Moon*, noted in his log: "So at three of the clocke in the after-noone they (the Indians) came aboord, and brought Tobacco, and more Beades, and gave them to our Master, and made an oration, and showed him all the country round." This was perhaps above the mouth of the Mohawk. Hudson sailed away but again returned to America, this time in English employ. Again he sought a northwest passage and again he left his name upon a magnificent body of water, Hudson's Bay, where, cast off by his crew, he died.

470 From the model by J. L. G. Ferris, in Independence Hall, Philadelphia

MODEL OF THE *ONRUST*, 1614

Little Holland, about to enter upon a twelve years' truce with Spain, was excited by the report of his explorations that Hudson sent to the Netherlands. Ambitious schemes for profit in the New World became the gossip of Amsterdam and Hoorn. Traders crossed the sea to the Hudson River to bargain with the Indians for furs and tobacco. Adriaen Block, one of these, lost his vessel by mischance in the region of the present city of Albany, and thereupon built another, the *Onrust*. He explored Long Island Sound, giving his name to Block Island. But in the early days the Dutch trade was desultory and its management by the government haphazard. Yet this same desultory trade served to open the eyes of Dutchmen to the possibilities of profit that were offered at the mouth of the Hudson. The model is an imaginary creation.

471 From Joost Hartgers, *Beschrijvinghe van Virginia, Nieuw Nederlandt, Nieuw Engelandt, etc.* Amsterdam, 1651

NEW AMSTERDAM — SO–CALLED EARLIEST VIEW

THE destinies of New Netherland were confided in 1621 to the Dutch West India Company. Peter Minuit, one of the directors whom they sent out, bought Manhattan from the Indians in 1626 and founded New Amsterdam. The Company's ships now brought out colonists' supplies and carried back furs. The powers of the Company were great. It had a monopoly of trade in Africa from the Tropic of Cancer to Good Hope, and on the American coast from Newfoundland to the Strait of Magellan. It was permitted to make alliances, to erect forts, to plant colonies, and to institute government. The States General, partners in all the Company's ventures, undertook to provide sixteen warships to protect its commerce. In 1626 engineers came from Holland to construct Fort Amsterdam, destined to be the chief bulwark of Dutch power in America.

LETTER RELATING THE PURCHASE OF MANHATTAN

ONE Peter Schagen wrote as follows from Amsterdam to the States General of the Netherlands at The Hague under date of November 5, 1626: "High Mighty Sirs: Here arrived yesterday the ship *The Arms of Amsterdam*, which sailed from New Netherland out of the Mauritius (Hudson) River on September 23; they report that our people there are of good courage and live peaceably . . . they have bought the island Manhattes from the wild men for the value of sixty guilders [$24] . . . the cargo of the aforesaid ship is: 7246 beaver skins, 178 1/2 otter skins, 675 otter skins, 48 mink skins, 36 wild-cat skins, 33 minks, 34 rat skins. Many logs of oak and nutwood. Herewith be ye High Mighty Sirs commended to the Almighty's grace."

At New Amsterdam under Minuit the little handful of settlers, save those who held public office, busied themselves with their private concerns. Some were traders; others were farmers; and there were a few artisans. Each morning the cows were driven to the *bouwerie* as the common was called. The cattle belonged to the company but the milk was the property of the settlers.

472 From facsimile in James Grant Wilson, *Memorial History of the City of New York*, New York, 1892

FORT ORANGE (ALBANY)

THE first settlement in New Netherland was made in 1624 at Fort Orange, now the city of Albany. Formerly a few traders had wintered there on an adjoining island and had built, in 1615, a fort called Fort Nassau; but this island was abandoned in 1617. The picture represents the town and river traffic later in the Dutch régime.

473 From the mural painting by Elmer E. Garnsey (1862–), in the Custom House, New York

NEW NETHERLAND UNDER THE DUTCH WEST INDIA COMPANY

COLONISTS at first were slow to leave the trim, fertile fields of the Netherlands for the uncertain wilderness of America. Among the earlier colonists were pioneers for conscience' sake, Protestant Walloons. Kiliaen van Rensselaer, a shrewd director of the West India Company, suggested the patroon system to build up an oversea population. Though he never came to America, he became the most famous of the patroons as the founder of Rensselaerswyck, near Fort Orange.

A patroon was a feudal lord who might receive a grant of land anywhere in the colony save Manhattan Island, which was reserved for the Company. Usually the holdings lay along the Hudson. The patroon must bring colonists to New Amsterdam, equip them and settle them on his estate. They were his tenants, he, in a sense, their feudal overlord. So Dutch colonists were brought out to America. But at its best this colonial system worked only fairly well, for conditions in undeveloped America were not favorable to the feudalism of mediæval Europe. Life in the American forest bred independence. The complicated legal arrangements of feudalism which were the result of hundreds of years of growth could not be transplanted to the primitive communities of America.

THE FUR TRADE

TRADE, not agriculture, was the basis of the prosperity of New Netherland. There was money to be made in shipping furs to the home land, and not many years passed before New Amsterdam assumed a solid and

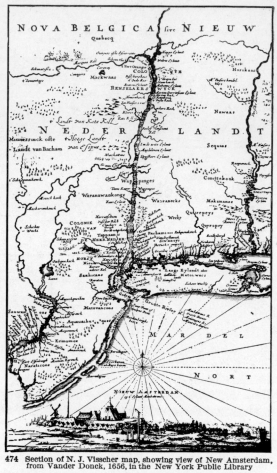

474 Section of N. J. Visscher map, showing view of New Amsterdam, from Vander Donck, 1656, in the New York Public Library

comfortable appearance. Houses of masonry appeared, sometimes even aspiring to a certain grandeur. The newness and uncouthness of the first days gradually disappeared, and Manhattan became the abode of a growing number of householders, in whose tidy homes the best Dutch customs were maintained.

475   From the mural painting *New Amsterdam* by Elmer E. Garnsey (1862–), in the Custom House, New York

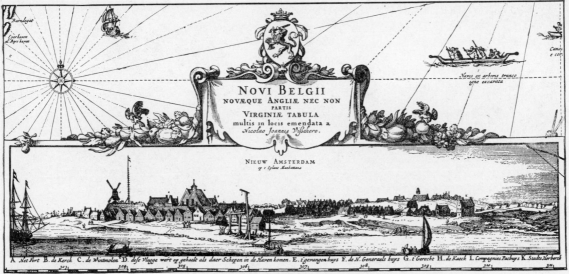

From the N. J. Visscher map of *Novum Belgium*, 1651–55, in the New York Public Library

NEW AMSTERDAM, ABOUT 1650

THE appearance of the little Dutch village, whose fortune it was to be the forerunner of the greatest metropolis of the western world, has long been a matter of interest and the early history of later famous streets has been diligently sought. A few sketches made during or shortly after the old Dutch days have been preserved. The earliest known is that of Hartgers (p. 229). Accompanying the *Novum Belgium* map (No. 476), so rich in drawings, is a second sketch of New Amsterdam in the days of Peter Stuyvesant, which sets forth in great detail the characteristics of this then prosperous colony and trading post.

The fort, the windmill and the flagstaff were prominent features of the little Dutch town. At the left of the mill may be seen the tops of masts of trading ships tied up to the wharves on the far side of the island. This little village was the center of an agricultural community that lay about the mouth of the Hudson and along the banks of the great river and also of a fur trade that reached far into the interior.

CATTLE FAIR AT NEW AMSTERDAM

IN 1641, Governor William Kieft founded the cattle fair at New Amsterdam. Not only cattle, however, were marketed there, but later all kinds of products were offered for sale. Cheeses, butter, laces, and linens were sold by the farmers' wives in their booths. Indian women from the neighboring districts brought baskets, cradles, wooden dolls, furs, and berries. Pleasure went hand in hand with business, and songs, and dances added to the joys of bartering. The Dutch early proved that they were as capable of adjusting their lives to the conditions in America as the Spanish or English. Like their neighbors they transplanted to the New World the customs which they had known in the old.

477   From the tapestry by Albert Herter, in the Hotel McAlpin, New York.

478   From the mural painting by Barry Faulkner (1881–), in the Washington Irving High School, New York

PIONEER WOMEN OF NEW AMSTERDAM

THE good *vrouw* of those days, in her voluminous petticoats and linen cap, stretched her skein of flaxen thread or wool. She was probably the best housekeeper on the whole seaboard; and her daughters were among those maids who trod the narrow paths through the meadows to soak their flax in the brook and do their laundry work.

479   From the mural painting by E. A. Abbey (1852–1911), in the Imperial Hotel, New York. © Brown Bros.

PLAYING BOWLS ON BOWLING GREEN

WHILE the sunset breeze slowly turned the windmill and carried the cool air from the bay over the narrow point of Manhattan Island, the sturdy burghers, their labors done, disported themselves on the Green. Nine pins was a favorite game. Bowling Green received its name sometime between 1730 and 1733, years after New York had come under English control.

480   From the mural painting by Francis Newton (1873–), at the New York Police Headquarters. © Curtis & Cameron

THE RATTLE WATCH

As dusk followed upon sunset, the Rattle Watch lighted their lanterns and made the rounds of New Amsterdam. It was house-time and bed-time for all good Dutch folk. Among other things they were required "to call out how late it is, at all the corners of the streets, from nine o'clock in the evening until *reveille* beat in the morning," and were to have a captain over them.

481 From the mural painting by Barry Faulkner, in the Washington Irving High School, New York

LONG ISLAND UNDER THE DUTCH

NEW AMSTERDAM was the hub and not the boundary of early colonization. Of the first settlers sent out by the West India Company on the *Nieu Nederlandt* in 1624, some went to the South River, now the Delaware,

482 From the painting *Edict of William the Testy*, by G. H. Boughton, in the Metropolitan Museum of Art, New York

and the main body went up the Hudson to establish Fort Orange, the present Albany. Later arrivals founded settlements on the rolling hills at the west end of Long Island, Vlackte-Bosch and Breuckelen, as the Flatbush and Brooklyn of today were then known. In time the Dutch became well established in America.

WILLIAM KIEFT

PETER MINUIT had first ruled New Amsterdam. He was followed by Wouter van Twiller who found difficult the task of directing the affairs of the colony. New England men encroached on the east and Virginians, aroused by the Dutch settlement on Delaware Bay, made threats. Van Twiller gladly relinquished his post to William Kieft. And Kieft had to face the first great Indian war of the colony which did not end before the Dutch had been reduced to distress. The picture illustrates a fictitious incident from Irving that the Dutch citizens of New Amsterdam smoked out a protest to Kieft's edict against smoking.

483 From the portrait, by Hendrick Couturier, in the New York Historical Society; courtesy of Miss Julia S. Winterhoff

PETER STUYVESANT, 1592?–1672

Now enters the last and mightiest Director-General of New Netherland, the redoubtable Peter Stuyvesant, brave as a lion and stubborn as a mule, a very able tyrant, who was perhaps just a shade better at stirring up trouble than he was at quelling it. He was a tall man with a large head, fierce little eyes, a big nose, square broad shoulders, and the voice of a thunder-god. He had lost a leg for his country and had replaced it with a wooden one. Proud indeed was Peter of his wooden leg. Though parsimonious enough generally, he lavished decorations upon this symbol of his military prowess: he bound it with silver bands and studded it with silver nails, and he polished bands and nails so that they glinted like a heaven of stars. Irreverent persons, behind his back, called him "Old Silver Nails."

THE LANDING OF PETER STUYVESANT

"I shall be as a father over his children," Stuyvesant announced to the reception committee of burghers who greeted him on his landing on May 11, 1647; and, that he might immediately inculcate in them the proper respect for parents, he kept them standing, with uncovered heads, for an hour while, king-like, he wore his hat. They soon learned that anyone who dared oppose the opinion of Peter Stuyvesant had "as much as the sun and moon against him."

484   From the painting by Stanley M. Arthurs, in his possession

"THE WRATH OF PETER STUYVESANT"

Proverbial has become the temper of the last and greatest of the Dutch Directors. Stuyvesant ruled the colony with an iron hand. "It may," he said, "during my administration be contemplated to appeal [to the home government]; but if anyone should do it, I will make him a foot shorter, and send the pieces to Holland and let him appeal in that way." "No one," wrote van Tienhoven, who was sent out to whitewash the Director's administration, "can prove that Director Stuyvesant has used foul language to or railed at as clowns any respectable persons who have treated him decently. It may be that some profligate person has given the Director, if he has used any bad words to him, cause to do so." A large number of worthy and respectable burghers, however, felt that they must be included in the list of "profligate" persons.

With all his faults, Peter Stuyvesant did more for the Dutch colony than any of his predecessors had done. He made treaties with the Indians, settled the vexed boundary question between the Dutch and English settlers on Long Island, and annexed the Swedish colony on the Delaware. He ordered the thoroughfares of New Amsterdam to be laid out as streets, and named.

But by his arbitrary rule he alienated public support during the very years when Holland was allowing the defenses of the colony to fall to pieces by ignoring Stuyvesant's appeals for military and financial aid. The picture is based on Irving's imaginary description of Stuyvesant's rage on learning of the surrender by the Dutch of Fort Casimir — he "thrust a prodigious quid of tobacco into his left cheek, pulled up his galligaskins, and strode up and down the room, humming as was customary with him when in a passion, a hideous northwest ditty."

485   From the painting by Asher B. Durand (1796–1886), in the New York Historical Society

THE FALL OF NEW AMSTERDAM

War broke out between England and Holland. New and Old England co-operated at once in an attack on New Netherland. Peter Stuyvesant, returning in haste from Fort Orange, saw four English ships at the mouth of the Hudson. Their commander, Colonel Richard Nicolls, demanded surrender of the "towns situate on the island commonly known by the name of Manhattoes, with all the forts thereunto belonging." That meant all New Netherland. Fort Amsterdam, long out of repair, was unfit for resistance, and Stuy-

486   From the painting by J. L. G. Ferris (1863–), in Independence Hall, Philadelphia

vesant was short of powder. He was, however, willing to fight, but the people dissuaded him from bringing useless bloodshed upon the colony.

487   From the painting by E. L. Henry (1841–1919), by permission of the Title Guarantee and Trust Co., New York

SURRENDER OF NEW AMSTERDAM, 1664

Nicolls sent to Stuyvesant letters written by Governor John Winthrop of Connecticut and himself requesting a conference "about the premises." The Director sparred for time, but capitulation was inevitable. Four days after the delivery of the English demand, six men, Sir Robert Carr, Colonel George Cartwright, Governor John Winthrop, Councillor Samuel Willys of Connecticut, Captain Thomas Clarke, and John Pinchon met with the representatives of Stuyvesant at the latter's bouwery house where, next day, September 6 (New Style), 1664, the articles of surrender were signed. The picture of the Stuyvesant house is an elaboration of a cut made nearly a century ago by Benson J. Lossing.

JAMES, DUKE OF YORK, 1633–1701

WHEN Stuyvesant's soldiers ran up the white flag at the fort on Manhattan Island, Holland saw the trading outpost which she had not taken the trouble to defend adequately pass into the hands of the British. Charles II turned it over to his brother James, the Duke of York, from whom New York thereafter took its name.

CORNELIUS STEENWYCK, MAYOR, –1684

NICOLLS as governor finished his term in 1668. He had been a tactful and intelligent official and had brought Dutch and English on the

Hudson into bonds of good feeling. On the eve of his departure a banquet was given in his honor by the Dutch Mayor of New York, Cornelius Steenwyck. Steenwyck was mayor for three years and once acting governor during the absence of Lovelace, who succeeded Nicolls. His great, square, stone house stood on the corner of the present Whitehall and Bridge Streets, a symbol of the stability and comfort of the little colony.

488   From *Cromwelliana*, Westminster, after an engraving in Guillem, *Heraldry*, 1679

489   From the portrait, 1667–68, painted in Holland by Jan van Goosen, in the New York Historical Society

DUTCH MAP OF 1673 — RECAPTURE OF NEW YORK

ONCE again, for a few brief months, the Dutch ruled in New York. On July 30, 1673, a fleet commanded by Cornelius Eversten and Jacob Binckes surprised the town, which was soon thereafter busy with the strengthening of the fortifications which had been long neglected. But when peace came, the treaty stipulated that the Hudson valley should revert to England. So for a third time a national flag was lowered on Manhattan. The map shows the Dutch fleet entering the harbor.

490   Retouched enlargement from the "Restitutio Map," 1673, in the New York Public Library

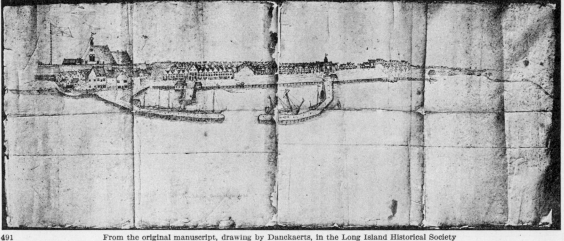

491   From the original manuscript, drawing by Danckaerts, in the Long Island Historical Society

VIEW OF NEW YORK FROM BROOKLYN HEIGHTS, 1679

JASPER DANCKAERTS and Peter Sluyter, two Hollanders of the Labadist sect, visited New York in 1679. Danckaerts kept a journal of their experiences and made drawings, among which are three pictures of old New York fifteen years after the British had first taken it. There are striking similarities between their drawing of the above view from Brooklyn Heights and that on the Visscher map (p. 231). In the quarter century and more that intervened between the two, the Manhattan skyline had been but little changed. But it was no longer a little trading village; it was already an infant city looking to a prosperous future.

THE STADT HUYS, 1679

LATER picture-makers have enlarged and touched up sections of Danckaerts' view, and their drawings have become current in the literature relating to early New York history. The Stadt Huys, found in the center of Danckaerts' drawing, had been erected in 1642 to serve as an inn. The building became the Stadt Huys in 1653 and was acquired by the city in 1655 to house the Dutch government. Under English rule it continued its dignified rôle in the political life of the colony.

492   From a reconstruction by J. Carson Brevoort (1818–87), of part of Danckaerts' drawing, in *Journal of a Voyage to New York and a Tour in Several of the American Colonies in 1679–80*. Edited by Henry C. Murphy and published in the collections of the Long Island Historical Society, 1867

Francis Lovelace, who became governor in 1668, built an inn against its west wall and opened a door between the hostelry and the courtroom — to mellow counsel with good cheer. The building like all the others which the Dutch built has long since passed away to make room for the busier life of a later age. Only in such old pictures as this can we catch a glimpse of the surroundings of the first phase of civilized life on Manhattan Island.

493   From an old print, enlargement and redraft of a section of Danckaerts' original,
1679, in the Long Island Historical Society

THE FORT AT NEW YORK

Ships from Holland or later from England sailing up New York harbor saw first the fort with its tall flag-staff rising above the ramparts. Failure to keep this fortification in a condition of adequate preparedness had contributed to the downfall of New Netherland. The houses outside the walls with their steep gabled roofs, stepped at the ends, were typical of the architecture the Dutch used in their solid homes. The boats tied up at the dock might well be fishing craft for use on the grounds off Sandy Hook and Long Island.

A VIEW OF NEW YORK FROM THE EAST, 1679

This reduction from the Danckaerts' original sketch is the view of the town as seen from a point on the shore of the East River near the corner of the present Fulton and Water Streets. The perspective is a rather distorted one due to the bend in the river. The black line in the background at the left is evidently intended for the Jersey shore. At the left end of the settlement appears the north side of the Long Dock, with a couple of river craft moored alongside. Following the line of the waterfront appear a row of quaint Dutch houses and then the orchard of Govert Lockerman, a prominent

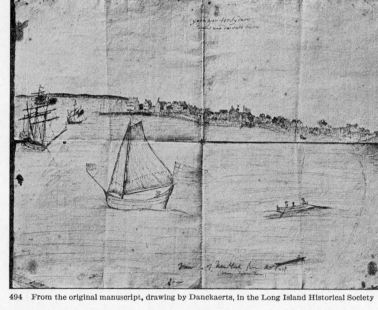

494   From the original manuscript, drawing by Danckaerts, in the Long Island Historical Society

landmark.   The large flag is on the Fort and next it is the church with a smaller flag.   Both buildings, on account of the perspective, seem to be too far away from their true positions.   Brevoort's reconstruction of

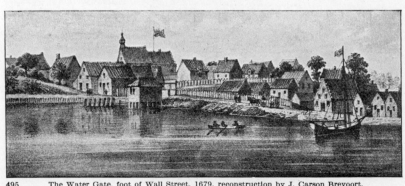

495   The Water Gate, foot of Wall Street, 1679, reconstruction by J. Carson Brevoort,
based on Danckaerts' sketch

the Water Gate at the foot of Wall Street (No. 495) is based on close study of this drawing by Danckaerts, and upon his own knowledge of the topography of the town. The sketch of a Dutch merchant ship is quite clear, and the sloop in the foreground, possibly the earliest view of an American-built vessel, is flying the British flag appropriate to the time.

VIEW OF NEW YORK FROM THE NORTH, 1679

THE picture "is taken from a point near the Hudson River and north of the present City Hall Park. It shows the great highway (present Broadway) and the two mills south of the Fresh Water, built respectively about 1664 and 1677. . . . The tower on the church in the Fort is greatly exaggerated. . . . Indeed, the whole topography is much confused." — I. N. P. STOKES, *The Iconography of Manhattan Island*. Brevoort's redraft (No. 497) clarifies the sketch.

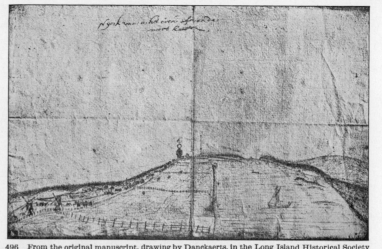

496   From the original manuscript, drawing by Danckaerts, in the Long Island Historical Society

497   From reconstruction by J. Carson Brevoort of Danckaerts' drawing, in *Journal of a Voyage to New York and a Tour in Several of the American Colonies in 1679–80*.   Edited by Henry C. Murphy and published in the collections of the Long Island Historical Society, 1867

ARRIVAL OF CAPTAIN KIDD IN NEW YORK HARBOR, 1696

IN days when privateering was the custom of the seas, piracy was of frequent occurrence. Long Island and New York became a pirates' nest. The Earl of Bellomont was commissioned governor to purge the colony of this commercial pest. He raised six thousand pounds and appointed William Kidd to drive the pirates from the sea lanes off Madagascar and bring home their booty. Kidd refitted and recruited in New York. The events that followed are blurred by conflicting accounts.

498   From the painting by J. L. G. Ferris, in Independence Hall, Philadelphia

RICHARD COOTE,
EARL OF BELLOMONT, 1636–1701

PERHAPS Kidd did turn pirate when he found his prey had vanished. Perhaps he was carried about unwillingly by an unruly crew. Perhaps he captured, as he had asserted again and again, only French boats which his commission authorized. Upon his return, Bellomont with unbecoming duplicity had him arrested in Boston and sent to England for trial. The evidence against him was feeble, and his own former record had been one of distinguished service. Nevertheless, he was convicted of piracy and murder and was hanged. In legend Kidd has now become one of the most famous and romantic of pirates, but there are many who believe that both trial and rumor were unjust to the adventurous captain.

Bellomont with whose name that of Kidd is forever linked served his colony well. Finding New York a nest of pirates and its politics shot through with corruption, he set out to bring decency into public life. His untimely death in 1701, after a brief rule of three years, brought to an end all his far-reaching schemes for the good of the colony.

499   From a contemporary engraving in Harvard University Library

500   From the painting by Stanley M. Arthurs, in Delaware College, Newark, Del.

DE VRIES CLAIMS THE DELAWARE FOR THE DUTCH

EARLY in the history of New Netherland, the Dutch had established the first settlement on Delaware Bay, building Fort Nassau in 1624 in the present Gloucester County, New Jersey. Then came more Dutchmen, led by David de Vries and two merchants named Godyn and Blommaert. Their colony, called Swannendael, near Lewiston, Pennsylvania, was destroyed by the Indians in 1632. Of this massacre De Vries wrote in his journal at the end of that year: "Found lying here and there the skulls and bones of our people and the heads of the horses and cows which they had brought with them . . . let the gunner fire a shot in order to see if we could find any trace of them the next day."

THE SWEDES ON DELAWARE BAY

IN 1638, Peter Minuit, who had founded New Amsterdam but had subsequently been dismissed from the Dutch employ, came out to the Delaware with a colony of Swedes and Finns. He settled on the site of Wilmington and named it Christinahaven, in honor of the infant queen. This territory he bought from the Minquas Indians, with whom he had at once entered into friendly relations. The artist in his representation of trade between the Swedes and the Indians seems to have copied his Indian battle from Champlain's drawing shown on page 298.

501 From H. T. Campanius, *Kort Beskrifning om Provincien Nya Swerige uti America*, Stockholm, 1702

PETER LINDSTRÖM'S MAP OF NEW SWEDEN

THE territory purchased by Minuit extended westward from the Delaware River between the mouth of the Schuylkill and Bombay Hook. The boundaries of New Sweden were enlarged when a new company was chartered, and the energetic Johan Printz was commissioned, in 1642, as governor. Printz built Fort Elfsborg in Jersey near the mouth of Salem Creek and established New Gothenborg, which he made his capital, near the site of the present Chester, opposite the Dutch Fort Nassau. At the mouth of the Schuylkill he built another fort. Meanwhile a band of English from New Haven had founded a settlement at the present Salem in 1641 and, a little later, built a fort at the mouth of the Schuylkill. In 1651 Stuyvesant sent men to build near New Castle Fort Casimir, which was seized by the Swedes in 1654. The map drawn by the engineer, Peter Lindström, shows the territory as it was when, for a brief year, 1654–55, it was all Swedish, the Dutch having been expelled and the English having failed and withdrawn.

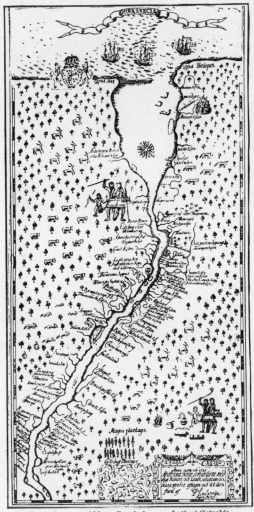

502 From the map of Nova Svecia in . . . *Lutheri Catechismus*, Stockholm, 1696, in the New York Public Library

503 From the portrait owned by the Swedish Colonial Society, New York, after a contemporary portrait in Sweden

JOHAN PRINTZ, THIRD GOVERNOR OF NEW SWEDEN

PRINTZ, who arrived as Governor of New Sweden in 1643, was a belligerent cavalryman, an energetic official, and a tactless neighbor. He built two forts on opposite sides of the Delaware River and ordered all ships to strike their colors and await his permission to pass. At this high-handed conduct every Dutch trader fumed.

DAVID DE VRIES

"IF it were *my* ship, I would not lower to these intruders," said David Pieterzoon de Vries, a passenger on the first vessel stopped by Printz's orders in 1643. The captain, more cautious, obeyed the Swedish command. That night De Vries, the strongest man in New Netherland, dined with the strong man of New Sweden. The evening was spent in talk over a jug of Rhenish wine. Such friendly intercourse between Dutchmen and Swedes, together with the growing aggressions of the English against the colonies of both finally led, in 1651, to a temporary alliance. Yet, through it all the Dutch resented the presence of their Swedish neighbors on the south.

504   From De Vries' *Korte Historiael*, 1655, engraving by C. Visscher, 1653

505   From Lindström's plan in H. T. Campanius, *Kort Beskrifning om Provincien Nya Swerige utt America*, Stockholm, 1702

FORT TRINITY

THE Swedes could not brook the Dutch post on Swedish soil. In 1654 they captured Fort Casimir. Lindström strengthened its bulwarks and renamed it Trefalldigheetz Forte — Fort Trinity.

THE FALL OF NEW SWEDEN, 1655

THE Dutch, on their part, considered that the Swedes were infringing on their rights. Twenty years of contest for this disputed region ended when a Dutch fleet forced New Sweden to surrender. Besieged by Stuyvesant and defended by Governor Rising, Fort Christina fell in 1655. Lindström's plan of the siege shows the fort (A) lying on a creek (B) between two swamps (P) and with the town of Christinahaven (C) behind it. The line of cannon at (M) marks the position of the besiegers. Stuyvesant's ships lie at the mouth of the Fishkill.

All the Swedish forts fell to the doughty governor of New Amsterdam. With them passed the power of Sweden in North America. For a few years the Dutch enjoyed the prestige of conquerors.

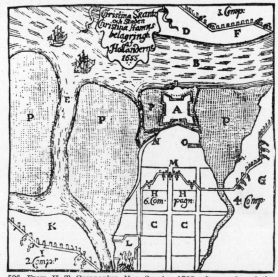

506   From H. T. Campanius, *Nya Swerige*, 1702, after a plan of the siege made by Peter Lindström, engineer of the Swedish colony

507   From the original Lease, June 23, 1664, in the New Jersey Historical Society

THE "LEASE AND RE-LEASE" OF NEW JERSEY

WHILE Nicolls was still crossing the ocean to take New York from the Dutch, the Duke of York was dividing the spoils of the anticipated victory. He assigned the territory of what is now New Jersey to John, Lord Berkeley and Sir George Carteret. The form of conveyance was known as "lease and re-lease." "In the 'lease' for the sum of ten shillings paid to him by the grantees James bargained and sold to them a described tract of land, while the 're-lease' stated that for a competent sum of money he had bargained, sold, re-leased, and confirmed to the grantees certain lands 'in as full and ample manner as the same is granted to the said Duke in the said letters patent,' namely, the grant by Charles II to his brother."—EDWARD CHANNING, *History of The United States*, New York, 1912. With this curious legal transaction began the separate history of New Jersey as an English colony. The authorities at New York were not pleased that jurisdiction over the country across the Hudson river from Manhattan Island should pass out of their hands. An effort was made to continue the control which the Dutch formerly had. But the attempt was unavailing, and the present state of New Jersey is the modern result of the Duke of York's "lease and re-lease."

508   From the original Re-lease, June 24, 1664, in the New Jersey Historical Society

509　　　　From the mural painting by Howard Pyle in the Essex County Court House, Newark, N. J.

THE LANDING OF PHILIP CARTERET IN NEW JERSEY

In 1664, the fall of New Netherland occurred, and the land about the Hudson River and to the west and south of the harbor of New Amsterdam fell into the hands of its new English proprietors. In England Berkeley and Carteret bestirred themselves to secure settlers for their lands. They offered liberal terms, liberty of conscience, an allowance of two hundred acres of land in each parish for the maintenance of a minister that the parish should elect, and an elected assembly which should share with the governor in the management of the province. Philip Carteret, a kinsman of Sir George, was sent out to take charge of the settlements that had been founded in the days of the Dutch, and that were growing as people found the flats of New Jersey more attractive than the hill country of the province of New York. In 1668, Carteret convoked the first assembly at Elizabethtown.

510

511　　　　　　　　　　　　　　　　512
From the mural painting by C. Y. Turner in the Essex County Court House, Newark, N. J.

ARRIVAL OF THE NEW ENGLANDERS AT NEWARK

The Elizabethtown assembly passed a code of laws that were reminiscent of the Biblical code in the Puritan colony of New Haven. In fact, two years before, in 1666, a group of considerable size had come to New Jersey from the New Haven and Connecticut colonies. Some had come from other parts of New England. Carteret had granted them land in the northeast corner of the province. He was glad to have the new settlers, but he disliked the tenacity with which they held to the organization of their Puritan church and to their New England ways. When they sought through the assembly to impress their ideas on the whole province, a struggle ensued which ended in the break-up of the legislative body. In 1672, the colonists took matters into their own hands, chose an assembly of their own and elected as president James Carteret, a son of Sir George, who chanced to be in the colony. When the colony had gotten completely out of hand, Philip Carteret sailed for England to lay his case before the proprietors of New Jersey and the king.

SIR GEORGE CARTERET, *ca.* 1610–80

THE story of New Jersey is a complicated one. The life of the colony was disturbed by the Dutch reconquest of New York which ended in 1674. New Jersey had been divided between Berkeley and Carteret. In 1673 Berkeley sold his half of the province to two Quakers who were finally confirmed in their rights to ownership and jurisdiction. William Penn, in pleading their cause before the Duke of York, became for the first time familiar with the opportunities in America. He pursued his new interest actively.

THE "QUINTIPARTITE DEED"

IN 1676, Sir George Carteret executed a "quintipartite deed." This instrument fixed a line of partition from Little Egg Harbor to a point on the Delaware, in 41° 40′ latitude. The land to the east of this line (East Jersey) was assigned to Philip Carteret. West Jersey went to William Penn and a group of Quakers. The Quakers' title, however, still bore a cloud growing out of the Dutch conquest. In

513   From the portrait by Sir Peter Lely (1618–80), in the possession of the family

1681–82 after several legal complications Penn and a group of Quakers secured possession of all of New Jersey. The province once more came under the control of a single group of proprietors.

514   From the original deed in the New Jersey Historical Society

515   Symbolical Coat-of-arms of New Netherland, detail from the mural painting by Barry Faulkner, in Washington Irving High School, New York

CHAPTER XII

THE QUAKER EXPERIMENT

FOR two generations and probably more, the men of William Penn's family had followed the sea; and part of their legacy to him was that love of freedom, that vigor, and that fearlessness in the presence of sudden peril or foe which are the gift of the sea to its sons. William's grandfather, Giles Penn, a merchant captain of Bristol, had a brush or two with French and Spanish ships and with the pirate fleets of the Levant. His father, William Penn, was a naval captain at twenty-one and became a vice-admiral at twenty-three. He won distinction in the first Dutch war and in the capture of Jamaica from the Spanish. In 1653, as admiral and general under Cromwell, he drew up the first code of tactics for the navy, which was to guide English sea fighters for generations after him. Admiral Penn hoped, by his service at sea, to win an earldom, that he might bequeath it to his son, for he wished to see that handsome lad living the life which he imagined he would have preferred for himself. He took William to sea for a week or so during one engagement so that the boy might prove his manliness under the eyes of the Duke of York. This end accomplished, he sent him swiftly home. In like manner he allowed his son a taste of battle in Ireland, and then refused the youth his choice of a military career. Old William would do the rough work; young William must be the finest puppet in England.

So young William, spurred by his heritage of vigor and courage and love of freedom, went adventuring in the only realm which his father could not close to him — the intellectual and spiritual domain. At Oxford, he took his stand with the liberals against ecclesiastical domination. He listened to the expositions of that remarkable Quaker, Thomas Loe; and in the Quaker concept of brotherhood and simple godliness William Penn found an ideal, and in the persecutions heaped upon a gentle people a battle-ground. He was imprisoned several times in England for his faith. He made a tour through Germany, where he preached the Quaker doctrine at the risk of his life. He found time to embody his ideas in several works on religion and on constitutional liberty. In the streets, and in prison, he proclaimed the rights of Englishmen. His profound study of English law and precedent was later reflected in the "frame of government" which he drew up for his colony and which insured to the colonists more liberty than was enjoyed at that time in England or in any other colony.

His father, who had driven him from home because of his religion, called him to his death-bed. "Let nothing in the world tempt you to wrong your conscience," he whispered; and one of his last acts was to send a message to the King's brother, the Duke of York, begging him, in memory of an old sea-dog's services, to protect William from persecution. He left his son a debt of £16,000 to collect from Charles II. The King had perhaps had a degree of real affection for the admiral, for he proved scrupulous about this debt. But as the King was poor in money and rich only in distant lands, he bestowed upon old Penn's son the region that we know as Pennsylvania.

WILLIAM PENN, FOUNDER OF PENNSYLVANIA, 1644–1718

THIS portrait of a handsome young man of twenty-two, clad in armor, is the familiar one we have of William Penn. It has not been authenticated. It is said to have been painted while Penn was at the Vice-regal court of the Duke of Ormonde in Ireland, where William had his first and only military experience in suppressing a mutiny.

The portrait represents an original likeness painted in oil in 1666 by an unknown artist, possibly Sir Peter Lely. It was, says Justin Winsor, one of two preserved at Stoke Pogis for a long time, and this one was presented in 1833 by Penn's grandson, Granville Penn, to the Historical Society of Pennsylvania.

516 From the portrait, artist unknown, in the Historical Society of Pennsylvania, Philadelphia

517 From the miniature by Sir Peter Lely, in the Historical Society of Pennsylvania, Philadelphia

ADMIRAL SIR WILLIAM PENN, 1621–70

"OLD PENN," as the royal brothers, Charles and James, affectionately dubbed the father of William, was a bold seaman and an efficient commander. He served the Commonwealth of Cromwell though suspected of being in correspondence with the Royalists. He commanded the expedition which captured Jamaica from the Spaniards, although but a few months before he had offered to carry the fleet over to the exiled king. Pepys called him a "mean fellow," and the character has been borne out somewhat by the investigations of later men. Yet he was a man of strength, a good fighter and a man of considerable importance in his day. It was a great sorrow to him to find the son of a British admiral espousing the cause of the despised Quakers who stood for pacificism. Apparently to his dying day he could not understand the mind of his son and he doubtless would have been amazed could he have known that young William's place in history was destined to be greater than his own.

518   From the mural painting by Violet Oakley (1874–), in the Pennsylvania State Capitol, Harrisburg. © Curtis & Cameron

WILLIAM PENN HEARS THOMAS LOE PREACH

WILLIAM, when scarcely seventeen and a student at Oxford, came under the influence of two men who were stirring the young thought of their day — John Locke, the philosopher, and Thomas Loe, the Quaker. Penn heard Loe discourse on the inner light, toleration, unostentatious, silent prayer, brotherly love, and the criminality of war. So deep was the impression the Quaker made that young Penn became a convert. And conversion turned his new life permanently into new channels.

519   From the mural painting by Violet Oakley, in the Pennsylvania State Capitol, Harrisburg. © Curtis & Cameron

PENN'S VISION

WHILE still a student at Oxford, William heard that the Quakers were planning to found colonies on the Delaware in order to escape the persecutions directed against them both in England and in the American colonies already established. The idea fired the freedom-loving imagination of young Penn. Forty years later he wrote, "I had an opening of joy as to these parts in the year 1661 at Oxford."

PENN DRIVEN FROM HOME

OLD PENN, more ambitious for his son than for himself, was mortified and enraged by William's conversion to the Quaker faith. On the advice of his friend, Samuel Pepys, he sent William to the gay French court to cure him. But the cure did not last; and one day, in an ungovernable fury, Old Penn beat his son with a cane and turned him out of his house.

520   From the mural painting by Violet Oakley, in the Pennsylvania State Capitol, Harrisburg.
© Curtis & Cameron

PENN'S ARREST

ON September 1, 1670, Penn was arrested in London for preaching in the street. It was not the first time he had been seized by the King's soldiers and clapped into prison. But, as he wrote, "the Tower was the worst argument in the world to convince me; for whoever was in the wrong, those who used force for religion never could be in the right."

Imprisonment but increased the bonds which held him to the Quakers. With so many others he too had suffered for an ideal.

521   From the mural painting by Violet Oakley, in the Pennsylvania State Capitol, Harrisburg. © Curtis & Cameron.

PENN IN PRISON

PENN spent his months of prison life in writing several works on religion and on constitutional liberty, the most important being *The Great Case of Liberty of Conscience.* This is a noble defense of complete toleration. His trial had far-reaching consequences. Trial by jury had become a farce, for the judges enforced their verdict on the juries. But Penn's spirited defense of himself inspired the jurymen to defy the judge and to assert their rights. The jury acquitted Penn, and the judge thereupon sent the jury to jail. The jury brought suit; the case was unanimously decided in their favor by twelve judges, and the former corruption of the system of trial by jury was at an end.

After Penn's release he made a missionary journey through Holland and Germany. At Emden he founded a Quaker society. Some of these Germans were later to aid him in the upbuilding of his great commonwealth in Pennsylvania.

522   From the mural painting by Violet Oakley, in the Pennsylvania State Capitol, Harrisburg. © Curtis & Cameron.

LETTER OF WILLIAM PENN TO HIS CHILDREN

THE character of William Penn stands forth in a letter to his children which has come down to posterity: "My dear Springer. Be good, learn to fear God, avoide evil, love thy book, be kind to thy Brother and Sister & God will bless thee & I will exceedingly love thee. Farewell dear child, Thy Dear Father. Wm. Penn. My love to all our Family & to Friends. 19th 6 mo. '82."

This is the passage addressed to his son Springer, on the brief page written to his three children.

CHARLES II, 1630–85

CHARLES II had borrowed freely from Old Penn's purse to outfit the navy. This debt at least, he felt, must be honored. Therefore, he made repayment, somewhat tardily, to Old Penn's son with a tract of land in America and, at the same time, gave the new colony its name, Penn's Woods, Latinized into Pennsylvania, in honor, not of William, but of Old Penn of the open purse.

523   From the original in the Historical Society of Pennsylvania, Philadelphia

524   From the portrait by M. C. Beale (1632–97), in the National Portrait Gallery, London

PENN'S "FRAME OF GOVERNMENT"

PENN drew up his constitution in 1681, in England, in consultation with Algernon Sydney and other noted English liberals. How modern was the mind of the great Quaker is seen in certain other ideas first formulated by him, such as that capital punishment should be inflicted only for murder and treason, and that all prisons should be places of work and reformation, instead of dungeons of horror. He touched upon the fundamentals of constitutional government when he said: "Liberty without obedience is confusion, and obedience without liberty is slavery."

The FRAME of the

GOVERNMENT

OF THE

Province of Pennsilvania

IN

AMERICA:

Together with certain

LAWS

Agreed upon in England

BY THE

GOVERNOUR

AND

Divers FREE-MEN of the aforesaid

PROVINCE.

To be further Explained and Confirmed there by the firſt *Provincial Council* and *General Aſſembly* that ſhall be held, if they ſee meet.

Printed in the Year MDCLXXXII.

525   From the copy in the Historical Society of Pennsylvania, Philadelphia

WILLIAM PENN'S SHIP *THE WELCOME*

PENN, along with other Quakers, had traveled among the Germans of the Rhineland, where a sect like their own was springing up.

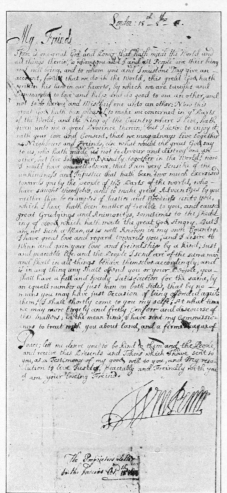

527 From a copy in the Historical Society of Pennsylvania, Philadelphia

526 From the model by J. L. G. Ferris, in Independence Hall, Philadelphia

When the great leader received his grant of land, pamphlets distributed in England and Germany urged the oppressed to emigrate to this refuge in the New World. On August 30, 1682, Penn sailed from England in *The Welcome*, with a hundred colonists aboard. Six weeks later the ship's company, mourning thirty who had died of smallpox at sea, looked out upon the autumnal splendor of the banks of the Delaware as, for three days, they made their way slowly upstream to their final anchorage.

WILLIAM PENN'S LETTER TO THE INDIANS, 1681

FROM London, on October 18, 1681, Penn wrote a letter to be presented by his commissioners to the "King or Kings of the Indians in Pennsylvania." It begins: "My Freinds: There is one great God and Power that hath made the World and all things therein, to whom you and I and all People owe their being and well being, and to whom you and I must one Day give an account, . . .; this great God hath written his law in our hearts, by which we are taught and Commanded to love and help and do good to one another, and not to do harme and Mischeif one unto another."

SUPPOSED MEETING–HOUSE OF FRIENDS IN UPLAND (CHESTER)

UPLAND had been settled by the Swedes in 1645, and it was the seat of the Swedish courts till 1682, when Penn entered it as proprietor of Pennsylvania and changed its name to Chester. Here met the first Assembly of the new colony; and here, in the winter of 1682, or the spring of 1683, Penn's "Great Law" was voted upon and adopted.

The Great Law contained sixty-nine sections and embodied Penn's Frame of Government and the English laws adapted to it.

528 From Sherman Day, *Historical Collections of the State of Pennsylvania*, Philadelphia, 1843

THE LANDING OF WILLIAM PENN, OCTOBER, 1682

"OH how sweet is the quiet of these parts!" Penn exclaimed, moved by the beauty and peace of the autumn woods. He wrote home glowing accounts of the meadows, the forests, the rivers, and the bird life, of his new domain. One new law he made immediately: for every five acres cleared, one acre must remain forested. During this winter, shipload after shipload of eager families came out to the rich bottom lands of the Delaware. Fortunately, the sufferings and privations of Virginia and New England were not repeated in Pennsylvania, and from the very beginning this colony was a success.

529   From the painting by J. L. G. Ferris (1863–), in Independence Hall, Philadelphia

530   From the painting by C. W. Jefferys, in possession of the publishers

PENN IN TREATY WITH THE INDIANS, 1683

"HAVING consulted and resolved their business, the King ordered one of them to speak to me. He stood up, came to me, and in the name of the King saluted me, then took me by the hand. . . . I have never seen more natural sagacity, considering them without the help (I was going to say the spoil) of tradition; and he will deserve the name of wise who outwits them in any treaty about a thing they understand. . . . We have agreed that in all differences between us, six of each side shall end the matter. Do not abuse them but *let them have justice and you win them*." — WILLIAM PENN.

THE PENN TREATY BELT

THIS belt, symbolizing faith and friendship unbreakable, is believed to have been presented to William Penn by the Leni-Lenape chiefs under an elm tree in 1683. There is no documentary proof of the existence of this treaty. Penn visited the Indians, lived with them, formed a high opinion of their good-will and integrity, purchased land from them by several treaties, and made promises to them which he kept.

Like the Pilgrims, the Quakers kept faith with the natives, and enjoyed peace for over fifty years. Such records are rare in the annals of English colonization in America. For the most part contact between the races led sooner or later to deadly conflict.

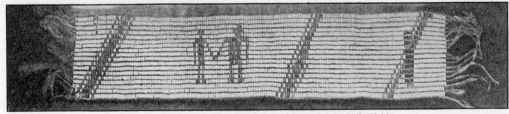

531   From the original in the Historical Society of Pennsylvania, Philadelphia

AN EARLY PENNSYLVANIA HOME

COLONISTS came to Pennsylvania more rapidly than houses could be built. Little habitations half-sunk in the hillsides served as temporary quarters for the people while farms were being laid out, crops prepared, and houses erected. Pastorius, the advance agent of the German Mennonites, was among those who began their New World career in such a humble setting.

532 From the drawing by Howard Pyle for Woodrow Wilson, *History of the American People.* © Harper & Bros.

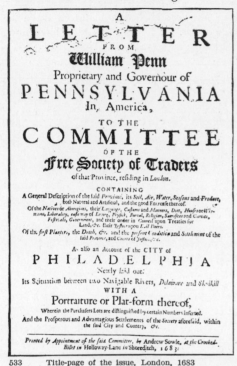

533 Title-page of the issue, London, 1683

PENN'S PAMPHLET ON PENNSYLVANIA

THIS is a sample of the advertisements of Pennsylvania that were distributed in England. Reading them on long winter evenings, quiet, industrious, well-to-do Quaker families discussed the advantages offered by the new colony, and reached the momentous decision to emigrate.

HOLME'S MAP OF PHILADELPHIA

"PHILADELPHIA; the expectation of those who are concerned in this province." Thus Penn described his city, and in his enthusiasm he added: "This I will say for the good providence of God, that of all the many places I have seen in the world, I remember not one better seated. . . . The situation is a neck of land, and lieth between two navigable rivers, Delaware and Schulkill, whereby it hath two fronts upon the water. . . . Delaware is a glorious river; but the Schulkill, being a hundred miles boatable above the falls . . . is like to be a great part of the settlement of this age."

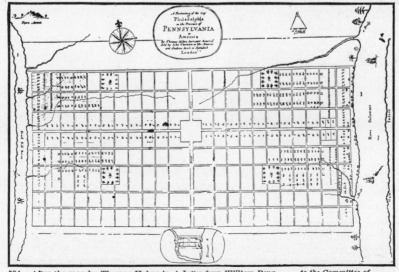

534 After the map by Thomas Holme in *A Letter from William Penn . . . to the Committee of the Free Society of Traders*, London, 1683. In the New York Public Library

MEMORIAL TO THE FOUNDER OF GERMANTOWN

THE Quaker following in Germany was large. The immediate success of the "Holy Experiment" held out hope to German Protestants suffering from intolerable persecutions and economically ruined by the Thirty Years' War. Germantown was founded in October, 1685, by Germans who had followed their agent, Franz Daniel Pastorius, to America. These new colonists were of many sects and from all classes. They were so industrious that Pastorius could write of them a few years later: "Our German society have in this place now established a lucrative trade in woollen and linen goods . . . besides this they have now purchased and hold over 30,000 acres of land."

536   From John F. Watson, *Annals of Philadelphia*, 1830

535 From the Pastorius memorial by Albert Jaegers (1868–) at Germantown, Pa.

THE SLATE ROOF HOUSE, 1700

PENN made his second visit to his colony in 1699. During his short stay he divided his time between his "slate roof house" in the city and the fine estate which he had previously laid out for himself on the Delaware.

537   From the contemporary painting by Peter Cooper in the Hall of the Library Company of Philadelphia

PHILADELPHIA IN 1718–20

BEFORE Penn arrived, his agents had laid out Philadelphia according to his design. "Be sure," said he, "to settle the figure of the town so as that the streets hereafter may be uniform down to the water from the country bounds," and, he added, "let every house be placed, if the person pleases, in the middle of its plot, so as to the breadth-way of it, that so there may be ground on each side for gardens, or orchards, or fields, that it may be a green town which will never be burnt and always wholesome." So rapid was the growth of Philadelphia that it soon became more than a country town and developed quickly into the chief commercial city of colonial America.

538   From *Views in Philadelphia*, published by C. G. Childs, 1830, engraving after a drawing by Hugh Reinagle

FRIENDS' MEETING–HOUSE, MERION

DURING the first fifteen years, the Welsh led in numbers all other immigrants. Most of them were Quakers; the others were Baptists and Anglicans. Forty thousand acres west of Philadelphia were assigned to them, and in this region the well-known names of St. Davids, Berwyn, Haverford, and Merion are present evidence of their vigor and industry.

539   From *The London Magazine*, October, 1761, after a sketch by George Heap, first published in 1754

PHILADELPHIA IN 1754

QUAKERS from England and Wales, Presbyterians chiefly from Ulster, and Protestants of all sects from Germany, flocked to Pennsylvania, where all creeds were tolerated. Within the first year eighty houses were built in Philadelphia, and three hundred farms were laid out round the town. Brick could be made and stone could be cut in the neighborhood; and thus Philadelphia rose chiefly a brick city, with houses on London models. In 1750 Philadelphia had a population of about 20,000, and Pennsylvania contained 150,000 inhabitants.

CHAPTER XIII

THE PLANTING OF MARYLAND

WITH the colonization of Maryland, in 1634, a new form of government, known as the proprietary system, was introduced into America. In 1632 Charles I granted a large territory lying north of Virginia to George Calvert, Lord Baltimore. Calvert desired to open in the new world a refuge for Roman Catholics, men of his own faith who — like the Puritans — suffered at home from interference with the free exercise of their religion. The new province was named Maryland in honor of Charles' Catholic queen, Henrietta Maria. As Lord Proprietor, Baltimore had various powers: to enact laws, — which, however, must agree with the laws of England and be approved by a majority of the freemen of the province; to create courts and to exercise the right of pardon; to make ordinances, provided that these did not deprive men of life, limb or property; to make manorial grants with feudal powers to the manor lords; to collect taxes, to found churches, and to appoint ministers.

From Gravesend in 1633 the *Ark* and the *Dove* set sail, bearing two Calverts "with very near twenty gentlemen of very good fashion," most of whom were Catholics, and about "three hundred laboring men well provided in all things," who were chiefly Protestants. At the Isle of Wight they took on two Jesuit Fathers, named White and Altham. By Baltimore's instructions the ships were to take the long West Indian route and avoid the Virginian coast, for Virginia was already heartily protesting against the Proprietor's patent. The voyagers should reach the mouth of the Potomac early in March, if no ill befell them on the way.

The spirit in which Lord Baltimore planted this first Catholic colony on American soil is exemplified in the rule of conduct which he gave to his Catholic colonists, a rule the wisdom and rightness of which have not grown old with time, nor have been limited in application to the behavior of one sect.

"His Lordship required his said Governor and Commissioners that in their voyage to Maryland they be very careful to preserve unity and peace amongst all the passengers on ship-board, and that they suffer no scandal nor offence to be given to any of the Protestants, whereby any just complaint may hereafter be made by them in Virginia or in England, and that, for that end, they cause all acts of Roman Catholic Religion to be done as privately as may be, and that they instruct all the Roman Catholics to be silent upon all occasions of discourse concerning matters of religion: and that the said Governor and Commissioners treat the Protestants with as much mildness and favor as justice will permit. And this to be observed at land as well as at sea." More than toleration, which is at best a negative state of mind, this rule called for the active exercise of that charity which alone neutralizes the bitter in life. It was an ideal worth laying as the moral corner-stone of a new colonial structure.

GEORGE CALVERT, FIRST LORD BALTIMORE, *ca.* 1580–1632

As Secretary of State, George Calvert had been an intimate councilor of King James I, and heartily in accord with the royal policy of friendship with Spain. His services had been rewarded with an Irish peerage in 1625. The next year he declared himself a Roman Catholic. He was a loyal national, a devout religionist, and a man of vision who had been long interested in English expansion. He had joined the Virginia Company in 1609; and from 1620 to 1628 had failed in his attempts to colonize Newfoundland.

540 From the portrait, artist unknown, in the State House, Annapolis, Maryland

541 From an engraving (about 1672) by A. Blooteling (1634–98), in the Maryland Historical Society, Baltimore, after portrait attributed to Sir Peter Lely

CECIL CALVERT, SECOND LORD BALTIMORE, *ca.* 1605–75

GEORGE CALVERT died before the charter for Maryland passed the seals. So the name of his son Cecilius, second Lord Baltimore, was inserted in the document. Opposition from Virginia, however, made it advisable for Baltimore to remain in England to protect his rights, and he therefore appointed his brother Leonard Governor and Lieutenant-General of Maryland.

A RELATION OF MARYLAND, 1635

FOR the benefit of those who might be interested in Maryland, Baltimore issued a pamphlet about the colony. It was read by many a group about Catholic firesides, and led to the seeking of a greater freedom in a new world on the part of those subjected to intolerance at home.

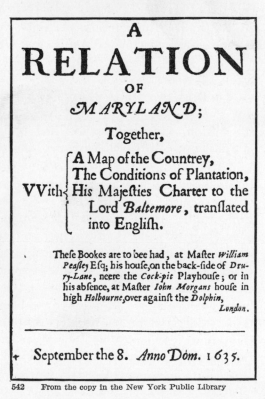

A
RELATION
OF
MARYLAND;

Together,

With { A Map of the Countrey, The Conditions of Plantation, His Majesties Charter to the Lord *Baltemore,* translated into Englith.

These Bookes are to bee had, at Master *William Peasley* Esq; his house, on the back-side of *Drury-Lane,* neere the *Cock-pit* Playhouse; or in his absence, at Master *Iohn Morgans* house in high *Holbourne,* over against the *Dolphin,*
London.

September the 8. *Anno Dom.* 1635.

542 From the copy in the New York Public Library

PLANTING OF THE COLONY OF MARYLAND

FATHER ANDREW WHITE, S.J., writes: "On the day of the annunciation of the Holy Virgin Mary, on the 25th of March in the year 1634, we offered in this island (St. Clement's), for the first time, the sacrifice of the mass; in this region of this world it had never been celebrated before. Sacrifice being ended, having

taken up on our shoulders the great cross which we had hewn from a tree, and going in procession to the place that had been designated, the Governor, Commissioners and other Catholics participating in the ceremony, we erected it as a trophy to Christ the Saviour, while the litany of the holy cross was chaunted humbly on the bended knees, with great emotion of soul." Translation by N. C. Brooks, in Peter Force's *Tracts*, Vol. IV, 1846.

543   From the painting, 1893, by F. B. Mayer (1827–1899) in the State House, Annapolis, Md.

MAP OF MARY-LAND, 1635

THE territory granted to Baltimore included what is now Maryland, as well as Delaware and a part of Pennsylvania. The fortieth parallel from the sea "unto the Meridian of the first fountaine of the River of Patowmeck," was its northern frontier; and to the south its line ran along the Potomac to Watkins Point and across Chesapeake Bay and the eastern peninsula to the ocean. Virginia sharply disputed the location of Watkins Point. The first expedition bestowed various place-names as it proceeded up the river.

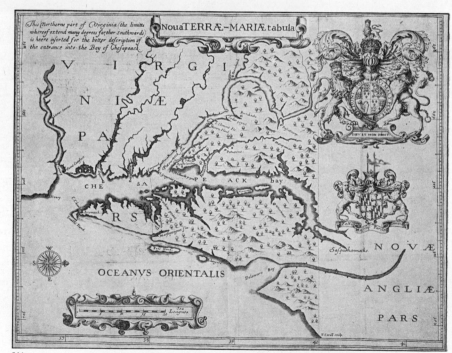

544   From *A Relation of Maryland*, London, 1635; engraved by T. Cecill

The Potomac was called St. Gregory; the islands in the river's mouth were named in order St. Clement's, St. Catharine's, and St. Cecilia's; the first tributary was called the St. George, and it was near its mouth that the site of St. Mary's was chosen.

545   From the mural painting by Edwin H. Blashfield (1848–), in the Court House, Baltimore.   © H. K. T. Company, by
permission of Gramstorff Brothers

A SYMBOLIC REPRESENTATION OF TOLERATION IN MARYLAND

THE Act of Toleration (*A Law of Maryland concerning Religion*) was passed by the Maryland Assembly, at Baltimore's instigation, in 1649, the year in which, at home, Charles I perished on the block, and the Puritan Commonwealth began. Baltimore, seeing how the tide ran, and wishing above all to keep Maryland, appointed William Stone, a Puritan, as governor, and placed three other Puritans in the council, which numbered five. The clause in the Act affecting freedom of conscience reads in part as follows:

"And whereas the inforceing of the conscience in matter of Religion hath frequently fallen out to be of dangerous Consequence, Be it . . . ordeyned and enacted . . . that no person or persons whatsoever within this Province, . . . professing to beleive in Jesus Christ, shall from henceforth bee any waies troubled, molested or discountenanced for or in respect of his or her religion."

546   From the copy of the "Toleration Act" in the New York
Public Library

WILLIAM CLAIBORNE, ca. 1589–1676

WILLIAM CLAIBORNE, on March 24, 1625, was commissioned by Charles I, as a member of the Virginia Council "and to be our secretary of State for the said colony and plantation of Virginia." In 1631 Charles granted him a patent, authorizing him to make discoveries. Claiborne discovered, partially planted, and settled the Isle of Kent before Baltimore's charter was drawn up; and his settlement was already represented in Virginia's House of Burgesses when Leonard Calvert arrived and claimed the Isle of Kent under his charter. The dispute that arose was not settled until 1660, when Baltimore's influence with Charles II prevailed and Claiborne was turned out as a "rebel."

547 From a portrait by Miss M. Gilmer in the
Virginia State Library, Richmond. After photograph of unauthenticated original in London

CHARLES CALVERT, THIRD LORD BALTIMORE,
1629–1714

IN 1675 Cecil Calvert died, and his son Charles succeeded him. Charles had a troubled reign in Maryland. He protested against the Pennsylvania grant which gave to William Penn the mouth of the Delaware. The religious and political strife in England, which led to the expulsion of James II, and the advent of William and Mary, was reflected in Maryland. In 1691 Lord Baltimore's governmental rights passed to the Crown, though his revenue from quit-rents and customs remained to him. His son, Benedict, became a member of the Church of England, and in 1720 his grandson Charles, fifth Lord Baltimore, resumed the government of Maryland under the Crown.

548   From an aquatint in the Maryland Historical Society, Baltimore

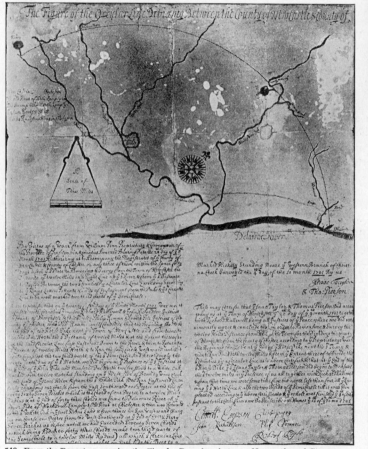

549   From the Report on running the Circular Boundary between Newcastle and Chester Counties, 1701, in the Historical Society of Pennsylvania, Philadelphia

550   From copy of an engraved map in Benjamin Franklin, *Articles of Agreement*. . . . Philadelphia, 1733

LORD BALTIMORE'S MAP, 1732

THE MASON AND DIXON LINE

THE dispute which arose between William Penn and Lord Baltimore about the borders of their colonies continued after the death of both parties. On May 10, 1732, an agreement was executed between the children of Penn and the great-grandson of the first Lord Baltimore, stipulating for a line due west from Cape Henlopen across the peninsula, from the center of which another line should be drawn tangent to a circle twelve miles from Newcastle, while a meridian from the tangent point should be continued to within fifteen miles from Philadelphia, whence should be traced the parallel of latitude westward that was to divide the provinces. Should the meridian cut a segment from the circle, the segment was to be part of Newcastle County. Attached to this agreement was a small map known as "Lord Baltimore's map." This parallel of latitude is the Mason and Dixon line which has become famous in history.

PHILIP JONES LAYING OUT BALTIMORE TOWN, 1730

THE Maryland provincial legislature long continued the practice of directing places to be laid out as towns, often in locations where there was little to justify a village. In 1729 this body directed seven commissioners to buy sixty acres of land on the north side of the Patapsco and lay it out in sixty equal lots as the town of Baltimore. Three years later the same body ordered the laying out of Jones-Town on the opposite site of Jones's Falls. In 1745 the two villages were consolidated. When the Revolution broke out, Baltimore

551 From *Harper's Weekly*, Oct. 23, 1880; original drawing by F. B. Mayer, in the City Library, Baltimore

was one of the chief cities of Maryland.

BALTIMORE IN 1752

THE houses and church of early Baltimore, the dock with the ship lying in the cove, the laden cart, the men on horseback and the tobacco field were all part of a life not essentially different from that of Virginia. Like the Old Dominion, Maryland raised tobacco on broad plantations. Wheat was a crop more common north than south of the Potomac, and the Maryland planters found its culture profitable.

Baltimore was the product of

552 Aquatint from a sketch, 1752, by John Moale, corrected by Daniel Bowley, "from his personal recollection," in the Maryland Historical Society, Baltimore

the eighteenth century. It was not laid out until nearly a hundred years had elapsed after the founding of St. Mary's. In 1752 there were only twenty-five houses and two hundred inhabitants in Baltimore.

But the farm lands of the interior, settled chiefly by Germans, were now productive, and the sea, the one highway to market, like a great magnet pulled the products of the land to the water's edge. In 1753 or 1754, a vessel of wheat was loaded for Scotland. In 1754, according to Governor Sharpe, Baltimore had "the Appearance of the most Increasing Town in the Province."

Baltimore was made a county seat in 1767 and a port of entry in 1780. In these years Baltimore passed rapidly from a small village to an important seaport.

553 From a lithograph, 1856, after a reconstruction, "Baltimore in 1752," by J. Backman, in the Maryland Historical Society, Baltimore

554 Courtesy of the Historical Society of
Pennsylvania, Philadelphia

555   From a wood engraving after a sketch, 1879, by W. T. Smedley (1858–)

MASON AND DIXON BOUNDARY STONE

THE Mason and Dixon boundary stones were set up at intervals
to mark the boundary between Pennsylvania and Maryland according
to a survey, finished in 1767 by Charles Mason and Jeremiah Dixon,
surveyors who came from England for the purpose. It was a difficult
and protracted task. They traced the line between the two states to a
point 244 miles west of the Delaware, where the work was halted by
Indians. The uncompleted line was not extended until 1783–84. The
stones were set up, one for each mile, every fifth stone having the
arms of Penn on one side, the arms of Baltimore on the other. Where
stones could not be set up, the line was marked by cairns.

556   The Great Seal of Maryland under the Lords of Baltimore, from the Maryland Historical
Society Fund Publications No. 23 (1886)

CHAPTER XIV

THE CAROLINA PROPRIETORS

WHEN Charles II returned as King of England there were men of power and influence in his realm whose support was needed to make the new monarch secure. Recompense for such support was only just. Hence, in 1663 Charles drew up a charter granting territory covering five degrees of latitude south of Virginia — and stretching westward without limit — to "our right trusty and right well-beloved cousins and counsellors, Edward, Earl of Clarendon, our High Chancellor of England, and George, Duke of Albemarle, Master of our Horse and Captain-General of all our Forces, our right trusty and well-beloved William, Lord Craven, John, Lord Berkeley, our right trusty and well-beloved counsellor, Anthony, Lord Ashley, Chancellor of our Exchequer, Sir George Carteret, Knight and Baronet, Vice-Chamberlain of our Household, and our trusty and well-beloved Sir William Berkeley, Knight, and Sir John Colleton, Knight and Baronet." Thus did the Proprietary of Carolina come into being. The first ships sailed in 1669, and in 1670 Charleston was founded.

The Carolina enterprise was a speculative venture, the aim being to make the Carolinas and the Bahamas centers of trade in semi-tropical products, such as almonds, silk and wine. One charter was granted in 1663 and a second in 1665. The latter was for the purpose of enabling the proprietors to incorporate in their colony settlements in the region of Albemarle Sound. The charter provided for a government under the direction of the proprietors with the assistance of a representative assembly. Religious toleration was also guaranteed.

Before the charters were granted settlement had been begun in what is now North Carolina, territory which Virginia considered to be part of her domain. The Virginia Assembly in 1653 had granted rights on Roanoke and Choan rivers "and the branches thereof" to one Roger Green, who desired to plant a settlement in this wilderness. Huguenots, Quakers, Ulstermen, poor and hardy men of all persuasions, followed Green into North Carolina to grapple anew with the forest. About 1660 a party of New Englanders looked in at Cape Fear river mouth, but soon abandoned the place; and five years later Englishmen from Barbados led by John Yeamans made a temporary settlement in the same region.

To the south of Carolina lay the Spanish settlements in Florida. Both Spain and England claimed the Carolina region. Its occupation became, therefore, a matter of political importance; to forestall the rival Spaniard was a patriotic duty. This argument weighed in the minds of the aristocratic proprietors who, at the same time, felt that the commercial resources of the country would fill their pockets with profit. In this they were doomed to disappointment. But out of their small beginnings grew ultimately two important commonwealths.

EDWARD HYDE, EARL OF CLARENDON,
1609–74

EDWARD HYDE, afterwards first Earl of Clarendon, was the chief adviser of Charles I in the struggle between King and Parliament. He urged the King to stand by the law. Charles, however, could not be restrained from autocratic and unlawful acts. As a result, the Commonwealth put royal power temporarily in eclipse. Clarendon was one of those largely responsible for the restoration of the monarchy in England in 1660 and for the hopeful and loyal spirit in which the people received Charles II. His significance in the history of America lies in the fact that he was one of the leading figures in the group of proprietors who received Carolina from the King.

557   From the portrait of the Earl of Clarendon by Gerard Soest, died 1681, in the National Portrait Gallery, London

GEORGE MONCK, DUKE OF ALBEMARLE, 1608–70

FOR both Cromwell and king, Monck was a loyal commander. He was an able professional soldier faithful to his engagements and was also a sagacious politician. After suppressing a military meeting against the Commonwealth Parliament he countenanced the election of a parliament which restored the monarchy.

558   From the portrait of the Duke of Albemarle by Sir Peter Lely, in the National Portrait Gallery, London

WILLIAM, FIRST EARL OF CRAVEN,
1608–97

CRAVEN'S loyalty to the Stuarts places him among the romantic Cavaliers of that troubled time between the accession of Charles I and the flight of James II. He had little capacity as a statesman, but he had a soldier's courage and he had wealth; hence he was of much assistance to the royal cause. Charles II, who was in debt for large sums, saw a convenient solution of the difficulty by creating Craven an earl and a lord proprietor of Carolina.

559   From the portrait of the first Earl of Craven by Gerard van Honthorst (1590–1656) in the National Portrait Gallery, London

ANTHONY ASHLEY COOPER, FIRST EARL OF SHAFTESBURY, 1621–83

LIKE Monck, Anthony Ashley Cooper was a firm pillar of support to the restored monarchy. As a reward for his services, Charles II made Cooper first Lord Ashley and later Earl of Shaftesbury. The king also designated him a patentee of Carolina. Shaftesbury, with John Locke, took the leading part in the settlement and management of the province.

560   From the portrait by John Greenhill (1649–76), in the National Portrait Gallery, London

561   From the portrait attributed to J. Closterman after Kneller (1648–1723), in the National Portrait Gallery, London

JOHN LOCKE, 1632–1704

A PHILOSOPHER and student of political economy, science, and theology, John Locke admits that "from the time that I knew anything I found myself in a storm." In common with Shaftesbury, he felt a keen interest in the development of the colonies overseas. At the latter's suggestion in 1669 he wrote the *Fundamental Constitutions* for the new Proprietary of Carolina. This document, built upon the theory of a feudal aristocracy, did not prove well adapted to primitive American conditions, however, and in course of time it gave place to a less artificial social and political organization within the colony. The *Constitutions* were not without their significance in Carolina history. They helped to foster the discontent which finally resulted in abolishing the proprietary rule. The feudalism of the *Constitutions* was out of adjustment with the needs of the colony.

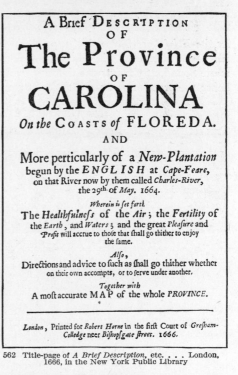

A Brief DESCRIPTION
OF
The Province
OF
CAROLINA
On the COASTS of FLOREDA.
AND

More perticularly of a *New-Plantation* begun by the *ENGLISH* at *Cape-Feare*, on that River now by them called *Charles-River*, the 29th of *May*. 1664.

Wherein is set forth
The *Healthfulness* of the *Air*; the *Fertility* of the *Earth*, and *Waters*; and the great *Pleasure* and *Profit* will accrue to those that shall go thither to enjoy the same.

Also,
Directions and advice to such as shall go thither whether on their own accompts, or to serve under another.

Together with
A most accurate MAP of the whole *PROVINCE*.

London, Printed for *Robert Horne* in the first Court of *Gresham-Colledge* neer *Bishopsgate street*. 1666.

562   Title-page of *A Brief Description*, etc. . . . . London, 1666, in the New York Public Library

"A BRIEF DESCRIPTION OF THE PROVINCE OF CAROLINA"

THE Carolina proprietors at once issued pamphlets extolling the value of the new land, and calling upon colonists to enter and enjoy the good things which Nature had provided. In 1666 there was published in London this *Brief Description*, in which were set forth the fertility of the country and its healthfulness.

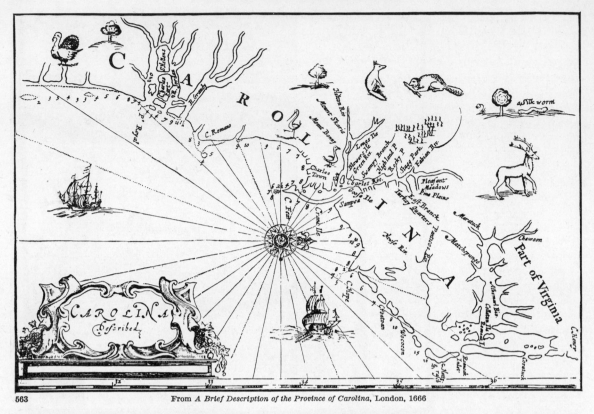

563   From *A Brief Description of the Province of Carolina*, London, 1666

THE EARLIEST MAP OF CAROLINA

In the *Brief Description* this map sets forth not only the coast line but the characteristics of the country. Already settlers from Virginia had overflowed into Carolina and had begun to build their cabins along Albemarle Sound, at the extreme right of the map. These newcomers were a mixture of good and bad elements; hence the proprietors sought to direct emigrants to a region farther south.

THE WARRANT TO MOVE TO THE NEW SITE, 1672

The settlers who came over in 1670 built the first Charles Town on the west bank of Ashley River. The site proved unsuitable for a settlement, consequently in 1672 Governor John Yeamans and the Council issued a warrant to John Culpepper, Surveyor General, to remove to the tongue of land between the two rivers—a much cooler and much more healthful situation. In 1680 the public offices of the colony were ordered transferred to the new town, and the old settlement was abandoned.

564   Facsimile of the original warrant, courtesy of A. S. Salley, Jr., Columbia, S. C.

PLAN OF CHARLESTON, 1704

"THE TOWN," wrote Thomas Ashe in 1682, "is regularly laid out into large and capacious streets. In it they have reserved places for Building of a Church, Townhouse, and other publick structures, an artillery ground for the exercise of their militia and wharves for the convenience of their trade and shipping."

Colonists came fast to Carolina. Barbados sent some and England, Scotland and Ireland contributed a share. French Huguenots came and a certain number of Germans.

In 1704 Charleston had five churches and numerous fine residences, such as that of Colonel William Rhett, facing his private wharf (17) on Cooper River.

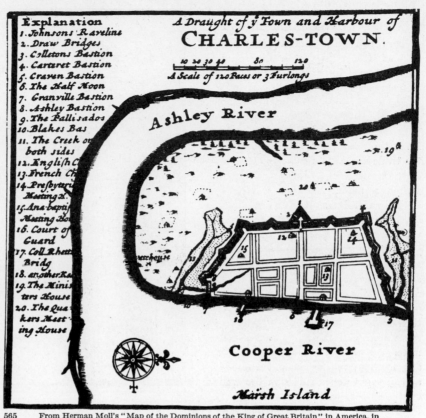

Explanation
1. Johnsons Raveline
2. Draw Bridges
3. Colletons Bastion
4. Carteret Bastion
5. Craven Bastion
6. The Half Moon
7. Granville Bastion
8. Ashley Bastion
9. The Pallisados
10. Blakes Bas
11. The Creek on both sides
12. English C
13. French Ch
14. Presbyteri Meeting H
15. Ana baptis Meeting Ho
16. Court of Guard
17. Coll Rhett Bridg
18. another Ra
19. The Minis ters House
20. The Qua kers Meet ing House

A Draught of ye Town and Harbour of
CHARLES-TOWN.
A Scale of 120 Paces or 3 Furlongs

Ashley River

Cooper River

Marsh Island

565   From Herman Moll's "Map of the Dominions of the King of Great Britain" in America, in
The World Described (1709–20)

566 From Captain Charles Johnson, *A General History of the Lives and Adventures
of the Most Famous Highwaymen, Murderers, Street-Robbers, Etc.*, London, 1736

BLACKBEARD, THE PIRATE

FAR from England and near the rich treasures of the Caribbean Sea, the sheltered coast of Carolina provided for many years a haven for the pirates. Of these marauders the most notorious was Captain Teach, commonly called Blackbeard, a figure fit to ship with the rogues of *Treasure Island*.

A contemporary thus describes him: "His beard was of an extravagant length, as to breadth it came up to his eyes. He was accustomed to twist it with ribbons, and turn them about his ears. In time of action he wore a sling over his shoulders, with three brace of pistols hanging in holsters, like bandoliers, and stuck lighted matches under his hat which, appearing on each side of his face — his eyes naturally looking fierce and wild — made him altogether such a figure that imagination cannot form an idea of a fury from Hell to look more frightful."

COLONEL WILLIAM RHETT

A DASHING Cavalier and a gallant soldier, Colonel Rhett first won his spurs on American soil by driving the French out of Charleston harbor. A few years later he made successful war upon the pirates who infested the Carolina coast; and in 1718 he captured the ferocious Stede Bonnet of Barbados, the worst terror of the trade route from these islands. Thus early in the history of this colony appeared a name that was to be heard again in Carolina. Rhett's activities are symbolic of a state of affairs that developed in the Carolinas in the early years of the eighteenth century. Defense against the Indians of the back country and the pirates of the coast became the responsibility of the settlers. The proprietors showed more and more plainly their inability to meet the situation, and the initiative in Carolina affairs passed more and more to the people who actually lived in the region and whose lives and fortunes depended upon the welfare of the settlement.

567   From the miniature by Fraser (about 1840) after an original pastel portrait by Henrietta Johnson, about 1710, both in the Gibbes Art Gallery, Charleston, S. C.

"A PERTICULER MAP FOR THE GOING INTO ASHLEY AND COOPER RIVERS"

THIS map shows the old and the new sites of Charleston and the adjacent plantations at about 1700. Edward Randolph, the King's Surveyor General of Customs, writes that "the great improvement made

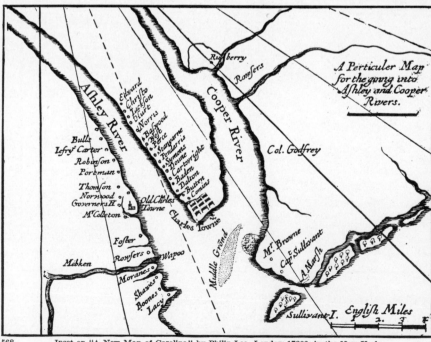

in this Province is wholly owing to the industry and labor of the Inhabitants. They have applied themselves to make such commodities . . . as Cotton, Wool, Ginger, Indigo, etc. . . . they are set upon making pitch, Tar & Turpentine, and planting rice . . . having about 50,000 Slaves to be employed in that service."

An act of Parliament in 1729 brought proprietary government to an end and set up royal governments in both North and South Carolina.

568   Inset on "A New Map of Carolina" by Philip Lea, London, 1700?, in the New York Public Library

569

From the line engraving by W. H. Toms, after a drawing by B. Roberts, published at London, 1739

CHARLESTON, 1739

In 1742 Eliza Lucas, an English girl who owned a large estate in South Carolina — and who afterward married Chief Justice Charles Pinckney and became the mother of Charles Cotesworth and Thomas Pinckney — wrote a description of the colony. "Charles Town the Metropolis is a neat pretty place, the inhabitants polite and live [in] a very genteel manner; the streets and houses regularly built; and ladies and gentlemen gay in their dress." Though the population was dominantly English, there were French Huguenots, Scotch, and Scotch Irish among them, and many who had come from Barbados.

No. 1

Persons Names to whom granted	Number of Acres	In what County Parish or Township or on what River or Creek Situated	Date of the Grant	Quitrents reserved thereon if any.	
Lady Margaret Yeamans	1070	on Yeaman's Creek	9th Febry 1674		
Anthony Earl of Shaftsbury	12000	on Ashley River	13th March 1675		
Joseph Pendarvis	137		1st Jany 1675.		
Mathew English & John Morgan	140	on Wandoe River			
John Smyth	1300	on Ashley River	25th Novemr 1675		
Stephen Bull	400	on Do	20th October 1676		
William Jones	210	on Stawan Island	20th Jany 1676		
Maurice Mathews	402	on Ashley River	28th April 1676		
John Boone	200		20th Febry 1676		
Sr Peter Colleton Bart & Thos Colleton Esqr	373	near Do	20th Sepr 1677		
Edward Mathews	570	on Cooper River	15th April 1676		
Robert Donne	150	near Charles Town	5th August 1676		

570

From *Colonial Office Papers, Class 5, No. 398*, in the Public Record Office, London

LAND GRANTS AND GRANTEES IN SOUTH CAROLINA, 1674–76

THE list of land grants from 1674, beginning with that to Lady Margaret Yeamans, wife of the first Governor, Sir John Yeamans, who founded the first English settlement, extends to October 31, 1765, by which date more than 11,000 names appear on the list.

CHAPTER XV

THE VISION OF OGLETHORPE

THE Proprietors of Carolina, alive to the menace of Spanish Florida, in 1717 arranged with Sir Robert Mountgomery, a patriotic Briton, to colonize the region we now call Georgia. The new province was to be called the Margravate of Azilia, and the Margrave must colonize it within three years or lose his rights. But Mountgomery failed to allure colonists, and Azilia never gained greater reality than its projected outlines on a map. In 1729 the Proprietors sold their rights to the Crown, and the two Carolinas became royal colonies. Still the southland between Carolina and Florida remained unoccupied — waiting the forceful claimant, be he English or Spanish.

James Edward Oglethorpe, distinguished soldier, patriot, and humanitarian, took up the issue for England. He formed a company of some twenty associates, obtained a charter from George II, in whose honor he named his province, and in 1732 sailed in the little ship *Anna*, with his first group of settlers. He founded Georgia as an asylum for the oppressed, and here poor Protestants from the continent were offered homes and freedom. Debtors and other unfortunates lying in English prisons were set free through his influence and were allowed to start life anew in Georgia. Parliament made several grants of money towards this noble scheme, and wealthy philanthropists contributed handsomely. From Europe came persecuted Salzburgers and Moravians. Jews came, and Highlanders, and Italians to teach silk culture. In February, 1733, the first cabins of Savannah rose on Yamacraw Bluff.

571 Oglethorpe Memorial at Savannah, Ga., from the sculpture by D. C. French (1850–)

MAP OF THE MARGRAVATE OF AZILIA

LIKE all good promoters, Mountgomery issued a luring "Discourse concerning the designed establishment of a new colony" (with a map of it as he saw it in his mind's eye), to — "so dispose the Habitations, and Divisions of the Land, that not alone our Houses, but whatever we possess, will be enclos'd by *Military Lines*, impregnable against the *Savages*, and which will make our whole Plantation one continued Fortress." The colonists, however, did not come, and Azilia ceased to exist elsewhere than on paper.

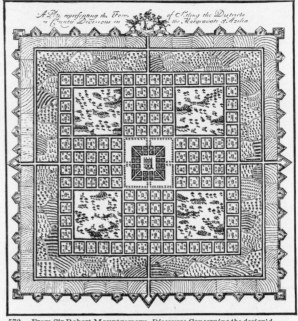

572   From Sir Robert Mountgomery, *Discourse Concerning the design'd Establishment of a New Colony to the South of Carolina*, London, 1717

573 From John Chaloner Smith, *British Mezzotinto Portraits*, London, 1884, from the portrait by Simon F. Ravenet (1706-74), engraved by Burford

JAMES EDWARD OGLETHORPE, 1696-1785

THE portrait shows Oglethorpe in the fire of his youth. The stretch of years between youth and age was lived chiefly for the good of humanity. At eighteen, he was fighting with Prince Eugene against the Turks, and a year later, on Marlborough's recommendation, he was made the Prince's aide-de-camp, and as such he served during the siege and capture of Belgrade. In 1722 he became member of Parliament for Haslemere and began to devote his energies to the relief of those unfortunates on whom the drastic English laws bore too heavily. It was out of these philanthropic efforts that the colony of Georgia was born.

OGLETHORPE WITH A COMMITTEE AT THE FLEET PRISON, 1729

OGLETHORPE with a committee of Parliament revealed shocking evils in prison conditions. Oglethorpe advised a new settlement in America where imprisoned debtors and other unfortunates might start life again, and at his request George II severed from Carolina the debatable ground between that colony and Spanish Florida. Oglethorpe was one of the trustees who should supervise the new colony for twenty-one years and then turn it over to the Crown. So Georgia was founded for the relief of human suffering.

574 From Lionel Cust, *The National Portrait Gallery*, London, 1901-02, after the painting, 1729, by William Hogarth

EARLIEST MAP OF GEORGIA, 1733

THE Altamaha River, the southern boundary of Georgia, was only a hundred miles north of St. Augustine; and a hundred miles was beginning to be a shorter journey than it had once been to the men of the New World. It was not far for ships to sail. Almost inevitably English ships from Georgia would look in on St. Augustine, or Spanish ships would take a nearer view of Oglethorpe's colonists.

575   From Benjamin Martyn, *Reasons for Establishing the Colony of Georgia*, London, 1733

576   From Benjamin Martyn, *Reasons for Establishing the Colony of Georgia*, London, 1733, engraving by T. Pine

EARLY VIEW OF COLONISTS' BUILDING, 1733

THE "town of Savannah" in the distance is based upon Mountgomery's plan of Azilia. The artist has in imagination anticipated the building of Savannah, which took no such checkerboard shape when at last it rose on Yamacraw Bluff.

"A VIEW OF SAVANAH 29TH MARCH, 1734"

THIS is dedicated by Peter Gordon, who drew the design, to the "Trustees for establishing the Colony of Georgia in America." A key accompanying the original indicates the location of the crane and bell to draw up goods from boats, General Oglethorpe's tent near the landing, the "pallisadoes" at the extreme left; a blockhouse in the far background; the parsonage house, the public mill, the house for strangers, the public oven, the draw wells, the "lott" for the church, the public stores, the guardhouse and battery of cannon at the left front.

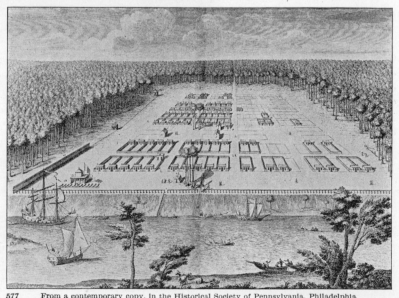

577   From a contemporary copy, in the Historical Society of Pennsylvania, Philadelphia

TOMO CHACHI MICO

THIS Indian was the principal Sachem of the district. He was an honest and friendly man who recognized in Oglethorpe a kindly spirit. Tomo extended respect and good-will to Oglethorpe's colonists; and young Georgia had no Indian wars. Tomo visited England in Oglethorpe's company and was made much of as a noble prince — which, indeed, he was.

578   From a contemporary engraving by John Faber after the painting by William Verelst in the British Museum

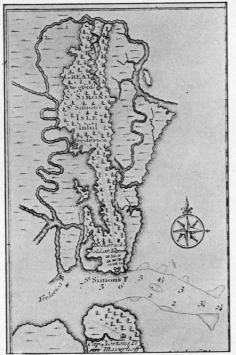

579 From *Urlsperger Tracts*, in the John Carter Brown Library, Providence, R. I.

FREDERICA, ON ST. SIMON'S ISLE

OGLETHORPE returned to Georgia in 1735 with Tomo and two shiploads of colonists, largely Highlanders — good fighting men for a new colony. On St. Simon's Island the new arrivals built Frederica. While stout houses were in building, the colonists lived in "Palmetto Bowers" which, being "in regular Rows looked very pretty, the Palmetto Leaves lying smooth and handsome, and of a good Colour."

Frederica was designed to be the British outpost nearest New Spain, and Oglethorpe was carrying out his instructions to make Georgia a fortified buffer state and to hold debatable land for England.

THE DEPARTURE OF THE SALZBURGERS FOR GEORGIA, 1732

IN the meantime in Central Europe, from the town gates in the Alpine province of Salzburg, from the narrow mountain valleys, from the homes of their ancestors, from the little farms and gardens so dear to the German heart, brave and persecuted men and women were emerging with little more than their faith, their families, and their cherished Bibles, to make their way to ports where they might take ship overseas to the Georgian wilderness.

580   After an engraving by David Ulrick Bocklin (1686–1748) in *The Salzburger Collection of Tracts*, 1732.   In New York Public Library

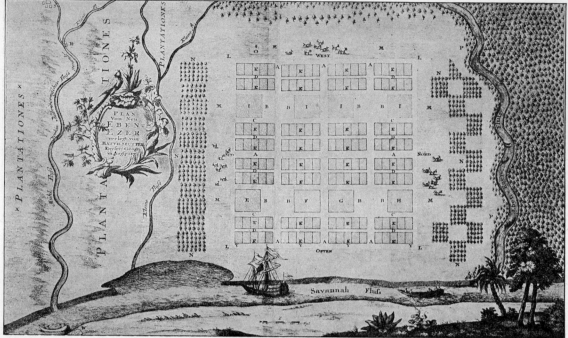

581   From a large folding plan in *Urlsperger Tracts*, in the John Carter Brown Library, Providence, R. I.

THE SETTLEMENT OF EBENEZER, 1734

IN 1734 Baron von Reck and two Lutheran pastors brought over 78 Salzburgers. More came afterward. One of the pastors tells of the reception given them by Oglethorpe and his other colonists. Cannon and huzzahs welcomed them; "a very good dinner was prepared for us"; the English clergyman took the pastors to lodge with him; in the morning a Jew fed all the Salzburgers a breakfast of rice soup; they were allowed to use the English church, and all the Jews attended their services for the delight of hearing again the German tongue. Twenty-one miles above Savannah they founded Ebenezer, saying with the prophet, "Hitherto hath the Lord helped us." In later years, however, the settlement unfortunately died out.

WAR WITH SPANISH FLORIDA

IN 1739 England and Spain went to war. Oglethorpe led an expedition against Florida, captured the Spanish outposts, but failed to take St. Augustine. The Spanish retaliated by an attack on St. Simon's Island, but they were beaten off. In 1740, Oglethorpe again descended on Florida and drove the Spaniards within their defenses at St. Augustine. The anxious Spaniards watched the English ships from their ramparts. But Oglethorpe withdrew because his forces were not sufficient for a successful attack on the city.

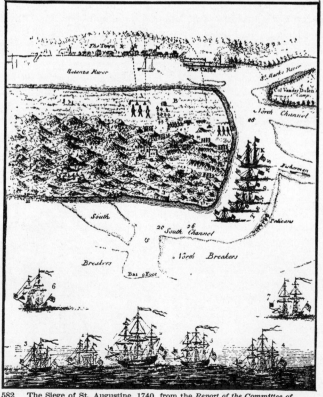

582   The Siege of St. Augustine, 1740, from the *Report of the Committee of both Houses of Assembly* . . . Charles Town, 1742

583   Ruins of Oglethorpe's Barracks at Frederica, by courtesy of the Southern Railway

SETTLEMENT OF THE BORDER DISPUTE BETWEEN ENGLAND AND SPAIN

IN 1742 the Spaniards landed troops before Frederica in a bold effort to take the English stronghold. Over a difficult terrain which at one place along the edge of a marsh required the attackers to advance in single file, the Spanish troops pushed forward to within two miles of the fort. Oglethorpe rushed to check the assault and defeated the invaders. The Spanish commander hurried up reinforcements to cover the retreat of his troops. They were ambushed by Oglethorpe's men and routed. So ended the fighting. But not until the close of the Seven Years' War was the border dispute between Spain and England settled.

"The treaty of Paris [in 1763, by which Florida was ceded by Spain to England] ended the long contest between England and Spain over the debatable land of Georgia. But it served also to revive an old quarrel between Georgia and Carolina. Before the treaty was ratified the governor of South Carolina proceeded to grant to Carolinians large tracts of land south of the Altamaha. Governor Wright [of Georgia] protested. Suddenly he had become a good Spaniard. Carolina's claim to the area on the ground of the grant to 29° was ridiculous, he said. . . . The home government took the Spanish view of the question — it was safe to do so now — and denied Carolina's claim. . . .

"Our story now soon ends. Two Gulf provinces, East and West Florida, were organized from England's new acquisitions. East Florida was delimited on the north by the St. Mary's River, and a line thence to the forks of the Apalachicola. The strip between the St. Mary's and the Altamaha was added to Georgia. It was no longer Debatable Land."— BOLTON AND ROSS, *The Debatable Land*, 1925.

584   Oglethorpe in the last year of his life, at the sale of Dr. Johnson's library. After the etching by Samuel Ireland, 1785

CHAPTER XVI

PIRATES AND PLANTERS OF THE WEST INDIES

BRITISH colonial schemes were not confined to the continent of North America. As the seventeenth century opened, it seemed as though the eyes of western Europe were fixed on the West Indies. Through the Caribbean Sea passed the silver galleons of Spain and no one knew what wealth might be concealed in the ring of islands that fringed it. The Spanish stronghold was at Española, although the power of Spain had waned since the defeat of the Armada. English, Dutch and French slipped in under the lee of the Spanish base and buccaneering grew enormously.

Piracy had long made perilous the route of the Spanish treasure fleet through the sheltered Bahama channel. As English, Dutch and French strengthened their grip on the continental seaboard, opening ports where ships could be built and overhauled and where markets were provided, piracy increased. Where formerly a sea captain would have good hunting if he cut out a straggling galleon, now a doughty pirate might have a fleet of ten or twenty stout fighting ships under his command. His need, therefore, was for neighborly harbors and convenient supply stations. Logically, the Indies provided them.

In the middle of the seventeenth century, the heyday of piracy, the buccaneers numbered several thousand. They came from all ranks of life. Some of the hauls they made were staggering; one of the greatest was that of the Dutchman, Piet Heyn, who descended at Matanzas harbor with thirty-one sails and captured the Vera Cruz fleet with its cargo worth fifteen million dollars. In such an atmosphere the tiny colonies on some of the islands were founded.

But the British had a way of testing out the soil of the islands they visited. Jamestown was still young when British plantations appeared on Barbados and St. Kitts. Tobacco and sub-tropical products were raised at first but when, about 1640, sugar was introduced, the prosperity of buccaneering took second place to that of agriculture. Barbados rapidly became the colony in which, of all her brood, the mother country was most interested. Rich Barbados with its great plantations, its large population of whites and its larger population of slaves became a center of interest for commercial England.

As the seventeenth century grew old buccaneering waned, but sugar planting grew in importance. Her colonies in the West Indies became a corner-stone of Britain's growing commercial empire. If necessary, how much better could she afford to lose any one of the continental colonies than her sugar plantations which were found on islands from Jamaica around the arc of the Antilles almost to South America.

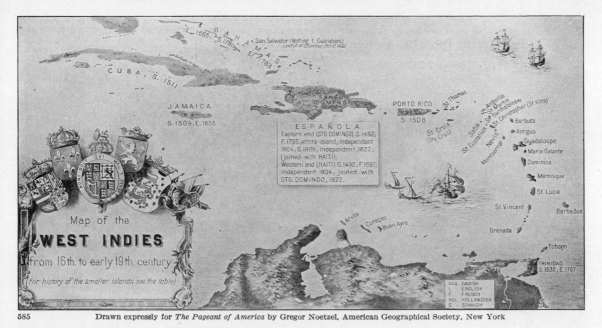

585   Drawn expressly for *The Pageant of America* by Gregor Noetzel, American Geographical Society, New York

The West Indies outline a rude arc of submerged mountain tops enclosing the Caribbean Sea and the Gulf of Mexico. They are divided into the Bahamas, the Greater Antilles — comprising Cuba, Jamaica, Haiti and Porto Rico — and the Lesser Antilles, including the Windward and Leeward Islands. By the end of the seventeenth century five nations had planted their flags in the Indies — Spain, England, France, Holland, and Denmark. The West Indies were under foreign control, as follows:

Anguilla, E. 1650; Antigua, E. 1632, F. 1666, E. 1667; Barbados, E. 1624–26; Barbuda, E. 1661–62; Buen Ayre, Curaçao and Aruba, Hol. 1634, E. 1798, Hol. 1802, E. 1807, Hol. 1814; Dominica, F. 1632, Neut. 1748, E. 1761, F. 1778, E. 1783; Grenada, F. 1650, E. 1762, F. 1779, E. 1783; Guadeloupe, F. 1635, E. 1759, F. 1763, E. 1794, F. 1802, E. 1810, S. 1810, F. 1814; Española, Eastern End (Santo Domingo) S. 1492, F. 1795 (French gained control of the whole island), Independent 1804, S. 1806, Ind. 1822 (joined with Haiti). Western End (Haiti) S. 1492, F. 1697, Ind. 1804 (1822 joined with Santo Domingo); Marie Galante, F. 1647–48; Martinique, F. 1635, E. 1762, F. 1763, E. 1794, F. 1800; Montserrat, E. 1632, F. 1664, E. 1667, F. 1782, E. 1783; Nevis, E. 1628, F. 1782, E. 1783; Saba, Hol. 1640; St. Bartholomew, F. 1648, Sw. 1784, F. 1877; St. Christopher, E. 1623, F. 1625 (divided between E. and F. 1628), E. 1666 (full control), 1667 (divided control), E. 1690 (full control), 1697 (divided control), E. 1702, F. 1782, E. 1783; St. Croix, E. and Hol. 1643, S. 1650, F. 1650, Dan. 1733, E. 1807, Dan. 1814; St. Eustatius, Hol. 1635; St. Lucia, F. 1650 (1666–1748 no settlement), 1748 declared neutral, E. 1762, F. 1763, E. 1778, F. 1783, E. 1803; St. Martin, Hol. and F. 1648; St. Thomas, Hol. 1657, E. 1667, Dan. 1671, E. 1807, Dan. 1815; St. Vincent, Neutral 1660, E. but no settlement 1668, Neutral 1748, E. 1762, F. 1779, E. 1783; Tobago, E. 1641, Hol. 1654 (South Coast), Dutch in full control 1658–1662, occupied alternately by English, French and Dutch 1662–1748, declared neutral 1748, E. 1762, F. 1781, E. 1793, F. 1802, E. 1803; Trinidad, S. 1532, E. 1797.

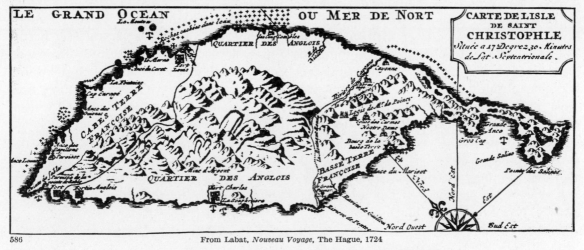

586   From Labat, *Nouveau Voyage*, The Hague, 1724

ST. KITTS IN THE EIGHTEENTH CENTURY

St. Kitts, or St. Christopher, was discovered by Columbus in 1493. It remained unoccupied till 1623, when the English landed and two years later set up a permanent settlement. The French settled to the west of them. In 1628 they made a peaceable division of the island, but in 1783 France ceded her part to England. On Nevis, the first island on the south, Alexander Hamilton was born in 1757.

THE ISLAND OF ST. LUCIA AMONG "LES ISLES CARIBES"

COLUMBUS is thought to have discovered St. Lucia in 1502. It is one of the southern islands of the archipelago. Englishmen attempted to settle it in 1605 and again in 1638, but on both occasions were driven off by the Caribs. The French planted a colony in 1650 but the English refused to acquiesce to their occupation and a long struggle for possession ensued. At the Peace of Paris, 1763, the island was assigned to France but, during the American War of Independence, it was captured by the British and used as a naval base. From St. Lucia Admiral Rodney sailed to his victory over the Comte de Grasse in 1782. At the end of the war the island was restored to the French, who held it until 1803, when it finally went to the British.

587   Detail (retouched) from Nicolas de Fer, *L'Atlas curieux*, Paris, 1703

PORT OF SPAIN, TRINIDAD

DISCOVERED by Columbus in 1496, Trinidad remained in the hands of Spain until 1797, when it was surrendered to a British fleet sailing from Martinique. Its first capital, San José de Oruna, was burned by Sir Walter Raleigh in 1595. Trinidad is very rich in asphalt, oil, timber and tropical agricultural products. Its capital, Port of Spain, is one of the finest towns in the West Indies.

588   From W. S. Andrews, *Illustrations of the West Indies*, London, ca. 1860

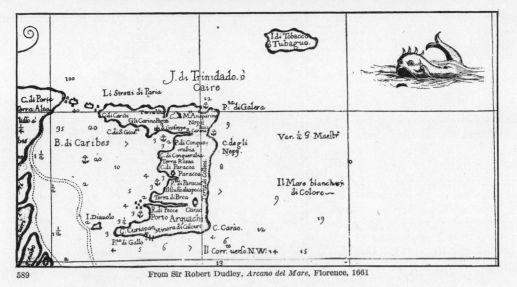

589

From Sir Robert Dudley, *Arcano del Mare*, Florence, 1661

MAP OF TRINIDAD, 1661

590

From *The European Magazine*, London, 1782

PORT ROYAL AND KINGSTON, JAMAICA

COLUMBUS called this island, discovered by him on May 3, 1494, Santiago. The Indian name was Jaymaca, "the island of springs." In 1523 the town of Sant' Iago de la Vega — the capital until 1872 — was founded. Twice, in 1596 and 1635, the British raided and plundered the island. After Spain surrendered it, Jamaica became the chief headquarters of the buccaneers.

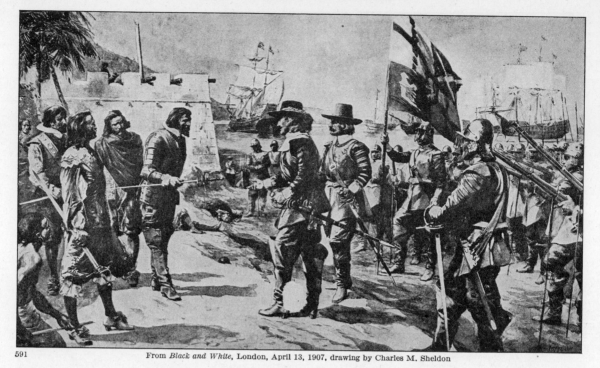

591   From *Black and White*, London, April 13, 1907, drawing by Charles M. Sheldon

SURRENDER OF JAMAICA TO ADMIRAL PENN

CROMWELL, who not only saw the value of England's overseas possessions, but foresaw hazard for them unless the power of Spain were broken, waged war with a mighty hand. An important incident among the results of his policy is pictured here. Admiral William Penn went ashore from the flagship *Swiftsure* on May 9, 1655, to receive the sword tendered him in surrender by the Spanish commander.

SIR HENRY MORGAN, THE PIRATE, *ca.* 1635–88

THE true story of this Welsh buccaneer outdoes fiction. Said to have been kidnapped in Bristol, sold in Barbados, Henry Morgan grew up in the harshest environment his times afforded, that of plantation slave-life. When about twenty he escaped to Jamaica, which Admiral Penn had just wrested from Spain. As Captain Morgan his name appears immediately on the records of English attacks on the Spanish islands. But the moral limits hedging an officer of the regular navy or army were not to his mind. By a series of daring and savage exploits he so won the hearts of the several thousand buccaneers in the islands that they made him their "Admiral." With ten ships and five hundred men in 1668 he took the Spanish city Puerto Principe and the stronghold of Porto Bello, evacuating the Isthmus only after the Governor of Panama had paid a heavy ransom.

Three years later, having meanwhile ravaged Cuba and sacked Maracaibo and Gibraltar, he returned to the Isthmus, ascended the Chagres River and took Panama. Haled to England to answer for his conduct, he won Charles' favor, was knighted and made lieutenant-governor of Jamaica. He used his position to assist and protect the buecaneers; and spent much of his time in mad carousals with them.

592   From Exquemelin, *De Amertcaensche Zee-Roovers*, Amsterdam, 1678

From Richard Ligon, *A True & Exact History of the Island of Barbados*, London, 1657

BARBADOS

Most important of the English colonies in the West Indies in the seventeenth and eighteenth centuries was Barbados, the easternmost of the Lesser Antilles. In 1605, an English ship found it uninhabited and took possession in the name of James I. Twenty years later a settlement was made. Since then the island has never passed out of British control.

ENGLISH PLANTERS IN BARBADOS

Sugar, introduced into the island in the middle of the seventeenth century, became its staple product and the foundation of its prosperity. Its inhabitants were drawn from all classes of the English people. At the time of the Civil War, when Cromwell overthrew the King's supporters, many Royalists fled to Barbados and took up plantations. By 1684 the population had grown to number twenty thousand whites and forty-six thousand slaves.

594   From Carolus Allard, *Orbis Habitabilis*, Amsterdam, ca. 1690

595   From an engraving by J. Kip (1653–1722) in the British Museum, after a sketch, 1695, by Samuel Copen

BRIDGETOWN, THE CAPITAL OF BARBADOS, IN 1695

BARBADOS was rich, the most important of England's sub-tropical colonies. The shiploads of sugar which its planters sent to the homeland helped to make England independent of the foreign supply. Seventeenth-and eighteenth-century Barbados was a cornerstone of the old British Empire.

596   From the painting by Frederick J. Waugh (1861–). © Detroit Publishing Co.

THE BUCCANEERS

THE members of a pirate ship entered into an agreement with one another when the voyage began. Agreement to commit Piracy, June 30, 1683: "Articles of Agreement between us abord of the *Camillion*, Nich. Clough Comander, that wee are to dispose of all the goods thatt are abord amongst us, every man are to have his full due and right share only the Commander is to have two shares and a half a share for the Ship and home the Captain please to take for the Master under him is to have a share and a half. Now Gentlemen these are to satisfy you, as for the Doctor a Share and half, and these are our Articles that wee do all stand to.as well as on and all."

597   View in border of Nicolas de Fer's map of America, 1705, in the Library of Congress

BUCCANEERS DIVIDING THE SPOILS

No better account of a pirate raid can be found than one published by Dr. J. F. Jameson in *Privateering and Piracy in the Colonial Period*, 1923. The anonymous chronicler tells of an unsuccessful fight in a river near Panama between a flotilla of buccaneers and the defenders: "Wee went into a river by the Assistance of a Pilott. capt. Sawlkings went ashore with about 45 men. the barkque went in as far as she could and came to an Anchor. they went up the River and landed Just against some Stockadoes. . . .

"Our Valliant Gen'll capt. Salkins landed him-self first and went into the Savana and saw aboundance of Peopple their. one Molatta mett him, whome capt Sawlkins Shott downe. Returnes back a little way, askt if the Party wear all landed and ready. Answer was made, 'Yes.' then said he, 'follow me and doe not lye behind, for if I doe amise You will all fair the worse for itt.' Hee went up corragiously with some brisk men with him, butt their was provided Mollattas and hunters with their launces which came to oppose him. He fierd his Pistole and shott downe one Musteese, the rest fiering and lodeing as fast as they could, but the Spaniards coming in uppon them so fast that kill'd capt. Sawlkins and 3 men more. thay tooke one alive. wee heard him make a dreadfull noyse butt could not rescque him, butt was forst to retreate to our cannoes, and goe off as fast as wee could, thay comeing downe so fast uppon us.

"Wee found in this River 2 barkques: one we burnt, the other wee brought out which was laden with pitch, She seemeing likely to sayle well. our peopple went aborde againe of capt. cooke, which lay with his barkque att the Rivers mouth, telling us that capt. Sawlkins was killd with 3 men more, to our greate sorrow. wee saild out with the barkque to the Key wheir the greate Shipp lay, about 5 leagues from this River, to the Southwards. when the parties came to know that capt. Sawlkins was kild and that thay could discover him to be our Admirall by the ring he had on his finger, a Present from the Governour of Pennamau, He sending him this token and with all to meete him on shoare with a hundred men to try their manhoods against one hundred of them. Capt. Sawlkins returns this answer, that in case he would bring out one hundred thousand pieces of Eight he would meete him, with one hundred men against his, to fight him for the money or Elce resolved to die in that Place." . . .

598

From the painting by J. L. G. Ferris, in Independence Hall, Philadelphia

THE DEATH OF BLACKBEARD

CAPTAIN TEACH, known as Blackbeard, was one of the most famous of the pirates. In 1716 he captured a large French merchantman. He christened her *Queen Anne's Revenge* and converted her into a warship armed with some forty guns. From the coast of Virginia to the Caribbean sea Blackbeard was known for his robberies. Daring and intelligent, Teach made himself a scourge of the Spanish Main. His winter quarters were on the shore of North Carolina where barrier beaches protect the bays and harbors.

For two years Blackbeard's piracies continued; then the governor of Virginia sent two sloops manned from the Royal Navy to destroy his pirate's nest. Lieutenant Maynard commanded the attacking forces. He boarded Teach's sloop. There was a hard fight. Blackbeard died in action, shot by Maynard himself. Not so fortunate were some of his contemporaries. Captain John Quelch, captured in piracy, was convicted and executed in Boston on June 30, 1704. An observer narrates the scene after he had mounted the scaffold: "The last Words he spake to One of the Ministers at his going up the Stage, were, 'I am not afraid of Death, I am not afraid of the Gallows, but I am afraid of what follows; I am afraid of a Great God, and a Judgment to Come.' But he afterwards seem'd to brave it out too much against that fear: also when on the Stage first he pulled off his Hat, and bowed to the Spectators, and not Concerned, nor behaving himself so much like a Dying man as some would have done. The Ministers had, in the Way to his Execution, much desired him to Glorify God at his Death, by bearing a due Testimony against the Sins that had ruined him, and for the ways of Religion which he had much neglected: yet now being called upon to speak what he had to say, it was but thus much; 'Gentlemen, 'Tis but little I have to speak; What I have to say is this, I desire to be informed for what I am here. I am Condemned only upon Circumstances. I forgive all the World: So the Lord be Merciful to my Soul.' When Lambert was Warning the Spectators to beware of Bad Company, Quelch joyning, 'They should also take care how they brought Money into New-England, to be Hanged for it.'"

CHAPTER XVII

NEW FRANCE

NEW FRANCE is a tragedy, complete in five acts.

(1534–1535) First, that eager explorer, Jacques Cartier, discovers the St. Lawrence, climbs what he calls "le mont royal," views from these heights of Montreal what is now a part of the United States; and then, returning to Quebec, the natural stronghold of New France, erects a scutcheoned cross to show that Church and State claimed lordship in this wild new virgin land.

(1608–1635) But two generations pass away before New France is really founded by the undauntable Champlain, who is forced by many an adverse circumstance to leave her still struggling for mere existence when he dies.

(1663–1713) The third act opens in a blaze of glory; for Louis Quatorze, "Roi Soleil" and "Grand Monarque," takes a personal interest in what he decides to make his Royal Province of New France. He sends a viceroy; also the famous veterans of Carignan; also the great Intendant, Talon, to supervise the settlers, who soon arrive in much larger numbers than before. His loyal subjects in New France extend his influence over the three great gulfs of St. Lawrence, Mexico, and Hudson Bay, along the two great rivers of the St. Lawrence and the Mississippi, and round the five Great Lakes. But even this third act closes under the double shadow of a France exhausted in Europe and driven from most of her footholds in maritime America.

(1713–1753) Old France and New are in partial eclipse under specious Louis Quinze; and neglected New France falls into a decline which eventually makes her the easy prey of her own corrupt officials.

(1753–1763) The fifth act begins with Washington's march to the Ohio and ends with the treaty which gave New France to Britain. (Volume VI, *The Winning of Freedom.*)

Why was New France a tragic failure? Because, for all her great heroic deeds, she lacked sea-power, man-power, government, and freedom.

British sea-power, both mercantile and naval, mastered her in peace as well as war. British oversea man-power was recruited by constant streams of settlers, against which her own one freshet had no chance whatever, even though it has multiplied far more than a hundred times in far less than three hundred years. Then, France had an autocratic government; but never any autocrat who could really govern on the spot: hence discord, division, and defeat. Finally, she had no adaptive freedom, like that which her English-speaking rivals enjoyed as colonials or won by independence later on.

599 From a tablet erected by the Historic
Sites and Monuments Board of Canada

SECTION I

THE FIRST EXPLORER OF NEW FRANCE

THE whole vast Gulf and River of St. Lawrence take their world-famous name from the odd fact that the pious explorer Jacques Cartier happened to be wind-bound in quite an unimportant little bay on the North Shore, opposite the island of Anticosti, on St. Lawrence's Day, the 10th of August, 1535. How the name that Cartier gave this anchorage was changed to Pillage Bay in after years, and how it was itself extended not only over all the gulf and river but likewise over the innumerable ranges of the oldest hills on earth, is too long and too conjectural a story for more than the merest mention here.

Our pictures naturally deal with 1535, the year of Cartier's greatest voyage, when he discovered Quebec, named Montreal, and, from this summit, gazed beyond the line that now divides the United States from Canada. But as he circumnavigated the gulf in 1534 and came out for the third time in 1541, these first and third adventurings should have at least a word in passing. During his first voyage to "the new country called *la nouvelle France*" he set up a Cross at Lobster Bay, on the Canadian Labrador, just inside the Straits of Belle Isle, and claimed the country for his king; though he found it "dry and half dead" and thought it must have been the land reserved for Cain. Making south he found Bird Rocks so thick with gannets and great auks that he could have loaded thirty boats with them within a single hour. Brion Island had "beasts as big as oxen, tusked like elephants, and living in the sea"; but it also had "peas as fine as those in Brittany, currants, strawberries, roses, grapes, sweet flowers, and sweet grass." On the New Brunswick coast he traded with Micmacs, who, to get a few trinkets, gave all their furs and other clothing, "so that they had to go naked." Luckily for them it was such a hot summer that Cartier called the neighboring arm of the sea *le Golfe de la Chaleur*. In Gaspé Bay he erected a Cross thirty feet high and bearing the loyal inscription LONG LIVE THE KING OF FRANCE! Then, in mid-August, he sailed home to St. Malo.

His third voyage in 1541 was an utter failure. He went out to found a colony for Roberval, whom Francis I had made Viceroy of a very nebulous New France. As all but one of the Indians whom Cartier had taken home five years before had died in France their friends at Quebec were naturally hostile. After a miserable winter at Cap Rouge, a few miles above Quebec, he sailed in search of Roberval, whom he met in Newfoundland. He then went home, while Roberval went on to an even worse winter at Cap Rouge. As the jails had provided most of the colonists, Roberval had a good deal of flogging, hanging, and shooting to do before returning home with the survivors in 1543.

JACQUES CARTIER, 1491–1557

ON an April day in 1534 the people of the French coast village of St. Malo saw two ships manned by some sixty-one men and commanded by their townsman Jacques Cartier put out to sea and turn westward. Many a fisherman from St. Malo knew the route across the Atlantic. For years now the French fishing boats as well as some from England and Portugal had been crossing the ocean to the Newfoundland banks to spend the summer catching and curing cod. But Cartier was not bound on a fishing expedition. His orders were to seek out that northwest passage to the Orient which, so thought the best geographers of the day, existed somewhere in America. He must have been a good commander; and we know, from an entry concerning a baptismal party, that he was a "jolly good fellow" too; *Jacques Cartier et autres bons biberons.* He was forty-four at the time of his famous second voyage; and splendidly fit in body and mind. How fit he was as a hydrographer any modern sailor can see for himself today by comparing the notes made in 1535 with the latest edition of the *St. Lawrence Pilot.* Jacques Cartier will not lose much by comparison in any case.

600   From the portrait by F. Ryss, 1839, in the Town Hall at St. Malo, France

601   From a photograph supplied by J. M. Clarke, State Museum, Albany

THE CARTIER MEDALLION

THE wooden medallion of Jacques Cartier, dated 1704, is a large circular shield about 20 inches in diameter which was originally nailed to the stern of the ship, *Jacques Cartier*, out of St. Malo. This ship, probably an old square-sterned schooner, is thought to have gone down in a storm in Gaspé Bay, for on these shores the shield was picked up by a fisherman whose descendants finally used the souvenir as a window-stop and sealed it up in the walls of their house. The house was torn down in 1909 and this portrait, thought to be the earliest extant representation of Cartier, was again brought to light. A full account of the discovery of the medallion is given in J. M. Clarke's *The Heart of Gaspé.*

JACQUES CARTIER'S
VOYAGES TO CANADA

——— 1st., Gulf of St. Lawrence , 1534
– – – 2nd., to Hochelaga (Montreal),1535-36
········· 3rd., to beyond Hochelaga, 1541-42

602   Drawn expressly for *The Pageant of America* by Gregor Noetzel, American Geographical Society, New York

JACQUES CARTIER'S THREE VOYAGES, 1534–42

THE first voyage took Cartier past the bluff western shore of Newfoundland. He made a circuit of the great estuary, the Gulf of St. Lawrence, catching sight of the broad river which entered it from the west. The next year he came out to determine whether this river was not in truth the passage to the Orient, sailed up it as far as the present site of Montreal and proved that the northwest passage did not lie there. When, in 1541, Cartier was again sent by the French King, it was to participate in a colonizing rather than an exploring enterprise. Yet Cartier did not miss the opportunity to make his way above Hochelaga for further study of the great river which he had been the first to enter.

CARTIER ERECTS A CROSS IN 1534

"ON Friday the 24th of July, 1534, we had a cross made, thirty feet high, which was put together in the presence of a number of Indians on the point at the entrance to this harbor." [That is, on what is called the Peninsula, opposite Sandy Beach Point, at the entrance to Gaspé Harbor, Province of Quebec, Canada,

just south of latitude 49° and west of longitude 64°, on the western side of the Gulf of St. Lawrence.] "Under the cross-bar we fixed a shield with three fleurs-de-lis in relief, and above this a wooden inscription, engraved in large Gothic characters: LONG LIVE THE KING OF FRANCE! When the cross had been raised we all knelt down, with our hands joined, worshipping it before the Indians. We then made signs to them, looking up and pointing to Heaven, to show them that it was by means of the Cross that we had gained our redemption. The Indians displayed many signs of admiration, constantly turning and gazing at the Cross." — Translated from the new *variorum* edition of Jacques Cartier's

603   From a crayon drawing by George Agnew Reid (1860–), in the Dominion Archives, Ottawa   works, H. P. Biggar, editor.

JACQUES CARTIER'S FLOTILLA, 1535

Grande Hermine, one hundred twenty-six tons, *Petite Hermine*, sixty, *Emerillon*, forty. Total crews, one hundred twelve. Cartier was both the first and last ancient seaman to sail the whole of the Lower St. Lawrence. Up to his time sails were mere windbags and the art of tacking was unknown. Therefore no progress could be made except with winds abaft the beam. In 1539, when Fletcher of Rye, shipwright to Henry VIII, tacked well to windward, with sails trimmed fore and aft, the

604   From an engraving after the painting by Gudin (1802–80), in the Hotel de Ville, St. Malo, France

modern sailing age was beginning to evolve. It made a change in transportation which, for its own time, was almost as great as that which steam made later on.

605   From the painting by C. W. Jefferys, in possession of the publishers

CARTIER AT HOCHELAGA (MONTREAL), 1535

TOUCHING, now here, now there, Cartier worked his way along the shores of the Gulf of St. Lawrence and up the mighty river of this name. He stopped at the Indian village of Stadacona, between the rock of Quebec and the river St. Charles, where he was well received by Donnacona, the Chief of Canada, a name then confined to the district of Quebec. Beaching two of his ships he pushed on upstream in the smallest to the Indian village of Hochelaga, where Montreal now stands. A thousand or more Indians — men, women, and children, — received the forty Frenchmen with songs and dances and endless shouts of welcome. They brought their chief and all their sick or maimed to be healed by the mere touch of Cartier's magic hand. But, true to his faith, Cartier opened his Testament and, in clear and solemn tones, read to the awestruck savages the opening verses of the Gospel of St. John: *In principio erat Verbum, et Verbum erat apud Deum et Deus erat Verbum.* "In the beginning was the Word, and the Word was with God, and the Word was God."

CARTIER FIRST TO SEE THE UNITED STATES FROM CANADA, OCTOBER, 1535

FROM his "Royal Mount" of Montreal, on a still, autumnal afternoon, Jacques Cartier gazed with rapture from where he "had view for more than thirty leagues all round" of mountains, north and south, and "between the southern hills, of country which is the loveliest that a man could see." No wonder; for he saw that wide magnificence of hill and plain, brightened by the long sheen of the St. Lawrence, just when the forest was aglow, as if a sunset glory shone the livelong day within the crimson of the maple leaves. But there was a terrible winter at Stadacona, whither Cartier returned. The Indians became hostile and scurvy broke out. One third of Cartier's little band died, the first Frenchmen to mingle their dust with the soil of Canada. In May, the party was glad to sail for home, leaving their cross of annexation: FRANCISCUS PRIMUS DEI GRATIA FRANCORUM REX REGNAT.

606   Drawn expressly for *The Pageant of America* by C. W. Jefferys

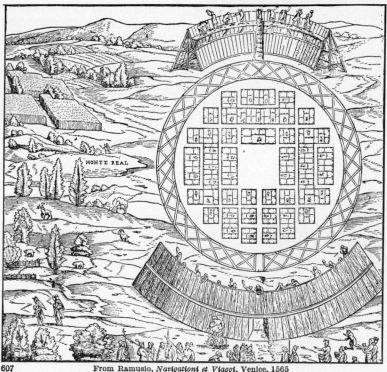

607   From Ramusio, *Navigationi et Viaggi*, Venice, 1565

RAMUSIO'S PLAN OF HOCHELAGA (MONTREAL)

BY the time a traveler's tales had been worked up by a draughtsman for a wonder-loving public the original evidence was apt to get perverted. Nevertheless Ramusio's plan agrees fairly well with Jacques Cartier's own description (1535). Hochelaga, says Cartier, was strongly fortified with three palisades, which had platforms from which the garrison could hurl stones on attackers. The houses were "finely and cunningly built": each of the fifty was about fifty paces long by twelve wide. There were splendid crops of corn all round. (Ramusio's sketch is criticized in *Transactions of the Royal Society of Canada* for 1925.)

SECTION II

THE FOUNDERS OF NEW FRANCE, 1600–1663

FOR a hundred and fifty years — from Jacques Cartier to La Salle — the greatly expanding area claimed by the French was thought to contain the shortest sea route to all the Indies and Cathay. But meanwhile the mines the Spaniards found in plenty farther south had set men searching for others in the north; and the lure of this northern Eldorado lasted as long as New France.

Failing the ready riches of the East, and failing any minable riches within its own domain, New France always relied upon fur. Fur was the next best thing to silver, gold, and jewels, because it was easily transported, found a ready market, and yielded enormous profits, owing to the ease with which the Indians could be cheated out of even the best pelts for the cheapest gewgaws, especially when plied with liquor first. Of course the English, Dutch, and other whites also cheated and debauched the Indians just as freely as the French did, besides being far less friendly, as a rule. And of course, in justice to the whites, it ought to be remembered that Indians valued gewgaws almost as much as whites valued furs. But the seamy side remains.

After treasure, trade; and after trade — and a long way after trade — came the founding of the real colony which resulted in *La Nouvelle France* of the old régime and the French-Canadians of the new. It is the peculiar glory of Champlain that he never, to his dying day, lost sight of settlement as the only firm foundation on which to build New France. His means were pitifully small, and the struggle for mere existence was intensely hard. But nearly all the settlers of this earliest time were Normans, akin, at least in part, to that magnificent race which changed the so-called "Anglo-Saxon" iron into steel and won the strenuous leadership in other lands, all over seaboard Europe.

The search for treasure, the business of trade, and the inrooting work of real settlement, all required the intervention of the State. But the insistent call of home affairs prevented the far-off, feeble voice of New France from being effectively heard at court (except, for once, by Richelieu) till this dire period closed. Yet in the very midst of it the Church won by far the greatest of all her glories in New France.

608 Canadian on Snowshoes,
from de la Potherie, *Histoire
de l'Amérique Septentrionale*,
Paris, 1722

TADOUSAC: FIRST ATTEMPT AT A TRADING–POST IN NEW FRANCE, 1600

At Tadousac, half way between the Gulf of St. Lawrence and the site of Quebec, the French planted their first trading-post in 1600. Pierre Chauvin of Honfleur was given the monopoly of the Laurentian fur trade for ten years on condition that he took out fifty colonists each year. But like most exploiters, he cared a great deal for the fur trade and little for colonization.

The numbers show depths in fathoms. Most of the letters explain themselves, especially when referring to natural features. F, however, deserves particular mention as "The Point of all the Devils," which it certainly is if you drag your anchor down-hill in the Bay (B) and fetch up on the Devil's own rocks. D is where the Indians camped; C where Chauvin landed his sixteen wretched "colonists." In three years Chauvin lost his monopoly because he failed in the vital matter of colonization. The honor of founding New France passed to another.

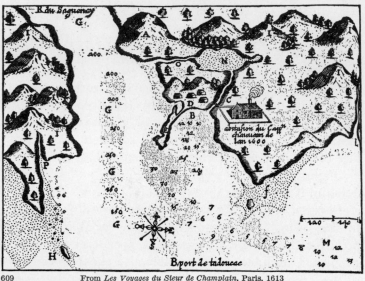

609   From Les Voyages du Steur de Champlain, Paris, 1613

610   From Carolus Allard, Orbis Habitabilis, Amsterdam, ca. 1690

FISH AND FUR

Fish and fur were the staple products of northern North America all through the seventeenth century. The French fished off Grand Banks and round the Gulf of St. Lawrence. Everybody "furred," that is, everybody who got the chance to do so.

611   From the Ducornet engraving of Champlain
in the Dominion Archives, Ottawa

SAMUEL DE CHAMPLAIN, 1567–1635

Samuel de Champlain, born in 1567 at Brouage, a village on the Bay of Biscay, was a soldier in the Wars of the League, devoted to the Catholic faith and King Henry of Navarre, with an inborn love of the sea, which he put to fine use as a captain in the French navy and an explorer of New France. But it is as the real founder of Quebec and New France in 1608 that he is numbered among the immortals. And it is because he made genuine colonization his supreme ideal that the seed he planted eventually took such firm root that all the storms of life could not prevent it bearing fruit a thousandfold and more. There is no authentic portrait known.

CHAMPLAIN IN THE WEST INDIES

CHAMPLAIN gained his first knowledge of the New World as a sailor to the Spanish Main. With rare powers of description he wrote the story of his adventures. The title of the translated Ms. runs: *Brief Narrative of the Most Remarkable Things that Samuel Champlain of Brouage observed in the West Indies.* He visited the Spanish ports and went overland to the City of Mexico.

612 First page of Champlain's Ms. account of his voyage to the West Indies, 1599–1601, in the John Carter Brown Library, Providence, R. I.

613 From Champlain's Ms. account of his voyage to the West Indies, 1599–1601, in the John Carter Brown Library, Providence, R. I.

CHAMPLAIN FIRST TO SUGGEST A PANAMA CANAL

L'on peult juger que sy ses quatre lieues de terre qu'il y a de Panama á ceste riviere estoient couppés, l'on pourroit venir de la mer du su en celle de deça, et par ainsy l'on accorciroit le chemin de plus de quinze centz lieus. "If these four leagues of land between Panama and this river [Chagres] were cut through, then passage could be made from the Pacific to the Atlantic, thus shortening the way by more than fifteen hundred leagues."

CHAMPLAIN'S BOOK ON HIS FIRST VOYAGE

IN 1603 Champlain was again in America, this time in the region which was to be the center of his thoughts and plans to the end of his life. He came out with a trading expedition and went up the St. Lawrence as far as Hochelaga, which the French found in ruined desolation as the result of Indian war. The title-page reads: "Of Savages, or the Voyage of Samuel Champlain of Brouage, made in New France in 1603: Containing:— The Customs, Ways of Living, Marriages, Wars and Dwellings of the Canadian Savages — The Discovery of more than 450 leagues in savage lands: what peoples live there: what animals are found: what are the rivers, lakes, islands, and main lands: what trees and fruits do grow — of the Acadian coasts, of the lands discovered there, and of the several mines which the savages report as being there."

614 Title-page of the original issue in the J. P. Morgan Library, New York

DE MONTS IN ACADIA, 1604–07

Upon his return from the St. Lawrence, Champlain joined company with a Huguenot nobleman, De Monts by name, who had secured from the king the first Acadian grant of the usual fur monopoly on condition of establishing a hundred settlers every year. De Monts became the head of a large company with a grant which included everything from Cape Breton to beyond New York. In 1604 he came out and established his settlement in Passamaquoddy Bay. Champlain was with him as geographer of the expedition.

No authentic portrait of De Monts is known. B. P. Poore was commissioned by the governor of Massachusetts to copy documents in the French archives. No original for the De Monts portrait has ever been found.

615 From *Acadiensts*, July–October, 1904, after "fictitious" portrait copied by Benjamin Perley Poore

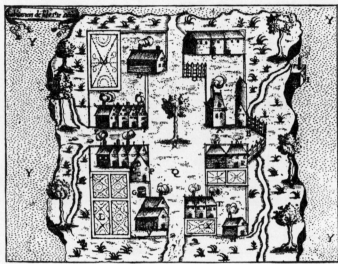

616   From Champlain, *Voyages*, Paris, 1613

THE FIRST ACADIAN WINTER, 1604–05

Champlain sketched the little settlement on the Island of St. Croix in Passamaquoddy Bay. The trim houses and snugly smoking chimneys proved to be but a whited sepulchre; for though De Monts had good workmen, with a fair spell of weather, after the first French colors in Acadia had been hoisted on the 25th of June, yet, when the searching cold, combined with fear of lurking Indians, had sealed up the whole colony for the winter, all the horrors of imprisonment and scurvy followed fast. Nearly half the wretched colonists died before spring let the enfeebled survivors crawl out.

CHAMPLAIN'S PLAN OF PORT ROYAL, 1605–07

A. WORKMEN'S QUARTERS
B. GUN PLATFORM
C. STOREHOUSE
D. PONTGRAVÉ & CHAMPLAIN
E. BLACKSMITH
F. PALISADE
G. BAKERY
H. KITCHEN
I. GARDEN
K. CEMETERY
L. RIVER
M. MOAT
N. HEADQUARTERS
O. SHIP'S STOREHOUSE

The next spring all hands rejoiced at sight of Port Royal (Annapolis Basin) "one of the finest harbors I had seen along the coasts," to which the survivors of St. Croix removed and built a new trading post. The following winter was so mild that "only a quarter of the people died." "Only a quarter" was not an abnormal death-rate for such places then.

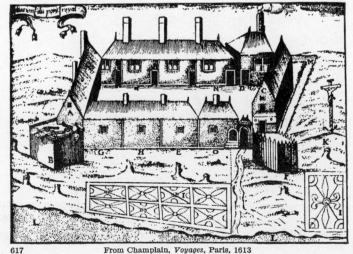

617   From Champlain, *Voyages*, Paris, 1613

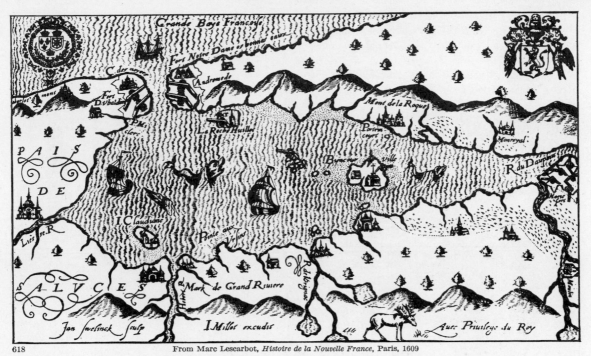

618   From Marc Lescarbot, *Histoire de la Nouvelle France*, Paris, 1609

LESCARBOT'S PORT ROYAL, 1606–07

AMONG the boatload of adventurers who came out to the little post of Port Royal in the summer of 1606 was Marc Lescarbot, a literary lawyer who would have made a splendid special correspondent for the Parisian press, had such men been invented then. Lescarbot in his *Histoire de la Nouvelle France*, 1609, told the story of Port Royal with all its alluring touches. Therefore he, and not Champlain, who gives little more than information, shall tell us of "The Order of Good Cheer" which Champlain proposed.

619   From the painting by C. W. Jefferys, in possession of
the publishers

THE ORDER OF GOOD CHEER

"EACH man was appointed chief steward in his turn. No one, two days before his turn, failed to hunt and fish for delicious fare. The chief steward, whom the Indians called Atoctegic, marched in at evening dinner, napkin on shoulder, wand of office in his hand, around his neck the Order's collar; then, after him, every single member of the Order of Good Cheer, each with his appropriate dish. At night, before giving God due thanks, the steward handed the collar to his successor, each then drinking to the other. We had abundance of game, such as duck, bustard, partridges, and geese; also moose, caribou, bear, and rabbits, whereof we made dishes better than those of the famous *Rue aux Ours* in Paris; for of all meats what can be tenderer than the best moose, or more toothsome than good beaver tail?"

But in France the Basques and Bretons were clamoring that they were being ruined because of the privileges of De Monts' company. His patent was revoked and Champlain brought the discouraged colonists home.

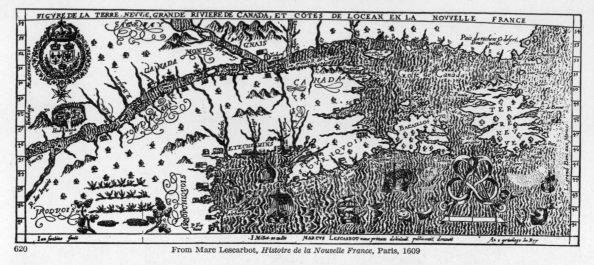

620   From Marc Lescarbot, *Histoire de la Nouvelle France*, Paris, 1609

LESCARBOT'S MAP OF NEW FRANCE, 1609

THIS was the first map after Champlain had founded New France in 1608 at Quebec. Tadousac, Hochelaga, and Stadacona all appear. Many of the names attached to the natural features are still in use, while others have been dropped. "Canada" was then applied to but a limited country around Quebec.

CHAMPLAIN'S *DON DE DIEU*, 1608

IN 1608 Champlain was again in American waters for De Monts, whom he had persuaded to abandon Acadia for the St. Lawrence country. Champlain's *Don de Dieu* was somewhat like a barque; though she carried a little square sail under her bowsprit and had no jibs, while her spanker was very lateenish. Her mainsail had good hoist and spread. She carried six sails on her three pole masts, and the tallest mast was 73 feet from step to truck. She had stone ballast, a rope-tackle tiller, and three cabins on the poop. She measured about 100 tons.

621   From the reconstruction made for the Quebec Tercentenary

622   From the painting by C. W. Jefferys, in possession
of the publishers

CHAMPLAIN BUILDING QUEBEC, 1608

IN 1607 the king had revoked the monopoly granted to De Monts, who, however, got a one-year monopoly of both the Acadian and Laurentian fur trade, freed from all obligation regarding colonists. De Monts then sent Champlain and Pontgravé to the St. Lawrence. Here, on the 3rd day of July, 1608, though coming to establish a trading-post, and regarding the St. Lawrence as the gateway to the real and fabled riches of the immemorial East, Champlain, by building his "Abitation" at the foot of the rock, near the present Notre-Dame-des-Victoires, founded Quebec, New France, and Canada.

ABITATION.DE QVEBECQ

623   From Champlain, *Voyages*, Paris, 1613

WINTER QUARTERS AT QUEBEC, 1608–1609

A. STORES
B. PIGEONRY
C. ARMORY
D. MEN'S QUARTERS
E. SUN DIAL
F. FORGE AND QUARTERS
G. GALLERIES
H. CHAMPLAIN'S QUARTERS
I. DOOR AND DRAW-BRIDGE
L. WALK, ALL ROUND
M. DITCH, ALL ROUND
N. GUN PLATFORMS
O. GARDEN
P. KITCHEN
Q. SLOPE TO RIVER
R. THE ST. LAWRENCE

BASQUE fishermen at Tadousac had attacked the van-ship and wounded Pontgravé. Now they plotted with some would-be mutineers from Champlain's men to kill Champlain and enjoy the "furring" rights themselves. The ringleader, Duval, "had his head put on a pike in our fort, as an example to those that remained." After mutiny, scurvy killed off all of the company but eight: "and half of these were ailing" added the undauntable Champlain.

CHAMPLAIN'S CONFERENCE WITH THE INDIAN CHIEFS

TILL the first French regulars arrived in 1665, Indian affairs were often matters of immediate life or death. The whites came out not only to a distant land but to a very much more distant age. It was as if the hand of time had been put back thousands of years, to an age when all our own ancestors were quite as wild and savage. This vast difference of course produced endless clashings; and, equally of course, the stronger whites took the usual advantage of the weaker reds. On the other hand, America could never have become civilized in so few centuries unless whites had mastered reds. Yet there were differences between the various whites, mostly to the advantage of the French. The Spaniards often treated Indians as their prey. The Dutch and English used them as they could for trade; but put them quite outside the pale in other ways. The French, with all their faults, were both more human and humane.

624   From the bronze panel by Mrs. S. J. Farnham in the Pan-American Union building, Washington

CHAMPLAIN FIGHTS THE IROQUOIS, 1609

In the spring of 1609 Champlain with two companions joined a war party of his Algonquin friends. He discovered the lake which bears his name and, near the present site of Ticonderoga, met the redoubtable Iroquois. Champlain has left an account of the fight. Both sides spent the night in warlike song and dance and in loud defiance of each other. The Algonquins carefully hid the three Frenchmen from the Iroquois till they marched to battle,

625   From Champlain, *Voyages*, Paris, 1613, after his own sketch

led by Champlain, while his two companions still remained hidden on the flank. Champlain's words are: "When I was within twenty paces the enemy, halting, gazed at me; as I also gazed at them. When I saw them move to shoot I drew a bead on one of the three chiefs. I had loaded with four bullets and hit three men at the first discharge, killing two on the spot. When our Indians saw this they roared so loudly that you could not have heard it thunder. Then arrows flew like hail on both sides. But when my companions fired from the woods the Iroquois, seeing their chiefs killed, turned tail and fled."

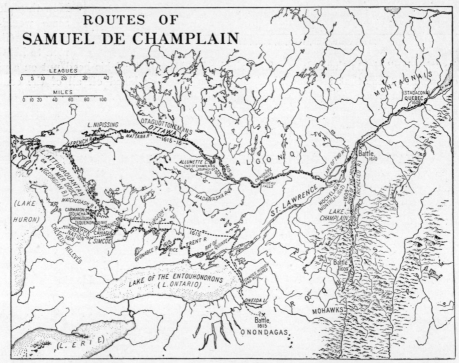

626 Drawn expressly for *The Pageant of America* by Gregor Noetzel, American Geographical Society, New York

CHAMPLAIN DISCOVERS THE GREAT LAKES, 1615

In 1613 Champlain went up the Ottawa to confirm a story he had heard from a Frenchman who had been living with the Indians, that by this way a water route lay to the sea. He did not find the ocean; but learned that the Indians of the country wished for nothing so much as his aid against the Iroquois. Two years later, in the summer of 1615, he joined a great war party, which adventure brought him to the shores of Lake Huron, where he was the first of all the whites to gaze upon those vast fresh-water seas that have assumed the name Great Lakes by the sheer force of natural right.

CHAMPLAIN'S SECOND BATTLE WITH THE IROQUOIS, 1615

THIS fight was brought on by the Indian interference with the fur trade. The Iroquois (or Onondaga) fort lay beside a pond a few miles south of Lake Oneida. The Hurons yelled like fiends, but behaved like a mob. Everything went wrong; and Champlain's Frenchmen could do nothing effective alone.

Champlain was wounded twice, "and suffered Gehenna while being carried bound and pinioned on the back of one of our savages." The defeated French and Indians took the long route back to Lake Huron. Then Champlain returned overland to Quebec.

627   From Champlain, *Voyages*, Paris, 1619, after his own sketch

CHAMPLAIN THE FATHER OF NEW FRANCE, 1608–1635

IN his work on *Navigation* Champlain says that "A good captain must be hardy and active and prove himself untiring at his work, so that whatever happens, he may be able to appear on deck and issue orders to his crew. Occasionally he should not disdain to lend a hand himself. . . . Prayers should be said night and morning, and the routine carried out in an orderly way. A captain should be quiet and affable, but peremptory in his orders. He must make sure that every man of each watch is doing his duty. . . . Should an accident happen the captain must give proof of manly courage, issue orders in a calm voice, and make light of facing

628   The Champlain statue by Paul Chevré (1898–), at Quebec

even death." Champlain, compelled to surrender Quebec to an English expedition (1629) returned to his post when Canada was restored to France. Here he died in his sixty-ninth year, still the Captain of New France.

LOUIS HÉBERT, FIRST HABITANT OF CANADA
(died 1627)

STRANGE to say, the first real habitant farmer was not a Norman peasant but a Parisian druggist, Louis Hébert, whose farm on the heights of Quebec was a constant joy to Champlain and the first missionaries, the Récollets, who had arrived two years before him, Hébert having landed at Quebec in 1617, the Récollets in 1615. Hébert heard the call of the soil with an enthusiasm which the modern townsman can hardly begin to understand.

629 The Hébert statue at Quebec, by Alfred Laliberté, (1878–)

THE FIRST SEIGNEUR, 1635

ROBERT GIFFARD had often come out as a ship's doctor and enjoyed great sport between Quebec and Beauport at a place still called La Canardière, from the duck-blind he built there. Now he was to be *Seigneur de Beauport* and settle his *censitaires* along that Côte de Beaupré (or Shore of the Beautiful Meadows) which bounds the North Channel just below Quebec. The French were accustomed to the seigniorial system at home; and, when properly applied to settlement in Canada, it worked very well and was fairly popular too. The seigneur held his lands in trust from the king, as his *censitaires* held theirs from him. He was the local immigration agent, the unpaid magistrate, the miller, and everything else that the curé, notary, and captain of militia were not; and he had to work hard to succeed. His milling rights often cost more than they were worth; for he had to build, repair, and run the mill, while getting only one bushel to every baker's dozen the farmer took away. His hunting and fishing rights were worth next to nothing, where people were few, the country

630   Drawn expressly for *The Pageant of America*, by C. W. Jefferys

vast, game plentiful, and wardens not to be had. As for seigniorial rents, they were often so small as not to be worth collecting except from the bigger *censitaires*. St. Martin's Day, November 11 (now best known from the Armistice of the Great World War) was rent day at the manor, where the seigneur kept such open house that many a *censitaire* got more in hospitality than he ever gave in rent. The seigneur's position, however, was an honorable one, often sought after by money-making upstarts; while home farms and "furring" might add a good deal to the very modest seigniorial income itself.

Alas that Champlain was not the governor to whom the first Canadian seigneur bent the knee! Champlain died on Christmas Day in 1635; and Giffard did homage on the following New Year's Eve, in the little Château St. Louis, to Monsieur de Bras de Fer, le Sieur du Chasteaufort, who was Champlain's lieutenant. "He of the Iron Arm, the Lord of Castle Strong" received the homage, invested Giffard with both sword and spur, and sent him forth as Lord of Beauport, ready to fight all enemies of France.

631 From a tercentenary medal, courtesy of Colonel William Wood

THE TERCENTENARY OF CHAMPLAIN'S
QUEBEC: 1608–1908

VERY notable was the commemoration at which France was represented by several envoys, King Edward VII by King George V (then Prince of Wales), and the United States by Vice-President Fairbanks. An international British, French, and American fleet anchored in the harbor of Quebec, where a facsimile of Champlain's famous *Don de Dieu* sailed in, exactly as she did in 1608.

632 From a tercentenary medal, courtesy of Colonel William Wood

Fifteen thousand Canadian soldiers paraded on the Plains of Abraham beside the three Naval Brigades; and several thousand more Canadians, clothed in the proper historic costumes, performed the pageant of Quebec's romantic past. How great the change and how short the time, as the world measures it, since the primitive days of Champlain and his garrison!

CARDINAL RICHELIEU, 1585–1642

RICHELIEU set out to unify France at home, make her the first Great Power in Europe, and win an empire overseas. Fostering French sea-power, and turning his spare attention to New France, he formed the Company of the Hundred Associates, which received in perpetuity a complete monopoly of "furring" rights, besides the control of all other trade for sixteen years, and dominion over North America from Florida to Labrador and from the Gulf of St. Lawrence to the great fresh-water seas discovered by Champlain. But Richelieu's attention was distracted nearer home; the Company failed to colonize New France; and when its charter was revoked in 1663 the entire white population was less than three thousand souls.

633   From the portrait by Philippe de Champaigne (1602–74), in the National Portrait Gallery, London

"FURRING" INDIANS GOING HOME

OF course the new company was ravenous for furs; and Quebec was keenly delighted when, in Champlain's last years, six hundred Huron braves arrived in a hundred and forty bark canoes all loaded down with pelts. The Indians drank and traded, danced, feasted, held a great pow-wow, and smoked the pipe of peace. Then, on the rising tide, the lightened birchbarks went gliding up-stream. So began the custom which developed into one of the most picturesque features of the life of New France. In later times each summer, except when some extraordinary circumstance prevented, a great fleet of Indian canoes from the interior of the continent paddled down to the French settlements along the St. Lawrence.

634   From copy of the painting, *Voyageurs on a Misty Morning*, by F. A. Verner (1836–)

RÉCOLLETS AND JESUITS, 1625

TEN years of mission work convinced the devoted Récollets that a richer, stronger, and better supported order than their own was needed in New France. So they welcomed the equally devoted but much more powerful Jesuits. These came year after year, directed by an organization marked by its zeal and fine intelligence. Singly and in pairs they went among the Indians in the service of their country and their God. All too often their fate was martyrdom with little glory. But they persisted; and their achievement also persists in the history of the land they served.

635   From the painting for *The Chronicles of Canada*, by C. W. Jefferys

FATHER LE JEUNE AND THE *JESUIT RELATIONS*

THE Jesuits had a fair field and much favor; for Huguenots and foreigners were forbidden after 1632. Fearless and tireless, the vanguard of the Lord of Hosts, the Jesuits could also write; and for their own time and place and people the *Jesuit Relations* were the best possible propagandist letters from the front. Father Le Jeune was one of the first three to arrive in 1625 and wrote a most appealing *Relation*. He likewise was the preacher at the funeral of Champlain.

636   From the portrait by J. Boyes in the House of the Immaculate Conception, Montreal

637   From the painting by Frank Craig, R. A. (1874–1918), owned by A. G. Doughty, Ottawa

ARRIVAL OF THE URSULINES, 1639

THE Ursulines are a teaching order; the *Hospitalières* are nurses. They both came to Quebec four years after Champlain's death. The central figure is that of La Mère Marie de l'Incarnation, first Superior of the Quebec Ursulines and the greatest woman of New France, dauntless and pertinacious as Champlain, a saintly leader, devoted teacher of both red and white, and ardent advocate of colonization. The *Hospitalières*, within their own sphere, were equally devoted to the service of both God and man. These self-sacrificing women, who came to care for the young and the infirm, brought gifts of love and service that only those who lived in a primitive frontier-post far from the land and scenes of their childhood could appreciate.

638   From the painting, artist unknown, in the Ursuline Convent, Quebec

MADAME DE LA PELTRIE

THOUGH of the *haute noblesse* of Normandy and a very rich woman in her own right, she was, like La Mère Marie, so moved by the *Jesuit Relations* that she gave up everything in France to found the Ursuline Convent at Quebec in 1639.

OLD URSULINE CONVENT, QUEBEC

HERE La Mère Marie de l'Incarnation used to teach the little Indian girls without trying to force premature "civilization" upon them. "They must see the woods. Loss of liberty makes them sad, and sadness makes them sick. We have not 'civilized' one in a hundred." Other classes were filled with the French girls of Quebec and the surrounding country. But teaching was not the only occupation. Whenever fire, sword, or pestilence swept through Quebec the Ursulines nobly did their duty. They have been through two fires and four sieges, besides nursing the sick and wounded of five battles and many a pestilential scourge.

639   From the painting, probably by one of the Ursulines, in possession of the Quebec Ursulines

HÔPITAL–GÉNÉRAL, QUEBEC

FOR nearly three centuries this famous hospital has nursed the sick and wounded of battle and disease. Indians, French, British, and Americans have all been treated with the same devoted kindness. There were American invaders here with Phips in 1690, Wolfe in 1759, and Montgomery in 1776, besides those brought in as prisoners during the War of 1812.

640   From a daguerreotype (*ca.* 1840) in the Hôpital-Général de Quebec, of a sketch, artist unknown

641   From the statue in Montreal by Louis Philippe Hébert

PAUL DE CHOMEDEY, SIEUR DE MAISONNEUVE
(died 1676)

MONTREAL is probably the only great commercial city in the world founded as a mission. A man of mighty faith was needed; for France, distracted at home, had no spare strength for Canada. But, like the purest Crusader come to life again, Paul de Chomedey, Sieur de Maisonneuve, swore that if every tree were an Iroquois he still would go. With forty-two companions, before an altar in the open air, the future town was dedicated to the Virgin by the name of Ville Marie in 1642.

JEANNE MANCE, 1606–73

FEELING a strong desire for service in New France, Jeanne Mance consulted Father Charles Lalemant, S. J., in Paris, and, accepting the rich and charitable Madame de Bullion's invitation to manage a hospital in Montreal, accompanied Maisonneuve and found her life work there. Her counterpart in education was Marguerite Bourgeoys, who began in a vacant stable the first school of that congregation of the Sisters of Our Lady which now extends from sea to sea.

642   From the portrait in the Hôtel Dieu, Montreal, artist unknown

FATHER JOGUES AMONG THE MOHAWKS

THE lot of Father Jogues took him among the Iroquois, who were hostile to New France from the very first. Preaching to, or negotiating with, the fierce Six Nations, was mortally dangerous for Frenchmen. But, like the other Jesuits, Jogues went forth unquestioning, readily accepting whatever might befall.

643   From the Champlain Edition of the works of Francis Parkman, drawing by Thure de Thulstrup (1848–). © Little, Brown & Co.

ISAAC JOGUES, 1607–46

WHEN asked to go on a last embassy to the Six Nations, his weary and weakened flesh shrank back. But his undaunted spirit urged him on. Then he went again, prophetically writing, "I go, but not to return." He felt this time that it was almost certain death. The Iroquois medicine men had traced the demon of an epidemic to the little black box which he had left behind. This and the encroaching establishment of Montreal were quite enough. Therefore he had to die.

JEAN DE BRÉBŒUF, 1593–1649

WHOEVER would see a champion of Jesuit Christianity at its noblest in New France could not do better than

644   From the Jogues statue by Sibbyl, at St. Joseph's Seminary, Dunwoodie, Yonkers, N. Y.

645 From the portrait of Brébœuf by J. Boyes in the House of the Immaculate Conception, Montreal

gaze upon Brébœuf (No. 645); for no Crusader ever went forth with nobler devotion to the cause of missions in that dread New World.

IROQUOIS MASSACRES OF JESUITS AND THEIR INDIAN CONVERTS, 1648–49

It was the first historic 4th of July in this New World, a Fourth as terrible to little, lost Huronia as the other Fourth is glorious to millions beneath the Stars and Stripes. Good Father Daniel had just pronounced the last words of the mass, *Ita missa est*, when sudden shrieks of Iroquois! Iroquois!! Iroquois!!! pierced the summer air. Stormers were hacking at the palisade and bullets were whistling in, when Daniel, pausing one sacred moment to bless

646   From P. Francisco Creuxius, *Historiae Canadensis seu Novae-Franciae*, Paris, 1664

his congregation, stepped forth unflinchingly, and, for another moment, awed even the Iroquois. Then, with fiendish yells, they cut him down and threw his body into his own flaming chapel.

Next year Brébœuf and Gabriel Lalemant were the foremost martyrs. This time the Iroquois were determined to slake their fury to the full; and even they must have been satisfied with keeping the gentle Lalemant under torture for fourteen agonizing hours. Brébœuf, a giant in stature and in strength, who used to carry Lalemant's loads across the portages, was racked with the most excruciating pains that they could think of. They poured boiling water on his head, to show their contempt for baptism. They hung a necklace of red-hot axe-heads round his naked shoulders. They girdled him with belts of fire. But never a word of anger or one cry of anguish could they wring from him. At last a furious war chief cut out his dauntless heart. (The picture is a composite showing the different forms of martyrdom suffered by many Jesuits at different times.)

FATHER DRUILLETTES MEETS GOVERNOR DUDLEY AT BOSTON, 1650

The Jesuit Druillettes and Noël Negahamet, an Algonquin chief, were well received at Coussinoe (Augusta, Me.) by John Winslow, who accompanied them to Boston. There Major Gibbons (whose friend, La Tour, we shall soon meet in Acadia) gave Druillettes a private room in which to practice his religion.

Governor Bradford gave him fish on Friday and paid for his journey home. John Eliot asked him to spend the winter. John Endicott of Salem took his petition to the General Court of Boston. But no treaty was ever made. New England wanted one for trade. But she would have none against the Iroquois, who had been neutral in the Pequot War.

647   Drawn expressly for *The Pageant of America*, by C. W. Jefferys

648 From an engraving by Claude Duflos in the Canadian Archives after a portrait attributed to Dion des Campeaux

BISHOP LAVAL, 1622–1708

FRANÇOIS DE LAVAL came of the famous fighting Montmorencys, among the noblest blood of France. He was the Jesuits' friend, a man of dauntless courage and unyielding will, ready to live without purse or scrip for himself, but always ready to use his power as head of the Church in New France in any way that seemed religiously right.

649 From the painting by Edwin Willard Deming (1860–), in the State Historical Society, Madison, Wis.

NICOLET IN WISCONSIN, 1634

THE mantle of Champlain, as explorer toward the west, fell on Nicolet and then on Radisson. Nicolet paddled along Lake Huron to Sault Ste. Marie and thence along Lake Michigan into Green Bay, where he met the Winnebagoes. He dressed in embroidered robes because he thought he must be getting near Cathay. But only Indians greeted him, and took him for a Manitou, a sort of wandering god.

650   From *Collier's Weekly*, Jan. 13, 1906, painting by Frederic Remington. © P. F. Collier and Son Co.

RADISSON AND GROSEILLIERS — FARTHEST WEST IN 1659

THESE lifelong chums were the first whites to enter the Mississippi basin, to explore Lake Superior, and to visit the great northwestern country of the Sioux, Assiniboines, and Crees. Later on they helped to fix the Hudson Bay Company's firm hold on the fur trade of the whole vast North.

"SANS MERCI" — "NO QUARTER"

THERE were times in the history of New France when habitant and Iroquois fought to the death — civilization against savagery.

DOLLARD: HERO OF CANADA'S THERMOPYLAE, 1660

EIGHT hundred picked Iroquois took the war path to blot out Montreal. But Dollard, commanding Fort Ville Marie there, knowing it might be fatal to await attack, went up the Ottawa for nearly thirty miles, to where, at the Long Sault Rapids, there was an Indian palisade. He had only sixteen French and forty-four Indians under Anohotaha and Mitiwemeg, the steadfast Huron and Algonquin chiefs.

651 From a bronze statuette by Louis Philippe Hébert, in Montreal

652 From the Dollard monument, Montreal, sculpture by Alfred Laliberté

DOLLARD'S LAST STAND AT THE LONG SAULT BLOCKHOUSE, 1660

FOR ten long nights and days the Iroquois raged round the tiny fort, where Dollard's men nearly died of thirst, after their one path to the river had been closed. Then all his Indians except the two chiefs and five of their followers deserted; whereupon seven hundred Iroquois advanced against the garrison of only twenty-three. Like one long living palisade, the enemy came on. The French muskets cut lanes of death through the attackers. But, like a storm-blown wave, the furious assault burst on the little fort and breached it. Anohotaha fell, mortally wounded, calling out with his last breath, "Lay my head on the fire; the Iroquois must never get my scalp."

Then Dollard's musketoon (loaded like a bomb, to hurl among the enemy) burst among the French, who were quickly hacked to death. But Montreal was saved; for the Iroquois council decided that a place defended by heroes like these could not be taken now.

653   Bronze relief on the Maisonneuve monument, Montreal, by Louis Philippe Hébert

654   From the "portrait anonyme" at Versailles

LOUIS XIV, KING OF NEW FRANCE, 1638–1715

WHATEVER his faults, neglect of New France was never among them. For more than fifty years he read all the Canadian dispatches; and there, to the present, they remain, with all his marginal notes. Nor was he lacking in ability. Moreover, Colbert was an almost ideal minister to direct colonial affairs from the home office. But an *enfant* colony three thousand miles away could never be an integral province of France; nor could it thrive if autocrat and bureaucrat combined to make it so.

Hard things were often said of Louis XIV; and that he rightly deserved some of them cannot be denied. But he was a worker, and a very hard worker too. The trouble was that he tried to do what no one man could do successfully, and that he extended the system of unification, needed in certain ways in France, to a country thousands of miles away at a time when months were required to exchange reports, ideas, and orders. He nearly made his bad colonial system work. But when the balance of sea-power turned against him New France was doomed.

SECTION III

THE AGE OF SETTLEMENT, 1663–1713

IN spite of heroes like Dollard and Brébœuf, in spite of founders like Champlain and Maisonneuve, in spite of the most devoted bishop, priests, and nuns, of habitants like Louis Hébert and seigneurs like Giffard, in spite of explorers like Nicolet and Radisson; and, strange as it may seem, in spite of the fact that France was not only the greatest power in Europe, most peopled and best armed, but rapidly rising to still greater heights; in spite of all this, it seemed as if New France was doomed. The wonder is how the stunted, starveling colony ever survived the terrible three years that began with Dollard's death in 1660. The company of the Hundred Associates (officially "of New France") was going to its ruin after a mixture of reckless exploitation, gross abuses, and the utmost possible evasion of all its duties, especially those of colonization. Less than three thousand French throughout America! Why, more than three thousand English had come out to Massachusetts alone, within a single year; and Virginia now had ten times the whites of New France! Moreover, the tide of Iroquois invasion had not been turned but only held back at one point and for a single season. Iroquois were killing Algonquins within a mile of where the new French governor was landing at Quebec in 1656. Even the Ursuline convent had to be garrisoned, and the nuns told off to regular siege duties — La Mère Marie taking the most dangerous one of all. Then, when the Iroquois receded, pestilence came in and proved worse than any massacre. Then came the earthquake year of 1663, when even the very hills seemed doomed. But the Church stood fast, heroically fast; and Laval actually chose this earthquake year to found the university which still bears his famous name. Yet from an agonizing people the cry of "Back to France!" went piteously forth.

The darkest hour, however, did, for once, precede the dawn. Every ship next year brought word of what great things the king would do, now that he was making his Canadian domain a Royal Province of glorious France herself. Then, in 1665, the royal might and glory were made manifest in this new, exultant province, which now received, besides a governor, a real viceroy, a regiment of veterans, fresh from a most victorious campaign, a king's intendant to manage the great prospective settlement, and, most significant of all, a goodly number of real settlers from different walks of life. Yes, the golden age had come; and for a generation its soaring spirit filled New France. Indian and English enemies were driven back; while eager French explorers went north and west and south, across the three great gulfs, along the two great rivers, and around the five Great Lakes, everywhere proclaiming the king of France to be the king of all unoccupied America!

When the era of expansion had passed, French claims extended northward to Hudson Bay, westward from the Gulf of St. Lawrence, and southward to the Gulf of Mexico. The interior of the continent was French. But, east of the Appalachians, the chain of English colonies grew in wealth and population; while here and there along the frontier the French and English clashed.

TRACY, VICEROY OF NEW FRANCE, 1603–70

THE Marquis de Tracy, great alike in council and the field,
landed in full state under the eager eyes of all Quebec. Here
were salvation, prosperity, and glory combined: ships, troops,
settlers, money, the king's own lieutenant; with a governor,
intendant, more ships, more troops, more settlers, and more
money still to come. New France went wild with joy. The
Church received the State befittingly. But Tracy refused the
special seat prepared for him, and knelt, with all his nobles,

on the stone
floor, the
most telling
example of
high-placed
humility;
for he was
the actual
vice-king
over all
French gov-
ernors.

655 From the engraved portrait of Tracy by Lenfant,
1660, in the Dominion Archives, Ottawa

656 From the portrait of Talon, said to be contemporary, artist
unknown, in the Hôtel Dieu, Quebec

JEAN BAPTISTE TALON, FIRST INTENDANT OF NEW FRANCE, 1625–91

WHAT could intendants do? Well, the real trouble is to
find out what they could not do; for they were everything the governor and bishop were not, while their
functions were also correlated with many of those performed by both of these great officials. Briefly, the
intendant was at the head of civil affairs in general and
of settlement in particular. Talon was an ideal intendant, perfectly adapted to New France.

THE SOLDIER–SETTLERS OF NEW FRANCE

THE famous *Régiment de
Carignan* not only fought the
Iroquois but provided many
settlers, who, with their increasing descendants, provided yet more soldier-
settlers. Talon got the king
to offer land to all who
would settle near the Richelieu, which the Iroquois used
already when invading New
France, and which the English would just as surely use
later on. The soldiers of
this regiment built the
French forts on the frontier
shown on the map.

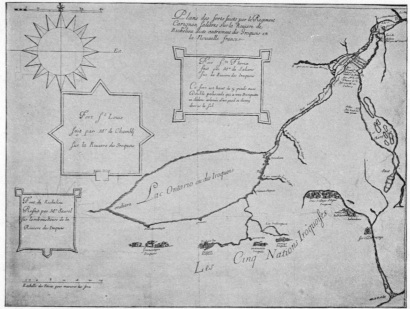

657   From the map of French frontier forts in the *Jesuit Relation for 1664–65*, Paris, 1666

THE MOTHERS OF
NEW FRANCE, 1665–1672

No wives, no settlements; no settlements, no future for New France. Now, there were five bachelors to every one unmarried girl. So Talon asked the king and Colbert for an immediate shipment of prospective brides; and out came the first consignment of the *Filles du Roy*, chosen from the Royal Orphanage of Paris. There was tremendous competition for the prettiest and sturdiest; but some others were left over, in

658   From the painting by C. W. Jefferys, owned by the Dominion Government, Canada

spite of the taxes and penalties enforced against bachelors and spinsters and even their unhappy parents too; also in spite of the bonus paid in cash and kind to every mated couple. Some wives proving too weak for the strenuous settlement life, Talon asked for Norman peasants; and several consignments of this kind — the very fittest of the fit — came out, with the encouraging result that every single one was wed. Then well-educated girls, suitable for officers' wives, were sent for, duly received, and quickly married off. But the first consignment was four short; fifteen were sent in rectification; and eleven were left lamenting. This was no fault of Talon's, for he was an excellent master of the matrimonial market when he got his own way. Moreover, the population trebled during his seven years in Canada; and half of this increase was due to the birth-rate. Up and down the St. Lawrence the habitant farms multiplied. About each habitant cottage played a brood of sturdy children.

What this birth-rate has been persistently, from his day to our own, may be imagined from these two very telling facts: first, that the three million French-Canadians in North America today are nearly all descended from less than thirty thousand French immigrants, most of whom came out under Talon's supervision; and secondly, that when the Quebec Provincial Government used to give a free hundred acres to fathers of twelve living children, it not infrequently received petitions from fathers who thought themselves entitled to double this acreage, because they had twenty-four children or more. Think of the following might-have-been. Had Talon's advice been taken, and at least one per cent (no more than that) of France's population come to Canada, then, at the rate which has actually been realized, there would be not three but twenty million people of French descent in the United States and Canada today.

Far more significant still is the fact that if immigrants had come out from France in the same proportion as they came from the old home folk of England, and if they had increased in the same proportion as the French-Canadians, then the French-Canadians of today would vastly outnumber the present population of the whole New World.

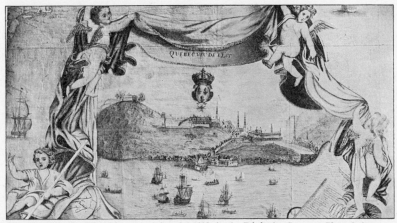

659   From De Fonville's Ms. map of Canada, 1699, in the Dépôt des Cartes et Plans de la
Marine, Paris

QUEBEC IN TALON'S
TIME, 1665–72

TALON built ships up to five hundred tons; founded a line between Quebec, the West Indies, and France; and employed three hundred and fifty shipwrights out of a population of only seven thousand. Furs were the most important commodity carried across the Atlantic to Europe.

CHARLES LE MOYNE, BARON DE LONGUEUIL, 1625-85

LE MOYNE, whose Canadian barony survives to the present day, was a glorious specimen of the seigneurs of New France. Tall, immensely strong, and very handsome, equally at home with red men or white, kind of heart yet keen of mind, and born to lead in either peace or war, he was exactly the sort of supremely fit Norman whom William the Conqueror would have delighted in. Fitter still, he married the belle of Montreal, whose brains well matched her beauty. Fittest of all, she bore him eleven sons, each one of whom was also well equipped both in body and in mind. All lived to reach high and well won rank in the army, navy, or administration, or died on active service at the front. Bienville, the ninth son, was the founder and first governor of Louisiana; while Iberville, the third, was no less an historic character than the great French hero of the three great gulfs — St. Lawrence, Mexico, and Hudson Bay.

660   From the Maisonneuve monument, Montreal, sculpture by Louis Philippe Hébert

662 From John Lambert, *Travels through lower Canada and the United States of North America*, London, 1810, from his own sketch

A CURÉ AND A FRENCH-CANADIAN LADY

THE curé was not only the minister of Providence but, in many a mundane affair, a sort of earthly providence himself. Yet, for all his worldly and his other-worldly power, the curé, then as now, was a most faithful shepherd of his flock.

661   From the painting by Walter Baker

LE CHATEAU DE LONGUEUIL

THE French-Canadian seigneur, as we have seen already, was never of the *haute noblesse*. Nor was he a landlord in any modern sense, much less a millionaire. He was, in certain ways, a semi-feudal lord of manor who led his tiny social world in both peace and war. Here, in the Château de Longueuil, we see his chateau at its very best — apart, of course, from ruins. The Longueuil barony, which still exists, dates from the military settlement formed by the veterans of Carignan who peopled the dangerous frontier just south of Montreal at the end of the seventeenth century, and who produced heroic women, like the first châtelaine, wife of Charles Le Moyne and mother to famous Iberville, or like Madeleine de Verchères.

THE PIONEER HABITANT

THE early habitant inherited that passion for his actual bit of earth which all French peasants have. But of course he "varied from environment" as well; and some of his sons were eager for new ground. But neither father nor even younger sons were ever, as a class, so eager for new ground as were their English-speaking rivals farther south.

663   From the drawing by C. W. Jefferys, in possession of the publishers

LE CANADIEN

KRIEGHOFF'S *Le Canadien* (No. 664) shows how true to type the habitant remained down to the middle of the nineteenth century.

664 From the painting by C. Krieghoff
(1812–72)

HABITANT PLOUGHING

HUOT'S *Habitant Ploughing*, though even later than Krieghoff's *Canadien*, shows the same persistence of type.

665   From the painting by Huot (1855–), location unknown

666 From the Maisonneuve monument at
Montreal, by Louis Philippe Hébert

THE HABITANTE

THE habitante was all that other wives of pioneers have been obliged to be, and more than most as well; for few of other lands have ever been such very prolific mothers. Families of twenty were not uncommon, and even thirty not unknown.

The habitante had to manage not only a most prolific household but one that was forced to be greatly self-supplying too. She had to weave and spin and bake, and do unnumbered odd jobs unknown to her descendants. Yet some old ways persist. And even now families of over a dozen are not at all uncommon.

667   From a photograph by Edgar Harting, Montreal

OLD HABITANT HOUSE

OLD habitant houses often were, and sometimes (like the one here) still are, substantially built of stone. Most were covered by roofs gracefully curved at the eaves; and many were carefully whitewashed.

FRONTENAC, 1620–98

THIS lion of New France, whose first term lasted from 1672 to 1682, was also the first and only governor who befriended popular representation in public affairs. He assembled the "Brandy Parliament" (to give evidence about the use and abuse of brandy in the fur trade), asked representative men to meet him officially and in conclave at Quebec, and cunningly devised the means whereby the captains of militia might be something not unlike a congressman at home. The king of course rebuked him, saying, through the mouthpiece of his minister, that Frontenac should "seldom or, to speak more plainly, never" call together any representative body not appointed by the Crown. (Frontenac's second term, 1689–1698, is dealt with in the chapter on the French and Indian Wars, Volume VI, *The Winning of Freedom*.)

669   Inset on Herman Moll's "Map of the Dominions of the King of Great Britain" in America, in *The World described* . . . 1709–20

668   From the statue by Louis Philippe Hébert at the Parliament House, Quebec

670   From *Advantures du Sr. C. Le Beau, ou Voyage Curieux et Nouveau parmi les Sauvages de l'Amérique Septentrionale*, Amsterdam, 1738, part I. p. 320

BEAVER DAMS

TRAVELERS' tales sometimes made wonderful pictures when put together in the hands of a bold eighteenth-century artist. Whatever else may be said, the idea in the sketch (of the prevalence and importance of the American beaver) rings true. The prosperity of New France largely depended upon this flat-tailed, dam-building rodent, whose pelts brought good prices in Europe.

LE BEAU'S MARVELOUS VISION

A GIANT beaver dam with beaver lodges in the background. But Sieur C. le Beau was not really the Canadian counterpart of Baron Munchausen. He served in New France for many years before publishing his *Voyage Curieux* in Amsterdam in 1738. He certainly exaggerated, but there was always some basis of fact.

EXPANSION OF
NEW FRANCE IN AMERICA
17TH AND 18TH CENTURIES

QUEBEC (FROM PT. LEVIS)

EXPLORERS
Champlain, 1609, 1615-16,
Nicolet, 1634,
Radisson & Grosseilliers 1658-61, -+-+-+-
Albanel, 1671, -+-+-+-
Joliet & Marquette, 1673, ...
La Salle, 1679-80,1682
Accau & Hennepin, 1680, -----
St. Denis, 1714-16,
La Harpe, 1719-22,
Bourgmont, 1724,
La Verendrye, 1731-1743
Mallet Bros. 1739-40

FRONTIERS
--- FRENCH
.... ENGLISH
.... SPANISH

MILES
100   0   100   200   300   400   500
FORT   ○ MISSION   ● SETTLEMENT

671   Drawn expressly for *The Pageant of America* by Gregor Noetzel, American Geographical Society, New York

THE SPREAD OF FRENCH INFLUENCE INLAND

I<small>N</small> the Mississippi Valley, as almost everywhere else, we view the struggle between the seaboard English and the inland French. French explorers were always first along the three great rivers St. Lawrence, Ohio, and Mississippi; first around the five Great Lakes; and first far west, until they saw the Rockies. But France failed to keep the seaways open and to send out a sufficient number of colonists. In the seventeenth century the Jesuit Albanel found the English flag on shipboard in Hudson Bay. The eighteenth saw the Gulf of St. Lawrence closed by the British conquest of Canada. The nineteenth saw the Gulf of Mexico lost with Louisiana.

672 From Ms. map by Joliet (known as his "Smaller Map") in the Dépôt des Cartes et Plans de la Marine, Paris

FRENCHMEN AT THE SOO IN 1671

TALON deserves the credit of having sent St. Lusson to the Soo (Sault Ste. Marie), in 1671, Albanel to Hudson Bay in 1672, and Joliet to the Mississippi in 1673. From Talon the quest was taken up by Frontenac. The chiefs of fourteen tribes met St. Lusson at the Soo when he proclaimed all the lands then or afterwards discovered, right up to the oceans of north and west and south, as being thenceforth annexed to New France.

673 Drawn expressly for *The Pageant of America* by C. W. Jefferys

THE FRENCH AND ILLINOIS, 1673

JOLIET, the prospector, and Marquette, the Jesuit, went up Fox River, across Lake Winnebago, and thence to the Wisconsin, from which, on the 17th of June, they were the first to reach the Mississippi and paddle down as far as the Arkansas. The Illinois received them as good friends.

FRENCH AMBITIONS IN 1673, AS SHOWN BY JOLIET'S MAP

BARRING Champlain, the first Frenchmen to explore the hinterland of the Gulf of St. Lawrence were mostly missionaries seeking to Christianize the Indians. When the vast extent of the interior began to be realized, laymen as well as churchmen were sent on definite exploring expeditions. To extend the boundaries of New France was to extend also those of the Catholic Church. Therefore Church and State co-operated in this truly imperial enterprise. French genius has rarely shown to better advantage than in this searching

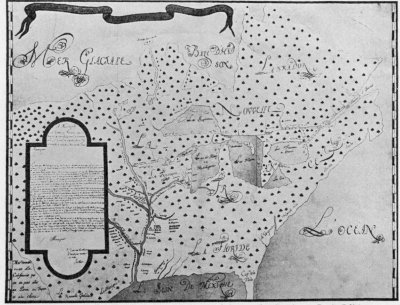

674   From Gabriel Gravier, *Etude sur une carte inconnue; la première dressée par Louis Joliet en 1674, après son exploration du Mississippi avec Jacques Marquette en 1673*, Paris, 1880

out of the very heart of North America. Joliet's crude map shows both the French dream and the surprising amount of information regarding the interior which their explorations netted.

Joliet inscribed in the panel in the lower left corner of the original of this map, a letter to Frontenac. The map gives, he says, the situation of the Lakes on which there is navigation for more than 1200 leagues from east to west. He adds that by one of the large rivers you will find a route to the Red Sea (*Mer Vermeille*), i.e. the Gulf of California, and from there to Peru, Japan, and China. (Winsor, Vol. IV, p. 209.)

675   From the bronze tablet by H. A. MacNeil, in the Marquette Building, Chicago

MARQUETTE'S FUNERAL AT THE MOUTH OF THE MARQUETTE IN MICHIGAN, 1675

MARQUETTE was more than an explorer. After his great trip down the Mississippi he returned to the Illinois country to plant a mission among the Indians. On his way he fell ill. A year later he again made the attempt and this time died. His energy, hardihood, and devotion were also typical of his brother Jesuits.

DULHUT AT LITTLE PORTAGE, MINNESOTA, 1679

NOBLEMAN, soldier, diplomat, explorer, trader, and king of the *coureurs des bois*, Dulhut was the successful rival of the Hudson's Bay Company all round Lake Superior (1678–1708), the peacemaker between Assiniboines, Crees, and Sioux, and the first white man who really blazed the western trail. His "furring" activities took him over great stretches of country and enabled him to supplement the information gained by the explorers.

676   From a mural painting by C. C. Rosenkranz (1871–) in the Glass Block Store, Duluth, Minn.

LA SALLE, 1643–87

FIRST to see Niagara, first to follow the Mississippi to its mouth, first to attempt the founding of Louisiana, La Salle (Nos. 677, 678) dreamed of a vast New France which should hold the heart and arteries of North America, and, like Iberville, he did much towards winning it.

To some, both in his own day and our own, he was a visionary. To others he was a discoverer and explorer. To others, again, he was the forerunner of a great Franco-American empire which ultimately failed through no fault of his. In truth he was all three.

677   From the "Waltner" engraving, Dominion Archives, Ottawa

678   From the engraving, earliest known portrait of La Salle, in the Bibliothèque de Rouen

679   From L. Hennepin, *A New Discovery of a Vast Country in America*, London, 1698

LA SALLE SEES NIAGARA

LA SALLE, Tonty, La Motte, and Hennepin seem to have discovered the famous Falls in 1678. Others had given Niagara a wide berth because of the savage Iroquois. The discovery of the Falls made it clear that a portage between Lake Ontario and Lake Erie was inevitable. La Salle, with deep insight, grasped immediately the commercial and military importance of the Niagara peninsula as an indispensable link with the West. A French fort here would defend the route which fur traders and soldiers would follow in going to the interior and would establish French control in the Great Lakes area.

680 From the painting, 1904, by Herman T. Koerner (1855–), in the Buffalo Historical Society

LA SALLE SAILS THE FIRST SHIP ON THE LAKES, *LE GRIFFON*, LAKE ERIE, 1679

LA SALLE, having all plans ready for his great adventuring into the unknown heart of North America, sent Father Hennepin ahead to Niagara, there to found a post and build a ship which should be ready to launch in the early spring of 1679. No Indian had ever seen, or even had imagined, so vast a white man's winged canoe as the little *Griffon* seemed when she sailed west, trading as she went, till at last she anchored in Green Bay. Thence, in September, she sailed back, with a fortune in furs aboard. But La Salle watched her departure with a very anxious heart. And his foreboding was fulfilled; for she foundered with all hands.

TONTY OF THE IRON HAND, *ca.* 1650–1704

HENRI DE TONTY was a soldier of such surpassing strength, courage, perseverance, and fidelity that, even in the wilds, he was more than the equal of two ordinary men who had both hands. He had lost one hand in the European wars. He and La Salle were friends till death; and their two glorious names are forever joined together in the story of how the Mississippi was explored for France.

681 From the bronze tablet by H. A. MacNeil, in the Chicago Historical Society

STARVED ROCK, WHERE LA SALLE BUILT A FORT, 1679

WHEN the *Griffon* had passed from sight La Salle and Tonty, with what remained of their followers, struck south, into the country of the Illinois. The explorers followed the Illinois River to a point near where Peoria stands today. Here La Salle's luck left him: his followers began to desert; and he foreboded attack by the Indians. Without supplies he could go no farther. So at Starved Rock he built a fort, called it Crèvecœur (or Heartbreak) and, leaving Tonty in command, hastened back both to get supplies for the building of a new ship at Crèvecœur and to learn the fate of the *Griffon*. He found that the *Griffon* had never been seen again. Undismayed, he secured new supplies and hurried westward, only to meet the staggering news that Tonty's men had mutinied. Hoping against hope that Tonty himself had been able to hold out, he then pushed on, only to find Fort Heartbreak utterly forlorn. A few months later Tonty, at Michilimackinac, told him the story of the whole disaster. But this only strengthened the indomitable fixed idea of being "more resolute than ever to continue the work and push on with further explorations."

682 From the painting, 1888, artist unknown, in the State Capitol, Springfield, Ill.

LA SALLE AT THE MISSISSIPPI

La Salle with Tonty returned to Fort Frontenac, replenished his supplies, and hurried west again. With what anxiety, and yet dauntless hope, must he have gazed upon this mighty Father of Waters, flowing through the very heart of his previsioned, vast New France. By February, 1682, his canoes were floating down the Mississippi. Past the Missouri and the Ohio they went on steadily southward until in April they reached the place where the great river divides to flow into the Gulf.

683   From *Collier's Weekly*, Feb. 10, 1906, painting by Frederic Remington
© P. F. Collier & Son Co.

684   From the painting (1902) by J. N. Marchand in La Salle High School,
New Orleans, La. Courtesy of Singer Manufacturing Company, New York

LA SALLE ANNEXES THE FUTURE LOUISIANA, 1682

Part of his dream had been achieved. With the solemnity due a great occasion La Salle set up a column hewn from the forest, affixing to it the insignia of the *fleur-de-lys*. Thus far had he brought the boundary of New France. The season was advancing, supplies were low, and it was a long paddle back up river. By August the party reached the country of the Illinois. Here La Salle and Tonty built a new fort, St. Louis, and spent the winter. The next year saw La Salle in France with a great project to lay before the king.

LA SALLE'S EXPEDITION TO LOUISIANA, 1684

The plan found favor at court. By midsummer four ships were at sea with men and supplies for the planting of a French post at the mouth of the Mississippi. But there were troubles enough on the way — disease breaking out, quarrels among the officers, and an attack by the Spaniards. The fact was that, what with her European troubles and her failure to develop a really national interest in colonization, France only put forth her left arm, and that spasmodically. She grasped the idea; but could not produce the people.

685   From the Champlain Edition of Parkman, after the painting by Gudin
(1802–79) in the Versailles Gallery. Courtesy of Little, Brown & Co.

686   From L. Hennepin, *Nouveau Voyage*, etc., Utrecht, 1698

LA SALLE'S CAMP IN TEXAS

FAR to the westward of the longed for Father of
Waters, La Salle camped his little band in Matagorda
Bay, while he searched vainly for the Mississippi.
La Salle's camp is indicated on the map in the
upper left corner, and the camp of the Indians to the right of it.   At the bottom is seen the French frigate
Le Jolly at anchor.

LA SALLE PUT ASHORE, 1685

THEN came the crowning misfortune (No. 686),
when the French admiral convoying La Salle put the
wretched colonists ashore far away to the westward
of the Mississippi.

687   From Ms. plan and sketch by an observer, in the Dépôt des
Cartes et Plans de la Marine, Paris

LA SALLE GOES FROM FORT ST. LOUIS TO HIS DEATH, 1687

LA SALLE had built a new Fort St. Louis as a base of operations.   For month after month he sought the
Mississippi in vain.   Finally he gave up and, with a small band, turned sadly northward in the hope of
reaching the Great Lakes.

688   From the painting by J. N. Marchand, about 1903. Courtesy of the Singer Manufacturing Company, New York

LA SALLE ASSASSINATED BY ONE OF HIS OWN MEN, 1687

LA SALLE had not yet got north of Texas before he was murdered. His determination to subordinate everything and every person to one exacting end was not fully shared by his men, who also resented the very firm hand with which he held them to their desperate task. So La Salle gave up his life in the midst of the wilderness which he had sought with such determination to win for New France.

WHERE LA SALLE'S PARTY WAS RESCUED

AFTER La Salle's assassination his followers were dispersed. The map below shows the location (at the left), several hundred miles west of the mouth of the Mississippi (at the right), of the cabins occupied by them at the time they were humanely rescued by the Spanish in the year 1689.

689   From L. Hennepin, *A New Discovery of a Vast Country in America,* . . . London, 1698

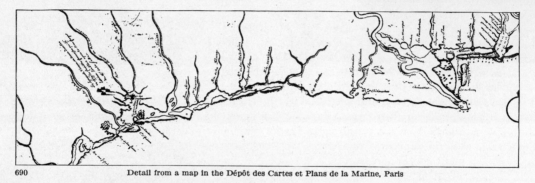

690   Detail from a map in the Dépôt des Cartes et Plans de la Marine, Paris

LANDING OF THE FRENCH UNDER D'IBERVILLE, AT OLD BILOXI, 1699

691   From the painting by Nesbit Benson, 1922, in the Historical Society of Mississippi, Jackson, Miss.

THE great event between the explorations of La Salle and the founding of New Orleans was Iberville's voyage of 1699, when (so far as that was possible with his handful of men) he confirmed La Salle's proclamation of French possession and anticipated the founding of a new French capital at New Orleans by building Fort Maurepas on or near the present site of Ocean Springs in Biloxi Bay. This was the first white settlement in Mississippi.

At the end of the same year Iberville came back and built a little fort eighteen leagues up the Mississippi. This was the first white settlement in Louisiana.

MADELEINE DE VERCHÈRES,
GIRL HEROINE OF NEW FRANCE: 1692

THE border seigniories which had been settled by the veterans of Carignan stood right in the line of Iroquois invasion; and after the appalling massacre of Lachine in 1689, when that whole settlement was blotted out by Iroquois, the very woods between the Richelieu and Montreal seemed ominous of doom, more especially because New France never had nearly enough men to garrison every little fort on every frontier seigniory. Madeleine de Verchères, however, proved herself well able to hold even Iroquois at bay.

MADELEINE AT BAY

ONE brooding day in October, when Captain de Verchères was on duty at Quebec, and his wife obliged to be in Montreal, his tiny fort at Verchères was garrisoned by three men, two boys, and one girl. The eldest man was over eighty. The Verchères were ten and twelve; their sister, Madeleine, fourteen. Suddenly, from the crimson forest came a burst of musketry. Then, through the smoke, came fifty yelling Iroquois. Madeleine, true daughter of the veterans, instantly ran in and barred the gate, put on a soldier's hat, took up her musket, armed both her brothers, and saw that they and all three men were properly posted at once. As quickly, she fired the single cannon, both to make the Iroquois think the

692   Statuette by Louis Philippe Hébert, made for the Dominion Archives, Ottawa, from a family portrait

fort well defended and to warn any *habitants* near by. Presently a family appeared at the river landing, between which and the fort there was a fire-zone of a hundred yards. Madeleine ran out and shepherded these people in, the Iroquois not venturing to break cover under that cannon's mouth.

For a whole week the dauntless Madeleine kept the murderous savages at bay. The word "All's well!" was duly shouted round the little fort, just as if it held a real garrison. Half the defenders were always on the watch; and no Iroquois could show himself without drawing fire. On the sixth day the news reached Montreal; and on the seventh Lieutenant de la Monnerie arrived with forty men. Madeleine, then not on actual guard, was dozing, with her musket on her knees, when her sentry challenged: *Qui vive?* "French: la Monnerie and forty men." Madeleine was all alert, and ready with the regulation word: "Advance one, and give the countersign!" When Monnerie complied she at once saluted, saying, "Sir,

693   From the painting by C. W. Jefferys, in the Dominion Archives, Ottawa

I hand over my command to you." Then, after he and she had made grand rounds together, and he had found everything in perfect order, she again saluted and asked the proper question in the proper way: "Sir, can you now relieve the guard: we've been on duty for a week?"

The problems of the frontier of New France that faced the Iroquois were not different from those of the English frontier that was destined slowly to work its way across the continent. Elsewhere, the French made friends with the Indians and had little trouble.

QUEBEC IN 1709

AT this headquarters of New France
the Governor, Intendant, and Bishop,
were often at cross-purposes — inevitably
so, where there was an autocratic system
without a local autocrat. Frontenac's
"Brandy Parliament" decided, against
Bishop Laval's most strenuous efforts,
that brandy was needed in the fur trade,
lest Dutch gin and English rum should
draw the Indians south. Again, Laval's
successor, St. Vallier, strongly opposed
the theater, and pronounced Molière's

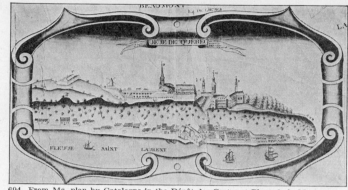

694 From Ms. plan by Catalogne in the Dépôt des Cartes et Plans de la Marine,
Paris; courtesy of Dominion Archives, Ottawa

Tartufe anathema. Frontenac as strongly favored it. He was in touch with the world of arts as well as
arms. But before Catalogne had drawn this plan, the *Cœur de Lion* of France had fought his last fight with
either foreign or domestic foes. His final public act, however, was diplomacy itself — the fêting of John

695   Drawn expressly for *The Pageant of America* by C. W. Jefferys

Schuyler, who had come from
the rival British colonies to exchange the prisoners of war after
the Peace of 1697.

CADILLAC FOUNDS DETROIT
July 24, 1701

THREE years after Frontenac's
death, Antoine de la Mothe
Cadillac, starting from La Salle's
Lachine with a brother of La
Salle's friend Tonty, and
traveling by Champlain's route
up the Ottawa and on to Lake
Huron, took a hundred men in
twenty-five canoes down to the
site of Detroit. Here he built
a picket fort (called Pontchar-
train), sixty yards square and
forty paces from the water.

ESTHER WHEELWRIGHT, PURITAN AND URSULINE

TAKEN by Abnakis during a raid on Wells, Me., in 1703, ransomed
five years later by the French governor, who sent her to school with
his own daughter, this little Puritan great-grand-daughter of John
Wheelwright had changed her English speech for Indian, her Indian
for French, and the faith of her fathers for that of the Ursulines by
the time the Peace of 1713 had let communications pass between
her old home and her new. Far stranger still, at the time of the
British conquest this daughter of the Puritans from the British colonies
was the Mother Superior of these French-Canadian nuns.

696   From a portrait in the possession of the
seventh generation of the Wheelwright family

THE FALL OF NEW FRANCE, 1713–1763

THE land had peace for thirty years. But the French were so exhausted by the later wars of Louis XIV that they acquiesced in being governed by the cradle and the grave throughout this period of decline. Louis XV came to the throne at the age of five in 1715, and Cardinal Fleury was seventy at his accession in 1723 to twenty years of power.

French Acadia was already in complete eclipse, having been ceded to the British by the Treaty of Utrecht; and the shadow was stealing across the Laurentian regions of New France. Only Louisiana looked, for one moment, bright; and that was really due to a purely artificial flare. In 1718 Bienville founded New Orleans, the tiny capital of Louisiana, which then included the whole Mississippi region, known and unknown.

The great French age of exploration ended with La Salle. But La Vérendrye and his four sons, all French-Canadians from Three Rivers, began in 1731 a quest for the Western Sea which reached its climax on New Year's Day in 1743, when the sons became the first Frenchmen who ever saw the Rockies.

Meanwhile the fur trade followed its checkered course, with all the usual interruptions from English-speaking rivals and the always hostile Iroquois. Montreal was the great emporium, where the Indians often came with pelts, as did the *voyageurs* and trappers who spoke French. Three Rivers was a much smaller trading center. But it had some business brought down by the St. Maurice; and, like Montreal, it was the seat of a Lieutenant-Governor.

In 1753 young George Washington, sent by Virginia to the Ohio country, warned the French to leave the region claimed by England. Their answer was a flat refusal. Then came the events of the last great war with England for colonial empire in the New World. Expeditions were sent by the English into the Ohio country. Others went up "the great war-path" by Lake Champlain to strike Montreal. Wolfe with his fleet and army finally penetrated the St. Lawrence and captured Quebec. Then the structure which France had reared in the valley of the St. Lawrence collapsed. But subsequent events were to prove that the dream of a French empire in America was not to die. Napoleon revived the old vision in his plans for Hayti and Louisiana; but failed to achieve his objective. When in 1803 he sold the vast territory west of the Mississippi to the young United States, the French flag passed forever from the continent of North America.

The French and Indian war destroyed the last vestige of French power along the banks of the St. Lawrence. Protestant England ruled over Catholic New France. The officials went home and the province was abandoned by its political and social leaders. Of all French institutions transplanted into the New World the Church alone remained. Faced with possible inundation by an alien and heretic people, the clergy of New France, supported by the liberal policy of the conqueror, sought to lead their flocks in such a way as to retain the unity of the French racial group. Modern French Canada is, to a large extent, the result of their foresight and statesmanship.

BIENVILLE, FOUNDER OF NEW ORLEANS, 1680–1765

FIVE years after the close of Queen Anne's War, Bienville, in 1718, founded New Orleans, which, four years later, became the capital of that vast province of Louisiana which stretched northward and westward no one knew how far. Bienville was one of the eleven sons of Charles Le Moyne, a famous French-Canadian seigneur. Iberville was another. New Orleans was the southernmost outpost of a French empire in North America like that of which La Salle had dreamed and had given his life to found. In area the domain of New France was vastly greater than the actual holdings of the English seaboard. England also claimed the continental interior.

But English traders and trappers venturing westward came upon French forts at strategic points. New Orleans was one of the greatest of these.

697 After the portrait in the possession of Mrs. R. A. Fergusson, Kingennie, Scotland, courtesy of Little, Brown, and Co.

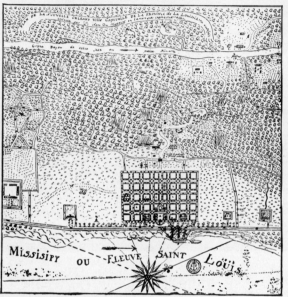

699 From an original sketch-plan of New Orleans, about 1720, in the Dépôt des Cartes et Plans de la Marine, Paris

PLAN OF NEW ORLEANS

CHARLEVOIX, chronicler and priest, described New Orleans as a little group of a hundred wretched hovels, in a malarious thicket of willows and dwarf palmettos, infested with serpents and alligators. Much of the population in the early days was of the most undesirable sort—deported galley-slaves and city scourings. There were also trappers and gold hunters accustomed to the wilds. All together they made a very turbulent population.

LA HARPE'S MAP OF LOUISIANA IN 1720

LA HARPE was very unassuming here. His boundaries for Louisiana are very restricted. Forty years later, in the map published in London by Thomas Jefferys at the height of the Seven Years' War, and at the very time (1760) of the last campaign against New France, Louisiana can be seen stretching from the Gulf of Mexico north to the Great Lakes and westward to the Rockies.

698 From an original sketch in the Dépôt des Cartes et Plans de la Marine, Paris

A GLIMPSE OF NEW ORLEANS, 1719

"THE Islets or dwellings of the citizens are surrounded by water for three months every year, when the river overflows, from the 25th of March. . . . In front of the town there is a levée, and behind it a ditch and other forms of draining."

700 From the original map in the Dépôt des Cartes et Plans de la Marine, Paris

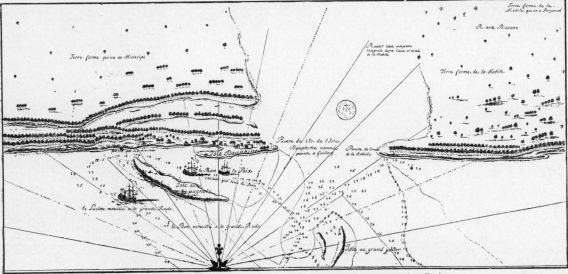

701   From a Ms. chart, not dated, in the Dépôt des Cartes et Plans de la Marine, Paris

THE FRENCH AT MOBILE

FRENCH influence and settlements spread eastward along the Gulf in the early eighteenth century. The map shows the site of the settlement on Isle Dauphine at the mouth of the Bay — the French settlement of Mobile, founded 1702 by Iberville, being to the north on the western side of the Bay. Mobile was the capital of Louisiana until 1720, when Biloxi became the capital.

THE SOUTH SEA BUBBLE

THE year after Bienville founded New Orleans the flare of preposterous speculation threw its distorting light upon Louisiana. John Law, a Franco-Scotsman, who was at first mistaken for a wizard of finance, pooled all the oversea French companies into a state corporation which people mistook for the actual owner of all the extra-European wealth of the whole world that did not already belong to the British, Spaniards, or Dutch. Louisiana was to be the modern Eldorado whence millions would come every day. When shares

rose to forty times par, and some real millions were consequently made overnight, the speculative public went mad. A few months later, in 1720, the "Mississippi Bubble" burst, to the utter ruin of all who, having lost their heads, never came to their senses in time.

703 From an engraving, 1720, by Leon Schenk

JOHN LAW, 1671–1729, CONTROLLER-GENERAL OF FINANCE, 1719–20

702   From the painting *The South Sea Bubble*, by E. M. Ward (1816–79), in the
National Gallery, London

LA VÉRENDRYE AND THE WESTERN INDIANS

THE great age of French exploration ended with La Salle. In those years the heart of the continent had been opened up and intrepid explorers had pushed both north and south. One more task remained, and that fell to the lot of La Vérendrye, a French-Canadian of Three Rivers, and his sons. Fur traders, bound for the Back of Beyond, they pushed their way westward over the treeless plains from tribe to tribe of Indians.

704 From *Collier's Weekly*, March 17, 1906, painting by Frederic Remington. © P. F. Collier & Son Co.

705   From an original drawing by C. W. Jefferys, in possession of the publishers

SONS OF LA VÉRENDRYE SIGHTING THE ROCKIES, 1743

AT last the sons of the old trader, the first Frenchmen to see the Rockies, saw the Big Horn mountains lifting their snowy peaks over the horizon. Without knowing it they were looking upon a boundary beyond which the claims of New France were never to go. Could they have looked southwestward a thousand miles or more they would have seen the ambitious Spaniards making their way northward into these same Rockies, creeping up the Pacific coast, and founding missions and settlements in California.

INDIANS IN MONTREAL

THOUGH the French pushed the fur trade far off into the western plains its center and emporium remained at Montreal. Here each summer was held the great fair and fur exchange, where Indians, fur traders, and merchants gathered to buy and sell, attesting the truth of the words of a contemporary chronicler:

"I would have you know that Canada subsists only upon the trade of these skins and furs, three-fourths of which come from the people who live around the Great Lakes."

706 From *Harper's Magazine*, April, 1892, after an original drawing by Frederic Remington

707 From an engraving by P. Canot after a drawing by Thomas Patten, for *Scenographia Americana*, London, 1762

MONTREAL FROM THE EAST

THERE were three "governments" in New France proper: the governments of Quebec, Three Rivers, and Montreal. Quebec, as the capital, had the Governor-General. Three Rivers and Montreal each had a Lieutenant-Governor. For many years after the French régime the habitants in these three governments were distinguished by the different colors of their *tuques*, i.e., knitted caps, long, and falling over on one side: Quebec, red; Three Rivers, white; Montreal, blue.

The Bluebonnets race-course still preserves the name originally given to this place near Montreal by the first English-speaking people there. Montreal never looked (or really was) half as strong as pictured here.

THREE RIVERS

THE sketch of the French center at Three Rivers was drawn upon the spot. The settlement grew slowly with the growth of New France. But it never achieved the importance of Montreal on the west or Quebec on the east.

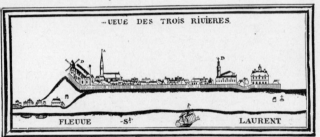

708 From inset on Catalogne's Map of 1709, in the Dépôt des Cartes et Plans de la Marine, Paris. Courtesy of Dominion Archives, Ottawa

PLAN AND VIEW OF QUEBEC IN 1729

QUEBEC remained the capital, where Church and State were ruled from France by a governor-general, bishop, and intendant, as before; and the few enlightened travelers of that age fully enjoyed its charm. But beneath the surface all true prosperity was withering away; and when the Intendancy fell into the rapacious hands of François Bigot, the most consummate thief with whom New France was ever cursed, the inevitable ruin came with the final French and Indian War. Of all French institutions transplanted into the New World the Church alone remained a really virile force.

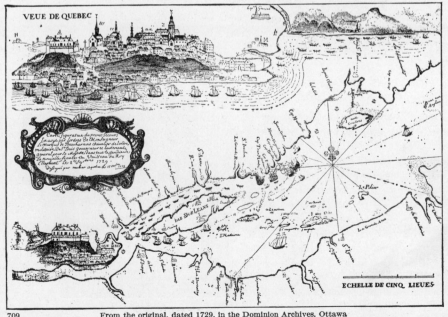

709 From the original, dated 1729, in the Dominion Archives, Ottawa

THE BASILICA, QUEBEC

THE Basilica, Quebec, was the headquarters of the Church throughout all the French dominions in America, right down to New Orleans, which was under its episcopal jurisdiction till the British Crown recognized the United States in 1783. The original building dated from 1647. It was rebuilt in 1749, burnt in 1922, and restored in 1925.

710   From a modern watercolor by
Walter Baker

TREASURY NOTE SIGNED BY BIGOT

THIS Treasury note for ninety-six livres was signed by Bigot, the last Intendant of New France, on the 1st of October, 1759, after the Battle of the Plains of Abraham, when the Government of New France had to leave its capital, Quebec, and retire to Montreal, where it finally capitulated within a year of the date written over the signature of the arch-thief Bigot.

711   From the original belonging to M. Cyrille
Tessier, Quebec

CARD MONEY SIGNED BY BIGOT

CARD money (piece for twenty-four livres) signed by La Jonquière as Governor-General, and countersigned by Bigot, who then, in 1749, was at the beginning of his perfectly unscrupulous career of absolute corruption, as the last Intendant of New France.

712   From the original belonging to M. Cyrille Tessier, Quebec

PALACE OF BIGOT, THE LAST INTENDANT

No authentic portrait of that consummate arch-fiend, François Bigot, apparently exists. But this picture of the Intendant's Palace at Quebec may serve to remind us of the difference between his ways of life and those of the heroic Montcalm, the last and greatest champion of New France. Montcalm lived in unpretentious winter quarters and ate scraggy horseflesh when the wretched colony was dying. Knavish Bigot and foolish Vaudreuil lived in all the luxury that New France could yield them by disgraceful means. When the whole country surrendered at Montreal in September, 1760, and the French and French-Canadians who had survived six desperate campaigns laid down their valiant arms, Vaudreuil (the Governor-General), and Bigot, to their eternal shame, made special terms for their own vile comfort and possessions.

713   From an engraving after a drawing by Richard Short, 1761, in the Dominion Archives,
Ottawa

CHAPTER XVIII

SPAIN IN THE SOUTHWEST

DURING the hundred years following the defeat of the Armada, years when the English were planting colonies on the Atlantic seaboard and the French explorers from Quebec and Montreal were penetrating the hinterland, Spain steadily declined. She had banished the Moors and Jews, two important factors in her economic structure. Treasure-seeking in the New World had diverted the energies of many of her people from productive activities. As the flow of treasure slackened, the impoverishment of national resources became increasingly apparent. Wars with the Dutch and with England sapped the Spanish military strength. One after another Spain's possessions in Europe slipped from her. Spanish power in the Netherlands, the Rhineland and Italy was curtailed or disappeared altogether. In 1640, Portugal revolted and became once more independent. With Portugal, Spain lost Brazil and the Portuguese colonies in the Far East.

But the same years that saw the waning of the Spanish power in Europe witnessed the growth of New Spain in America. Steadily the Spanish viceroys spread the laws and language of Spain and the faith of the Catholic Church over peoples and lands more and more remote from the Mexican capital. Explorers made their way northward across the dry country of northern Mexico. Missionaries and colonists followed them. In 1609, two years after the English planted their first permanent colony at Jamestown, Santa Fé was founded. From New Mexico the Spanish frontier in course of time pushed into Texas. The eighteenth century saw a Spanish advance in another direction. A foothold was first won on the peninsula of Lower California. Then Spanish missions and presidios (forts) appeared in the valleys of California.

Almost always the missionary was to be found leading the advance. The wild tribes that lay to the west and north of the seat of the Aztec power offered little to the seeker of gold; hence the seeker for souls for a time had a free hand. The missionary taught the gospel and trained the Indians to be self-supporting in a rudimentary civilization. Wandering tribes were gathered into pueblos beside the missions and sometimes held there by force. Close on the heels of the mission came the presidio or fort, which marked the establishment of military and political power. Both mission and presidio were looked upon as transitory. The officials of New Spain looked forward to a day when their holdings would be consolidated and when New Spain would take on something of the settled quality of the motherland.

714 Old Pecos Mission near Glorietta, N. M.,
photograph by the Department of Roads, Washington

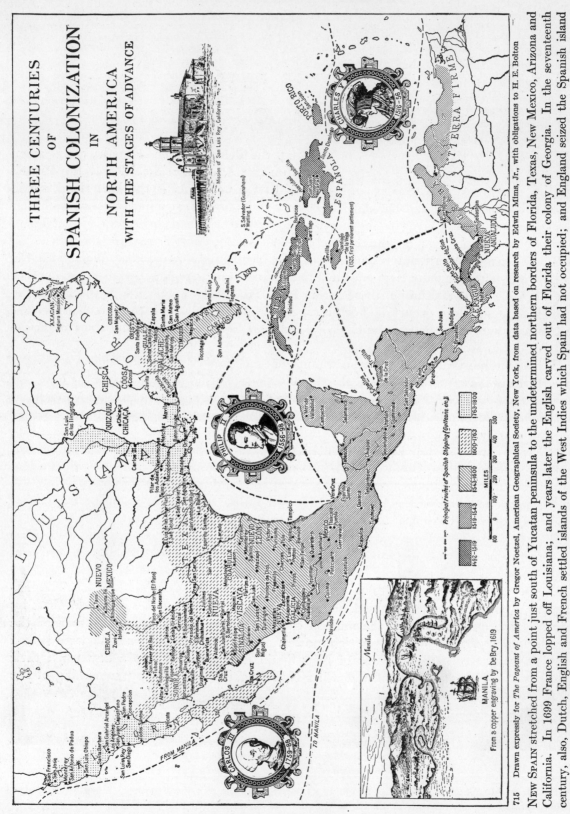

THREE CENTURIES
OF
SPANISH COLONIZATION
IN
NORTH AMERICA
WITH THE STAGES OF ADVANCE

Mission of San Luis Rey, California

MANILA

MANILA.
From a copper engraving by de Bry, 1619

1492-1519	1519-1543	1543-1600	1600-1763	1763-1800	

MILES
100   0   100   200   300   400   500

Principal routes of Spanish Shipping (Galleons etc.)

715   Drawn expressly for *The Pageant of America* by Gregor Noetzel, American Geographical Society, New York, from data based on research by Edwin Mims, Jr., with obligations to H. E. Bolton

NEW SPAIN stretched from a point just south of Yucatan peninsula to the undetermined northern borders of Florida, Texas, New Mexico, Arizona and California. In 1699 France lopped off Louisiana; and years later the English carved out of Florida their colony of Georgia. In the seventeenth century, also, Dutch, English and French settled islands of the West Indies which Spain had not occupied; and England seized the Spanish island of Jamaica. With the Seven Years' War, she lost Florida to the English, and gained Louisiana from France.

PALACE OF THE VICEROYS

WITH her decline as a power in Europe, Spain looked more and more to her New World possessions to supply her with gold and to uphold her prestige. To Mexico she looked to guard her frontier from English and French encroachment. The vice-regal palace housed a succession of strong men, who kept high state and dignity in the capital, were bold and ruthless in the quelling of revolt, and energetic in sending out exploring and conquering expeditions north by land and sea. They wrote Texas, New Mexico, Arizona and California upon the map of New Spain.

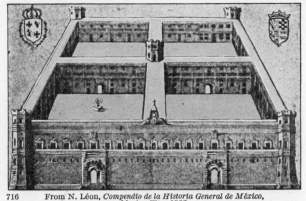

716   From N. Léon, *Compendio de la Historia General de México*, Mexico City, 1902

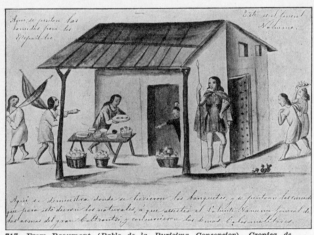

717   From Beaumont (*Pablo de la Purisima Concepcion*), *Cronica de Mechoacan*. Transcript of Ms. about 1750. In New York Public Library

NATIVE LIFE PICTURED BY FRIAR BEAUMONT

FRIAR BEAUMONT (see No. 236) here pictures a banquet scene in which natives have prepared a feast for General Nañuma and the Spanish military chiefs.

To this crude sketch the good Friar attached in his own hand a few notes in Spanish which illustrate the complete subserviency of the simple natives to the military authority of the invaders.

718   From Alexander Humboldt, *Vues des Cordillères* . . . etc., Paris, 1810

OLD CATHEDRAL IN MEXICO CITY

IN the life of Mexico the Church was a symbol as imposing as the vice-regal palace. The great cathedral, which stands on or near the site of the Aztec temple, was begun in 1573, and finished in 1811. During the seventeenth and eighteenth centuries it was the most imposing and most beautiful building in America.

THE UNIVERSITY OF MEXICO

In 1553, under the influence of a vigorous viceroy, Mendoza, the University of Mexico was founded. It was the first university in North America, and the building is now used by the Conservatory of Music.

719   From Manuel Rivera Cambas, *Mexico Pintoresco Artistico y Monumental*, Mexico City, 1880

720   From the painting *Capture of the Spanish Treasure Ship*, by Carlton T. Chapman, courtesy of the artist

DRAKE IN THE PACIFIC

The news of Sir Francis Drake's raid in the Pacific in 1578–79 shook New Spain like a reed. Old Spain was stirred. Wild rumors flew overseas between Madrid and Mexico. Philip II ordered the Mexican Viceroy to send out expeditions by sea and land to discover and fortify the western mouth of the Strait and to colonize the land once traversed by Coronado.

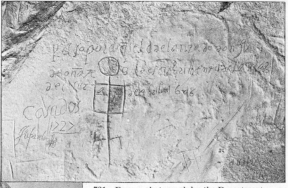

721   From a photograph by the Department of the Interior, Washington

722   From a photograph by the Bureau of Ethnology, Washington

EL MORRO ROCK WITH OÑATE'S INSCRIPTION, 1606

Delays occurred, partly because of Philip's belief that his Armada would destroy England's power in both hemispheres. But his Armada was beaten. Again he ordered the Mexican Viceroy to make secure for him his far western lands. In 1598 Juan de Oñate led a colony into New Mexico. He explored widely from Kansas to California but did not reach the sea.

On El Morro Rock (Valencia County, N. M.) he inscribed this legend: "Passed by here the *adelantado* Juan de Oñate to the discovery of the sea of the South on the 16th of April, year 1606."

THE GOVERNOR'S PALACE, SANTA FÉ

OÑATE'S successor, Pedro de Peralta, founded Santa Fé in 1609. A map of America north of Mexico as it was in that year would show English Jamestown, founded in 1607, French Quebec, founded in 1608, Spanish St. Augustine, 1565, and, far to the west, Spanish Santa Fé, 1609, and, at Manhattan Isle, Henry Hudson taking possession for the Dutch — a scene set for a long and mighty conflict.

723   From the painting by Oscar B. Jacobson (1882-), in the University of Oklahoma, Norman, Oklahoma

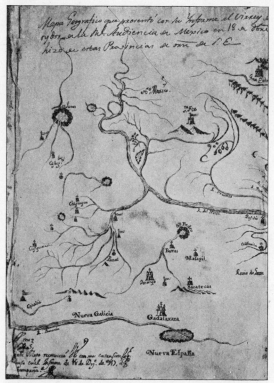

724   From the original map accompanying the Report of the Viceroy of New Spain, December, 1717, in the Archives of the Indies, Seville, Spain

MAP OF NEW MEXICO IN 1717

THE Spaniards colonized New Mexico. By 1617 zealous Franciscans had built seven churches and baptized fourteen thousand Indians. But the Spanish hand lay heavy on the native tribes. The deeply rooted religious customs of the Indians were suppressed; severe penalties followed infringement of the rules of the Church; tribute was levied on the conquered people. In 1680 the Indians revolted. Four hundred Spaniards were massacred and New Mexico passed again into the control of its ancient rulers.

This curious old map shows New Mexico after the Spaniards had returned. The missions are shown by small buildings surmounted with crosses. Santa Fé appears behind two mountains. The number and distribution of the Spanish centers show the extent of the occupation of the New Mexican region.

THE REOCCUPATION OF NEW MEXICO

DURING the years of their independence the Indians attempted to destroy the vestiges of the Spanish civilization. The churches, particularly, were objects of their wrath. But in 1692, a new commander, Don Diego de Vargas, approached from the valley of the Rio Grande. He came to Santa Fé and persuaded its people to surrender. The Cross was again raised in New Mexico and the Spanish power ruled in the pueblos.

725   From R. E. Twitchell, *Leading Facts of New Mexican History*, Cedar Rapids, Iowa, 1911–12, drawing by Kenneth M. Chapman

726 From the Champlain Edition of Francis Parkman;
drawing by Adrien Moreau (1843–). Courtesy of Little,
Brown and Company

DE LEÓN'S AND TERÁN'S MARCHES INTO TEXAS

NEWS of La Salle was transmitted by special
messenger from the Spanish ambassador at
Louis' court to his King; and was carried as swiftly as galleons could sail to Vera Cruz. The viceroy
selected the experienced frontiersman, Alonzo de León, to lead an army northeastward across the Rio Grande,
to destroy the colony which La Salle might plant on the Missis-
sippi River. On his third journey León found La Salle's abandoned fort, which was set afire presently by Father Massanet,
who accompanied him. After Alonzo's death Domingo Terán,
in 1691, entered Texas but, like León, failed to make a permanent establishment.

728 From Isidro Felis de Espinosa, *El Peregrino
Septentrional Atlante*, Mexico City, 1737

LA SALLE AT THE FRENCH COURT

ENGLAND had challenged New Spain on the Pacific. France
now threatened from the region of the Mississippi. La Salle,
having gone south from Canada, and, having reached, in a
canoe, the mouth of the Father of Waters in 1682, claimed
the region for Louis XIV. Returning to France he asked and
received the monarch's assent to build a fort at the mouth
of the great river. (See pp. 320 and 321.)

727 Drawn expressly for *The Pageant of America* by Gregor Noetzel,
American Geographical Society, New York

FRA MARGIL PREACHING TO INDIANS

THE Frenchman Pierre Le Moyne d'Iberville, in 1699, settled
a colony near the Mississippi and named the country Louisiana.
His brother Bienville later came to govern the region. Frenchmen explored the Mississippi, the Mobile and the Red Rivers.
France in the north built forts from Detroit to St. Louis and
then at the mouth of the Mississippi. (See p. 315.) French
traders went into Texas. It was indeed time for Spain to
make Texas hers.

PRESIDIO OF SAN ANTONIO, 1722

As a result of the efforts of Father Margil, a number of missions were established in Texas. To strengthen these outposts and secure a base of operations against the French, the Spanish authorities decided to erect a military post and settlement on the San Antonio River. Early in 1718 sixty-two settlers were sent out accompanied by friars and soldiers. By these the presidio of San Antonio was erected, just three months before Bienville founded New Orleans. About the pre-

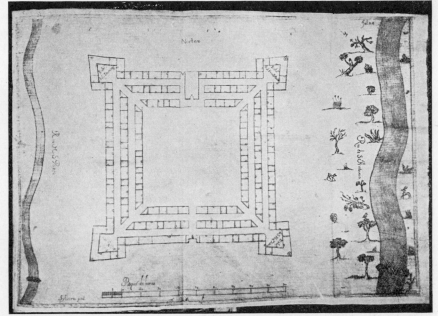

729 From Antonio de la Peña, *Derrotero de la expedicion en la Provincia de Texas*, Mexico, 1722, in the Archives of the Indies, Seville

sidio were established a settlement and the San Antonio, or Alamo, mission.

Two other establishments fastened the Spanish hold upon Texas. They were the mission and presidio of Nacogdoches, far to the eastward near Louisiana, and Bahia del Espiritu, near the site of La Salle's fort on Matagorda Bay.

PLAN OF PRESIDIO AT ADAES, 1721

THE most important French post in this debatable southland was Natchitoches on the Red River commanding western Louisiana. In 1721 a Spanish force led by the Marquis of Aguayo erected the Presidio of Los Adaes, now Robeline, La., fifteen miles from Natchitoches. "On the top of this elevation, which commanded the whole plain," wrote La Peña in 1721, "his lordship laid out and began at once to build the

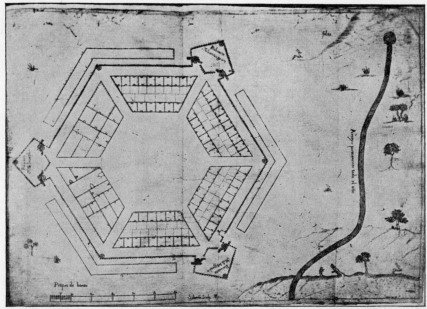

fortification. He gave it the form of a hexagon, making each side about fifty-five yards long. He left three bastions unconstructed and made the other three smaller than he had planned. These he placed at the alternate corners so that each should protect two sides of the fort. He made these changes in his plan to suit the nature of the land and the few soldiers assigned to the fort." — BOLTON AND BARKER, *With the Makers of Texas*, New York, 1904.

Here at the border, facing the French, the Spaniards fixed the capital of Texas.

730 From Antonio de la Peña, *Derrotero de la expedicion en la Provincia de Texas*, Mexico, 1722, in the Archives of the Indies, Seville

731 From Bon Marc de Villiers du Terrage, *Les Dernières Années de la Louisiane Française*, Paris, 1904. After a contemporary painting, artist unknown, in El Museo Naval, Madrid

ULLOA, FIRST SPANISH GOVERNOR OF LOUISIANA

SPAIN entered the Seven Years' War (1756–63), as the ally of France; and by secret treaty in 1761 acquired Louisiana. France had lost Canada to England and was trying to prevent Louisiana also from falling into the same hands.

In 1766 Spain sent Juan Antonio de Ulloa (No. 731), as first governor of Spanish Louisiana. Ulloa was a well-known scientist and naval officer. He had once been captured by the English, taken to London as a prisoner of war and there, as a scientist, made a member of the Royal Society of London.

732 From the portrait by Andres Molinary (1847–1915), in the Louisiana Historical Society, New Orleans

GOVERNOR O'REILLY, *ca.* 1730–94

THE French inhabitants resented the transfer of their allegiance by treaty. They hampered Ulloa in every way and finally chose a new governor backed by a military force. In 1768 Alejándro O'Reilly, the new governor (No. 732), determined to stamp out rebellion and to make an example of Louisiana. He secured information regarding the leaders of revolt, arrested them while they were his guests at a reception and had them summarily executed. Spain thus took control of Louisiana in fact as well as in name.

OLD SPANISH PALACE AND CATHEDRAL, NEW ORLEANS

BIENVILLE had founded New Orleans in 1718 and made it the capital of Louisiana in 1722. It was originally a swampy, unhealthful place and its growth was slow; but it was a favorite rendezvous for gold-hunters, trappers, buccaneers, many of whom were deported galley-slaves. The raising of the Spanish flag made little change in New Orleans. The larger part of the city was destroyed by fire in 1788. Its real development began with the sugar industry which was put on a sound basis in 1795. In 1803 it had about 10,000 inhabitants to witness the ceremonial transfer of Louisiana to the United States.

733　　　　From a print, about 1820, in the Louisiana State Museum, New Orleans

AN "ISLAND CALLED CALIFORNIA"

THE story of California differs from that of Texas. In 1510 an author named Montcalvo published a romance titled *Esplandián* in which he said: "Know that on the right hand of the Indies there is an island called California very close to the side of the Terrestrial Paradise . . . in the whole island there was no metal but gold." Hence the name California, which Cortés is said to have bestowed on the "island" of Lower California, where he went in search of the gold and the other marvels described by Montcalvo.

734 From Herrera, *Novus Orbis* (with vignette map showing California an island). Amsterdam, 1622

SALVATIERRA, MISSIONARY, 1648-1717

735 From the portrait in the National Museum, Mexico City

JUAN MARIA DE SALVATIERRA, a Jesuit of great ability and energy, undertook to convert the natives of Lower California. His efforts with the docile Indian were successful. Missions were established from San Bruno, just north of La Paz, to Santa Maria, just south of Velicata. The Jesuit missions, with their fields of grain and fruit and herds of cattle, prepared the way for the exploration and colonization of Upper California.

THE MISSIONS OF CALIFORNIA

GRADUALLY the missions worked their way northward. They had a dual purpose. With the Fathers, of course, the chief aim was the Christianization of the Indians and the saving of souls. But to the secular powers the missions were the outposts of Spanish sovereignty. Spain at home had been crippled. She could no longer gather shiploads of colonists for distant lands. She looked, therefore, to the missionaries to domesticate the natives, collect them in villages, make loyal subjects of them, and thus provide her new lands with a well disciplined people to hold those territories for her against the encroachments of other nations.

736   After a sketch of San Juan Bautista by Vischer, 1865

737   After a sketch of San Buenaventura by Vischer, 1865. (Courtesy of the University of California, Berkeley, Cal.)

738 From the portrait by A. R. Mengs (1728–79), in the Musée du Prado, Madrid

CARLOS III, KING OF SPAIN, 1716–88

CARLOS III ascended the Spanish throne in 1759, the year in which Portugal exiled the Jesuits and in which Quebec fell before the armies of Wolfe. He entered the Seven Years' War as France's ally and secured Louisiana from her by secret treaty. But he lost Cuba and the Philippines to the English. To get them back he was forced to surrender Florida. The English now held the Atlantic coast, the Ohio Valley, and Canada. Carlos determined to secure the Pacific coast by planting fortified colonies at strategic points in Upper California. Military power had come to strengthen the hold of the missionaries.

JOSÉ DE GÁLVEZ, 1729–86

JOSÉ DE GÁLVEZ was sent out by Carlos III to carry out the order for expulsion of the Jesuits and to effect various reforms in the government of New Spain. Gálvez arranged for the transfer of the missions of Lower California, then occupied by Franciscans, to the Dominicans.

740 From *Lettres Edificantes* (etc.), Vol. v, Paris, 1724, in the New York Public Library

739 From L. Alamán, *Disertaciones sobre la Historia de la República Mejicana*, Mexico City, 1844–49

KINO'S *PIMERÍA ALTA* MAP, 1705

AFTER the establishment of Salvatierra's missions Spaniards believed California to be an island. Not so Father Kino, the great missionary of the southwest. Kino made over fifty journeys. He traversed the sandy Devil's Highway; crossed many times the country between the Gila and Magdalena Rivers; and in 1702, he explored the Colorado from the Gila's mouth to the Gulf of California. His map first clearly showed the land route to Lower California, and that this country was a peninsula and not an island.

PADRE JUNIPERO SERRA, 1713–1784

FRAY JUNIPERO SERRA, superior of the Franciscans in Lower California, was chosen by Gálvez to head the missionary enterprise in the north. Serra, a man of great gifts, had renounced honors and distinction in Europe, in order to serve the heathen in the New World. He is rightly regarded as the leading pioneer of the present state of California.

741   From the statue by Douglas Tilden (1860–) in Golden Gate Park, San Francisco

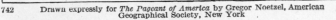

742   Drawn expressly for *The Pageant of America* by Gregor Noetzel, American Geographical Society, New York

SPANISH EXPANSION INTO CALIFORNIA

WITH the problem of the missions in Lower California out of the way Gálvez proceeded to his next task, the occupation of Upper California. He organized an expedition into the desired region and gave command to Don Gaspar de Portolá. The expedition was divided into three parts, one to advance northward by sea and two by land. Early in 1769 three Spanish ships carrying colonists sailed for San Diego. An advance party set out from Velicata in Lower California to cut a road to the same point. In May Portolá, with the main body, advanced overland into California. In less than a decade the Spaniards pushing northward by sea and land had reached the Golden Gate and had established San Francisco.

PORTOLÁ DISCOVERS THE GOLDEN GATE

LEAVING Serra at San Diego, Portolá set out on July 14 for Monterey, with several friars, Rivera and his soldiers, and the Indian road-builders. They passed Monterey Bay without recognizing it. Only when they saw Drake's Bay stretching before them did they realize that they had overshot their goal. They pitched camp. A party of hunters went into the hills after game, and presently emerged from the forest to see far below them a great smooth harbor, the huge rock pillars at its entrance glowing in the sunset. It was San Francisco Bay.

743   From the painting, 1896, by Arthur F. Mathews (1860–) in the San Francisco Art Association, San Francisco

SAN CARLOS MISSION

SAN CARLOS mission on Carmel
River, five miles from Monterey,
was Serra's home during the
fifteen years of his labors in
California. In Serra's day there
was only a small adobe church
beside the orchards of olive and
fruit trees which he had planted.
Half a stone's throw from the
church stood Serra's cell.

744 From Vancouver, *A Voyage of Discovery*. . . . London, 1798, after a sketch by J. Sykes

745 From a lithograph, 1865, of Santa Barbara Mission, by Vischer, in the
collections of the University of California, Berkeley, Cal.

SERRA HANGING THE BELLS OF SAN GABRIEL MISSION

SERRA founded nine of the twenty-one permanent missions
which the Franciscans built in California. They were
San Diego, 1769; San Carlos, 1770; San Gabriel, 1771;
San Antonio de Padua, 1771; San Luis Obispo, 1772;
San Juan Capistrano (the first, not the present, structure)
and San Francisco de Assisi, 1776; Santa Clara, 1777;
and San Buenaventura, 1782.

746   From a painting by George Melville Stone (1858–),
in the Mission Inn, Riverside, Cal.

747   From the painting by George Melville Stone, in the Mission
Inn, Riverside, Cal.

SERRA CROSSING THE DESERT

SERRA had desired to make his own the spirit of
St. Francis of Assisi. Efficient organizer and executive
as he was, yet it is as a Christian and a humanitarian
that he stands out against the colorful background of his
California. Spaniards and Indians alike were devoted
to him. His co-workers in the Faith reverenced him
as one who has attained in this world something of
the invisible Kingdom of Heaven. The keynote of
his life and labors was sounded in the first words with
which he greeted his dark-skinned "children," whether
in the mission *patio*, in the vineyard, or the road-
ways — "Love God."

PALOU ADMINISTERING ABSOLUTION TO SERRA

In his cell at San Carlos, furnished with a chair and table, a bed of boards and a blanket, where, at noon, the shadow of the great cross he had erected fell full upon him, Serra died. His pupil and biographer, Fray Palou, heard his last confession and absolved him. From many miles round the Indians trudged to Carmel to strew his coffin with the flowers he had loved.

To both Indian and white Serra personified the highest type of religious leadership. His life represented the activities of his Church at its best.

748   From the painting in the National Museum, Mexico City

749   From George Vancouver, *A Voyage of Discovery*, London, 1798

THE PRESIDIO OF MONTEREY

Life was pleasant in the old capital of California. Mission Indians did what little work was necessary in the fields and withindoors tended the cookpot. The houses, of adobe or wood, were primitive and rather bare. Gentlemen lavished expense on their own gay clothes and trappings for their horses. On feast days there was mirth and color.

DON JUAN BAUTISTA DE ANZA

To fortify San Francisco Bay and plant a colony there and to open a land route were first among the important tasks to be done to protect California from attack by way of north or south. Both were performed by the dashing frontiersman and

750   From the painting *To the Fiesta*, by Lester D. Boronda (1886–), in the Mission Inn, Riverside, Cal.

751 From the portrait in the possession of John F. Biven, San Mateo, Cal.

commander at Tubac, Arizona, Juan Bautista de Anza. He crossed desert and mountains to San Gabriel. Then in October, 1775, he started again from Tubac with his colonists. In April he left them at Monterey and went on to San Francisco to select sites for a presidio and mission. The presidio was founded in September, 1776, and the mission a month later. While Anza surveyed its site in the summer of 1776, couriers were hastening north and south from Philadelphia with the news of the birth of a new nation — one hundred and sixty-nine years after the founding of Jamestown. Another seventy-five years would see the American flag flying over the presidio of San Francisco.

NOTES ON THE PICTURES

THESE notes are predicated on the obvious fact that while historical pictures as visual aids giving swift mental impressions have a recognizable value for the teacher, student and general reader, they also have definite limitations. They vary in reliability. The original source of each picture is indicated in the attribution printed under the cut and this in many cases sufficiently establishes its authenticity. In some cases the text carries criticism or correction of the pictures. The many pictures of the sort called "fanciful" by historians, creations of the imagination of well-known painters, will call for reservation because of the very nature of their conception and execution. Comment and criticism on many such pictures are given in the notes that follow. An historical painter's reconstruction of an event which he did not witness may well express the spirit of the event and its local setting. More than this it cannot do. The painter can infuse a picture with the moral or religious significance of a great occasion, can translate a great moment of history in terms of its political meaning for posterity, or re-create a scene which has all the elements of a thrilling adventure. Pictures of the imagination, however, still remain what they are intended primarily to be, — works of creative art and not historical works. As such, they are here subjected to criticism. They should be studied more for what they suggest than as literal renderings of the facts. With such considerations in mind the following notes, which make no pretense of completeness, have been prepared as preliminary aids to any who would examine the individual pictures more fully.

THE EDITORS

3, 4. Drawn from life in water color. Accurate though the drawing is crude. White was with the Raleigh expedition to Roanoke, 1585.

5. Modification by European influence is shown in these cuts.

6. Portrait from life.

7. Engraving after a lost original by Jacques Le Moyne, who was with French expedition to Florida in 1564. His sketches of Indians from life, through influence of Richard Hakluyt, obtained for de Bry's *Grands Voyages*. Theodore de Bry (1528–98) was a German engraver and publisher at Frankfort. His son, Johannes Theodorus de Bry, carried on work after his death. De Bry's engravings illustrate explorations in both East and West. They vary from faithful copies of originals like the White drawings to purely fanciful sketches based on travelers' tales. He frequently took many liberties with originals. Historical value of each de Bry picture must be determined separately.

9. Accurate in essentials. The draftsman of the 19th century tried to visualize word descriptions of early Indian life in villages.

11. Indian palisaded village copied with Dutch legend from William Janszon Blaeu, whose *Nieuwe Atlas*, Amsterdam, 1642, has illustrations based evidently on de Bry.

12. Drawn from life by army officer.

13, 14. Artist studied in Paris under Gérôme, whose influence he shows. Painted several Indian subjects, essentially accurate in detail and spirit.

15. Drawing by Champlain on his travels in America. Essentially accurate.

16. See 7.

18. Essentially accurate.

19. Captain Seth Eastman, teacher of drawing at West Point, 1833–40, saw service in Indian country. Was chosen to illustrate *Historical and Statistical Information respecting the History, Condition and Future Prospects of the Indian Tribes of the United States*, 1850–57, issued by the U. S. government. Work marked by accurate knowledge and careful detail.

20, 22, 23. See 3.

26. Lafitau (died 1740), a Jesuit missionary who lived many years among northern forest tribes, says in his work that some of the illustrations are based on de Bry. Referring to one of the sketches he says: "The engraver has forgotten to envelop the Indian in furs as the season demands."

27. See 19.

28, 29. See 7.

37, 38. See 19.

39. See 7.

40. See 26.

41. Essentially accurate.

42, 43. See 7.

45. Artist formerly member of staff American Museum of Natural History.

46. See 12.

47. See 26.

48. Accurate. Drawn from observation by French writer who spent 16 years (1718–1734) in Louisiana. Picture represents peace ceremony in presence of Bienville.

50. See 3.

54, 55. See 7.

56, 57. See 3.

58. See 19.

59. See 3.

60. See 12.

61. Accurate in detail and in spirit. Painting done under the direction of Arthur C. Parker, Archæologist of the State Museum, Albany.

62. Artist about 1834 made many accurate drawings of Plains Indians from life, signed *pinx ad nat.*

63, 64, 66, 67. See 62.

68. A portrait painter who in 1832 went to live and work among Plains Indians, visiting more than fifty tribes. His paintings of Indian figures and customs faithful and sympathetic. Many of his originals are in the U. S. National Museum.

69, 70. See 48.

71. By German artist trained at Düsseldorf. Visited Plains Indians about 1855.

72. See 68.

73. Essentially correct.

74. Accurate, drawn from observation.

75, 76. See 68.

77. Artist, resident of Montana, familiar with modern life of plains.

78, 79, 80. See 68.

81, 82. See 62.

83. See 19.

84, 85. See 62.

86, 87. See 68.

88. See 62.

90. See 19.

91, 92, 93. See 62.

94, 96, 97. Accurate.

98. Impressionistic but essentially accurate.

99. See 62.

100. Accurate.

101. See 19.

103, 104. See 62.

105, 106. Essentially accurate.

107. See 19.

108. See 62.

109, 110. See 68.

111. Accurate. Artist familiar with Indian life.

113, 114, 115, 116. Sketched from life by government artists.

123. Accurate, painted from observation.

124. Accurate.

125. Impressionistic but essentially accurate. Sculptor born in Utah, studied in Paris, has made Indian types a specialty.

126, 127. Essentially accurate. Sculptor has specialized some in Indian subjects.

129. See 128, 130, 131, and 132.

130. See 128, 131, and 132.

140. See 128, 130, 131, and 132. Artist one of the founders of the Norwegian National School (died Oct., 1925).

141. See 128, 130, 131, and 132.

142. Conjectural.

144. Accurate in spirit.

146, 147. Vander Aa published several large works full of engravings. Many were copied from de Bry and Montanus. Others, like the two cuts here shown (from Vol. I of his *Collection*) were constructed from travelers' accounts by engravers who knew nothing at first hand of the scenes pictured.

150. Original a highly colored, fanciful decoration. Strange lands visited shown by islands in foreground.

152, 153, 154. Modern copies of originals done in 1375. Of value only as curious European conceptions of Asia before the age of discovery.

159. Accurate view, detail from large colored picture. The publisher known also for faithful pictures of Palestine (15th century) drawn on the spot.

173. Artist an authority on costume and known for many historical paintings, and illustrations in textbooks and magazines.

175. The picture is fanciful, as are most of those in Montanus.

178. After a family portrait at Nuremberg.

180. J. B. Thacher (*Columbus*, Vol. III, p. 18) says the Florence portrait was painted by Cristofano dell' Altissimo for the Duke Cosimo of Tuscany from an original in the Jovian Gallery, between 1552 and 1556.

190. "I am unable to discover that anybody here knows Crespo or where his Presentation picture hangs." (Letter from researcher in Madrid.)

191. An ideal conception of an event which probably did not take place. Painting, by a notable Italian painter of the modern school, accurately expresses ecclesiastical hostility to and ridicule of Columbus' scheme.

193. By a Spanish artist. Studied in Paris under Bonnat. His Columbus pictures based on his own study of scenes in Spain which figure in the Discoverer's career. The mounting of the globe is of a type about one hundred years later.

194. According to Señor Machado of the Junta de Iconografia Nacional, Madrid, portrait was done by Isabella's order in her lifetime and by her presented to the Cartuja (Carthusian Order) of Miraflores, whence it passed into the possession of Philip V.

195. Artist studied abroad, and in 1881 went to Spain to collect first-hand material for this painting, which in 1883 was purchased by order of Congress for the capitol.

196. For the painting here reproduced artist was awarded the Cross of Carlos III at the National Exposition at Madrid, 1877.

197. Von Brožik studied at Prague and Munich. Influenced by Piloty and Gabriel Marx, also by Munkácsy. He painted large canvases on historical subjects. Director of National Academy at Prague, 1893. The picture well illustrates modern conceptions of the importance of the signing of Columbus' agreement with the Spanish sovereigns. As this took

place at Santa Fé, in the Spanish military camp in the plain before Grenada, architectural details of the picture are much overdone. No evidence to show that the occasion was one of such ceremony and splendor. The jewels displayed on the table perpetuate an exploded fiction. See 196, text.

198. Accurate view from colored wood engraving, over five feet long. See 159.

199. Artist painted many pictures on Spanish history for that government by invitation of the Minister of War.

200. Replica, made for the Columbian Exposition, 1893, of the flagship of Columbus, from specifications supplied by the Spanish government.

202. Artist was Director of the Academy at Prague, 1841–52.

203. Artist, an American much of whose life was spent abroad, was commissioned by the U. S. government to paint this picture, for which he received $10,000. It shows little trace of the artist's earlier style or ability (e.g., his *Marius on the Ruins of Carthage*). Bishop William I. Kip alleged that the picture was partly the work of a clever Frenchman, whom Kip had seen at work on it in Paris (*The Atlantic Monthly*, February, 1867). The friar behind Columbus and the kneeling boy are inaccuracies.

204. Sketch done at Watling Island of conjectural landing place of Columbus. Cronau's conclusions as to this and other points in the Columbus story are discussed by C. K. Adams in *Some Recent Discoveries Concerning Columbus*, in Annual Report of the American Historical Association, 1891.

205. By a Spanish artist, student at School of Fine Arts, Valencia, exhibitor at Expositions in 1886 and 1887, Madrid, later Director of School of Fine Arts, San Fernando. Exhibitor at Royal Academy, London, 1909. Picture well expresses the wonder of the red men. Indians at the landing carried lances, not bows and arrows.

208. Portrait of Indian woman much idealized. The live parrots and stuffed birds to which, according to Las Casas, Columbus pointed as he addressed the sovereigns, do not appear in the picture. According to Peter Martyr (1455–1526), who was present, the sovereigns invited Columbus to be seated in their presence.

211. By an Italian painter who in 1856 was awarded the gold medal of the Academy of Bologna for historical painting. Later painted portraits in this country and in 1874 became Director of Art Department of the University of Notre Dame.

213. No basis in fact for this sculptural conception of Cabot. It, however, well symbolizes the Cabot tradition.

214. A decorative picture by a British painter of religious and historical subjects, exhibitor at the Royal Academy. Probably Cabot's departure was not accompanied with very much pomp and ceremony.

215. The original Holbein portrait then in Royal Galleries, Whitehall, London, was destroyed by fire in 1842. There is another copy by Chapman in the Massachusetts Historical Society.

216. Illustration shows only a detail of La Cosa's map.

218. Sometimes claimed as a portrait from life by Bronzino (1502–72), painter of portraits of Dante, Petrarch and Boccaccio.

220. Taken from a part of an enormous Portuguese chart, found at Munich in a collection of old sea charts, dated *ca.* 1504–05.

221. Sketch made at the Isthmus of Panama, 1890. See 204.

222. By a Canadian artist, student and illustrator of the history of the United States and Canada.

228. A reduced copy of section of Kohl's facsimile, 1860, of a Map of the World, 1529, by Diego Ribero, Spanish cosmographer. Spanish legends appear here in English. Original in the Vatican, Rome.

231. See 222.

233. The map is from a rare copper plate, dedicated to Hakluyt by "F. G." (supposed to be Francis Gualle). It records the voyage of Cabot ("Bacallaos ab Anglis, 1495"), Frobisher's discoveries ("Meta Incognita, 1576"), voyage of Amadas and Barlowe ("Virginea 1584"), and of Drake ("Nova Albion Inventa An. 1580 ab Anglis").

234. Accurate, based on accounts by observers.

243. From one of several collections of illustrated voyages of the 17th century. View probably fairly accurate.

244. One of several Montezuma portraits in Mexico, none authentic.

245. By a Mexican painter. Costumes and architecture in general accord with Aztec design.

247. An interesting example of historical painting in the century after the conquest.

260. The destruction of the Aztec capital and the building of the new Mexico City on the same location makes an accurate reconstruction of the old Aztec buildings improbable. Cf., 252, 253, 254, 255, 256, 257, 258, 259, 261, 262, 263.

265. By a Spanish painter of historical pictures and winner of first prizes. Of little historical value except as an artist's study of the mounted figure of Cortés.

268. Example of modern school of historical painting, correct in spirit. Artist for many years professor of drawing in the Circulo de Bellas Artes, Madrid.

269. See 222.

270. Portraits in oil of all the Incas are in the New York Historical Society and are said to

be the originals from which the portraits in Herrera were engraved. Portraits cannot be authenticated.

283. American painter of historical subjects. Artist received $10,000 from U. S. government. Painting shows influence of romantic school, little effort at historical investigation.

284. See 173.

285. Drawn by a member of the staff of the School of American Archæology, Santa Fé, N. M.

291. See 7.

292. Only one of Le Moyne's originals known to be in existence. Artist actually saw the Indians. Earliest known depiction of Indians made by an eyewitness in America.

293, Drawing out of proportion. Cf. with page 153.

302. See 146.

306. It is known that from 1574 for some years Zucchero was painting portraits in England.

307. No known authentic portrait of Hawkins. For Hawkins portraits and those of other navigators, see *Dictionary of National Biography*, London, article by J. K. Laighton.

309. Probably a portrait of Gilbert.

310. See 146.

314. By a noted American mural painter of historical subjects.

315. See 314.

316. See 3.

317. See 7.

320. Extremely doubtful if Drake corrected the map as intimated by a note inscribed on it near bottom.

323. By one of the leading Dutch map-makers, 16th century.

325. Probably a portrait of Cavendish. See 307.

330–333. The tapestries on which the Pine engravings were based were woven at Delft, Holland, by H. Cornelius Vroom of Haarlem. All but two were destroyed by fire in 1835.

334. By a well-known British painter.

335. Inscription on plan says it was "taken out by John Hunt in the viii day of October in the yeare of our Lorde 1607."

345. By a Dutch engraver who worked about ten years, from 1613, in England engraving many portraits of royal and other personages, some of them signed.

349. See 314.

350. Cut of ship is the same as that in *Newes from Virginia*, London, 1610. See Vol. XI, 1.

352. By a pupil of Howard Pyle. Paintings marked by conscientious attention to correctness of costume.

358. See 7.

365. Inscription at bottom of portrait, according to the present owner, was done in the 18th century to cover up a slight scorch. Owner can trace portrait back to great-great-grandfather (1729–98).

370. Picture an example of nineteenth-century sentimentalization of Pocahontas. Setting and most of costumes quite improbable. Pocahontas' uncle and two brothers were present at wedding but apparently no Indian women.

375. By the leading American painter of marine subjects, member of the National Academy.

395. Painted in 1845 by order of the U. S. government by instructor in drawing at West Point Military Academy, 1834–46, later professor there. Spent some time in research in Holland. Portraits wholly fictitious; thousands of engravings were sold, each accompanied with a "key to the portraits," eighteen in number, including a "boy belonging to Winslow family."

396. A model of a ship of the same type as the *Mayflower*.

400. The painter's last work and left unfinished. Studied in Paris, Rome, Florence and Düsseldorf. Picture suggests a former tendency to hold up the Plymouth plantation covenant as one of the world's great constitutions. Nothing is known about the signing of the compact except a few lines by Bradford.

402. Artist, English-born, known for his carefully drawn pictures of ships. For seven years followed the life of a sailor. His "Battle of the Iron-clads," 1887, was purchased by the U. S. government.

403, 404. Illustrations of the landing of the Pilgrims were common in popular histories and schoolbooks of the early nineteenth century. No attempt was made to invest the landing with the moral and religious significance which later paintings were to express.

405. Painter a pupil of Benjamin West. The painting was the first ambitious attempt to depict the Pilgrim "landing." When exhibited in 1815 made considerable stir. As history it is worthless. Picture referred to by Webster, in Plymouth oration, 1820.

406. Lucy's painting is in harmony with the moral and religious significance which was given the landing by Webster's Plymouth Rock oration, 1820, and Longfellow's poems. Picture shows strong French influence in figures and costumes, Lucy having studied art and painted this picture in France.

407. Gisbert's "Landing" carries the religious aspect to an extreme. Artist was Director of the Prado Gallery, 1867–70. Repeats an error in Lucy's picture of cliffs rising above the water.

408. Picture strikes a new note. Religious aspect subordinated. A determined facing of the wilderness most striking feature.

409. Artist shows influence of Bougereau and Jean Paul Gérôme, under whom he studied. His fifty or more canvases on American history reveal a frank striving for rich color effects.

and are invested with deep sentimental feeling. His knowledge of early costumes and of early ships comes from long study of this field.

410. Artist, English born, came to America in boyhood. His paintings on the Pilgrims and other American subjects have a delicacy and sympathy which won for them a wide popularity.

411. Only Pilgrim portrait that is authentic. Done probably from life while Winslow was in England as agent for Massachusetts.

412. Portrait cannot be authenticated. It was found in Philadelphia by the present owner. (See his account in Massachusetts Historical Society *Proceedings*, Oct., 1877, p. 324.)

414. Attempt at reconstruction by amateur. Correct in general features.

415. An artist's creation, not based on any evidence.

416. Reconstruction. See 414.

425. See 409.

434. Another portrait, painted in England from life, by a pupil of Van Dyck, is in the American Antiquarian Society.

435. See 402.

437. See 410.

438. A crude portrait of Richard Mather has been in the American Antiquarian Society since 1815. It may have been done by John Foster as preparation for this woodcut.

441. Portrait undoubtedly fictitious, following closely an engraving in Watson's *Annals*, 1830, of Benjamin Franklin. (See S. S. Rider, *An Inquiry Concerning the Authenticity of an Alleged Portrait of Roger Williams*, Providence, 1891 — Rhode Island Historical Tracts, 2nd Series, No. 2.)

442. Painted while Saltonstall was in Holland as ambassador.

444. Artist the creator of a new school of historical painting. Faithful student of events and of period costume.

450. Believed to be a family portrait.

452. An idealization. No portrait is known.

453. By a successful painter of landscapes, pupil of Thomas Cole; painted notable pictures of Niagara, and of Mexican and South American mountain scenery.

454. Conjectural study done as a wall decoration, by a competent mural painter.

464. Portrait found in a London shop in 1851. Inscription in upper left-hand corner believed to be modern.

469. See 409. The journal of Juet does not refer to a negro (porter) among Hudson's crew, which was half English and half Dutch. No authentic likeness of Hudson.

471. This has been called the first engraved view of New Amsterdam, and absurd claims have been made for it. It is undoubtedly a Dutch engraver's endeavor to visualize verbal descriptions, in which respect he has been unsuccessful. Even the respective locations of town and fort have been reversed.

473. A reconstruction, by a mural painter of standing, known for his historical pictures in public institutions. River traffic exaggerated for this time.

475. See 473.

477. See 454.

478. A fanciful decoration. Costumes essentially correct for the period.

479. Essentially accurate conception by an American painter known for his painstaking study of the archæology of his pictures.

480. By a pupil of Howard Pyle. Conception based on data in early records of New Amsterdam.

481. Decoration by one of the younger generation of mural painters.

482. See 410.

483. Painter of this portrait identified by V. H. Paltsits, of the New York Public Library. (See Stokes, *Iconography*, I : 95–96.)

484. See 352.

485. Artist originally an engraver, famous for his plate of Trumbull's "Declaration of Independence." Later painted portraits of several Presidents. Original of the illustration done as a caricature for Irving's *Knickerbocker History of New York*.

486. See 409.

487. Artist studied in Paris. Student of American history and life. Exhibitor at Centennial, 1876, and at Paris, 1878. Painted many clever *genre* pictures and historical pieces.

498. See 409.

500. See 352.

509. See 444.

510, 511, 512. See 314.

516. The only Penn portrait with any claim to resemblance, according to Charles Henry Hart, is a bust carved from memory, after Penn's death, by Sylvanus Bevan, an apothecary.

518, 519, 520, 521, 522. Artist educated in Paris. Made a special study of William Penn and his contemporaries, preparatory to painting for the state of Pennsylvania a frieze containing eighteen panels entitled "Founding the State of Liberty Spiritual." Another series of nine panels, "The Creation and Preservation of the Union," is in the Senate Chamber, Harrisburg.

526. See 409.

529. See 409.

532. See 444.

534. The original map is in British Museum, Add. Mss. 5414, Roll 23.

536. Built about 1698, according to Scharf, by James Porteus for Samuel Carpenter, and stood until 1867 on S. E. corner of Second Street and Norris Alley, Gothic Street.

538. Built of stone 2 ft. thick in 1695, in the form of a T. Picture shows the building at date of the print.

543. Artist studied abroad and exhibited at the Paris Salon. The picture an idealization but authentic in spirit.

544. Map is based on the map of Virginia, engraved by William Hole, in Smith's *True Relation of Virginia* (Oxford, 1612).

545. An idealization by a talented American painter of mural decorations on historical subjects.

547. Portrait presented to Virginia State Library by American descendants of Claiborne. Not authenticated.

548. Authenticity of portrait is not established.

553. Apparently under the inspiration of Moale's sketch, 552.

591. Artist a well-known illustrator for English journals.

595. Exaggerated view probably published as propaganda for colonization.

600. No authentic portrait of Cartier.

603. Original by a well-known English painter for the Quebec Tercentenary, 1908.

607. According to Justin Winsor, the plan was simply a bird's-eye view of an Indian camp, added by Gastaldi, map-maker for Ramusio's account of Cartier.

611. The so-called Champlain portrait here reproduced is from a lithograph done in 1854 by Louis César Joseph Ducornet (1806–1856), a French artist deformed from birth, having neither arms nor thighs and but four toes to his right foot. All alleged portraits of Champlain have been derived or adapted from it directly or indirectly, and no authentic portrait of Champlain exists. See "A Critical Examination of Champlain's Portraits," by V. H. Paltsits, in *Acadiensis*, Vol. IV (1904). Curiously enough some of these adaptations have been attributed to Balthazar Moncornet, another French artist (born 1615). H. P. Biggar, in *The Canadian Historical Review*, Vol. I (1920), reproduces a portrait of Michel Particelli, Controlleur-Général des Finances, engraved by Moncornet in 1654, proving that, with variations of background and other modifications, it is the source of the Ducornet lithograph that was metamorphosed into a portrait of Champlain just two centuries later.

615. This alleged portrait of De Monts is without the least right to authenticity. It has been used a few times, derived from a water color in Vol. I, p. 441 of a collection of copied documents from France, made for Massachusetts in 1845 by Benjamin Perley Poore. For a critical exposé by V. H. Paltsits, see *Acadiensis*, Vol. IV (1904), pp. 303–05.

620. Lescarbot, who drew this map, was a French lawyer who joined the first settlement in New France.

628. See 611.

643. By a well-known painter and illustrator for books and magazines, specializing on American history.

645. Portrait possibly derived from the standing figure of Brébœuf at right of plate 646.

646. Imaginary conception based on accounts in Jesuit narratives.

648. Artist studied in Paris under Boulanger and Lefebvre. Made special study of Indian life.

675. Sculptor studied abroad and since 1896 has created many impressive studies of Indian life, also sculptures for memorials.

677. This portrait of La Salle, according to Justin Winsor (Vol. IV, p. 242) first appeared in M. Pierre Margry's *Mémoires et Documents*, etc., Part I, Paris, 1876. It was copied from the figure of La Salle in the copper-plate by Vander Gucht for Hennepin's *Nouvelle Decouverte*, 1697, (689), drawn reversed. The engraver merely made an enlargement of the head and shoulders from the murder scene, this being used as a frontispiece in M. Margry's work. It has since been commonly known as the Waltner engraving. The only portrait of La Salle which has any standing is that seen in the small cut, 678. This was reproduced for *The Pageant of America*, by M. de la Roncière of the Bibliothèque Nationale, from a print in that institution from an engraving in the Bibliothèque de Rouen.

680. Conjectural; nothing is known about La Salle's ship. Probably it was much smaller than represented. Apparently derived from the Hennepin picture (686).

684. By a well-known illustrator; essentially correct.

688. Very doubtful if the French built so formidable a palisade, La Salle's party at this time being a small one.

691. Topography correct, picture otherwise conjectural.

INDEX

Titles of books under author are in italics; titles of illustrations under producer are in quotation marks.

366 INDEX